RACE AND GENDER AT WAR

WRITING AMERICAN MILITARY HISTORY

EDITED BY
LESLEY J. GORDON
AND
ANDREW J. HUEBNER

THE UNIVERSITY OF ALABAMA PRESS
Tuscaloosa

The University of Alabama Press
Tuscaloosa, Alabama 35487-0380
uapress.ua.edu

Typeface: Garamond Premier Pro

Cover image: Above,Susan Baptist, a projectionist, shows training films for the troops, 2011648277; below, formation of Black soldiers after the Spanish-American War, 2007682340; Library of Congress Prints and Photographs Division

Cover design: Sandy Turner Jr.

Publication made possible in part by the generous support of the Charles G. Summersell Chair of Southern History at the University of Alabama.

Cataloging-in-Publication data is available from the Library of Congress.
ISBN: 978-0-8173-2211-3 (cloth)
ISBN: 978-0-8173-6168-6 (paper)
E-ISBN: 978-0-8173-9529-2

RACE AND GENDER AT WAR

Contents

Illustrations

Acknowledgments

This volume originated in March 2019 with a one-day conference we organized at the University of Alabama. It was called "Race and Gender Explorations: A Symposium on War and Military Service in 19th & 20th Century America," and many of the original panelists from that symposium expanded their papers for our volume. Then, to round out the collection, we also invited additional contributors. We are grateful to all our authors for their patience and hard work over several years (and through a pandemic) to see this book through to publication. For helping make the symposium a success, we also thank Charissa Threat, Holly Pinheiro, Aaron Phillips, Sea Talantis, Marla Scott, Ellen Pledger, and Morta Riggs. We were very fortunate to have generous financial assistance provided by the College of Arts and Sciences, the Charles G. Summersell Chair of Southern History, the Frances S. Summersell Center for the Study of the South, and the Departments of History, American Studies, and Gender and Race Studies at the University of Alabama. Finally, we are grateful to the two external reviewers, who offered valuable suggestions to improve the collection. For soliciting those reviews and shepherding the project on to completion, we offer our heartfelt thanks to Claire Lewis Evans, Dan Waterman, and the staff at the University of Alabama Press.

Introduction

Lesley J. Gordon and Andrew J. Huebner

The US military has long carried gender and race to war. Whether in the way the state builds its armed forces or justifies the conflicts it fights, or in the way citizens understand service or experience its benefits and burdens, or in the repercussions military policy holds for the uniformed ranks and civilians alike—in all these ways and more, the politics of race and gender have persistently shaped the course of US military history. Scholars of the last few decades have increasingly recognized this feature of American life, producing a rich body of work on the implications of gender and race for the nation's military past and present. Some works have sought to supplement the broader "grand narrative" of war and the US military; others have raised fresh questions about specific roles women and minorities have undertaken in times of war. Still others have used the categories of race and gender to reframe our understanding of the role of the military as a social institution and instrument of the state. If armed conflict often provides a sharper lens to understand human behavior, then it is hardly surprising that wartimes can expose, disrupt, or confirm the deeper dynamics of race and gender.[1]

Our volume, which originated in a one-day symposium at the University of Alabama in 2019, seeks to contribute to this expanding historiography. Here readers will find essays on topics dating from the mid-nineteenth century to the late twentieth century and addressing diverse questions of race and gender in US military history. Topics range widely from Choctaw who served with the Confederate Army, to gendered ideologies and violence on the Texas frontier, to the varying roles of women in the armed services, to firsthand accounts of white soldiers in the 1898 war against Spain, and to the hypersexualized visual imagery of World War II.

No collection of this size could hope to offer comprehensive coverage of all periods and themes. Our ambition, rather, is to showcase historians with varied research agendas working in the field of war and society, a rich, mature area of inquiry that shares space with operational studies inside the broader field of military history. These scholars bring different interpretive interests and methodologies, and mine different kinds of sources, collectively auditioning some of the approaches that have defined, and are defining, the field. Some of our authors draw on the theoretical conceptions of race and gender in their research; others look at the lived historical experiences of minorities and women at war. There are also explorations of how and why white Americans' racial and gendered views changed (or failed to change) during wartime. Each essay seeks to highlight long overlooked and understudied aspects of American military history, though in some cases, fortunately, ongoing scholarship is redressing those imbalances.

Beyond their shared sensitivities to race and gender as analytic categories, our authors together focus on matters including martial rhetoric, state militias, citizenship, army recruitment, and imprisonment. Chapters are arranged chronologically, beginning in the 1830s with the Texas Revolution and continuing into the twentieth and twenty-first centuries. Methodological approaches range from close primary source analysis to broad synthesis, demonstrating how and why military conflict and service reflect and shape larger societal trends. In short, this collection offers nothing like full coverage of the chronological or thematic sweep of American military history, but rather a sense of the of the war and society approach, a sampling of current scholarship within a vibrant and expansive field. Readers interested in a wider lens, however, should peruse the further reading section at the back of the volume, which is arranged by chapter. Readers will also find within each essay references to the wider historiography, assessing the broad interconnections of gender, race, and the military.

The volume opens with Patrick T. Troester's "'Let Us Be Men and Texas Will Triumph': Race, Gender, and Nation in the Texas Revolution." The piece examines Anglo-American war rhetoric in Texas between 1835 and 1836, focusing on the ways in which agitators and rebel leaders used gendered, racialized, and sexualized rhetoric in public and private to shape responses to and understandings of the developing war with the Mexican central government. Troester finds that a common pattern in this rhetoric conjoined Mexican national authority with groups of perceived racial Others within and near Anglo-Texan society—independent Native Americans, enslaved African Americans, and the "hireling" soldiers of the Mexican Army. Rebel leaders imagined racialized threats leveled against white homes and families, the practical and symbolic building blocks of the nation-state. Anglos within and beyond the bounds of Texas used this discourse to rally local communities, individuals, and resources; to legitimize a weak and divided government; to enlist outside capital and manpower; and to lend sacred meaning to individual and collective participation in the war. Perhaps most importantly, however, these ideologies helped transform the political conflicts of a few regional elites into a popular, indeed national, war. As they drew in people and resources from across the continent, what began as a small-scale multiethnic uprising within Mexico became an Anglo-dominated war for independence. As Troester demonstrates, gendered and racialized ideologies of shared national danger were essential to forging and sustaining the volatile and bitterly contested new nation-state project of the Republic of Texas.

Historians have paid a good deal of attention to white, native-born soldiers in the Civil War, but much less to Native Americans serving with both armies. Fay A. Yarbrough's "Red Soldiers in Gray: Enlisting Confederate Choctaw Soldiers in the American Civil War" looks at the experiences of Civil War soldiers in Indian Territory by closely examining their Compiled Service Records. These records are useful sources for all Civil War troops, but they are particularly valuable for recovering the experience of Native soldiers, who left few diaries, journals, or letters home. The Compiled Service Records of Confederate Choctaw soldiers indicate the details of their enlistments and the duration of their service. These archival records, while uneven and unpredictable, offer further glimpses of daily life for the troops. They track the movement of Confederate prisoners of war from camp to camp and show that some soldiers chose to swear the oath of loyalty and even join federal units. Other prisoners of war were exchanged. The records also include more mundane, though consequential, information, such as petitions for promotion, letters of resignation, and certificates of disability. In short, a picture emerges of enthusiastic Choctaw enlistees at the beginning of the war, and of their waning support for the war as poor provisions and desertion plagued their ranks. In the end, Yarbrough contends, Choctaw Confederates were not so different from white Confederates in many respects.

Black soldiers served in significant numbers in the Union army, and Amanda Bellows's piece, "African American Military Service and Citizenship in Late Nineteenth-Century America," tracks the significance of Black men in US uniform both during and after the Civil War. Their service was not a given, with many African Americans passionately debating the merits of service to a country that failed to protect their civil or political rights. While some advocated military service as a pathway to citizenship or increased legal protections, others cited continuing discrimination and racial violence in opposing it. Bellows's essay further probes the decades that followed the Civil War, examining the experiences of Black soldiers stationed in the postemancipation South and West. These men, many of them Civil War veterans, continued to fight against racism by proving their abilities as soldiers and asserting their rights as citizens through military service. Ultimately, their contributions to the reconstruction of the South and the conquest of the American West challenged lingering racist beliefs that African Americans were unfit to serve in the army and helped affirm their rights as citizens.

Large numbers of Black men serving in the U.S. military proved a complicated question for the Confederacy. Caroline Wood Newhall's "'It Is Not the Policy nor the Interest of the South to Destroy the Negro': Black Prisoners of War and the Intersection of Race, Property, and Law in the Confederacy" shows how the Confederate government tried to adapt its extant state slave codes and federal laws to the demands of warfare. In accordance with its civil and criminal legal systems, the Confederacy interpreted the laws of war in ways that significantly affected the Black US soldiers who faced Confederates in battles, sieges, and surrenders. Historians emphasize the Confederacy's refusal to recognize soldiers of color as legitimate combatants as a reason for the small number of Black prisoners of war who reached military prisons, and point to this lack of protection under the laws of war as a significant factor in atrocities committed against Black troops. Newhall argues, however, that Black prisoners of war were in fact categorized as legally recaptured property under a principle of wartime law called *postliminy*. As the Civil War progressed, the Confederate government actively encouraged military commanders to show leniency toward Black prisoners in order to mobilize their labor for the increasingly desperate war effort. Using the testimony of Black prisoners of war in their military pension files, Newhall concludes that the majority appear to have been reclaimed by former enslavers, sold to new enslavers, and appropriated as labor by the military, rather than summarily executed or sequestered away in prison camps.

After the Civil War, with an army smaller yet more diverse, the notion of the southern military tradition lingered. In "Race and Region in Post–Civil War US Army Recruiting," Kevin Adams examines African American and white men who enlisted in the US Army after the creation of segregated infantry and cavalry regiments in 1866. Adams's essay, based on analysis of a sample of over four thousand enlistment records of white and Black soldiers between 1870 and 1890, investigates those men who chose to join the army during the period of warfare against Native nations in the late nineteenth century. While some of the data lines up with previous studies of army demographics, this sample provides important new insights about the army's recruitment of Black and white southerners during and after Reconstruction. Although many nineteenth-century contemporaries waxed poetic about martial culture in Dixie, army recruiting reveals that southern Black men, much more than whites, converted such a culture to actual service in the armed forces during and after Reconstruction.

The significance of southern Black men's military service in the nineteenth century is further underscored in Gregory Mixon's essay, "Robert Brown Elliott: Assistant Adjutant General, National Guard, South Carolina." Current biographies outlining Elliott's political career briefly trace his tenure leading the South Carolina National Guard, but these studies do not explain his actions, decisions, and personal assumptions about the South Carolina National Guard, Black political power, and the Black and white effort to democratize South Carolina during Reconstruction. Mixon utilizes secondary sources on Elliott's life and political career, but also untapped records from the state adjutant general's office. In a reading that reflects broader scholarship on the African diaspora, Mixon sees Elliott's rise to power as part of the hemispheric Black efforts to define freedom, citizenship, and nation-state formation during the long nineteenth century.

The 1898 war against Spain in the Caribbean and Pacific still gets limited attention from scholars, despite the important work that has been done on imperialism, the savage fighting in the Philippines, and Teddy Roosevelt's hypermasculine Rough Riders. Kari L. Boyd-Weisenberger's essay, "'A Class of People Far Superior': White Soldiers, Civilians, and Perceptions of Race and Class in the Spanish-American War," looks closely at the diaries and letters of northern volunteers to explore their firsthand experiences of war in what they perceived to be a very foreign land. As Boyd-Weisenberger argues, these men left their homes with high hopes for their military service, eager for battle and a chance at glory. But as the probability of combat service faded, or proved less glorious than expected, they faced bitter disappointment, leaving them feeling resentful of the new people and places they saw while in the service and revealing their underlying prejudices. Their descriptions of southerners and people of color became more racialized too, revealing that the dehumanizing effects of warfare could extend far beyond the front line.

The final two essays address gender and sexuality in the twentieth century. Michele Curran Cornell's "The Problem with Wolves: American Servicemen's Sexuality across the Two World Wars" surveys military policies and newspapers, including cartoons, and the mixed messages they sent about white American soldiers' collective sexuality. During World War I, the US Army designed sex policies to shelter the American public from doughboy promiscuity, despite high venereal disease rates among the troops. In contrast, Cornell finds, after a generation of changed social standards, military sex policies loosened during World War II, allowing freer sexual license among servicemen. In this climate, ribaldry surfaced in military newspapers, perhaps best depicted in Leonard Sansone's recurring cartoon *The Wolf*, which appeared to champion sexual aggression, at least among white soldiers. Thus, dual images of American servicemen as both chaste protectors and sexual predators inevitably presented conflicting ideas about America's wartime mission in the early twentieth century.

Heather Marie Stur's essay, "Gender, Sexual Orientation, and the US Military," looks broadly at efforts to integrate women and openly gay or lesbian individuals into the military in the 1990s as well as the angry reactions rooted rhetorically in concerns over sex and privacy. These strong public responses reveal the deep commitment of American civilians to the idealized image of the US soldier as a heterosexual man and to traditional ideas about gender, sexuality, power, and martial citizenship. Exploring debates over women and openly gay or lesbian individuals in the military in the context of contemporaneous issues such as the Anita Hill/Clarence Thomas hearings, the Tailhook scandal, and the AIDS crisis, Stur concludes that in the end, inclusion reflected and affected broader American attitudes.

Chad L. Williams closes the collection with an epilogue titled "African Americans, World War I, and the Boundaries of Military History." This piece, based on his remarks as keynote speaker at our 2019 symposium, delves into ongoing debates over the alleged decline of history and the disconnect between academic historians and the public. Williams raises important questions that continue to be relevant to how we define and legitimize fields of history broadly, and military history specifically. He recounts his own experiences with labels and assumptions about what military history is—and, by default, who gets to write it.

These essays, chronicling more than 180 years of American history, demonstrate that the tensions and injustices surrounding race, gender, and military history remain relevant and controversial, continuing to roil American politics, society, and culture to this day. Recent and recurring controversies over female soldiers in combat, military posts named after Confederates, sexual assault within the armed forces, and the service of transgender people, just to name a few, remind us that the military as an institution evolves over time. But they also show the stubborn durability of racial and gender discrimination both within and outside the military—a record of bigotry with deep historical roots.

Overall, this collection seeks to showcase the war and society approach and thus reinforce and broadcast its well-established place within the field of military history. Taken together, the essays here offer our readers ways of integrating familiar sources, and varied methodologies crafted to present a more complete picture of military service in the nineteenth and twentieth centuries. They collectively chart the transformation of a largely white, male institution into the more diverse body that serves the United States today, and testify to the implications of that change for the association of military service with national citizenship. The episodes that make up this volume, as well as the broader literature on gender, war, and the military, demonstrate just how uneven, complex, and often expensively purchased those transformations have been.

RACE AND GENDER AT WAR

1

"Let Us Be Men and Texas Will Triumph"

Race, Gender, and Nation in the Texas Revolution

Patrick T. Troester

On May 2, 1836, Anglo-Texan diplomats attended a Philadelphia meeting in support of their ongoing rebellion against Mexico's central government.[1] Days later, Stephen F. Austin gushed to Missouri senator Lewis Fields Linn about the "enthusiastic and ardent" event held in the same "Temple of Liberty where, in '76 those principles were proclaimed which have ever since been a beacon-light to the benighted and enslaved of all nations." For Austin, this seemed apropos, to say the least. "The *spirit* of '76 was there," he wrote, as if describing some supernatural being. "*That* spirit, and [the] *hearts* of the vast multitude, told them what to do. No cold or selfish influence of policy or party cast its chilling breath."[2] Austin was not alone in such sentiments. In spring 1836 Anglo-Texans old and new constantly invoked their revolutionary heritage, portraying the current war as a reprise of the American Revolution. They were right to some extent, but not always for the reasons they said.

Austin's letter soon turned to a well-worn script that had developed alongside the Texas conflict. "A war of extermination is raging in Texas," he warned Senator Linn, "a war of barbarism and of despotic principles, waged by a mongrel Spanish-Indian and Negro race, against civilization and the Anglo-American race." Austin had strayed far from his long-cultivated persona of model adopted citizen and leading mediator between colonists and the central government. Now caught between an advancing Mexican army and a stubbornly neutral Jackson administration, he pushed Anglo-Texan war rhetoric to its limits, desperately seeking the intervention of men like Linn. Austin claimed that he was a true American—one who had served his nation well indeed. In "laboring like a slave to *Americanize* Texas," Austin had created a bulwark around the Mississippi Valley and its thriving cotton industry more effective "than a standing army of

10,000 men." But now for diplomacy's sake, Andrew Jackson was throwing everything away. "It is to be broken up," Austin railed, "because it will not do for the United States government to interfere with a usurper, a base, unprincipled, bloody monster . . . who desolates Texas under the bloody flag of a pirate, and whose avowed intention is to excite the Indians and negroes, and crimson the waters of the Mississippi, and make it the eastern boundary of Mexico. . . . No. This monster cannot be interfered with, because a treaty was made. . . . Oh! spirit of our fathers, where are you?" Treaties and borders were not supposed to keep Americans from helping one another in times like these.[3]

Austin's letter is emblematic of the nationalist project that emerged alongside what is conventionally called the Texas Revolution. In 1835–36, as long-simmering conflicts over regional sovereignty and the future of chattel slavery in Texas erupted into war between mostly Anglo colonists and the Mexican central government, rebel leaders developed a racial and familial vision of nationalism premised on the supposed danger of racial others within and nearby Anglo-Texan society. The ways in which they portrayed the war and its violence imagined a gendered, racialized, and sexualized threat to the white families that composed the nation at the local level. With minor variations, the story went like this: a "tyrant" Mexican dictator at the head of a racially mixed mercenary army sought to enlist savage Indian neighbors and rebellious enslaved Black people to consummate a "war of extermination" against white colonists. Anglo-Texan rebels publicly and privately used these ideologies for a host of vital tasks in ways strikingly reminiscent of their revolutionary ancestors.

As recent work has explored, early American nationalists relied on the counterpoint of racial others to bring together divided colonial societies into a national coalition and pursue what they called the "common cause." Six decades after US independence, similarly divided Anglo-American colonists in Texas reprised those same discursive tools to forge a new common cause. Like their predecessors, Anglo-Texans perceived, portrayed, and responded to their emerging national interests largely through a racialized and gendered sense of shared danger, much of it provoked or even created by rebels themselves. Authors within and beyond the bounds of Texas used the common cause to rally local communities and their resources, to legitimize a weak and divided government, to enlist massive amounts of outside capital and manpower, and to lend sacred meanings to individual and collective participation.[4]

This ideological work transformed the political grievances of a few regional elites into a popular—indeed *national*—war, invoking a familial vision of American nationalism that stretched easily beyond the boundaries of the United States. As the common cause drew in participants and resources from across the continent, what began as a small-scale multiethnic uprising within Mexico became an Anglo-dominated war for independence, led and funded in large part by proslavery cotton and land interests in the United States. Recent literature on the Texas borderlands has emphasized the fundamental importance of chattel slavery, the cotton boom, and fears of Mexican abolition in bringing about the rebellion, providing an overdue corrective to long-standing narratives that downplayed the role of slavery. However, traditional and revisionist histories alike examine only in passing the racialized and gendered fear rhetoric that suffused the war.[5] A close analysis of the common cause and its political impacts shows the fundamental roles that this discourse and related ideologies of gender, race, and nation played in shaping the war's outbreak, course, and results. Most importantly, it uncovers how rebels marshaled popular support at the local and transnational levels by framing their movement as a defense against existential threats—not merely threats against slavery, but threats against the nation, the family, and the very frameworks of race and gender that ordered Anglo-American society.[6]

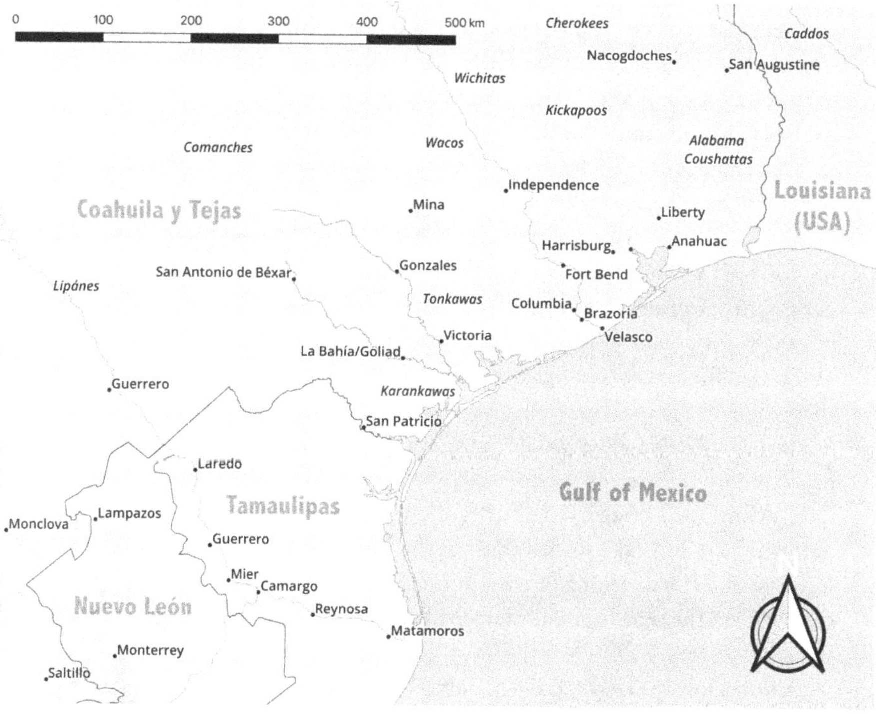

FIGURE 1.1. Northeastern Mexico, 1835–36. Courtesy of Patrick T. Troester.

Prior to the outbreak of war in 1835, Anglo-Texan politics had been anything but unified (figure 1.1). Although most colonial elites saw slavery and cotton as the keys to the province's future, they agreed on little else. Growing conflicts between Mexican officials and Anglo agitators through the early 1830s only deepened the rifts, pitting leaders like Austin who favored conciliation against more pugnacious figures like Brazoria planter William Wharton and his loose group of allies, eventually dubbed the "radical party." In 1834–35, when centralizing reforms to the national government sparked rebellions in other Mexican states and presented yet another threat to the future of Texas slavery, Anglo colonists remained divided, unable to agree on even the basic realities of their situation, much less a common course of action.[7]

On June 22, 1835, shortly after a small group of Anglo agitators seized the small Mexican army garrison at Anahuac, Robert Williamson addressed a citizens' meeting at San Felipe de Austin, making one of the earliest appeals to the common cause. "United we stand, divided we fall," he began, in a winding speech that conjoined the alleged threats of military despotism, Catholicism, aristocracy, Indian savagery, and abolition. Recent acts of the Mexican Congress, Williamson claimed, had replaced the republic with a dictatorship. Having subdued liberal resistance in Zacatecas and elsewhere, Santa Anna's men now marched on Texas to finalize the conquest: "They are coming to compel you into obedience . . . to compel you to liberate your slaves; to compel you to swear to support and sustain the government of the Dictator; to compel you to submit to the imperial rule of the aristocracy, to pay tythes and adoration to the clergy." Soldiers were already landing in Texas for these purposes, he claimed, and Anglo citizens were preparing for war. Williamson closed with an argument many would echo—Anglo-Texans must capture and hold San Antonio de Béxar or lose Texas entirely. "Five hundred troops can so fortify San Antonio as to resist the united attack of all Texas." Failure to capture Béxar would "permit an enemy to be there stationed that will send the Indians continually upon you." If Mexico's tyranny was strictly political, its Native allies would bring something else entirely: "instigated and protected by the Mexicans, the Indians will be your constant enemies; they will be the continued ravagers of your country and the destroyers of yourselves. . . . You will hear around your habitations the Indian yell, mingling with the Mexican cry, and the shrieking of your murdered wives, rousing the slumbers of the cradle, from the midst of your burning buildings will tell you, when too late, of the error to your policy."[8]

Williamson made the danger immediate, intimate, and gendered. Anglo-Texans' foes had a single target—white homes and families—and the imagined violence was both physical and sexual. Others soon piled on. The anxieties evoked in the common cause ran deeply enough in Anglo-American culture to require little coordination. Weeks later from Lampazos, Nuevo León, Benjamin

Milam forwarded troubling rumors from the Mexican interior. "Their intention," he wrote, "is to gain the friendship of the different tribes of Indians; and if possible to get the slaves to revolt. These plans of barbarity and injustice will make a wilderness of Texas and beggars of its inhabitants, if they do not unite." Such appeals drew a direct line between national politics and the nuclear family, linking the idea of the nation to the individual households that composed it at the local level. According to their logic, the imagined nation already existed; the only problem was convincing Anglo-Texans of their shared perils before it was too late.[9]

Through June and July, however, numerous Anglo-Texans worked to deescalate tensions, condemning what they characterized as a handful of dangerous troublemakers and affirming their loyalty to Mexico. Just after the publication of Williamson's address, a meeting at Columbia condemned "the conduct and acts of individuals (less than a majority) calculated to involve the citizens of Texas in a conflict with the Federal Government of Mexico. . . . They denounce said persons as foreigners, and disclaim all participation in the act whatsoever." Colonists in Mina were similarly unimpressed. "It would be the blindest credulity," they declared, "to believe to the full extent, the idel exaggerations, that for some time past have agitated the public mind." They lamented how "the misconduct of a *few designing men* is attributed to the *whole* community" and pledged to uphold the constitution as loyal Mexican citizens.[10]

Other Anglo-Texans appealed directly to Mexican officials. Edward Gritten, for instance, wrote to General Domingo Ugartechea at Béxar multiple times that summer, asking him to dispel the rumors being "spread maliciously" in the Anglo colonies and urging him not to send troops. "That district is very alarmed," Gritten reported, "for they have been made to believe that there are now troops en route to exterminate them." Still, he insisted, the problem was a brash minority. "The sane part of the population does not want a break with the Mexicans, but to conserve with them peace and union." Over the next two months, Ugartechea and other officials wrote to discredit the rumors, dismissing them as the work of "perverse" outsiders.[11]

Some Anglo-Texans went even further. Not long after pledging support for the Anahuac agitators, Brazos Department *jefe político* (district political chief) James Miller got cold feet. After resigning and making his own entreaties to Ugartechea, Miller wrote a friend in Béxar with a plan that might forestall war entirely. Keeping the peace required decisive action, Miller argued, namely, arresting the lead agitators as the government had recently ordered. "They should *now* be demanded of their respective chiefs—a few at a time—at first, Johnson, Williamson, Travis, and Williams—and perhaps that is enough."[12]

One of these wanted men, William Barret Travis, offers a window into the mindset of the men agitating for rebellion in Texas and the central problem they faced. Travis embodied a particularly aggressive strain of mid-nineteenth-century Anglo-American masculinity and a near-ubiquitous Anglo-Texan story. Immigrating illegally in 1831 at the age of twenty-one, he left behind a failed marriage, a son, and an unborn daughter in Alabama. Texas offered Travis a chance to escape and overwrite his previous failures. Travis prospered in Texas as a lawyer, dealing primarily with commerce and land speculation—both of which tied him closely to emerging battles over slavery and federal authority in the province. Within a year, he had become a prominent figure of the radical party, leading violent clashes against military and customs officials at Anahuac in 1832 and 1835. Travis saw his life as a gendered and racialized project of mastery. His surviving 1833–34 diary records tireless work as an agent in Texas for US-linked commercial networks. It is not incidental, however, that amid endless shorthand accounts of financial and legal transactions, he also tallied his sexual conquests in broken vulgar Spanish.[13]

Orchestrating revolution was similar business. For Travis and others, "the Cause of Texas" was a project of white masculine regenerative violence and mastery that could take many forms. During the summer of 1835, the main task was still instigating conflict and creating common interest. Since most Anglo-Texans focused on the familial and the local, Travis and his allies insisted that the only thing that could unify them was a shared danger. Over the coming months, they effectively created that danger, shaping its meanings from the start. Writing to fellow radical David Burnet in April, Travis argued that Mexican military intervention would be a turning point. "Such a measure would kindle a flame in Texas that would burn in twain the slender cords that connect us to the ill fated Mexican confederation." Though rumors of an "invasion" then seemed far-fetched, Travis was certain that Texas would join the United States before Jackson left office. Things moved slowly that spring, but Travis insisted that "all are determined to defend the country within our own limits to the last extremity." By late August, Travis could feel the momentum shifting when the Mexican government ordered the arrest of him and six other agitators. "This was too much for the people to bear," he told Andrew Briscoe, also a wanted man. "Their wrath was turned against the Torries and Spanish-Americans. . . . They have become almost completely united." With a statewide meeting of Anglo-Texan delegates approaching, Travis congratulated his friend: "You have shown yourself the real white man and uncompromising patriot. . . . Let us be men and Texas will triumph."[14]

The exiled Mexican liberal Lorenzo de Zavala was less optimistic. "There is no unified patriotism," he told Austin weeks later, because "the inhabitants are scattered and believe themselves free from all danger. They will defend their private rights until death; but they still do not realize the necessity for co-operation." The common interest Zavala described would need to be created, and the ideology of the common cause became a central way in which Anglo leaders did so.[15]

Although unity remained elusive, the political and discursive space for dissent was rapidly disappearing. Perhaps the ultimate barometer was Austin himself. On September 18, two weeks before the outbreak of hostilities, he published a circular warning that General Martín Perfecto de Cós was inbound toward the colonies, and Anglos now had no choice but to immediately prepare to fight. "War," Austin declared, "is our only resource. There is no other remedy but to defend our rights, ourselves, & our country . . . by force of arms. To do this, we must unite." Days later, Branch Archer and the Columbia Committee made the point more starkly: "The evidence is so clear, so convincing that an honest difference of opinion can no longer exist. . . . He who says that there is no just cause to apprehend danger, and recommends a supine course, is a *traitor*, and as such should be punished. . . . We have a common cause and a common foe, and we should be united." Archer went on to elaborate the common cause in familiar terms. The Mexican military had "lately made a treaty with the Comanches, and other tribes of the savages, and have engaged them to fight against us." Quickly defeating Cós, Archer argued, would keep these Indians out of the war. He also emphasized the sexual danger, admonishing wavering Anglo men: "Behold your wives and daughters, are you prepared to yield them to the embraces of a brutal soldiery?"[16]

Archer's call for absolute adherence was not bluster. Something was changing. Indeed, his own election as chair of Columbia's vigilance committee was one indication. Less than three months earlier, Columbia had joined other Anglo towns declaring loyalty to Mexico. Individuals and communities alike were now changing course. Around the same time, James Miller, who in July had advocated turning in agitators, publicly recanted. In a pamphlet to the "People of Texas," Miller explained that he had meant only to follow his constituents' wishes. Until recently, he insisted, the vast majority favored neutrality, but "times have changed, and with the times, many circumstances have transpired to show that many of the dangers, once supposed to be fanciful, are too real." He restated the emerging party line in his own words, affirming that the Mexican government was "fitting up a formidable invasion of the rights and properties of Texas, that the ruin of her commerce, the emancipation of her slaves, the abolition of the system of colonization, the prostration of her local militia, and other oppressive measures are within her scheme." How deeply Miller believed all this is unclear, but that made little difference. "Texas is up now," he explained. "She sees but with one eye."[17]

Why did this narrative come into focus so quickly and prove so effective? Of course, the anxieties behind the common cause had deep and enduring roots in Anglo-American culture, but they were also *timely*. During the 1830s, these anxieties ran prominently through society and politics in Texas and surrounding regions, though in more complex ways than Anglo-Texans emphasized. Like the rebellion itself, their current manifestations stemmed in large part from the rapidly expanding cotton boom, which sent wealthy planters, poor white people, enslaved African Americans, and displaced Native people into Mexico's far northeast at the same moment when Mexicans were moving both to centralize national power and to abolish chattel slavery.

By 1835, Texas had transformed. When Anglo colonists began immigrating in 1821, as many as 40,000 diverse Native people lived in Texas, outnumbering the Hispanic Tejano population ten to fifteen times over. Anglos arrived slowly at first, but by the 1830s, what had begun as a trickle grew to a torrent. As the slave-based cotton industry transformed the greater Mississippi Valley, a massive influx of land-hungry settlers and speculators poured into Mexican Texas from slaveholding regions of the US South. Arriving at a rate of roughly 3,000 per year and matching the flow of cotton's expansion through the trans-Appalachian Southwest, migrants from the United States more than doubled the colonial population of Texas between 1830 and 1834, the very period during which Mexican officials sought to seal the border. In 1835, some 24,700 Anglos and enslaved African Americans lived in the province. By 1836, ongoing immigration and thousands of US volunteer troops had shifted that figure to perhaps over 30,000. Along with Anglos and enslaved people came Native migrants too. Cherokee, Creek, and other groups of refugees from the United States had begun arriving in Texas around the time of the Louisiana Purchase, forced west as cotton cultivation seized their southeastern homelands. By 1830, there were some 10,000 Native immigrants living in Texas, with thousands more across the Red River in US Indian Territory. Their numbers continued to grow over the coming decade as the United States carried out its Indian removal policy.[18]

Nor were the changes merely demographic. Through the early 1830s, Texas found itself increasingly tied to the burgeoning print and commercial networks of the Lower Mississippi Valley, which bound Texans to their US neighbors through shared systems of communication, trade, finance, and culture. As Anglo-Texans and many Tejano elites sent growing volumes of cotton and hides into the Atlantic World via New Orleans and imported outside capital and a range of manufactured goods, they wove Texas into the emerging slave-based capitalism of the American South. It was no coincidence that 74.4 percent of rebel troops immigrated to Texas *after* 1830, during the cotton boom's peak years. The war accelerated these changes. As US capital and military manpower flooded in and immigration continued apace, Anglo-American political influence within Texas grew rapidly. When leaders spoke of mobilizing "the people," they were dealing with a moving target.[19]

During the early 1830s, Texas morphed from a Mexican frontier colony toward something that increasingly resembled an informal social, cultural, and economic colony of the southern United States. This was visible first in the constant slippage and vagueness of the term *American* as a national, ethnic, and racial identifier in Texas, but it appeared in other ways as well. The actions of many Anglos in Texas reveal a view of the region as what historian Amy Kaplan calls "foreign in a domestic sense"—part of the United States, though outside it.[20] In May 1835, for instance, a group of US travelers arrived in Harrisburg only to be detained by a Mexican customs schooner. As an outraged friend explained to William Travis, "the passengers had no passports—not thinking it necessary and demanded to have the privilege of returning to the United States." Similar logic appears in Jonas Harrison's December 22, 1835, address to the San Augustine Committee of Vigilance. Recounting the war's origins, Harrison portrayed the Mexican government's 1830 ban on further US immigration as an act of violence against Anglo kinship networks, which "totally separated many of the first emigrants from their relatives and friends, who intended to have removed to the country. . . . Families and the nearest ties of kindred and friendship were thus severed." One of the starkest indications of this thinking materialized toward the war's end. As they designed their new nation-state, Texan lawmakers constitutionally banned the importation of enslaved people *except* from the United States, expressly prohibiting any future law from denying US immigrants the right to bring along human chattel. Outsiders too minded the blurred distinction between Anglos on either side of the Sabine. When a Mexican agent asked Caddo Indians near the Texas-Louisiana border to attack Anglo-Texans, they refused. According to a report sent to a US Army officer in Louisiana, the Caddo explained that "the Americans (whites) were the same on both sides of the [Sabine river], and should they kill or plunder those in Texas, the Americans (whites) on this side would kill them."[21]

Such rapid change brought instability, virtually all of which traced to the cotton boom and its resulting land rush. Perhaps the most pronounced manifestation was the fear of slave insurrections. Although endemic in the early United States, this fear became even more frenetic during the 1820s–30s. As soaring profitability hurled slave-based cotton production westward, the society around it became progressively more threadbare. Enslavers' paranoia reached new heights, occasionally erupting in spasmodic mass violence. Historians have examined insurrection scares in Texas slave society during the rebellion itself, but that unrest and the anxieties surrounding it fit into a broader regional context. Just as the crisis in Texas escalated during summer 1835, large sections of nearby Mississippi were ablaze in fears of slave insurrection. At the climax of these panics, planters in Madison County, which had grown apace with Texas between 1830 and 1835, tortured and executed at least sixteen enslaved people and seven white people to contain a slave conspiracy that may have never existed.[22]

Relations with Native peoples were similarly volatile. In the spring and summer of 1835, violence erupted in eastern Texas between Anglo colonists and several Indigenous groups, primarily due to Anglo settlers' encroachment on Native territory. Amid rumors that Indians were planning a general attack on the colonies, Anglo rangers carried out campaigns against Caddo and Wichita, while strained negotiations kept tensions with immigrant Cherokee and Creek at a bare simmer. By October, those leading the summer campaigns against Native peoples pivoted to join the "Army of the People" in expelling Mexican garrisons from Texas.[23]

Texas in 1835 was thus at the epicenter of several interwoven westward-spreading conflicts, which became only more volatile as they collided with a rival nation-building project that was both abolitionist and racially plural. These conflicts and the racial anxieties surrounding them further linked Anglo-Texans to US society and culture, and they account in large part for the power and salience of the common cause within Texas and beyond. Meanwhile, the human geography and limited communication infrastructure of Texas played their own roles. Despite their growing numbers, Anglo-Texans in 1835 were spread across some thirty-five thousand square miles, with no single settlement housing more than a few hundred people. As the common cause narrative took root that summer, leading agitator William Wharton at Brazoria controlled the only printing press in the colonies. The radical party thus enjoyed a near monopoly on the flow of information both among dispersed Anglo-Texan communities and into the neighboring print networks of the Mississippi Valley. These agitators would use it to their spectacular advantage over the following months, churning out a steady stream of disinformation and inflammatory rhetoric through their weekly newspaper, the *Texas Republican*, and in a flurry of broadsides.[24]

Unifying Anglo-Texas was only one part of the problem. Successfully resisting the Mexican army would require soldiers, money, and political allies beyond the province. In fall 1835, Anglo-Texans began reaching out through networks in the United States to mobilize the manpower and resources necessary for their emerging war. In December, Austin and his longtime rivals Wharton and Archer departed Texas on a trip to "approach the authorities of our Mother Country" and solicit donations, loans, and other aid from US citizens. Others focused on recruiting troops. In early October, Samuel Houston, soon-to-be commander-in-chief of Texan forces, promised would-be volunteers from the United States "liberal bounties of land. We have millions of acres of our best lands unchosen and unappropriated." Houston and others also invoked the ties of kinship and national heritage linking Anglo-Texans to the United States, with declarations like, "The people of the United States will respond to the call of their brethren in Texas!" Appeals for volunteers developed a well-worn formula, and by spring 1836, the Anglo-Texan state established a detailed quota system, assigning rank to arriving officers based on the number of enlisted troops they brought along.[25]

US citizens responded with great enthusiasm. In late October, M. E. DeGreve of Jackson, Mississippi, informed Houston that his letter in the local newspaper had been electrifying. Though DeGreve could not come personally, he promised, "I will do you all the good I can. . . . I have commenced the fire for Liberty, and I assure you it already begins to Blaze in our little Vilage." Several of DeGreve's "young friends" wanted to fight, and he promised to teach them drill and tactics while they awaited Houston's orders.[26] Similar reports and offers to aid the common cause poured into Texas, with men, money, and other resources close behind.

Throughout the conflict, Anglo-Texans and their US allies carried on a sort of nationalist call-and-response, invoking and affirming the bonds of kinship—both real and fictive—that bound them to a common national family. In late October, Texas General Council chair Richard Royall declared in a written appeal to the US public, "We are but one people. Our fathers, side by side, fought the battles of the revolution. . . . You are united to us by all the sacred ties that can bind one people to another. You are, many of you, our fathers and brother[s]—among you dwell our sisters and mothers." A meeting in Louisiana proclaimed similarly, "the majority of the people of Texas are bone of our bone and flesh of our flesh . . . united to us by the ties of nativity and kindred. . . . They are engaged in the same cause" for which "their and our forefathers bled and died," proving themselves "genuine Americans." Arriving volunteers chimed in too. In December, a company from Georgia announced to its new commander, fellow Georgian James Fannin, "As Americans we hail you as the champion of Liberty! As Georgians we hail you as a brother."[27]

Anglo courtship of the United States employed one additional key ingredient, a simplified historical narrative known as the Texas creation myth. It went like this: invited by the Mexican government to settle and secure its frontier, Anglo settlers had accomplished what Mexicans could not, redeeming Texas from the wilderness through privation and hardship. In return, Mexico had stabbed them in the back. After suddenly banning further immigration, the central government abolished the republican Constitution of 1824, to which colonists had pledged loyalty, and then unleashed a string of abuses climaxing in Santa Anna's 1836 "invasion." It was a story familiar and straightforward enough to appeal broadly to Anglo-Americans across the continent. What was striking, however, was the ease with which newcomers wove themselves into it. Men and women arriving from the United States used the myth to cast themselves as rescuers and long-lost kin rather than conquerors, even claiming places among the betrayed citizens of Texas after the fact—all while demonizing Mexico as a foreign invader in its own province.[28]

US volunteers combined these narratives to lend sacred meaning to their participation, portraying Texas as a site of masculine heroism and regeneration and a place where Anglo men could achieve a host of interlocking personal and national goals. Like Travis, many volunteers saw the chance to correct past failures, perhaps none more so than John Sowers Brooks. In summer 1835, twenty-year-old Brooks left the US Marine Corps eleven months into a four-year enlistment, officially citing "ill-health and general dissatisfaction" but complaining privately that the service had felt like "bondage." Soon after his discharge, news from Texas offered hope of redemption in the eyes of his family. Having failed in the only career he had ever wanted, he saw Texas as a second chance. But there was more to it. "Something in the cause of the Texians," Brooks wrote his father, "comes home to the heart of every true American. Its near similarity to the glorious struggle of our own ancestors in 'Seventy-six' must produce a sympathy for them in every part of the Union." Confident that his peers had "inherited enough of the spirit of their fore-fathers," Brooks imagined a sweeping project through which his entire generation could honor their national family as the last heroes of the American Revolution were passing away. But Brooks's dearest ambitions remained personal. He asked his father in the event of his death, "forget all my errors and follies, and believe . . . that I have never for a moment forgotten your kindness or affection. . . . I love you with an affection so intense that it almost breaks my heart." After months of unanswered letters to his family in the United States, Brooks confessed to his sister his fear "that you had forgotten your poor, wayward brother. Why is it so?" Although he admitted, "my life has indeed been a wayward and useless one," Brooks now engaged in "the only pursuit in which I could feel a throb of interest; and the cause in which I now exercise it, renders it still dearer, and more ennobling to me." Indeed, the cause made all the difference. Brooks told his sister of the Mexican army's determination "to murder all Americans indiscriminately," in "a war of extermination, not directed solely against the armed soldiers in the field, but against the peaceful citizen, the helpless female, and the defenceless infant." Whatever the outcome, "if I die . . . it will be in a good cause."[29]

Texas offered other forms of gendered redemption too. Micajah Autry hoped the promised land bounties could help him achieve a domestic ideal that eluded him in the United States. He sought not to defend Anglo-Texan families, but to conquer a space for his own. Volunteering after a failed law career in Tennessee, Autry assured his wife, Martha, "I feel more energy than I ever did in anything I have undertaken. I am determined to provide for you a home or perish." A month later, he added encouragingly, "Be of good cheer Martha, I will provide you a sweet home. I shall be entitled to 640 acres of land for my services in the Army and 4444 acres upon condition of settling my family here." Autry also invited his family members to join him in Texas: "Tell Brother Jack to think of nothing but coming here with us." He was not alone. Many volunteers made similar calls to specific individuals or to their communities in general.[30]

Better-connected volunteers did so on a much broader scale. As Mexican troops closed in on the Anglo colonies in March 1836, newly arrived Florida planter and speculator Thomas Jefferson Green urged a departing friend to rally additional US volunteers, weaving together images of violence against Anglo-Texan families with promises of the rewards awaiting their prospective saviors: "Tell them our women have been assaulted, our virgins defiled, and our men treated as devils, rather than Christians. . . . Inform them of the advantages, of our munificent land bounties, of our fat cows and hogs—Now is the time for enterprize and honor and fortunes." Days later, Green personally returned home to raise additional volunteers. As news of rebels' defeat at the Alamo spread across the United States, he implored Americans "in the name of every tie which binds blood to blood" to aid Anglo-Texans, "the children of your loins." Despite arriving in Texas only a month prior, Green rendered the Texas creation myth in first-person plural as his own shared experience. "It would be too tedious," he explained, to give "a minute history of our settlement and wrongs. Let it suffice, for this occasion, that your kinspeople and children . . . did through much want and privation, danger and bloodshed, settle and bring into enviable notice, the then unknown, but fairest portion of heaven's works." In return, "our most intelligent citizens, whose greatest offence was intelligence," were "abused and imprisoned, our women insulted and driven to menial service, our prisoners of war cruelly massacred. . . . Ought I, shall I tell the rest? *Their bodies were burned to ashes with savage delight*, in the presence of *wives, mothers, and daughters*!!" Only swift action could now save Anglo-Texans and the national mission they represented.[31]

Nor was the honor available only to white men. In February 1836, the Nacogdoches vigilance committee dispatched Haden Edwards to solicit donations from "the fair sex of our mother country" for a unit to be known as the "Ladies Battalion or Regiment." He was to record each benefactor's name for display at a banquet honoring these virtuous republican mothers. A week later, women at a two-thousand-person meeting in Nashville, Tennessee, "immediately pledged themselves to arm and equip a company of 200." Within a week, sixty men had already enrolled. A thoroughly impressed Austin wrote his cousin Mary Holley, "This generous and disinterested act of patriotism is worthy of imitation, and will find a bright page in the brilliant record of female magnanimity. . . . I hope that the great and patriotic State of Kentucky will join her Sister States of the South in aiding us."[32]

These thousands of volunteers and millions of dollars arriving from the United States did not merely bolster Texas's common cause, they transformed it. As US participants and backers began to claim the war as their own, their actions and understandings shaped its meaning and outcomes in definitive ways. Most importantly, they pushed a wavering Anglo leadership toward an unambiguous declaration of independence. Anglo-Texan diplomats repeatedly admonished the provisional government that securing further loans, donations, and enlistments from the United States hinged on independence. The rebel army pushed in the same direction. Though it was originally a force of mostly permanent colonists, over the winter of 1835–36, the composition of the "Army of the People" shifted toward a US volunteer majority. These recently arrived soldiers used their jealously acquired citizenship to vote and publicly advocate independence. By 1836, newcomers also increasingly steered Texas governance: 42 percent of delegates to the March 1836 convention had immigrated in the previous two years, and nearly a quarter only in the past year. It is no coincidence that the Texas Declaration of Independence arrived at that meeting prewritten by a man who had spent mere weeks in the province. Sure enough, the founding document echoed its predecessor's invocation of dangerous racial others: "[Mexico] has, through its emissaries, incited the merciless savage, with the tomahawk and scalping knife, to massacre the inhabitants of our defenceless frontiers."[33]

Another mark of growing US influence was the shifting place of Tejanos and Mexican federalists in the rebellion and its rhetoric. Early on, many Anglos hoped to forge interethnic alliances, linking their own movement with others throughout Mexico. However, as Mexican dissent cooled and Anglo war aims shifted toward independence in early 1836, these hopes rapidly disappeared—along with many Tejano participants. Convention candidate Thomas Borden captured an emerging Anglo consensus when he addressed Austin voters in January. Mexican alliances were a red herring, Borden argued. Certainly *some* Mexicans were "friendly to the Americans of the United States," but "as a nation, I look upon them as our enemies; and since we are compelled to fight, let us fight for something." He closed by quoting John Adams, "Independence now, and independence forever!!!!"[34]

The impact of new arrivals reached far beyond rhetoric and high politics. After rebels captured Béxar in early December 1835, most Anglo-Texan troops went home, and elites turned back toward fighting one another. Those remaining at arms were overwhelmingly newly arrived volunteers from the United States. Together, the garrisons at Béxar and Goliad constructed a narrative casting themselves as defenders of all Texas, arguing that if their positions fell, Texas fell with them. In doing so, they took the gendered logic of the common cause to its extremes, affixing themselves to the families and communities that composed the emerging Texan nation-state. In a remarkable bait and switch, these small groups of Anglo-Texan agitators and US volunteers made themselves a metonym for all Anglo-Texan society. When they forced the hand of the Mexican government on the battlefield, the results simultaneously proved and sanctified the idea that a "war of extermination" against Texas was afoot. Most did not intend to become martyrs, but their deaths only made the rhetoric more effective. Throughout this process, rebel leaders closely followed the logic of southern honor. As historian

Kenneth S. Greenberg explains, "Free and honorable gentlemen, unlike the slaves they governed, were not afraid to die." That idea rested on a common justification for chattel slavery, that enslaved people had "chosen" servitude over death. For a "real white man," that choice was unthinkable. Battlefield death was the ultimate refusal to be submissive or dependent—the highest embodiment of mastery and manly independence.[35]

Throughout February and March 1836, William Travis and James Bowie at Béxar wrote feverishly to the eastern Anglo colonies. "We will rather die in these ditches than give it up to the enemy," declared Bowie: "Public safety demands our lives rather than to evacuate this post." Travis elaborated, citing a Mexican proclamation supposedly "denouncing vengeance against the people of Texas" and threatening "to exterminate every white man within its limits." Though Travis hoped Anglo-Texans would rally, he suspected it was "useless to waste arguments upon them—*The Thunder of the Enemy's Cannon and the pollution of their wives and daughters—The cries of their Famished Children and the smoke of their burning dwellings, will only arouse them.*" The following month, he added, "if my countrymen do not rally to my relief, I am determined to perish in the defense of this place, and my bones shall reproach my country for her neglect." Travis underscored the war's racial character by repeatedly urging Anglos against trusting Tejanos. For him, Béxar's Tejano majority had made their loyalties clear when all but a handful refused to help reinforce the Alamo: "Let the government declare them public enemies, otherwise she is acting a suicidal part." As the Mexican army surrounded Béxar, Launcelot Smither rushed to Gonzales, informing Anglo colonists that the Alamo's garrison would "defend it or die on the ground," for Mexicans "intend to show no quarter." He left out—or was unaware—that Travis had been offered the chance to surrender, but "answered the demand with a cannon shot." Smither admonished colonists to send reinforcements, or "suffer your men to be murdered in the Fort. If you do not turn out Texas is gone." A company of thirty-two men from Gonzales, including several who had helped fire the war's first shots there in October, were the only colonists to answer Travis's calls.[36]

After rebels' defeat at the Alamo on March 6, early stories of the "last stand" struck similar chords. Convention delegate Benjamin Goodrich took the news more personally than most. "Texas is in mourning," he wrote home to Tennessee: "Among the number of your acquaintances murdered in the Alamo, were Col. David Crockett, Micajah Autry . . . John Hays . . . and my unfortunate brother, John C. Goodrich: but they died like men, and posterity will do them justice." The loss left him determined: "The blood of a Goodrich has already crimsoned the soil of Texas and another victim shall be added to the list or I shall see Texas free and Independent."[37]

Around the same time, Houston wrote to James Fannin at Goliad, including the story of an Alamo defender named Almeron Dickinson. One of the few longtime Texas residents defending the makeshift fort, Dickinson had brought his wife and daughter inside. As Mexican troops overran the old mission compound, he supposedly "tied his child to his back, leaped from the top of a two story building, and both were killed by the fall." Houston added ominously, "the wife of Lieut Dickinson is now in the possession of the officers of Santa Anna." Others seized on Susanna Dickinson's story, passing starkly sexualized versions of it to US newspaper editors. According to one, she had been "the only white person" to survive the assault, which culminated with the last two Anglo men being "pursued into her room" after trying to surrender. Mexican soldiers defiled the domestic space by subjecting the men "in her presence to the most torturing death," in a scene rendered with phallic and penetrative imagery: "They were even raised on the points of the enemy's lances, let down, and raised again and again . . . till they . . . expired in convulsion." A letter to the *New Orleans Bulletin* even inflicted an imagined rape on Susanna Dickinson: "She was taken and suffered from the Mexican officers the most odious pollution that ever disgraced humanity. She barely escaped with her life—but is diseased, and in a situation exciting pity and horror."[38]

Long before the Alamo fell, Fannin was up to similar work at Goliad. In February 1836, he received a letter from a US volunteer named Robert Morris, which passed along reports that Mexican forces at Matamoros were confiscating private property and subjecting residents to forced labor. But that was not all: "soldiers have assassinated many of the most influential citizens, and the wives and daughters are prostituted—the whole country is given up to the troops to induce them forward." Fannin took these ideas and ran. Appealing to the Texas General Council for reinforcements, he declared, "not the least doubt should any longer be entertained . . . of the design of Santa Anna to overrun the country, and expel or exterminate every white man within its borders." He asked, "in sober earnestness, 'Why halt ye between two opinions?'" Aghast at Anglo-Texan indecision, Fannin spun Morris's rumors into a racial and sexual nightmare: "What can be expected for the *Fair daughters* of chaste *white women*, when [Mexicans'] own country-women are prostituted by a licensed soldiery, as an inducement to push forward to the Colonies, where they may find *fairer game*?" The letters from Morris and Fannin soon appeared in the provisional government's official newspaper, alongside pro-independence tracts from Austin and the Nashville citizens' meeting, showing colonists they were in danger, but not alone.[39]

Béxar and Goliad were strategically unimportant, but viewed in the context of ideology they seemed priceless. Indeed, by conjoining Béxar and the threat of independent Indians, Anglo agitators had enshrined it as the linchpin to Texas from the beginning. The common cause made these two garrisons of mostly foreign volunteers into symbols and martyrs for "the people" of Texas, focusing a long-elusive national unity by creating a vivid sense of common danger.[40]

The demographics of rebel forces illustrate the full importance of this ideological work. According to historian Paul D. Lack, 50.3 percent of all rebel troops with verifiable arrival dates had spent a year or less in the province, while a full 40.2 percent arrived as US volunteers only after the war began. However, Lack's data is incomplete. If we factor in the 1,286 men with unknown arrival dates, the overall proportion of US volunteers may have been higher still. Most importantly, at least 78 percent of those with known arrival dates at Béxar and Goliad were US volunteers. With few exceptions, the martyred troops of Travis, Bowie, and Fannin were not the idealized settler citizens to whom Anglo-Texan leaders appealed. They had never sworn allegiance to Mexico nor been lured by false promises—at least not *Mexican* promises. They arrived after the shooting started. The endurance of Goliad and the Alamo as Texan national myths and the mass panic they inspired in their wake thus underline the effectiveness of the common cause in incorporating and naturalizing outside actors.[41]

Carefully framed by ideology, the Béxar and Goliad defeats were electric in the Anglo colonies. Inhabitants interpreted and responded to the news in ways that emphasized the dangers from racialized others in their midst. A citizens' meeting in Brazoria responded in panic to the already capitalized "Fall of the Alamo," warning of the now-unopposed march of "the enemy into the heart of Texas, with the avowed purpose of a general extermination of ourselves, our wives, our children and all who inhabit this country." It got worse: "We have moreover been appraised of the horrid purpose of our treacherous and bloody enemy, to unite in his ranks as instruments of his unholy and savage work, the negroes, whether slaves or free, thus lighting the torch of war, in the bosoms of our domestic circles." Others cast their suspicions toward Tejanos. Writing days later from the countryside west of town, Benjamin White warned Brazoria, "news is that all Americans in Guadaloupe were butchered by the citizens, Spaniards. . . . Unless you can rally and send on men forthwith, to cover [the] retreat, all must be lost." In some Texas plantation districts, as white families fled en masse, those remaining feared that enslaved people would make their own common cause with nearby Indians. One report claimed, "The negroes high upon the Trinity . . . have endeavoured to enlist the Coshatti Indians on their side and come down and murder the inhabitants & join the Mexicans." Farther east, reports from Nacogdoches of a Mexican envoy courting independent Indians even prompted US military leaders in Louisiana to request volunteers from nearby states, in case Indians "on our side of the boundary line" joined "in the war of extermination now raging in Texas."[42]

Such fears spurred drastic action. As Mexican general Joaquín Ramírez y Sesma's forces approached Gonzales, they found an abandoned wagon, surmising that the driver had "returned violently" to warn the town. Fearing this "would alarm the population," the general sent a proclamation in English to assure peaceful colonists they would not be harmed. "In spite of this," he wrote horrified, "they have consummated their barbarity, burning entirely three homes on this side of the river, and the whole *Villa*, including seeds, tableware, and whatever else they had . . . they set fire to everything and fled." Another officer, José Enrique de la Peña, met a young Tejana in Gonzales who described how Anglo-Texans and US volunteers had used common cause rhetoric and violence to ensure the town's evacuation and destruction. "She . . . assured me, as have many other people, that some of the families who did not participate in the war had resolved to wait for us so that they could salvage their possessions, but . . . armed men set fire to their dwellings, by this barbarous method forcing them to flee." When some still refused to leave, the men told them "of the death scenes at the Alamo and at Goliad, which they narrated with all the vehemence of which they are capable." "So it was," he lamented, "that the owners who did not themselves set fire to their homes saw them go up in smoke by other hands, principally by the volunteers who had come from the north and had nothing to lose." For Peña, the domestic detritus left behind in the "Runaway Scrape"—he found a young girl's abandoned hair curlers particularly upsetting—testified to innocent families hoodwinked by the framers of the common cause, "dragged into the war by those who promoted it, who painted us in the blackest colors, describing us to them as savages, as men more ferocious than beasts."[43]

Even Houston was taken aback when San Felipe residents followed suit and "immediately set fire to their own houses and reduced the place to ashes" after the Mexican army crossed the Colorado. He reassured Anglo-Texans, "Let the people not be in any dread of danger, if the men will turn out like men." Perhaps the destruction was unnecessary, but forced evacuation was becoming official policy. On April 2, Houston wrote to Wyly Martin at Fort Bend, responding to rumors that some residents nearby, and one family in particular, had "openly declared" their intent to "join the enemy at the first possible opportunity—under the protection of a white flag." He ordered Martin to investigate and, if the rumors were true, "arrest them instantly, and send them to the Sec. of Govt. at Harrisburg with a copy of the charges against them." Why was the commander in chief personally concerned with the neutrality of a single Anglo family? At that moment, Anglo-Texan independence hinged on the idea of a danger that was, at base, untrue. Indeed, throughout the entirety of the war, the private correspondence and public proclamations of Mexican officials confirmed that despite the policy of executing armed foreigners as pirates, they had no intention of making the alleged "war of extermination" against all Anglo-Texans.[44]

Evacuating people was one thing; making them fight was something else altogether. Rebel leaders' efforts to organize a military defense amid the Runaway Scrape reveal the challenges of unifying people who, despite cultural and other ties, were fundamentally *local* actors. Some policymakers eventually turned this to their advantage, combining rhetoric with coercion to simultaneously rally troops and offer nominal safety to Anglo families. In March, upon taking office as president of the Republic of Texas, David Burnet called for an end to the infighting that had hamstrung three successive Texan governments over the past five months. The common danger made unity the only choice: "let no American lay the secret hope to his heart that *he* would be exempt from the general destruction; for the delusion may be fatal to himself and pernicious to others." The following day, Burnet underscored the gendered nature of that danger, declaring, "Rally, then, fellow-citizens, to the standard of your country. While the army is between your families and the enemy, they are safe. Reinforce and sustain that army, and our wives and children are secure from pollution." Officials repeated this appeal over the next two months, emphasizing the martyrdom of "our gallant brothers slaughtered at the Alamo" and warning Anglo men that inaction would "abandon helpless women and children to their fate."[45]

As rhetoric proved its limited value, Anglo-Texan leaders made military participation the law of the land, ordering the arrest and return of all deserters, and stating that anyone found fleeing or hiding "shall forfeit his right to citizenship and all his lands. . . . Every name of those who defend the country shall be recorded, and those whose names are not on the list will be considered as abandoning his country." Days later, Burnet ordered "all families now on the road [to] stop their further progress eastward" and proceed to the south side of Buffalo Bayou, across the water from Mexican troops. A lottery selected a few men to guard women, children, and enslaved people, while the remainder joined the army. In this way, the newborn Anglo-Texan state bound its own fate to the lives of its citizens, offering limited protection for the families of would-be soldiers, while at last securing access to what remained of the colonies' scattering manpower.[46]

Individual Anglo-Texans did indeed engage in and experience the war as a project of nation-making, but it was one firmly embedded within immediate kin and community relationships, even if they now sometimes stretched across borders. Writing many decades later, Dilue Harris, who had been ten years old at the time, recalled an essentially *local* experience of the war. When early reports of invasion reached her family's plantation during corn planting season, they were initially dismissed: "we had heard this news before, but didn't know whether it was true." As reports became more reliable, Harris played her own small part in mobilizing local resources for the national war, casting bullets for the expected fight. News of the Alamo's capture arrived alongside waves of fleeing colonists. This too was personal. As her family and their enslaved laborers joined the mass migration eastward, Harris recalled "weeping all day about Colonel Travis" with her sister. The girls had met him months earlier, and he had left a personal token in the form of some small books, which they were forced to leave behind. Though the only Mexican soldiers Harris met were either dead or imprisoned, the experience proved fatal to one family member—an infant sister who sickened and died on the road.[47]

Harris's turn-of-the-century account joined a wave of genealogy and commemoration that had more to do with that era than the 1830s. But it reflected something that was true in both periods. People on all sides understood the growing power of nation-states in the US-Mexico borderlands within the gendered context of families and local communities. Especially early on, these fluid and unstable projects were most salient when they directly affected those intimate realms—especially if that impact took the form of violence, whether real or imagined. The seamlessness with which Harris and her peers remembered and portrayed the grassroots mobilization of Texas communities sixty-five years later illustrates the success of the common cause and its authors.

In less than a year, elite proslavery agitators had used gendered and racialized ideologies of shared danger to create a new national project in the borderlands. With the help of these narratives, they steered Texas politics toward war and independence, while marshaling vast quantities of manpower and resources from across Texas and the United States. Moreover, they made the process seem totally organic—a spontaneous movement of noble colonists defending themselves from "extermination." The contested new nation-state they built not only seized huge swaths of territory from Mexico and Native nations; it erected unprecedented protections for the expansion of chattel slavery while promoting ongoing immigration and ever-growing social and economic ties with the United States, despite the political barriers to annexation. In the decade after 1836 and beyond, similar familial ideologies of race and nation would remain crucial to Anglo-American nationalism in Texas and across the slaveholding South. As a range of individuals and institutions used such rhetoric to mobilize local participation and resources, they bound the emerging political constructions of the nation-state to both the intimate relationships and the racialized and gendered meanings that structured everyday life.

2

Red Soldiers in Gray

Enlisting Confederate Choctaw Soldiers in the American Civil War

Fay A. Yarbrough

> Den jest as we starting to leave here come something across dat little prairie sho' nuff! We know dey is Indians de way dey is riding, and de way dey is all strung out. Dey had a flag, and it was all red and had a big criss-cross on it dat look lak a saw horse. De man carry it and rear back on it when de wind whip it, but it flap all 'roun de horse's head and de horse pitch and rear lak he know something going to happen, sho!

> Bout dat time it turn kind of dark and begin to rain a little, and we git out to de big road and de rain come down hard. It rain so hard for a little while dat we jest have to stop de wagon and set dar, and den long come more soldiers dan I ever see befo'. Dey all white men, I think, and dey have on dat brown clothes dyed wid walnut and butternut, and old Master say dey de Confederate Soldiers.
>
> —Lucinda Davis, oral history, circa 1937

Lucinda Davis, a woman who had been enslaved by Tuskaya-hiniha, "a full-blood Creek Indian," offers one of the few existing accounts of the Battle of Honey Springs in July 1863. She describes the approach of Native troops carrying the Confederate battle flag, the changing weather conditions, and the arrival of white Confederate troops. Her account goes on to detail the roar of gunfire that sounded "lak hosses loping 'cross a plank bridge way off somewhar."[1] Davis offers compelling testimony about the far-reaching and destructive effects of battle on the civilian population and on the landscape, but what I am most interested in for this essay is the experience of Native soldiers. What do we know of those soldiers on horseback whose riding style was so distinctive that Davis and her fellow spectators identified them as Indians from a distance? What can we say about their experiences with the Confederate army?

In the wealth of scholarship produced about the Civil War, Native groups, when they are discussed at all, tend to appear as a footnote or, perhaps, a chapter, often about military tactics or land loss or as part of a larger effort to consider who constituted the Southern population.[2] In general, there is a dearth of historiographical material that studies Native participation in the American Civil War from the perspective of Native peoples. Scholars have devoted a few volumes to the participation of Cherokee in the war, but the Choctaw Nation has not yet been a focus of study.[3] Recent studies by Mary Jane Warde and Bradley R. Clampitt have looked at the war's impact in Indian Territory as a whole, and Megan Kate Nelson has focused farther west, connecting the Civil War to settler colonial policies.[4] And in classic studies that remain valuable nearly a century after their publication, Annie Heloise Abel explored the ties between the Confederacy and various Indigenous groups.[5]

Thus, one goal of this work is to capture Choctaw voices by using sources produced by the Choctaw Indians themselves whenever possible. The service records for the First Choctaw and Chickasaw Mounted Rifles provide enlistment information about Choctaw troops and occasional insights into the experiences of individual soldiers. These records demonstrate that Choctaw men were early and enthusiastic supporters of the Confederate war effort. Their enlistment patterns often included surges after military battles or when fighting occurred close to Indian Territory. And as with many Southerners, Choctaw fervor for military service faded as the war dragged on and soldiers dealt with supply shortages, inferior supplies when they did finally arrive, and families who suffered at home while the men fought. Choctaw Confederates were not so different from white Confederates in many respects.

Perhaps this conclusion, revealed by the Choctaw military records, is surprising: Choctaw Confederates experienced the Civil War in ways familiar to white Southerners. Where the Choctaw experience differed is in the meaning they attached to their war participation. That is, their identities as Choctaw likely shaped the significance they attached to their fighting, given the traditional importance of warfare to achieving manhood in Choctaw society. Enlistment, then, provided a way for Choctaw men to access full manhood in a world where the federal government discouraged warfare between Native groups. But these ideas are not revealed in the military records. Likewise, these sources do not address the political calculus of Choctaw lawmakers as they contemplated whether to remain neutral in the war, or slavery's role in the Choctaw decision to ally with the Confederacy. The Confederate government offered the Choctaw multiple inducements, including assuming the federal debt owed to the Choctaw and promising to protect Choctaw sovereignty. And Choctaw were active participants in the enslavement of people of African descent, with some Choctaw engaged in large-scale plantation agriculture. For more on martial masculinity, the Choctaw practice of slavery, and the decision to ally with the South, I point readers to my monograph *Choctaw Confederates: The American Civil War in Indian Country*.[6] Here my focus is on extracting information from the service records to provide a snapshot of Choctaw soldiers' military experience during the war.

The service records I rely on to illuminate the soldiers described by Lucinda Davis come from the National Archives: Compiled Service Records of Confederate Soldiers Who Served in Organizations Raised Directly by the Confederate Government.[7] From the outset, however, these records are something of a misnomer. This title suggests that authorities from the Confederate States of America enlisted these troops into service; however, the Choctaw were quite committed to their alliance with the Confederate States of America. They had early allied with the Confederacy and agreed to place a regiment of Choctaw troops numbering one thousand men, under white officers, committing to pay $500,000 to arm and equip said troops.[8] Which authorities, Choctaw or Confederate, enlisted these troops, then, is less clear than the records' title would suggest, which will also be demonstrated by my examination of the enlistment documents. In addition, I supplement the service records with firsthand accounts from Civil War soldiers more broadly to create a fuller picture of Choctaw soldiers' experiences.

Before I discuss what these records reveal about the soldiers' experiences, however, I describe these records in detail. I do this for several reasons. First, while scholars often assume that written records about Native people are sparse, these records represent thousands of pages of documents. Second, although some might question the reliability of documents that appear to be an artifact of the twentieth century, I contend that these records accurately represent the often difficult-to-trace quotidian activities of common soldiers during the Civil War. Third, the transfer of this information onto government forms reinforces how numerous the records are: federal officials spent money to design and print these forms to organize a large body of information. Finally, this deep dive into the minutiae of the evidence reveals something of my methodology; in short, I want to give readers a sense of how I attempted to wring meaning from what may appear to be brief and generic forms. In particular, the records reveal patterns of enlistment that I contend represent Choctaw enthusiasm for the war, an enthusiasm that seemed to decline after the Battle of Honey Springs.

The majority of the enlistment records consist of preprinted forms compiled by the War Department to facilitate efficient and rapid determinations of individual eligibility for pensions and other veterans benefits. Each record includes a jacket with the soldier's name, company, and rank, as well as a list of the other cards associated with his record. This jacket also indicates whether the soldier's records appear under a different spelling of his name. There were sufficient numbers of Choctaw troops that an official created preprinted jackets or envelopes stating, "1 Choctaw Mounted Rifles. Also known as Cavalry. (Confederate.)." The jacket often contains a fill-in-the-blank-style company muster roll. The company name and the information "(Confederate.) 1 Choctaw and Chickasaw Mounted Rifles" appear preprinted on this form as well. The form lists the date, location, and term of enlistment. One version of the form asks for the enlistee's age; a later version does not. Especially useful is the remarks section. In most cases it merely indicates whether an enlistee was still present at the end of his term of service, but sometimes it includes rich tidbits about absence without leave, promotions, or work duties. A frequently included payroll form states whether the soldier received a commutation for clothing for six months, generally in the amount of twenty-five dollars. Sometimes a bounty pay and receipt roll for fifty dollars is on file as well, along with petitions or official correspondence regarding the soldier. Less frequently, other miscellaneous documents, often handwritten, are included in the soldier's jacket.

The contemporary Choctaw Nation estimates that approximately 1,200 Choctaw troops had served on the side of the Confederacy by the middle of the Civil War.[9] I have collected the service records of over 3,100 individuals for the totality of the Civil War. If one counts only those records for individuals who enlisted in 1861 and 1862, there are over 1,800 individuals, which is closer to Edward Elmer Prag's finding that the Choctaw and Chickasaw Confederate forces comprised 1,885 men in June 1861, the third month of the war.[10] Prag's number includes Chickasaw Confederates, whom I do not discuss here, but even so, the 1,200 estimate by the middle of the Civil War is likely quite low. To be sure, there is likely some duplication in my records, but if the information differed in any detail for two records with the same name, company name, or age, for instance, I retained both entries. There are separate records for Chickasaw soldiers; thus, the individuals I included appear to be from the Choctaw Nation.

The 3,100 troops represented in the records translate into roughly 17.2 percent of the total Choctaw population, or 20 percent if one excludes the enslaved population. In the United States, soldiers accounted for approximately 14.6 percent of the Northern population (2.7 million served out of a population of 18.5 million) and 8.3 percent of the Confederacy and border states (approximately 1 million served out of a population of 12 million). If one excludes the enslaved population of the South, however, 12.5 percent of Southerners served in the Confederacy (the Southern population drops to 8 million if one excludes enslaved persons).[11] Thus, while 3,100 troops may seem like a small number in the aggregate, as a proportion of the Choctaw population it is large. Of course, this figure of 3,100 troops is much lower than the 10,000 troops that Colonel Douglas H. Cooper, writing to Confederate president Jefferson Davis, predicted that the Choctaw and Chickasaw would provide, a number all the more astonishing given that the combined Choctaw and Chickasaw population at this time was less than 23,000 people, including their enslaved populations.[12] Cooper wrote: "The Choctaws and Chickasaw can furnish 10,000 warriors if needed. The Choctaws and Chickasaws are extremely anxious to form another regiment."[13]

The data included in the Compiled Service Records not only tells us about individual soldiers but reveals aspects of the changing nature of Choctaw society. For instance, the names on these records simultaneously demonstrate the influence of Euro-Americans and the resilience of traditional naming practices. Names include John Simpson, several Thomas Jeffersons, and Jefferson Davis (a private, aged twenty-five), but also Cubbee, Eahantubbee, Haiokonubi, and Shumpalubbee. Some listed names are a blend of traditional Choctaw names and European names: William Eyashahopaye, Shiaheka Thompson, or Lewis Himakambi. The surnames of prominent families within the Choctaw political arena also appear: the Fulsoms, Leflores, and McCurtains are three examples, each family having produced district or principal chiefs of the Choctaw Nation during the nineteenth century.

The age data on soldiers from the First Choctaw and Chickasaw Mounted Rifles provides some opportunity for comparison with data on American soldiers in the Civil War and again confirms a parallel experience. The average age for the Choctaw enlistees was 27.9, with a median age of 25. The average age of Union soldiers was 25.8, and the median age was 23.5. Similar data for Confederate soldiers does not exist; however, Civil War historian James M. McPherson offers some numbers based on a small sample size of 429: 26.5 years of age on average at enlistment, with a median age of 24.2.[14] These Native soldiers, then, were slightly older than their American counterparts. The age data and name data also suggest relationships between soldiers. Were the cluster of five Greenwood enlistees, aged twenty to twenty-eight, related to one another in some way? Allen, Gibson, Harris, Hogan, and Sesson Greenwood all mustered into Company 1-E as privates at Black Jack Court Ground on July 3, 1861, so perhaps they were. Similarly, Joseph Hunter, aged forty-three, and Stilon Hunter, aged eighteen, both joined the Maytubby Company at Goodland Station on September 2, 1864. Could they have been a father and son joining together in hopes of watching out for each other? The sources are maddeningly silent about such connections, though we know other relatives did enlist together during the Civil War.[15]

The question of company assignment may seem straightforward: individuals mustered into Company A or 2-K or 2-D, among many others. As was common among other Confederate and federal troops, some Choctaw companies were also known by names connected to their commanding officers. Captain Sinta Nowa's company, for example, was also known as Walking Snake Company and Company I. Other companies were known as Captain Coleman E. Nelson's company or Captain Edmond Gardner's company or Captain Shemontah's (John Gibson) company. This information is preprinted on enlistment records, reinforcing the idea that these companies were well known by these less-standard names.[16] The use of both Choctaw and English language in the names is also noteworthy. *Sinti* is snake in Choctaw, and *nowa* means a walk or to walk. Walking Snake was thus a translation of Captain Sinta Nowa's name. Shemontah may come from the Choctaw word *shema*, meaning to dress up or embellish.[17] Perhaps Captain Shemontah is the same John Gibson who appeared on the Dawes Rolls as a "full-blood" Choctaw, aged sixty-five in 1899.[18] He was certainly the right age to have served as a captain during the war. The presence of these Native names in Civil War military records exemplifies the way that this quintessentially American event included peoples who did not identify as Americans.

The data on the date and place of muster reveals patterns in where and when soldiers enlisted into the First Choctaw and Chickasaw Mounted Rifles. Almost 70 percent of the records include this information.[19] Careful preservation of the enlistment date was crucial to determining when a soldier's term of service was complete. As one would expect, a surge of young men signed up to fight at the start of the Civil War, in spring 1861. Of the records that include date and muster location data, half indicate enlistments that took place in 1861. June and July 1861 were especially popular months to enlist: the records include 950 enlistments for these two months alone. This Choctaw enthusiasm for the Confederacy is remarkable, given that the Choctaw did not sign a treaty with the Confederacy until July 1861.[20] Thus, Choctaw citizens committed to fight in the war even before the Choctaw legislature had officially sided with the Confederacy.

Historian Annie Heloise Abel notes that the work of consolidating Indian support began before any formal treaties were signed between the Choctaw Indians and the Confederate government.[21] The Choctaw government passed a resolution in support of the Southern states in February 1861, five months before the formal treaty alliance, so gathering Choctaw support may not have been so difficult.[22] Surely the Choctaw resolution was a response to the February 4 meeting of six states in Montgomery, Alabama, to form a provisional government and establish the Confederate States of America.[23] The Choctaw may have been waiting for the seceding states to create a more formal body before expressing support. US Indian agent (and soon Confederate colonel) Douglas H. Cooper enrolled Indians for service as early as April 1861, again before an official treaty of alliance had been signed.[24] Muster rolls show over one hundred Choctaw troops enlisted in May 1861, specifically on May 13 in Skullyville, Indian Territory. Perhaps this enlistment fervor was prompted by the neighboring state of Arkansas's decision to join the Confederacy less than one week prior, on May 7, 1861.[25] Moreover, Skullyville is located near the far eastern border of the Choctaw Nation, very close to the shared border with Arkansas and Fort Smith, and was described by some Choctaw as a particular center for the settlement of enslavers due to agricultural conditions favorable to plantations.[26]

In 1862, enthusiasm for the war among Choctaw Indians was still strong: nearly eight hundred men enlisted in the regiment during the second year of the war. January, March, and July were especially popular times. The almost two hundred men who joined the regiment in January may have been spurred to action by the November and December battles that took place in Indian Territory: Round Mountain, Chusto-Talasah, and Chustenahlah. All three engagements were efforts to subdue wealthy Creek Indian Opothleyahola and his followers. Initially hoping to remain neutral, the Creek leader disagreed with the Creek Council's decision to ally with the Confederacy. While other Indian nations were negotiating treaties of alliance with Confederate officials, Indians loyal to the American federal government were coalescing around Opothleyahola. Though his wife was an enslaver, he promised freedom for enslaved people, and many in nearby Indian nations ran away to join him.[27] Phoebe Banks, whose parents were enslaved by the Creek Perryman and McIntosh families, recalled her family joining "Old Gouge," as Opothleyahola was known: "All our family join up with him, and there was lots of Creek Indians and slaves in the outfit when they made a break for the North. The runaways was riding ponies stolen from their masters."[28] Moreover, many free Black people also favored his Unionist stance and joined the loyal Creek camps, which were growing in size. Some contemporaries estimated that Opothleyahola had as many as 9,000 followers, but only 2,000 would have been fighting men. Colonel Cooper led over 1,400 Native Confederates, supplemented by the Ninth Texas Cavalry, to attack and then pursue Chief Opothleyahola and his band. The three November and December battles punctuated Opothleyahola's flight to Kansas.[29]

Of the 105 deaths noted in the records over the course of the war (four of which were horses), seven were the result of this campaign against Opothleyahola. Cherokee Presbyterian minister Stephen Foreman wrote in his diary in January 1862 that he had heard "about 14" men were lost in the fighting. Perhaps the additional deaths noted by Foreman came from the Ninth Texas Cavalry, which Colonel Cooper had called in as reinforcements.[30] Despite these losses, the Confederate forces could claim a victory because they had forced so many loyal Indians into Kansas and neutralized the threat represented by Opothleyahola. But would this threat remain outside of Indian Territory? Missionary Joseph Murrow worried that once weather conditions improved, "there will be squally times in this territory again, unless there is a considerable force of Confederate troops on the Kansas border to oppose 'Old Posey' [a nickname for Opothleyahola] and his wild Indians and wilder Jayhawkers."[31] If this feeling was widespread within Indian Territory, and among the Choctaw in particular, it may explain the burst of enlistments in January 1862. The men joined the regiment at Eagletown, Lukfahtah, and Doaksville, all located in Apukshunnubbee District, in the southeastern corner of the nation, close to Texas and Arkansas. Nearly 230 more men enlisted in March, again from this same area: Lukfahtah and Nowood in Red River County in the southeastern corner of the district. The companies raised in Red River County formed on March 10, most likely in response to the Battle of Pea Ridge (Elkhorn Tavern in nearby Arkansas) on March 7–8. The First Choctaw and Chickasaw Mounted Rifles failed to arrive on time at Pea Ridge, and the federal forces defeated the Confederate troops. The Confederate general Albert Pike pulled back his forces, leaving Indian Territory isolated. The proximity of the fighting and the threat of Southern failure may have spurred Confederate Choctaw companies to form. June and July brought still another two hundred troops into service.

The October 1862 Tonkawa Massacre, which took place in the Leased District, west of the Chickasaw Nation, highlights the internecine conflict that the Civil War represented within Indian Territory. The Wichita Agency in the Leased District was at the center of the action. The Wichita Indians claimed that their treaty with the Confederacy had been signed under duress, but that groups such as the Comanche and Tonkawa had signed willingly. The Confederate government was not able to meet its obligations for supplies and medicine included in the treaty. As Texans continued to make incursions at the agency despite their shared loyalty to the Confederacy, tensions rose to the point that Indian agent Matthew Leeper moved his family to the safety of Sherman, Texas. When Union raiders, who reportedly included members of the Shawnee, Delaware, Kickapoo, Seminole, Cherokee, and Osage tribes, infiltrated the agency, some Confederate Indians joined the raiders because of their frustrations with Leeper and the Confederate government's unkept promises. Reports of the death of a Caddo boy and the suspected cannibalism of the Tonkawa suddenly focused the various groups' ire sharply on the Tonkawa. The Tonkawa reported to Superintendent S. S. Scott that they lost "twenty-three of their warriors, and about a hundred of their women and children" in the massacre.[32] The American Civil War, then, could exacerbate tensions within Native groups and between Native groups. The war pitted more than white brother against white brother or white friends against each other. Rather than stoke enthusiasm for the Confederacy, the Tonkawa Massacre sowed discord, revealing how convoluted the alliances between groups could be and how old grievances persisted.

The use of conscription to fill the military ranks was an apparent difference between the Confederate and Choctaw governments. By April 1862 President Davis pushed a conscription act through the Confederate Congress to reinforce troop strength with soldiers who served longer enlistments and to centralize control over the Confederate forces.[33] However, fear that the promised bounties and furloughs would not attract enough soldiers was also an impetus for the 1862 act and the Confederate conscription laws to follow. Each successive act enlarged the age pool of the men eligible for the draft: from an initial pool of ages eighteen to thirty-five, then eighteen to forty-five, then finally seventeen to fifty, with men up to age sixty serving on home guards.[34] The Choctaw, on the other hand, did not resort to a draft to augment their troop strength. Rather, when principal chief George Hudson issued a proclamation in June 1861 stating that "all citizens and residents of said nation between the ages of 18 and 45 years, subject to military duty, are required to enroll either in the volunteer or the reserve militia, according to law," with an aim of a troop strength of 700 men, more than 950 men responded in June and July alone.[35] Historian Annie Heloise Abel describes Chief Hudson's proclamation as "in effect, a conscription act."[36] The lack of coercive measures such as penalties for noncompliance and the flood of men who enlisted suggest that the proclamation was not quite a draft, despite Hudson's forceful language.

The Choctaw, instead, appear to have relied on voluntarism and inducements such as bounties and clothing commutations to fill the ranks of the First Choctaw and Chickasaw Mounted Rifles. As late as January 1865, principal chief Peter Pitchlynn recommended that the Choctaw Council pass a "general Military law, which recognizes the volunteer system as just and efficient."[37] Again, Pitchlynn's language reinforces the idea that Hudson's proclamation was not regarded as a draft among Choctaw. Pitchlynn's, and Choctaw Indians', commitment to a volunteer force came at a time when the Confederacy had already passed multiple conscription acts and was even debating arming the enslaved for the war effort.[38] There is no evidence of a discussion of slave enlistment in the Choctaw legislative records.

By 1862, officials were offering Choctaw enlistees a $50 bounty at the time of enlistment. Almost four hundred Choctaw soldiers received the bounty, and the enlistments were concentrated in Doaksville, Eagletown, and Lukfahtah. Almost all the bounty recipients were members of George E. Deneale's company. The $50 bounty may have contributed to the high enlistment rates for 1862 (nearly eight hundred Choctaw) and for the creation of this company in particular. According to a letter from Pitchlynn to William Cass written in January 1862, President Davis sent Colonel Deneale to the Choctaw Nation "to raise a Regiment of Choctaw Warriors to go to Virginia." Pitchlynn stated that guns, horses, and clothing would be provided, and he asked for "healthy men" between the ages of eighteen and forty-five. The men were to meet at Eagle

County Court House and Doaksville. The monthly pay varied by rank: captains would receive $120, first lieutenants $94, and warriors (enlisted men) $24. In addition, warriors would also receive $25 for an initial purchase of clothes and a monthly clothing allowance of $2.50. By the end of the war, Pitchlynn reported, the warriors would receive a $40 bounty, which is less than the $50 listed on the enlistment records.[39] Pitchlynn himself served as a first lieutenant and received a $50 bounty but not the clothing commutation. While his letter suggests that officers in Deneale's company would not receive the clothing commutation, the enlistment records indicate that officers such as Captain Ho Tubbee and Second Lieutenant Wilson Webster did. And not every warrior received the clothing commutation, according to these records.[40]

Choctaw officials likely expected the Confederate government to pay the bounties. The Confederate States of America had agreed to furnish the Choctaw with "the above sum of five hundred thousand dollars to arm and equip said Regiment and maintain in the field for that length of time [twelve months], and after the war and peace is established to reimburse the Choctaw, in said amount by the said Government of the Confederate States."[41] Likewise, soldiers in the various state militias and armies were offered bounties as an inducement to serve. By December 1861, however, it had become clear that a short war was not to be, and Confederate officials worried that the experienced soldiers would not continue to serve when their terms soon expired. Hence, the Confederate Congress passed an act to provide its own $50 bounty and furlough of sixty days to those men who reenlisted.[42] Perhaps the $50 Confederate bounty in the rebelling states replaced the $40 mentioned by Pitchlynn. The bounties also represented a growing worry that there were not enough willing men to serve, regardless of experience.

Over one thousand members of the First Choctaw and Chickasaw Mounted Rifles also received a $25 clothing commutation. For more than 60 percent of these entries, no date or place of muster is included, but the remaining records overwhelmingly represent enlistments that took place from May 1861 to June 1862. The offer of bounties and clothing commutations mirrors recruitment efforts in the larger Confederacy. In February 1862, Joe Thompson's artillery company advertised a $50 bounty and $25 commutation for "able-bodied men who wish to take part in driving the foe from Georgia's soil" near Savannah. In Dalton, Georgia, a regiment raised by Colonel Jesse A. Glenn announced a bounty of $50, $50 annually for clothing, and a monthly wage of $11 for enlistees. Colonel Glenn hoped to attract one thousand volunteers with these inducements.[43]

Despite the promises made by Confederate authorities in the alliance treaties, the Choctaw experienced shortages in supplies and currency. In February 1862, less than a year into the conflict, Major Mitchell LeFlore approached the Choctaw Council to describe the condition of the Choctaw army. LeFlore said that the troops were "suffering sickness & deaths" and presented a verbal petition for the appropriation of money for the army. He averred that if the council members saw the headquarters of the Choctaw troops, they would be convinced of the army's serious need. By October, presumably in response to a different request, the council discussed, amended, and passed an act allocating $2,500 to purchase munitions for the home guards and militia.[44] Despite the Confederacy's inability or unwillingness to meet its treaty obligations to supply the Choctaw war effort, Choctaw soldiers continued to enlist in large numbers. The numbers reflect the strong Choctaw commitment to the Confederate war effort.

By 1863, enlistment numbers had declined sharply: only 189 soldiers enlisted, in contrast with the more than 1,000 enlistments in 1861 and nearly 800 in 1862. The Civil War had by this time gone on much longer than anyone (Choctaw or Confederate) expected. The realities of fighting, familial separation, and poor provisioning extinguished Choctaw enthusiasm for the war. As Confederate officer Edward W. Cade wrote to his wife in 1863, "I am sick of war" and "the separation from the dearest objects of life."[45] Surely many Choctaw soldiers would have agreed with this sentiment. Captain David Perkins, for instance, resigned his command of Company E in the First Choctaw and Chickasaw Mounted Rifles in 1863 because of physical infirmity, but also stated, "And last but not the least reason is, I have so many little children, unless I stay at home and provide for them they must necessarily suffer—as they have been during my first campaign."[46] These men felt the tug of family and home and knew the suffering of civilians as the war continued.

The Choctaw enlistments that did occur in 1863 clustered in February, March, and April, with no enlistments occurring after July. Of course, on January 1, 1863, Abraham Lincoln's Emancipation Proclamation took effect, ending slavery in rebelling states and parts of states. While it was unclear whether the proclamation applied to Indian Territory, news of emancipation spread across this land.[47] If nothing else, US troops often informed enslaved people in Indian Territory of their change in status: Charlotte Johnson White learned of emancipation when soldiers arrived at her Cherokee enslaver's plantation.[48] Perhaps more relevant to Choctaw military enlistments was the activity in the Cherokee Nation in the first part of 1863. A pro-Union faction of Cherokee claimed rightful authority to govern and established a new legislature in February. One of its first acts was to abolish slavery in the Cherokee Nation.[49] While many Cherokee enslavers did not recognize the legitimacy of this new government and likely ignored this act, the fact remains that these actions brought abolition and the prospect of emancipation to the heart of Indian Territory. For some Choctaw, events in the Cherokee Nation may have hardened their resolve and led to the clusters of enlistments in Skullyville and San Bois, locations in Moshulatubbee District, close to the Cherokee Nation.[50] Conversely, perhaps Cherokee emancipation and Lincoln's proclamation led other Choctaw to see the Confederate chances for success declining, softening overall enlistments.

In July, two battles took place in Indian Territory, at Cabin Creek and Honey Springs, possibly affecting Choctaw enlistment numbers. Cabin Creek was located along Texas Road, an important route for moving military supplies from Fort Scott, Kansas, to Indian Territory. The battle consisted of a series of skirmishes as Stand Watie's forces attempted to capture federal supplies. The Confederates eventually failed, and Watie blamed the defeat on his lack of cannons.[51] More remarkable is the diversity of forces present: troops from Colorado, Wisconsin, and Kansas; the Indian home guards; Confederate Indian troops; Texas Partisans; and the First Kansas Colored Volunteers all clashed on the battlefield.[52] Private Christopher Kimball of the Ninth Kansas Cavalry described the federal forces attempting the crossing: "Maj. Foreman assumed command, which consisted of the Indians, five companies of the colored regiment, the mounted men of the 2nd Colorado, and Capt. [Charles J.] Stewart's company, the 9th Kansas. Maj. Foreman, followed by Capt. [Bud Gritts], of the 3rd Indian, advanced into the stream."[53] Private Kimball's words paint a portrait of men of different races fighting together to preserve the country. In fact, historian Mark Lause suggests that the Union's triracial army in the West could have been a model for future race relations in the United States.[54]

Like Cabin Creek, Honey Springs was also located along the important supply route of Texas Road. In the aftermath of the loss at Cabin Creek, Confederate forces used Honey Springs as a staging ground to prepare an attack on Fort Gibson and push federal forces out of Indian Territory. Soldiers amassed at Honey Springs and brought in supplies in preparation for the march to Fort Gibson.[55] Again, the fighting would include men of Native ancestry, men of African descent, and Euro-Americans, a fact not lost on the men involved. As they waited for the command to advance, Colonel James M. Williams told the men of the First Kansas Colored Volunteers, "This is the day we have been patiently waiting for; the enemy at Cabin Creek [gave] you [the] opportunity of showing them what men can do fighting for their natural rights and for their recently acquired freedom and the freedom of their children and their Children's children."[56] Colonel Williams also assessed his men's performance after the fighting: "they [the rebels] received a lesson which in my opinion, taught them not to despise on the battlefield, a race they had long tyrannized over as having no rights which a white man was bound to respect. I had long been of the opinion that this race had a right to kill traitors and this day proved their capacity for the work."[57] Colonel Williams certainly understood the meaning of Black troops' presence on this battlefield, for themselves and for the men they faced. Private Edward Folsom of the First Choctaw and Chickasaw Mounted Rifles was on the other side of the battle lines, and the Black troops made an impression on him as well.

He remarked, "It was not long before the Federal cavalry found us and came over with Negro troops and give us fight. We had one side of Elk Creek and they the other. It was a stand up fight I never did see so many wounded Negro troops in a small fight."[58] Soldiers everywhere, not just in the South, were impressed and sometimes unsettled by the combat action of Black troops during the war.

The Confederates failed at Honey Springs because of inferior munitions supplies and, in part, the combined actions of the First Kansas Colored Volunteers and the Indian home guards. The Confederates outnumbered the federals two to one but were outgunned three to one. And the inferior quality of Confederate gunpowder meant that the downpour during the battle on July 17 rendered their arms useless, according to Douglas H. Cooper, by now a general.[59] As the fighting raged on, the federal Indian home guard regiment inadvertently misled the Twentieth and Twenty-Ninth Texas Cavalry into thinking the federals were retreating. The Texans pursued, only to be met with a volley of bullets from the First Kansas Colored and forced to pull back. Then federal troops picked up the Texans' colors.[60] Tandy Walker arrived with Choctaw and Chickasaw troops late in the fight and was able to hold the federal forces as the Confederate forces continued to retreat. Dallas Bowman, a private from the First Choctaw and Chickasaw Mounted Rifles, remembered, "The Feds followed us about a half mile out on the prairie at which time our battalion charged on them and held them in check until the train could get out of the way."[61] Native troops, then, were important to both Confederate and federal forces in the battle. As the troops fled, General Cooper ordered the destruction of supplies and munitions located in Honey Springs. Corporal W. K. Makemson of the Confederate Indian brigade led the squad that set fire to the commissary and quartermaster stores.[62] Henry Clay, who had been enslaved in the Creek Nation, remembered the smoke and fire as "the Yankees burn up Honey Springs," but in reality, he likely saw not federal action but Confederate efforts to keep supplies out of enemy hands.[63]

Some enslaved people also witnessed the battle and described the fighting and retreat years later. Creek freedwoman Lucinda Davis heard "de guns going all day, and along in de evening here come de South side making for a getaway. Dey come riding and running by whar we is, and it don't make no difference how much de head men hollers at 'em dey can't make dat bunch slow up and stop."[64] Davis's description matches Private Bowman's comments that Confederate troops scattered, "which caused confusion and we had a general stampede." Likewise, Private Folsom reported that his company's picket "stampeded and broke for the mountains and most got away."[65] Phoebe Banks's uncle Jacob told her that the fighting at Honey Creek "was the most terrible fighting he seen, but the Union soldiers whipped and went back into Fort Gibson. The Rebels was chased all over the country and couldn't find each other for a long time the way he tell it." Banks's family had been enslaved by a Creek family and followed Opothleyahola to Kansas. Uncle Jacob had returned to Indian Territory with federal troops to "fight the Indians who stayed with the South."[66] A disheartened Private R. McDermott from the Twentieth Texas Cavalry seems to confirm Uncle Jacob's account: "I belive they will whip us and whip us all the time until we are reinforced from Texas or some other point. I know it for I have tried them and they are as good as we are, better drilled and better armed. We got so much scatteredness in the stampede that we was 3 days getting together and not all have come in yet."[67] It seems that Confederate soldiers truly had scattered across the country and did not immediately regroup for a counterattack or another engagement.

The Battle of Honey Springs proved to be the largest battle fought in Indian Territory in terms of numbers: approximately ten thousand men met in battle there, nearly six thousand Confederates and some four thousand Union soldiers. The Confederate loss left Texas Road open for Union control and allowed federal troops to take Fort Gibson. Some view Honey Springs as a turning point for Confederate forces in Indian Territory, after which white troops no longer defended the area in an organized manner. Moreover, the victory gave federal troops an avenue into the Choctaw Nation, "the fiercest and most steadfast of the Indian Nations in the Confederacy."[68] Given the scale of the fighting and the defeat, it comes as no surprise that the First Choctaw and Chickasaw Mounted Rifles did not see any new enlistments for the remainder of the year. The federals sent troops to Fort Gibson to strengthen their position in the territory, and July 1863 handed Confederate forces major losses.[69] Confederates were back on their heels, and Choctaw soldiers may have viewed the Southern effort as a losing one overall.

Historian Whit Edwards states that the "desertion rate in the Confederate army in the Indian Territory was alarming" and attributes many desertions to the increased federal presence at Fort Gibson after the Battle of Honey Springs. However, the military records of the First Choctaw and Chickasaw Mounted Rifles indicate that the vast majority of incidents of this unit's soldiers being absent without leave (AWOL) came before the action at Cabin Creek or Honey Springs.[70] Rather, Choctaw soldiers left their stations without permission most frequently in May 1863. May was a busy time for Choctaw agriculturalists. Soldiers may have returned home in order to plant crops with their families for the fall harvest.[71] And many soldiers returned to their companies in June, before official rolls were taken on the last day of that month. Perhaps soldiers had to appear on the June 30 roll to receive payment for their duty, or, again, perhaps they had simply returned home to complete specific tasks and then returned to the fighting. War fatigue instead of the events of July may have been the culprit for permanently absentee Choctaw soldiers. Nearly 25 percent of the deserters had enlisted in 1861 for a twelve-month term, but remained on active duty in the summer of 1863. Another 30 percent were in the middle of two-year enlistment agreements, while 41 percent were in the middle of three-year service terms. Such soldiers may have left their posts because of a weariness of the war in general, not because of the specific battle losses.

The records for the Confederate Choctaw companies also reveal that desertion rates were higher in two companies in particular: Company 2-C and Company 3-H. Captain Willis Jones led Company 2-C, in which thirty-five soldiers appeared as absent without leave. The soldiers enlisted in July 1861 for twelve months and then reenlisted in July 1862 for two more years.[72] Thus, by May 1863, these soldiers had been serving for nearly two years. Surely some frustration with the length of the war was setting in. One officer, Second Lieutenant Abel McAfee had been absent without leave since July 1862, when the company had reorganized and members reenlisted. In Company 3-H, the numbers are more startling: sixty-nine soldiers were listed as absent without leave. The company formed in March 1862, with men enlisting for three-year terms. Clearly, something drove the mass absenteeism in this unit in May 1863. Captain Lycurgus Pitchlynn (son of Peter) led the group, supported by Lieutenant Belvin Wilson. By November 1862, Lieutenant Wilson was dead, which likely decreased group morale. Moreover, Captain Pitchlynn himself was listed as a deserter and dropped from the rolls by order of General Cooper in June 1863. Did the May absenteeism lead Pitchlynn to desert, or, rather, was his desertion symptomatic of a larger problem in the company?[73] Perhaps Pitchlynn's leadership was lacking and the soldiers voted with their feet. Or Pitchlynn may have tacitly approved of the men's actions because he himself planned to return home. Given Pitchlynn's own troubled past, which included a conviction for assault and battery with intent to kill and an admitted alcohol problem, the company's de facto dissolution under his command should come as no surprise.[74]

In 1864, the already sharply declining enlistment rates among the Choctaw dropped even further: there were only fifty-seven recorded enlistments, all of them in September at Goodland Station and under the banner of the Maytubby Company. Goodland Station was located on the grounds of Goodland Academy, in the southeast corner of Pushmataha District, near the Choctaw Nation's border with Texas. Presbyterian and Congregational missionaries founded the academy in 1848, and during the war Choctaw regiments camped on the school's grounds.[75] The company's namesake, Peter Maytubby, initially enlisted in June 1861 as a first lieutenant in Company 2-D, formerly known as Company 1-H.[76] As a captain, he formed the Maytubby Company in 1864. The entire company enlisted for terms of "3 years or the war." This slight boost in recruitment in 1864, which seems late in the war, may have been a response to some success achieved by General Cooper in consolidating his command and ambushing the Sixth Kansas Cavalry at Massard Prairie, Arkansas, close to Fort Smith and Skullyville, on July 27. Earlier in July, just prior to the events of Massard Prairie and the September bump in enlistments, the council also passed an act directing the principal chief to form a brigade in conjunction with the Chickasaw for Confederate service for three years or the duration of the war.[77] So there may have been a broader push for recruits in the Choctaw Nation that led to the September enlistments. In 1865, the final year of the war, the records show just one enlistment in the Choctaw Confederate service, in March.

The Compiled Service Records for the soldiers of the First Choctaw and Chickasaw Mounted Rifles provide a window into the experiences of Civil War soldiers in Indian Territory. These troops often did not leave journals or diaries, and letters home were rare indeed. Service records include important information about when and where soldiers mustered for battle and for how long they enlisted. Like their fellow American soldiers, Choctaw rushed to serve early in the war, but their commitment waned as the war dragged on for longer than anyone had anticipated: half the men in the regiment enlisted in 1861. In particular, fighting at Pea Ridge and Opothleyahola's opposition to allying with the Confederacy may have sparked some Choctaw enlistments. Age data from the records indicates that Choctaw soldiers were a little older than their American counterparts. And a wave of desertions in May and June 1863 may have had more to do with seasonal agricultural patterns than with specific battles or events. Thus, a picture emerges of the enlistees: enthusiastic at the beginning of the war, but plagued by poor provisions, desertion, and waning enthusiasm as the war progressed. It is a picture that is surprisingly and perhaps uncomfortably similar to the story we know about white Confederate soldiers' experience of the war.

3

African American Military Service and Citizenship in Late Nineteenth-Century America

Amanda Bellows

On January 22, 2021, retired four-star army general Lloyd Austin became the first African American secretary of defense, following his Senate confirmation.[1] Austin issued a statement on Twitter, declaring, "It's an honor and a privilege to serve as our country's 28th Secretary of Defense, and I'm especially proud to be the first African American to hold the position."[2] A momentous occasion, Austin's selection as secretary of defense served as a reminder of the slow pace of change in the US armed forces over the course of the twentieth and twenty-first centuries. Just months earlier, the *New York Times* published an article decrying the underrepresentation of African Americans at the highest levels of the US military, noting that three-quarters of a century after its desegregation, its "upper echelons remain[ed] the domain of white men."[3] Although nearly half of male enlisted recruits in 2016 for all branches of the military were African American, Hispanic, American Indian, Asian, or Native Hawaiian, the *New York Times* reported in 2020 that "of the 41 most senior commanders in the military . . . only two [were] black."[4] These findings direct attention to the topics of African American military service, citizenship, and discrimination, subjects that have been deeply intertwined throughout US history.

From the nation's founding in 1776 to the twenty-first century, African Americans have served as soldiers, sailors, airmen, and marines. Historians of colonial America recall the sacrifices of Crispus Attucks, a formerly enslaved man who was killed during the Boston Massacre (1770), and the enslaved and free Black men who died while fighting in the Continental Army during the Revolutionary War (1775–83). Although they helped free the colonies from British rule, Black soldiers could not liberate the hundreds of thousands of African Americans who remained in captivity at the birth of the American republic.[5] The nation's founding documents promised liberty to its people but failed to abolish slavery or grant citizenship to enslaved African Americans. Slavery grew in the South and expanded westward during the early republican period, when Black and white abolitionists vociferously called for its destruction. On the eve of the US Civil War (1861–65), four million African Americans remained enslaved and were denied the rights of citizenship. To end slavery and preserve the Union, almost two hundred thousand African Americans, many of whom escaped from bondage in the Confederate South, enlisted in the Union army. By defeating the Confederacy, they helped secure a victory that resulted in slavery's abolition. In the aftermath of the war, freedpeople gained citizenship but continued to face discrimination and racial violence. During Reconstruction and the oppressive Jim Crow era that followed, African Americans served as soldiers who rebuilt and enforced order in the postwar South, expanded the western frontier, and furthered American imperial ambitions abroad.

This essay focuses on the links between military service and citizenship for African American soldiers between 1861, when the Civil War began, and 1898, when the United States won the war against Spain in the Caribbean and the Philippines. Following the ratification of the Fourteenth Amendment in 1868, freedpeople collectively exercised their privileges and immunities as constitutionally recognized citizens for the first time. During the critical thirty-year period that followed, African Americans would not only fight against white Americans on the home front who sought to disfranchise, subjugate, or terrorize their community, but also participate in military conflicts domestic and foreign.[6] This essay examines the reasons that African American men decided to serve in the US military during an era defined by civil war, national rebuilding, imperial expansion, and racial oppression. Their decisions to enlist were never easy; at key historical moments, African Americans passionately debated the morally fraught question of whether they should further the interests of a government that did not guarantee or adequately protect their rights. While some African Americans advocated military service as a pathway to citizenship or to increased legal protection after the ratification of the Fourteenth Amendment, others opposed it due to continued anti-Black discrimination and violence.[7] Military service provided opportunities for personal growth, but life in the segregated army during the late nineteenth century was difficult due to racism that limited possibilities for advancement and shaped daily life.

In addition, this essay investigates the experiences and outcomes of military service between 1861 and 1898, focusing on material conditions for Black soldiers as well as the instances of discrimination that they experienced from fellow soldiers, commanding officers, and citizens. It looks at the consequences of service and the ways in which soldiering advanced collective and national interests.

By fighting for the Union, which sought to end slavery in the Confederacy following President Abraham Lincoln's issuance of the Emancipation Proclamation in 1863, African Americans secured liberty for millions of enslaved people. After emancipation, they helped restore order in the Reconstruction-era South and enforced laws that outlined important new rights for freedpeople. Finally, African Americans furthered the nation's imperial ambitions by pushing the frontier westward during the late nineteenth century and helping defeat Spain during the Spanish-American War (1898).

AFRICAN AMERICAN SOLDIERS IN THE UNION ARMY

In 1861, the national divisions between those who supported slavery and those who advocated its abolition had immeasurably deepened. When rebel troops in South Carolina fired on Fort Sumter in April of that year, the outbreak of civil war seemed unavoidable, but African Americans' role in the conflict remained undefined. Two subsequent years of war led to thousands of deaths, but by 1863 neither the Confederacy nor the Union could claim victory. The federal government hoped to gain the upper hand against the Confederates in part through the enlistment of a new group of civilians, free and formerly enslaved African Americans. In January 1863, Lincoln issued the Emancipation Proclamation, a document that liberated enslaved people in the Confederacy and permitted the enlistment of African American soldiers into the Union army, ultimately emphasizing for the first time slavery's abolition as a central military aim. The War Department enacted its General Order 143 four months later, formally announcing the creation of the Bureau of Colored Troops, which would manage the registration and training of Black US Army soldiers. It remained uncertain, however, whether African Americans would join the fight to defeat the Confederacy and preserve a nation that did not yet legally recognize them as citizens.

Black Americans considering the prospect of enlisting in the army in 1863 harbored significant concerns. With military service came the possibility of death from violence, disease, exposure, or accident. As soldiers, they had to leave behind their families for an uncertain future. From the Civil War's outset, abolitionist Frederick Douglass urged the destruction of the South, advocating what historian David W. Blight describes as "a long and merciless war that would not only root out and destroy secession but [also] the 'monster' of slavery itself."[8] Born into slavery in Talbot County, Maryland, Douglass successfully escaped from bondage at the age of twenty-eight and made a new life for himself in the North as a powerful writer and orator who forcefully championed the abolition of slavery.[9] His personal experience instilled in him a lifelong hatred of the institution and a drive to secure the liberation of the millions of African Americans who remained enslaved in 1861. Douglass advocated Black military service from the outset of the war and lamented the federal government's initial refusal to permit the enlistment of African Americans. In his autobiography, he recalled how he "spoke as [he] believed, all over the North, that the mission of the war was the liberation of the slave, as well as the salvation of the Union; and hence from the first [he] reproached the North that they fought the rebels with only one hand, when they might strike effectually with two . . . and that the Union cause would never prosper till the war assumed an anti-slavery attitude, and the negro was enlisted on the loyal side." Douglass used his pen and his influence to share his convictions, he recalled, "in every way possible—in the columns of [his] paper and on the platform, by letters to friends, at home and abroad."[10]

Shortly after the issuance of the Emancipation Proclamation, Douglass's sons Lewis and Charles answered their father's call for African American men "to fly to Arms!"[11] They joined the Fifty-Fourth Massachusetts, an all-Black regiment that displayed tremendous bravery at the Battle of Fort Wagner in South Carolina, in July 1863. A third son, Frederick, traveled to Mississippi to encourage African Americans to enlist.[12] But some African Americans remained hesitant to fight for a country that denied them citizenship and failed to protect them. Some feared the prospect of capture by Confederate troops and the particular dangers that awaited Black Union soldiers. Confederates openly threatened to murder Black Union soldiers or sell them into slavery, words that troubled the federal government and likely deterred potential enlistees. To reassure Black soldiers and to prevent Confederates from committing war crimes, President Lincoln's administration issued General Order 100 on April 24, 1863, which urged Confederates not to abuse imprisoned Black soldiers and to obey international law.[13] But some Americans argued that this executive order did not adequately protect Black Union soldiers. For instance, in a letter published in the *Liberator* in May 1863, abolitionist Gerrit Smith expressed his skepticism about the ability of the Union army to recruit Black soldiers because the federal government "ha[d] not the manliness to promise to see to it that captured blacks shall, instead of being murdered or sold into slavery, as the rebels threaten, to be treated as prisoners of war."[14]

The prospect of unequal pay discouraged other potential recruits, who faced serving in segregated units under dangerous conditions. General Order 163 stated that African American soldiers would receive a salary of ten dollars per month, from which an additional three dollars would be deducted to cover the expense of clothing.[15] William Woodlin, a member of the Eighth US Colored Troops, decried what he called the "paltry sum of $7 per mo[nth]." In May 1864, Woodlin recorded in his diary the dissatisfaction of his fellow soldiers, writing that "excitement was quite high in reference to the smallness of the pay."[16] Woodlin was not alone in his criticism of the unjust treatment of Black Union soldiers. An article published in January 1864 in *Harper's Weekly*, one of the most popular illustrated periodicals of the nineteenth century, emphatically encouraged readers to support equal pay for Black and white soldiers because of their shared duty of personal sacrifice for the Union cause. "Now that, in obedience to the demands of national common-sense," the article declared, "colored men are enrolled as soldiers, every citizen ought to insist that they shall have exactly the same treatment, chance, and pay as other soldiers."[17]

Despite Democratic disapproval, the US Congress passed legislation six months later ensuring that Black and white Union soldiers would receive equal salaries. The Act Making Appropriations for the Support of the Army promised to give back pay to formerly enslaved soldiers for terms of service up to January 1, 1864, and to free Black soldiers for the full length of their service.[18] The legislation also sought to correct additional areas of disparate treatment by ensuring that African Americans "who have been or may be mustered into the military service of the United States shall receive the same uniform, clothing, arms, equipments, camp equipage, rations, medical and hospital attendance, pay and emoluments, other than bounty, as other soldiers of the regular or volunteer forces of the United States of like arm of the service."[19] Although this law was enacted less than one year before the Civil War ended, it serves as an important marker of the federal government's evolving position regarding the protection of Black soldiers' rights.

A final deterrent to military service was the racism expressed by white Union army soldiers who opposed Black enlistment. James Lindsay Smith, a formerly enslaved man, recounted in his autobiography in 1881 the abuse that many Black soldiers experienced during the Civil War. Although African Americans supported the federal government in its hour of need by enlisting to defeat the Confederacy, he wrote, "Many of them were . . . knocked down by [white Union soldiers], and maltreated in every way. The treatment . . . [they received] was equal to slavery. All this was because the white soldiers did not want to stand side by side with them. . . . Pen can not begin to describe the extreme sufferings of the colored men in this respect."[20] Another Black Union army soldier, Private Burke, was assaulted by his own commanding officer while marching in a procession to honor President Lincoln. A fellow soldier recorded in 1865 that "not being properly drilled, and being perhaps a little awkward in his movements, this devoted soldier of the United States army [Burke] was struck senseless and bleeding to the ground with a tremendous blow from a sword in the hand of an arrant coward and brute, his Company commander."[21] The attack was particularly shocking since it came from an officer who was supposed to protect the soldiers he led, indicating that racism could pervade all ranks of the military. Unfortunately, African American soldiers like Burke had few avenues for rectifying wrongs committed by their military superiors, since, the anonymous observer lamented, "to complain in the present instance would be deemed insubordination."[22]

Despite the dangers of enlistment, the material inequality that characterized the experience of soldiering, and the racism of white troops, 179,000 African Americans fought for the Union army and 19,000 joined the US Navy over the course of the war.[23] They accounted for more than 10 percent of the total fighting force and made a significant contribution to the war effort. The vast majority of African American soldiers hailed from the US South and border states, a fact that suggests that most soldiers were formerly enslaved men who had a personal stake in defeating the slaveholding Confederacy.[24] Formerly enslaved African Americans who fought for the Union cause ultimately helped secure liberty for themselves and millions of others. Eight months after the Confederacy's surrender at Appomattox, Virginia, on April 9, 1865, the required majority of states ratified the Thirteenth Amendment, which formally abolished slavery in the United States. During the tumultuous years that followed, Congress passed the Fourteenth Amendment, which granted citizenship to all persons born or naturalized in the United States, and the Fifteenth Amendment, which gave Black men the right to exercise their political voices by voting. Through their military service to the Union army, African American soldiers helped secure these critical victories in the fight for Black rights.

AFRICAN AMERICAN SOLDIERS IN THE POSTWAR SOUTH

After the conclusion of the Civil War, a conflict in which more than 750,000 soldiers perished, African Americans continued to experience violence and discrimination during the turbulent period of Reconstruction (1865–77) and the subsequent Jim Crow era.[25] Black soldiers, who had given up so much during the war, decried the unjust postwar treatment of African Americans, which persisted despite the ratification of the Reconstruction amendments. Richard McDaniel, an African American man from Indiana who served in the Eleventh US Colored Heavy Artillery, pointed out white northerners' hypocrisy in 1865. In a revealing letter, McDaniel recorded his frustrations after the war's end, writing that "the colored men have fought their battles, achieved their victories, and saved the Union. Now they say that we can't all live on the same soil, and we will have to make some provision to dispense with the negro!" McDaniel recognized that African Americans' fight for freedom was just beginning and expressed his hope that "our people [will not] . . . let this thing go on without opposition."[26] In the years ahead, many African Americans would view continued military service as a pathway for securing liberty and for achieving personal or national advancement as the United States rebuilt its fractured country and expanded westward.

In 1866, Congress established six new all-Black regiments: the Thirty-Eighth, Thirty-Ninth, Fortieth, and Forty-First Infantry, and the Ninth and Tenth Cavalry. Further restructuring three years later produced the Twenty-Fourth and Twenty-Fifth Infantry Regiments, which joined the Ninth and Tenth Cavalry in the western part of the continental United States.[27] African American soldiers' decisions to continue serving in the US Army after the Civil War were difficult. The transition from wartime to peacetime left some soldiers with an uncertain future and limited means with which to support their families, particularly when the federal government did not live up to its promises to veterans.[28] For instance, two African American soldiers argued that their families received inadequate rations from the US government shortly after the war ended, in the spring of 1865. Richard Etheridge and William Benson, members of the Thirty-Sixth US Colored Infantry Regiment, stationed near Richmond, Virginia, petitioned Union army general Oliver Otis Howard for better conditions for their families, who were living in the Freedmen's Colony of Roanoke Island in North Carolina. They declared that they had "served in the US Army faithfully and don [their] duty to our Country," but the government was not compensating them fairly for their sacrifices. The men explained that their families were starving because the government had reduced the rations owed as a condition of their enlistment. To make matters worse, Etheridge and Benson continued, the assistant superintendent of Negro affairs on Roanoke Island stole and resold their remaining rations, taking "no notice of their [wives' and children's] actual suffering."[29] These circumstances made Benson's and Etheridge's continued military service challenging, due to their inability to provide for their kin. Their petition to General Howard serves as evidence of the unfair treatment that Black soldiers and their families received from the US government during the aftermath of the Civil War.

African American soldiers who remained in the army contributed significantly to the rebuilding of the war-torn nation and protected the rights of freedpeople, who gained citizenship and the franchise during Reconstruction. Historian Gregory P. Downs argues that Black soldiers "continued to play an outsize role in shaping life on the ground in the South" after the Civil War ended. They kept order in former Confederate states, where federal troops maintained a significant presence, and shaped postbellum race relations between freedpeople and white southerners.[30] In 1866, a soldier succinctly outlined the duties of the troops to the commanding officer of the Sixty-First US Colored Infantry; their assignment was to "keep the country quiet, arrest criminals, protect the weak and defenceless from wrong and outrage, and generally enforce obedience to the laws and orders."[31] Such responsibilities differed greatly from those of wartime, but were no less important in holding together the fragile union and securing liberty for African Americans. In the immediate aftermath of the war, African American soldiers made up 36 percent of army forces, continuing to serve bravely across the South, where they challenged white supremacists who sought to restore the repressive antebellum social and political order.[32]

Among the US Army's most important jobs during the postwar period were the suppression of violence, which exploded during political elections, and the protection of African Americans' ability to vote. The Reconstruction Acts of

1867–68 guaranteed the franchise to men regardless of race in former Confederate states and authorized the US Army to uphold voting rights using force. Scholar Gabriel J. Chin argues that "the Reconstruction Acts were highly effective in enfranchising African-Americans as the victorious U.S. Army directly enforced them during its occupation of the former Confederacy."[33] Even with the presence of the US Army, however, violence frequently erupted during election season. Downs writes of two notable episodes during Reconstruction. In 1868 in Arkansas, white supremacists assassinated US congressman James Hinds and threatened a group of Republican politicians sheltering in the state capitol. Afterward, Arkansas's governor ordered two thousand Black and white militiamen to restore order throughout the state by crushing Klan violence and holding trials. Three years later, violent upheaval in Texas prompted Governor Edmund Davis to "declar[e] martial law and [send] black officers to arrest almost 6,000 civilians."[34]

Episodes of brutality flared up across the South during the years when US Army troops and Black militiamen struggled to keep peace; indeed, their very presence stirred the violent disaffection of southern white people. Another striking example of African Americans' role in protecting Black voters and politicians occurred in 1878, when US congressman Robert Smalls of South Carolina endured an attack led by hundreds of white supremacists. Smalls was a courageous man who escaped from slavery during the Civil War by sailing a Confederate ship into Union hands. He subsequently served as a pilot for the US Navy and as an elected official in the South Carolina House of Representatives, the South Carolina Senate, and the US House of Representatives.[35]

At a political meeting in the town of Gillisonville, South Carolina, in 1878, however, Smalls found his life in danger. Educator Laura Towne, who was teaching at a school for freedpeople on Saint Helena Island at the time, recorded in her diary that shortly after the election that year, eight hundred white supremacists descended on Gillisonville. They began terrorizing the Black population, "slap[ping] the faces of the colored women coming to the meeting, whooping and yelling and scattering the people on all sides."[36] Smalls retreated into a store with a contingent of armed supporters, but the white supremacists fired shots into the building and threatened to "set fire to the house and burn him up in it." Hundreds of African Americans rallied to Smalls's defense before he escaped by train. Towne recorded that Smalls subsequently was met at every station by "troops of negroes, one and two hundred all together, all on their way to Gillison to the rescue."[37] Towne's description does not make clear whether these troops were active soldiers in the US Army; however, they may have been militiamen or Union army veterans. Their courageous work in protecting the Black population of South Carolina and one of the state's most prominent politicians stands as an additional example of the critical role that Black soldiers played in defending the rights of citizenship for African Americans after emancipation.

The election of Republican presidential candidate Rutherford B. Hayes in 1877 heralded the winding down of the US military's role in the former Confederacy. During the Hayes and subsequent Garfield administrations, Congress and the US Supreme Court weakened the powers of the US Army. Whereas soldiers were expected to maintain order and quell domestic violence during Reconstruction, Congress passed the Posse Comitatus Act in 1878, which restricted federal soldiers from acting as a police force.[38] Violence subsequently increased during the Jim Crow era, when white supremacists targeted Black men and lynching rates rose further. African American soldiers who continued serving in the US Army during the late nineteenth century, however, would increasingly participate in the federal government's project to gain control of the western frontier.

AFRICAN AMERICAN SOLDIERS ON THE WESTERN FRONTIER

After Reconstruction ended, African American soldiers, many of whom had originally joined under the Union army, continued their military careers out west. As part of all-Black regiments created in 1866, they served on the American frontier, a term that scholar James N. Leiker describes as "the peripheral edge of white settlement socially and geographically."[39] The members of these units took on the complex job of furthering the settlement of western territory. Leiker characterizes their task as fraught because, as "black males, themselves victims of white prejudice, [they] voluntarily aided the subjugation of Native peoples for the benefit of Anglo expansion," a phenomenon that "illustrates the complicated, even paradoxical nature of American race relations" during the second half of the nineteenth century.[40]

The Ninth and Tenth Cavalry eventually adopted the name Buffalo Soldiers, a moniker likely conferred on them by the Native Americans they encountered.[41] Not long afterward, the term Buffalo soldiers was more broadly applied to African Americans serving in the all-Black regiments on the frontier. Their tasks ranged from the construction of infrastructure projects that increased the efficiency of westward expansion to participation in conflicts with Native Americans who opposed encroachment and dispossession. The pay statements of soldiers in the Tenth Cavalry and the Twenty-Fourth Infantry indicate that they typically served five-year terms during the 1860s and 1870s, earning approximately thirteen dollars per month.[42] Their salaries were comparable to those of white soldiers during the same period, due in large part to the passage of the Enrollment Act on March 3, 1865, which affirmed that Black and white soldiers would receive equal pay.[43]

Although the first Buffalo Soldiers served in no sustained, major war, their lives on the frontier were not without danger. In his diary from 1868, Samuel K. Thompson, a lieutenant in the Fifty-Fourth Infantry during the Civil War and a soldier in the Twenty-Fifth Infantry thereafter, composed a comprehensive "last will and testament" owing to, he wrote, "the uncertainty of life (of men in the Army)" despite the fact that he was then "in good health and in [his] right mind."[44] Thompson's decision to write a will while serving out west attests to the inherent insecurity that soldiers faced on the frontier, where they were exposed to severe weather, substandard living conditions, the spread of disease, and the threat of death during violent conflicts.

Despite their efforts to meet the challenges of military service as infantrymen and cavalrymen, Black soldiers encountered discrimination, racism, and abuse from civilians, soldiers, and administrators in the West. When serving in the field, African American soldiers regularly dealt with individuals who treated them with scorn and disrespect. For instance, in his account of an 1867 military expedition of Black soldiers from Fort Leavenworth, Kansas, on the Santa Fe Trail, US Army surgeon W. Thornton Parker recorded that "their advent astonished everyone. The frontiersmen looked upon them as a military caricature . . . the officers detailed to serve with them were half ashamed to have it known. The white soldiers who came into contact with these recent slaves, now wearing the uniform of the regular army, felt insulted and injured; and their redskin adversaries heaped derision" on them.[45] Two decades later, in 1892, African American soldiers from the Ninth Cavalry serving in northern Wyoming, where a violent dispute between cattle ranchers and settlers caused significant upheaval, also endured racism from local white residents. In his research about an incident recorded as the "Suggs Disturbance," historian Frank N. Schubert found evidence that Black soldiers were "verbally harassed," "denied accommodations in the local hotel," and insulted at gunpoint by white people in the town of Suggs, Wyoming, which was located near the soldiers' military outpost of Camp Bettens.[46]

At other historical moments, however, Buffalo Soldiers were praised for their bold actions in the line of duty, earning national fame that challenged racist notions about Black soldiers' abilities. In one representative case, Corporal William Othello Wilson of the Ninth Cavalry was praised for his role protecting a military wagon train in South Dakota in 1890 that was, according to his lieutenant, "attacked by hostile Indians" one day after the tragic Wounded Knee Massacre at the Lakota Pine Ridge Reservation. Wilson volunteered to "send word" for additional help, an act that "involve[ed] much risk as the Indians, knowing what was intended, would endeavor to intercept the messenger and [if he was] overwhelmed by numbers certain death would follow."[47] Wilson received a medal of honor. So, too, did seventeen other Buffalo Soldiers during the late nineteenth century, for deeds ranging from the rescue of fellow soldiers to bravery during skirmishes with Native Americans.[48] Another medal of honor recipient, soldier Emanuel Stance, described the decoration as a gift that he would cherish "as a thing of priceless value" that would motivate him to "endeavor by [his] future conduct to merit the high honor conferred upon [him]."[49]

For Stance and other African American soldiers, the US Army's recognition of their courage served as a source of great pride, particularly during the Jim Crow era, when southern states passed discriminatory laws that segregated and disfranchised Black citizens, and violent acts against Black people occurred regularly across the nation. Although the federal government failed to protect Black rights during the late nineteenth century, its bestowal of significant awards on African American soldiers may have helped foster in the broader populace a growing appreciation for their service. Army surgeon Parker argued in 1899 that "from such discouraging beginnings has developed a military organization of brave and efficient soldiers, who have since [1867] . . . made excellent records for themselves. . . . The 24th and 25th Infantry, and the 9th and 10th Cavalry are a credit to the U.S. Army."[50] His description of how Black military service evolved in the years after the Civil War attests to changes in the perception of Black soldiers' abilities and contributions over time.

BLACK SOLDIERS AND THE SPANISH-AMERICAN WAR

As new American citizens following the ratification of the Fourteenth Amendment, Black soldiers contributed to the reconstruction of the US South and the settlement of the American West during an era of deep discrimination and racial violence. But their participation in a war on foreign soil at the close of the nineteenth century would generate further calls for the recognition of their rights. Thirty-three years after the Civil War ended, Black soldiers in the US Army found themselves involved in a new endeavor: an international war driven by imperialist goals. In the spring of 1898, the Spanish-American War erupted, following an explosion on the USS *Maine* in Havana Harbor on February 15, which downed the ship and led to the deaths at least 260 Americans aboard.[51] The US Congress declared war on Spain on April 25, launching the nation into battle against a colonial power whose oppressive rule in Cuba threatened American business interests and regional political stability.

The Spanish-American War, which began just two years after the Supreme Court ruled that segregation in public facilities was constitutional in the case *Plessy v. Ferguson*, prompted debate among African Americans about whether to serve in the military. Journalists writing for newspapers with predominantly Black audiences expressed varying opinions: while some urged Black citizens to fight out of duty to their country, others argued that African Americans should not fight for a nation that trampled on their civil rights at home.[52] African American soldiers ultimately played a substantive role in the Spanish-American War: they accounted for 25 percent of soldiers in Cuba and helped secure victory for the United States in a matter of months.[53] Their distinguished service elicited praise from national newspapers and demands from the Black community for the government to protect African Americans' civil rights.

Four all-Black regiments, the Twenty-Fourth and Twenty-Fifth Infantry, and the Ninth and Tenth Cavalry, fought in the war against Spain. The two cavalry regiments fought alongside the unit that gained the most fame during the conflict, the Rough Riders.[54] Volunteers and "immune" regiments, selected by the government based on the racist assumption that Black soldiers could endure the climate and illnesses endemic to Cuba, also served.[55] They fought in three significant battles, Las Guasimas, El Caney, and San Juan Hill, as American forces sought to gain control of the island. During the war's most famous encounter, the Battle of San Juan Hill, the four all-Black regiments helped capture the hill, though much of the fame has gone to the Rough Riders.[56] Newspapers heaped praise on the fighters, and President William McKinley promoted six African American noncommissioned officers to the rank of second lieutenant in recognition of their service.[57] On August 12, 1898, combat ceased and both countries began to hammer out the terms of surrender. As part of the peace settlement outlined in the Treaty of Paris in December of that year, the United States annexed Puerto Rico, Guam, and the Philippines.[58]

As in previous conflicts, African American soldiers experienced difficult material conditions, discrimination, and racism during the Spanish-American War, particularly in connection to the segregation of the army and the issue of promotions: it was impossible for an African American man to reach the rank of anything higher than a lieutenant.[59] But Black service led to public requests for changes to the army and energized those fighting for the protection of African Americans' civil rights. For instance, in the June 1898 article "Epaulets or Chevrons?," General Thomas J. Morgan contended that with "the magnificent record of [African Americans'] fighting qualities on many a hard contested field, it is not unreasonable to ask that a still further opportunity shall be extended to them in commissioning them as officers as well as enlisting them as soldiers." Critically, Morgan linked the issue of military ranking to citizenship, arguing that "it is very important that [African Americans] should be made to feel that their citizenship is not a mere name, but is a solid reality; that citizenship means manhood; in no other way . . . [can they] feel a sense of their real dignity as men and citizens more quickly than by effacing the color-line in military appointments."[60] After the war's end, the *Philadelphia Press* concurred, running an article that concluded, "In discipline, in courage, and in patriotism, no one can challenge the record made by the negro. He has stood ready to the death to meet the duties of American citizenship. He ought to find a growing readiness to give him all its rights."[61]

African American soldiers returning from the Spanish-American War, however, would find that their rights as citizens were still under attack. Although they had advanced the United States' imperial ambitions and freed Cubans from Spanish rule, African Americans did not enjoy liberty at home. They came back to a country where the lynching of Black men and women continued unabated, and segregation became increasingly widespread. Military service did not guarantee African American soldiers or members of the broader Black community their civil rights. The Methodist newspaper *Zion's Herald* drew attention to this tragedy in the article "The Hard Fate of the Negro," which ran in November 1898. "It was only yesterday that we were hearing chanted the praises of the Negro soldiers in Cuba," the article began. "Today we are reading of the killing of ten Negroes in a Mississippi town and probably as many more in North Carolina, of several lynchings in Georgia and Texas, and the troubles of colored miners in Illinois." The publication denounced widespread violence against African Americans as well as their disfranchisement in many states across the South, where Black citizens "[had] no political rights worth naming."[62]

Others decried the nation's imperialist policies, which they perceived to be a distraction from domestic problems like the denial of rights to African Americans in the Jim Crow South. In a powerful open letter, the Colored National League, an activist organization based in Boston, presented such a position to President McKinley. Writing in 1899, its authors denounced the "crisis and extremity in the life of our race in the South" and asked McKinley to "pause, if but for an hour, in pursuit of [his] national policy of 'criminal aggression' abroad to consider the 'criminal aggression' at home against humanity and American citizenship, which [was] in the full tide of successful conquest at the South."[63] Despite the request of the Colored National League and others, however, no such shift in policy would follow. McKinley's assassination two years later led to his replacement by Vice President Theodore Roosevelt, a Spanish-American War veteran who generally disregarded Black rights. At the turn of the century, the fight for African Americans' liberties and for equal treatment in the US military remained unfinished.

In the many decades after the Civil War, when two hundred thousand African Americans to whom citizenship was denied served their country, African Americans continued to fight for equal treatment under the law. Throughout the oppressive Jim Crow era, they combated discrimination and white supremacist violence as civilians and soldiers. Indeed, the march toward equality in the US military continues to this day. In 2020, 9 percent of US military officers were Black, although African Americans composed 17 percent of those serving.[64] But events like the January 2021 confirmation of Lloyd Austin as secretary of defense and the June 2020 confirmation of General Charles Q. Brown Jr. as chief of staff of the US Air Force represent important signs of progress. In a video address delivered amid national Black Lives Matter protests following the Minneapolis police's murder of an African American man, George Floyd, in May 2020, General Brown discussed the circumstances surrounding his promotion as the first Black military chief. He reflected on the contributions of the Black soldiers who preceded him, acknowledging that their sacrifices made "this opportunity possible." Although General Brown said that he would not be able to "fix centuries of racism in our country," nor to "fix decades of discrimination that may have impacted members of our Air Force," he promised to seek the "wisdom and knowledge to lead those willing to take committed and sustained action to make our Air Force better." General Brown ultimately joined a long line of African Americans before him, connecting his military service to citizenship and "the equality expressed in our Declaration of Independence and the Constitution that [he had] sworn [his] adult life to support and defend." Ultimately, like his predecessors in centuries past, he would seek to make the military a more equitable place and to "make a difference" in an imperfect nation.[65]

4

"It Is Not the Policy nor the Interest of the South to Destroy the Negro"

Black Prisoners of War and the Intersection of Race, Property, and Law in the Confederacy

CAROLINE WOOD NEWHALL

> Sir, In the skirmish of the 22nd July 1864 a negro man named Wilson was captured by the Confederate forces. He is wounded . . . and is receiving such medical attention as we have. When he is well if his owner lives in the Confederate lines he will be delivered to him, if not he will be held to slavery by the Government. I have to inform you that negroes are not considered prisoners of war, but all who surrendered to us are treated as property and either delivered to their original owner or put at labor by the Government.
>
> —CAPTAIN WILLIAM B. HARDEMAN TO COLONEL H. A. MCCALEB, JULY 30, 1864

"INSTEAD OF A FEELING OF terror you have aroused a spirit of courage and desperation that will not down at your bidding," declared Union major general Cadwallader C. Washburn in a fiery communication to Confederate major general Nathan Bedford Forrest in June 1864.[1] Washburn sought to rebuke and intimidate Forrest in the wake of several massacres of Black US soldiers that spring and summer. Washburn had received reports of atrocities committed against several regiments of the US Colored Troops (USCT) at Brices Cross Roads in Mississippi on June 10, and he promised "consequences . . . fearful to contemplate" if Forrest and his commanding officer, Major General Stephen D. Lee, did not disavow the massacre and punish the perpetrators. Or, if "it is contemplated by the Confederate Government to murder all colored troops that may by chance of war fall into their hands, as was the case at Fort Pillow," Washburn continued, then "it is but fair that it should be freely and frankly avowed." If the Confederacy intended to subject Black soldiers to "indiscriminate slaughter," Washburn reasoned, then Black soldiers would "cheerfully accept the issue" and treat Confederate soldiers in kind.[2]

Forrest denied that the Confederacy sought to destroy Black soldiers out of revenge or hatred and gave clear voice to his and the Confederacy's treatment of Black combatants as enslaved property incapable of participating in legitimate warfare. "I regard your letter as discourteous to [Lee] . . . and grossly insulting to myself," responded Forrest. Rather than deign to address Washburn's accusations of Forrest's culpability in the murder of Black troops at the Battle of Fort Pillow in Tennessee back in April (in which many of the 282 Black soldiers present were lined up and executed after surrendering), Forrest bluntly stated his and the Confederate government's position on Black soldiers. "I regard captured negroes as I do *other captured property* and *not as captured soldiers*," Forrest proclaimed, stating that if Washburn wanted further information on what was to be done with Black prisoners of war (POWs), he should confer with the "authorities at Richmond." Furthermore, Forrest wrote, "I have captured many thousand Federal prisoners, and they, including the survivors of the Fort Pillow massacre (black and white) are living witnesses of the fact," claiming that none had ever been "insulted or in any way maltreated" by his order or with his knowledge or consent. "It is not the policy nor the interest of the South to destroy the negro," asserted Forrest. "On the contrary," he wrote, the Confederacy's policy was "to preserve and protect him."[3]

The formal entry of Black soldiers into the US armed forces during the American Civil War marked a significant step toward recognizing Black freedom, personhood, and equality—and the Confederacy responded to this threat by denying Black soldiers' legitimacy. Confederates thus murdered, imprisoned, and, most significantly, enslaved Black POWs as forms of emasculation that upheld white supremacy, the Confederacy's stated raison d'être. By late 1862, the US Congress had expanded on the existing Articles of War (compiled and adopted in 1806) to pass the first and second Confiscation Acts and the Militia Act.[4] The Articles of War made no mention of race or slavery, whereas these three acts specifically used military authority to emancipate select groups of enslaved people in Confederate territory and begin the process of formally enlisting Black soldiers.[5] The Confederacy (which had adopted the US Articles of War) immediately announced its refusal to recognize any Black men as combatants; it would instead treat them as recovered property.[6] In doing so, Confederates actively—and symbolically—attempted to emasculate Black soldiers and delegitimize their role in the war. Confederates treated Black soldiers, both in rhetoric and in combat, as enslaved insurrectionists who were incapable of engaging in civilized warfare. Yet treating a Black soldier as a recaptured slave also resulted in treating him with degrees of restraint that meant that hundreds of Black POWs survived their captivity. Taking Black POWs alive served the purposes of white supremacy and the Confederate war effort in much the same way that executing Black soldiers did.[7]

Throughout the antebellum period and into the Civil War, militant Black men met various fates that followed a simple logic: they had to be unmade as men and remade as slaves to maintain the slave states' social order and, subsequently, the Confederate war effort. As such, Confederates engaged in both terrorizing violence and degrees of restraint toward Black US soldiers. Returning captured Black soldiers to their supposedly rightful position as slaves fulfilled the Confederacy's demand for Black labor and at the same time satisfied the emotional needs of southern white manhood. Whiteness and masculinity were closely intertwined in the South, such that white supremacy was explicitly tied to the creation and maintenance of white manhood.[8] Black men's performance of manhood through their military service during the Civil War, and the presence of tens of thousands of formerly enslaved men in the ranks, brazenly transgressed the Confederacy's established racial and gendered order.[9] Edward Baptist has noted that in the "grammar of American manhood" that developed over the course of the antebellum period, "enslaved men were not men at all."[10] Yet as paid, uniformed, and armed representatives of the United States (a sovereign power recognized by the international community), formerly enslaved and freeborn Black soldiers alike could, by 1863, legally make war on Confederates. Black soldiers unmade the very cornerstone of the Confederacy and, by extension, its system of racial, chattel slavery. The United States rationalized its enlistment of Black men using past precedents and the demands of war, and the Confederacy responded in kind to vindicate its treatment of most Black soldiers and POWs as slaves. Though the United States might consider Black soldiers to be men and legitimate combatants, Confederate officials argued that based on existing laws and the Articles of War, the Confederacy had no obligation to abide by US wartime policy once Black soldiers fell into Confederate hands within Confederate boundaries.

Confederate officials and military leaders alike justified treating Black soldiers, particularly formerly enslaved Black southerners, as slaves based on the principle of *jus postliminium*, also called postliminy. Postliminy, according to legal theorists such as eighteenth-century Swiss lawyer Emer de Vattel, stipulated that "persons and things taken by the enemy are restored to their former state, on coming again into the power of the nation to which they belonged." Furthermore, it was the duty of a sovereign "to restore" recaptured persons and things "to their former condition," and "to give back the effects to the owners—in a word, to replace everything on the same footing on which it stood previous to the enemy's capture."[11] Confederate government officials and military commanders such as secretary of war James A. Seddon, prisoner exchange agent Robert C. Ould, and General Robert E. Lee repeatedly cited postliminy in communications with US officials and commanders to justify the treatment of Black POWs as recaptured enslaved property rather than as POWs subject to protections under the Articles of War. Thus, according to Confederates, any escaped or "stolen" enslaved people captured back from the United States (uniformed or not) would become enslaved once more, regardless of their status while in US custody.

Confederates' decisions to take more than 2,200 Black POWs alive in the aftermath of even the worst battles from late 1862 into early 1865 served several interests.[12] Forrest's correspondence with Washburn, for example, demonstrates military commanders' commitment to postliminy, even if Forrest did not use the term itself to describe his treatment of Black POWs as captured property.[13] Ould specifically referred to "the *jus postliminii*" when he told US exchange agent Major General Benjamin Butler that under Confederate policy, "on recapture" formerly enslaved Black soldiers "followed the rule of all property" on par with horses or livestock and "reverted to their former condition" of slavery.[14] Seddon referred to the "principle of *postliminium*" in a communication with Ould in June 1863, wherein he outlined postliminy's applicability to enslaved people according to "international law" and past practices in the United States.[15] Meanwhile, members of the Confederate Congress such as House representatives Thomas D. S. McDowell of North Carolina, Charles F. Collier of Virginia, and Henry S. Foote of Tennessee debated how best to use Black POWs to benefit both individual Confederates and the war effort by treating them as war booty.[16]

The emasculation of enslaved Black men lay at the heart of antebellum slave codes and the treatment of Black POWs, and Confederates argued that applying postliminy to human beings on the basis of race and former status was legal within both US and Confederate borders during the Civil War.[17] Indeed, by the time of the Civil War, the United States had long-established processes to reclaim escaped enslaved people in times of peace or from enemy belligerents in times of war, and to compensate affected enslavers for their losses during postwar processes. The United States had sought compensation from foreign adversaries for the loss of enslaved people after both the Revolutionary War and the War of 1812. It was successful following the latter conflict, when US enslavers received monetary reparations for the loss of enslaved people who had successfully found refuge with British forces. After the Second Seminole War (1835–42), the Congressional Joint Committee on Claims (a majority of whose members were enslavers) approved payment to the heirs of a Florida enslaver whose enslaved servant Louis Fatio had been captured and claimed as a slave by the Seminole Indians.[18] The Fugitive Slave Acts of 1793 and 1850 had likewise established a national legal obligation to preserve enslavers' rights over enslaved people, even within the boundaries of the free states. Escaped enslaved people did not, under the Fugitive Slave Acts, become free even if they had escaped into a free state or foreign country. These "fugitives" still owed a lifetime of labor to their enslavers under the law—any removal of enslaved people from the slave states, by escape or otherwise, was considered theft of labor.[19] The unauthorized physical removal of an enslaved person from an enslaver's control constituted a violation of enslavers' rights to full authority over enslaved people and their bodies. Despite northern states' defiance of this federal law through state-level personal liberty laws, the US Congress and the Supreme Court had on numerous occasions ruled that refugees from enslavement did not cease to be enslaved within the boundaries of free states or even foreign countries.[20] Confederates, who now considered themselves to be a sovereign state separate from the United States, cited this body of US and state laws to justify treating some US soldiers as recaptured property based on their race.

At the center of this legal sparring lay Confederates' abject refusal to treat nonwhite people as capable of restrained, or "civilized," warfare. Confederates took up antebellum portrayals of Black men as barbarians who would commit atrocities against Confederate soldiers and innocent white women and children alike under the "pretended freedom" offered by the United States through military service.[21] Confederates such as Seddon decried the use of Black soldiers as "a barbarous system of warfare" employed by the United States, one that violated the principles of civilized warfare by encouraging "atrocity and violence." According to Seddon, "the savage passions and brutal appetites of a barbarous race are to be stimulated into fierce activity" by Black men's inclusion in the US military as uniformed combatants.[22]

White Americans defined and fought the Civil War within bounds—developed and codified in the eighteenth century—that allowed for both violence and restraint. However, the scale and unprecedented demands of this war necessitated new interpretations and applications of the laws of war. According to historian Wayne E. Lee, Americans' prior experiences with warfare against enemies considered to be "brothers" (namely Europeans) followed a "vision of regulated war" developed over the eighteenth and nineteenth centuries in Europe in order to increase "the value of restraint and the social power devoted to it."[23] Following the Peace of Westphalia in 1648, for example, theorists such as Vattel outlined acceptable wartime behaviors designed to limit the "damage of war," and by 1802, the US Army and Navy trained in codes of conduct that were developed, printed, and disseminated by military officials who studied Enlightenment-era treatises on ideal conduct in warfare on land and sea.[24] On the other hand, Lee states, Anglo-Americans viewed warfare through ethnocentric, racial, and gendered frameworks and deemed the wartime practices of "barbarians" (namely Native Americans and enslaved people) as atrocities. Although Anglo-Americans also committed atrocities, this practice was considered not a descent into "uncivilized" warfare, but rather an accepted response to "barbaric savagery" in the form of a reprisal or retaliation.[25] Anglo-Americans' retaliation against enemies guilty of atrocity, in their view, fell within appropriate conduct outlined by European theorists.[26] Nineteenth-century white Americans therefore were no strangers to the excesses of war, whether they were fighting with Europeans, Native American nations, or enslaved people.[27]

In contrast, enslaved people of African descent fell into a gray area not clearly outlined in theorists' writings on accepted forms of treatment of people and property in warfare, with their acts of war cast as *rebellion* rather than retaliation. For example, Vattel only referenced enslaved people in terms of ancient Roman law, which did not clearly apply to the issues introduced by racial, chattel slavery in the Atlantic World.[28] Indeed, few Europeans opined on the issue of dealing with enslaved Black people in treatises on the laws of war—though enslaved people regularly engaged in combat—because Europeans and Americans failed to consider enslaved people as legitimate combatants and their actions as declarations of war.[29] Enslaved people, according to antebellum US, international, and Confederate laws, were only capable of rebellion or insurrection—they were not considered to be perpetrators of just war and thus could not be treated as legitimate belligerents.[30] Enslaved people, in the eyes of North American and European courts, committed atrocities if they used any violence in their freedom struggles, because codes of conduct in war did not apply to small groups of nonstate actors.[31] Past precedent in issues of captivity and slavery in North American warfare thus aided the Confederacy in its creation of policies for handling enslaved people, combatants and noncombatants alike.

With no formal Confederate policy in place regarding Black soldiers by late 1862, however, Confederate soldiers in the field took small numbers of Black troops whom they encountered captive rather than resorting to summary execution. The participation of armed and uniformed Black men in at least one early engagement in November 1862 forced military commanders to make decisions themselves and seek guidance from Richmond after. By this time, the US Congress had passed its two Confiscation Acts (August 1861 and July 1862) and the Militia Act (July 1862), which allowed Union forces to define refugees from slavery as "contraband of war" taken from states in insurrection, and to allow Black people to support the military as laborers.[32] President Abraham Lincoln's preliminary Emancipation Proclamation of September 1862 further declared that Black soldiers could be enlisted into the US Army after January 1, 1863.[33] On November 14, 1862, Confederate brigadier general Hugh W. Mercer reported that four Black men were captured on Saint Catherines Island near Savannah, Georgia, wearing US uniforms and carrying arms. One of the prisoners, Manuel, had since been acquired by Savannah slave traders named William C. Blount and Edmond M. Dawson.[34] Mercer deemed the issue a military matter rather than a civilian one, seized Manuel from the traders, and placed him in jail. What happened to the other three men is unknown, but it seems at least one other captive was still alive when Mercer wrote to his commanding officer, Brigadier General Thomas Jordan, asking for instructions.[35] Mercer requested "that these negroes be made an example of," for they "are slaves taken with arms in hand against their masters and wearing the abolition uniform," and "some swift and terrible punishment should be inflicted that their fellows may be deterred from following their example."[36]

This early capture signified that Confederates were willing to apply both restraint and violence toward Black POWs as individual commanders deemed necessary. In the wake of this first action involving a small number of Black POWs, Confederate secretary of war Seddon outlined a flexible policy toward Black soldiers that allowed for their execution as well as their captivity and enslavement. Seddon referred the matter of the Saint Catherines Island combatants to President Jefferson Davis, and both agreed on November 17 that Manuel, now reduced to being called "the negro," should be executed "as an example," which Seddon relayed back to army commanders, including General P. G. T. Beauregard.[37] Seddon made no mention in this instruction of the other three Black soldiers captured alongside Manuel. While there is no known record as to what Mercer ultimately did with the four captives, it is likely that he ordered their execution.

Beauregard, who commanded the Confederate defenses along the Eastern Seaboard, indicated that he did not assume that execution was standard policy, and perhaps expected different instructions in dealing with larger groups of Black soldiers. He asked for "the general instructions of the War Department . . . in such cases" so that they could be swiftly handled in the future.[38] Seddon outlined his and Davis's general views on the subject on November 30, 1862. He summarized the legal questions and existing laws and warned Beauregard of the consequences of treating Black soldiers as legitimate combatants. Seddon stated that "slaves in flagrant rebellion are subject to death by the laws of every slave-holding State."[39] The existing slave codes in every Confederate state (as well as the slave states that remained in the United States) prescribed execution for enslaved individuals who rebelled against enslavers. The aftermath of prewar plots and rebellions, such as Denmark Vesey's in 1820 and Nat Turner's in 1831, had resulted in widespread massacres of enslaved people to instill terror as a measure of deterrence. Massacres, however, were only one of many tactics that white people had used against enslaved and free Black populations throughout the United States. White southerners had also relied on restraint and semblances of due process in the wake of suspected and thwarted rebellions, including those of Vesey and Turner.[40]

Throughout the antebellum period, white southerners demonstrated their ability to show restraint toward suspected Black rebels by keeping them alive and profiting from their punishment. White southern men regularly formed all-white civil tribunals to try suspected enslaved rebels, with many of these Black survivors pardoned or sold out of state. As deeply flawed as these procedures were, enslaved people still, according to historian Ariela Gross, "received real defenses, often by prominent lawyers, and their appeals and writs of habeas corpus were heard all the way up the state court systems." The very existence of trials for enslaved people, says Gross, "exemplified the problem of slave resistance," for when enslaved people challenged their status, "they forced the law to deal with them as People."[41] Nevertheless, as abolitionist minister William Goodell observed in 1853, enslaved people were only ever treated as people under the law when they faced punishment for acts deemed threatening to white authority; in all other relations, enslaved people were treated as property.[42]

Seddon argued against the use of trials during the war, contending that the use of civil actions in wartime would cause both delays and "military inconvenience," likely over the question of which courts actually held jurisdiction over such cases.[43] By terming captured Black men such as Manuel "slaves in flagrant rebellion," Seddon indicated that the Confederate military should define Black soldiers as property, not as regular or irregular combatants. The possibility of treating Black soldiers as irregular combatants, such as guerrillas, does not appear to have ever been a consideration.[44]

Seddon and Davis did not recommend that commanders should make examples of all Black combatants through their execution, however. Executions were practicable in the case of Manuel because such a small number of captives had been taken alive, and Mercer persuasively argued that the military should make examples of these Black men as a means of deterrence to others. Seddon knew all too well, however, the "possible abuse of this grave power under the immediate excitement of capture" and the "over-zeal" of subordinates. At this stage of the war, the Confederacy still hoped for foreign intervention and recognition, particularly from the British. Confederate diplomats asserted in their meetings with foreign dignitaries that Black soldiers' involvement would result in a race war against innocent white citizens.[45] Seddon therefore "deemed [it] judicious" that "the general commanding the special locality of the capture" exercise "discretion," meaning his judgment, when determining whether to execute Black soldiers.[46] Seddon thus explicitly placed power over Black POWs in the hands of commanding officers heading various geographic departments. Executing Black combatants was acceptable so long as it was commanding officers who gave the order to do so. Seddon sent a copy of his directive to Major General John H. Forney, then commanding the Departments of Alabama and West Florida, who had already received inquiries from subordinate officers about what to do with

Black men in arms. Only commanders, stated Seddon, had the "discretion of deciding and giving the order of execution."[47] He did not address, however, what should happen to the Black POWs who *survived* capture, and he did not propose consequences for any Confederate soldiers who killed Black POWs in violation of commanding officers' orders.

US officials rejected Confederates' reasoning for treating Black soldiers as slaves rather than as men and soldiers. Black soldiers *were* regular soldiers of the United States, regardless of the Confederates' feelings on the matter—Black POWs were indeed legitimate combatants and should have been subject to agreed-on standards of warfare, particularly because the United States was already recognized as a legitimate nation with a legitimate military.[48] For one, the United States had decided early on to treat Confederate soldiers as legitimate POWs, despite denying the legitimacy of the Confederacy itself and refusing to recognize it as a legitimate belligerent. US officials thus sought to protect Black soldiers by arguing that their status as uniformed combatants rendered them subject to appropriate protections and treatment even more so than Confederates, who were being treated as uniformed combatants solely out of a desire to reestablish the Union. Furthermore, according to General Order 100, which was drafted in 1863 by the jurist Francis Lieber at the instruction of US general Henry W. Halleck, enslaved people "complicat[ed] and confound[ed] the ideas of property (that is, of a *thing*), and of personality (that is, of *humanity*)." Slavery in the United States, Lieber wrote, existed "according to municipal or local law only," and thus neither the United States "nor any officer under their authority can enslave any human being." In the context of war, in which the laws of *nations* dictate military treatment of property and people, "fugitives escaping from a country in which they were slaves . . . into another country, have . . . been held free and acknowledged free by judicial decisions of European countries." Lieber wrote that "a person so made free by the law of war is under the shield of the law of nations" forever after, and local and state laws simply ceased to apply to them.[49]

Lieber thus struck a blow to Confederates' claims that they could apply postliminy to enslaved people freed by a nation with which Confederates were at war. He argued that the "former owner or State can have, by the law of postliminy, no belligerent lien or claim of service." Lieber walked a fine line in his analysis, however, by stating that enslaved people fleeing to "another country" were free. By using this argument against the Confederacy to justify treating Black soldiers as freemen no longer subject to postliminy, Lieber risked acknowledging the Confederacy as a separate country from the United States. He specifically did not address the circumstances that might affect postliminy in the case of a civil war.[50] However, the United States eventually came to adopt this stance after passing the Confiscation Acts, the Militia Act, and the Emancipation Proclamation.

Though the Confederate government proved consistent in its refusal to treat

Black POWs (both freemen and formerly enslaved men) as legitimate POWs subject to exchange, questions over what to do with these captives remained. The Confederate government and military struggled to determine who held proper authority over captured Black soldiers, most of whom had been enslaved prior to their military service, though some had been free their entire lives.[51] In anticipation of the Emancipation Proclamation, President Davis publicly declared the official Confederate position on Black soldiers and POWs on December 23, 1862, but left the details vague. Davis declared that "all negro slaves *captured in arms* be *at once* delivered over to the executive authorities of the respective States to which they belong to be dealt with according to the laws of said States."[52] Historians generally interpret Davis's order, called General Order 111, as a blanket approval to kill rather than capture Black soldiers, and point to the actions of Confederate soldiers at infamous engagements such as the Battle of Fort Pillow and the Battle of the Crater as upholding this argument.[53] Though General Order 111 allowed for "such captives to be transferred to civilian courts for trial, if convenient and if done without delay," according to one scholar, "the same result," meaning Black soldiers' murder, "would follow."[54] Indeed, throughout the antebellum period enslaved rebels, real and suspected, had been swiftly judged and executed with the approval of all-white courts, and many other enslaved people had often been murdered out of fear and retribution upon the exposure of emancipation plots. Davis's and Seddon's recommendations to commanders and state governors throughout 1863 and 1864 however, much like their recommendation to Mercer and Beauregard in late 1862, suggest a somewhat different approach than indiscriminate slaughter when facing Black soldiers.

Though Confederates repeatedly subjected Black POWs to brutalization and murder, postliminy provided some safeguards for the Black men who survived capture. Enslaved men in rebellion and combat were dangerous, but they remained, under Confederate interpretations of the law, subject to state laws regarding enslaved people. Davis's wording in General Order 111 is significant for it conferred a modicum of protection on Black POWs by defining them as enslaved people, and thus as potentially valuable property.[55] Confederate commanders would have to keep Black soldiers alive to deliver them "at once" to the proper state authorities. Davis thus modified Seddon's November 1862 instructions in such a way as to discourage executions committed by the military, and to make the capture of Black POWs a civil issue by placing Black POWs under the final authority of state governments rather than individual department commanders. State governments historically dealt with slave trials, slave rebellions, fugitives, criminals, and conflicting property claims over enslaved people, and continued to do so during the war where civilian courts and governments remained in operation. Davis thus rendered Black POWs subject to similar treatment as other refugees from slavery as outlined in the Fugitive Slave Act of 1850.[56]

Between December 1862 and June 1863, the Confederate military and Congress therefore approached the issue of Black captives on an ad hoc basis, in part because some of the initial prisoners were small groups of unarmed northern freemen (most of whom were sailors). These men posed less of a threat than full regiments of Black soldiers numbering in the hundreds. At least four free Black sailors captured in North Carolina and South Carolina in January 1863 simply remained incarcerated in Charleston, South Carolina, military prisons due to their race. Clarence Miller, a "freeman by birth" hailing from Philadelphia, was captured from the USS *Columbia* with his white crew when the gunboat was shipwrecked off Wilmington, North Carolina. The crew was sent to Richmond, where they were confined at Libby Prison until the white sailors were exchanged. Miller wrote to government officials a year after his capture that "though nearly white," he remained in prison, as the Confederates "do not recognize me as a soldier entitled to treatment as a prisoner of war."[57] How Confederates determined Miller's race is unknown, though it is likely they seized the *Columbia*'s records, which might have listed Miller as a "mulatto." His status as a freeman would also have been included in these records. Neither white nor enslaved, Miller remained in limbo, and he remained in Libby for at least a year after his white comrades had been exchanged. What happened to him unfortunately remains unknown. Around the same time Miller entered Libby, in January 1863, Confederates captured the US gunboat *Isaac Smith* and its crew in South Carolina. Confederates exchanged the white crew members within weeks, while the three Black crew members—Orin H. Brown, William H. Johnson, and William Wilson (all of whom came from New York)—remained behind in a Charleston jail until the end of the war.[58] Though it is unclear whether any of these men served as enslaved laborers during their incarceration, Confederates made a distinction between them and the white POWs regardless.[59] These three men, however, managed to survive their captivity and return to the United States.

Black men's free status thus did not necessarily protect them against enslavement (although this would change in 1864, as I will discuss). The first Black men captured in US uniforms who were sold into slavery were unarmed freemen from Massachusetts who served as officers' valets in a white regiment. In January 1863, Confederates captured two Black adolescents along with the members of the Forty-Second Massachusetts Volunteer Infantry in Galveston, Texas. Despite their clear status as free northerners, Charles Fairfax Revaleon and Charles Gerrish Amos were enslaved until the end of the war, and Revaleon changed hands several times. It seems that their youth and presence in a white regiment may have rendered them more of an opportunity for profit than a threat. The white officers and soldiers imprisoned with the adolescents reported that they were sold two or three days after their capture, with Revaleon apparently meriting a "pitiful sum of $47."[60] Their sale outraged the men of the Forty-Second Massachusetts, at least one of whom sent letters to Massachusetts governor John Andrew, President Lincoln, and Union army major general Ethan A. Hitchcock, who served as an adviser to the US secretary of war, Edwin M. Stanton. Major General Edward R. S. Canby regretfully informed Governor Andrew on April 15 that "at present it appears to be impossible to do anything in this case except as a result of success in the war."[61] Held deep in Confederate territory in Texas, both Amos and Revaleon managed to survive their enslavement and return home, but only after the close of the war. Northern freemen's imprisonment, it will be seen, would become a major concern following captures of men from the Fifty-Fourth and Fifty-Fifth Massachusetts Colored Infantries in July 1863, but these two young men remain the only known sales of freeborn Black men during the war.

Large groups of Black soldiers participated in engagements beginning in June 1863, which presented thornier issues for the Davis administration than had the small groups taken prisoner from October 1862 to May 1863. Rumors of massacres abounded following the first major engagements with Black troops: at Milliken's Bend on June 7 and at "Mound Plantation" near Goodrich's Landing on June 29 and 30, both in Louisiana.[62] Confederates took dozens of Black soldiers from the Forty-Sixth and Forty-Ninth US Colored Infantry (USCI) alive after these battles, subjecting them to a number of fates, including execution, imprisonment, enslavement, and sale. The exact numbers remain unknown, but as many as 113 enlisted men from the Forty-Sixth and 29 men from the Forty-Ninth were taken prisoner; at least 83 of these men survived.[63] One Confederate soldier, Private John Simmons of the Twenty-Second Texas Infantry, stated that about a dozen Black soldiers from the Forty-Sixth died immediately after their surrender.[64] At least 49 men from the Forty-Sixth and Forty-Ninth likely did not survive capture or captivity. What happened to most of them remains unclear, but several POWs reported that Confederates killed at least one man on the forced march to Monroe, Louisiana, along with brutalizing and threatening the wounded Black soldiers who had trouble keeping up. It is likely many men died in the immediate aftermath, but the majority were ultimately distributed throughout Louisiana and Texas to be put to work on fortifications and, in at least one instance, sold to a new enslaver.[65]

At times, atrocities committed or threatened against Black POWs at this early juncture of the war appear to have even violated orders. Private William Hunter of the Forty-Ninth USCI recalled that after his capture at Milliken's Bend on June 7, 1863, he and his fellow Black POWs were transported to Monroe. The Confederates, who were part of the Third Brigade, Texas Division, "carried us to the court house yard, and said they were going to hang us, and had the rope," despite the fact that Brigadier General Henry E. McCulloch, commanding, had said that the Confederates "should not do anything until they consulted with him." Private Hunter heard "Gen. McCullock [*sic*] tell Gen. [Thomas J.]

Churchill that we had to be treated as prisoners of war and he would *wade to his saddle skirts in blood before we should be hung*. He said the owners by proving property should come and take them."[66] McCulloch managed to stop his men from carrying out their intent, at least in this instance. McCulloch's alleged specification that Black prisoners were to be kept alive for the purposes of reclamation is significant, and suggests that some commanders attempted to make use of Black POWs early on. Whether Seddon communicated with McCulloch on this point is unknown, but given Seddon's instructions to Governor Milledge Bonham of South Carolina and Lieutenant General E. Kirby Smith in the Department of the Trans-Mississippi in July and August 1863, it seems possible that Seddon was already recommending that Black POWs be kept alive so as to be enslaved (or reenslaved). US threats of retaliation may have been the impetus for Seddon's recommended course of action.

As more Black soldiers engaged Confederates in battle, Seddon became increasingly explicit throughout the summer of 1863 in his suggestions to commanders to use Black POWs as labor rather than executing them, and he began to make distinctions between northern freemen and formerly enslaved men. The capture of free northern Black soldiers in South Carolina in July 1863, for example, pushed Seddon to advocate more diverse approaches to handling Black POWs of various backgrounds to avoid "embarrassments."[67] On July 22, Governor Bonham demanded that General Beauregard hand over all Black POWs captured in engagements on July 11 and 18 near Charleston. The POWs taken in this action came from the Fifty-Fourth and Fifty-Fifth Massachusetts Colored Infantries, as well as the Second South Carolina Colored Infantry (later organized as the Thirty-Fourth USCI). Governor Bonham stated that per President Davis's General Order 111, he held authority over the free- and slave-born POWs from South Carolina. In terms of legal action against and punishment of freemen from northern states, however, Bonham stated that his authority was less clear, "till I can correspond directly with the War Department as to [the POWs'] disposition."[68]

Neither Beauregard nor Bonham knew the proper course of action regarding the men of the three captured regiments in the summer of 1863, given that Davis's December 1862 proclamation had stipulated that Black POWs "be at once delivered over to the executive authorities of the states *to which they belong*."[69] Though Bonham presumed that northern freemen would simply be dealt with by the authorities of the state in which they were captured, his July 22 letter to Beauregard sought elucidation, since these particular Black POWs were not simply escaped property subject to reclamation by private citizens.[70] Seddon, Davis, Beauregard, and Bonham consulted back and forth throughout August 1863 regarding who held authority over white USCT officers and northern freemen, as well as what course to take with them.[71]

Seddon ultimately advised Bonham to hold northern freemen in prisons for indefinite periods rather than place them on trial or execute them. Seddon recommended to Davis on August 23 that a definitive policy regarding northern freemen be announced to avoid further confusion. Seddon stated to Davis that authorities had two courses of action. They must either "promptly" execute northern freemen or deal with them "in some exceptional way to mark our stern reprobation of the barbarous employment of such inciters to insurrection with all its attendant horrors in our slave-holding States." Seddon advocated for the latter course, preferring to hold northern freemen to "hard labor." Such a course would not only "deter" slave insurrection, it would "meet the requirements of our own people" to benefit from the captives' forced labor.[72] Two days later, Davis responded to Seddon, stating that as president he held authority over the handling and punishment of white USCT officers, not that of any "captured negroes" in US uniform. Such a determination, according to Davis, was not his to make, and was instead up to the governors of the states.[73] Davis declared that the power to "commute penalty" such as execution had been granted to the governors so as to "make discriminations . . . to avoid the *danger of sinking the spirit in the letter of the law*."[74] Though Davis did not recommend any specific course of action, his analysis of the scope of authority and punishment with regard to the northern Black POWs gave Seddon leeway to recommend clemency.

By the time Seddon communicated this recommendation to Bonham on September 1, however, the governor had already set the process in motion for a trial to be convened to determine the guilt of four Black POWs who had previously been enslaved. According to lawyer Howard C. Westwood, Bonham directed his attorney general to prosecute the case, and a five-man tribunal composed by the police court for the Charleston District, "sometimes called the provost marshal's court, with criminal jurisdiction over slaves and free blacks," began proceedings to determine what to do with the four POWs.[75] The court, however, punted the issue back to the Confederate military after ruling that it did not have jurisdiction over cases involving Black soldiers in the uniform of an enemy belligerent, particularly when none of these men were native to South Carolina. Seddon, for his part, stated to Bonham on September 1 that "I venture to recommend further, that the captured negroes be *not* brought to trial; or, if condemned, that your powers of executive clemency be exercised to suspend their execution."[76] Following the tribunal's ruling and Seddon's guidance, Bonham let the Black POWs remain in Charleston for several months, until they were transferred to the military prison at Florence, South Carolina.[77]

At the same time that Seddon communicated with Governor Bonham, he also advised Lieutenant General E. Kirby Smith on what to do with Black POWs that had been taken prisoner contrary to Smith's wishes. In June 1863, a week after the large group of Black POWs had been taken alive at Milliken's Bend,

Louisiana, Smith (who commanded the Department of the Trans-Mississippi) wrote to Major General Richard Taylor that "I hope this may not be so, and that your subordinates . . . in command of capturing parties may have recognized the propriety of giving no quarter to armed negroes and their officers." Smith then stated that giving no quarter to the Black soldiers would have relieved Confederates of "a disagreeable dilemma."[78] However, the fact remained that several dozen Black POWs were now in military custody, and Smith wrote to Seddon seeking instructions. Smith received the following response from the War Department on July 13: "a different policy than that suggested by you is recommended. Considering the negroes as deluded victims, they should be treated with mercy and returned to their owners."[79] On August 12, Seddon repeated this to Smith, clarifying that he was against executing Black POWs except when absolutely necessary, and that they should instead be "returned to their owners." Though Seddon did not "design these as positive instructions," they were "suggestions which I hope will receive the concurrence of your judgment and become your rule of action." While he may not have intended his advice to be interpreted as an order, Seddon thus advocated showing "mercy" to Black troops, advising that "the *white men* leading them . . . had better be dealt with red-handed on the field or immediately thereafter."[80] The only instance in which Seddon appears to have openly advocated the massacre and execution of enemy soldiers was the capture of white USCT officers.[81]

Seddon's communications with Bonham and Smith made clear that executing Black soldiers of any background was an unwise invitation to US retaliation. On July 30, 1863, President Abraham Lincoln had issued General Order 252. "For every soldier of the United States killed in violation of the laws of war, a rebel soldier shall be executed," the order stated. Furthermore, for "every one enslaved by the enemy or sold into slavery, a rebel soldier shall be placed at hard labor on the public works, and continued at such labor until the other shall be released and receive the treatment due to a prisoner of war."[82] US commanders such as Major General David Hunter had already threatened retaliation against Confederate POWs for violence toward Black POWs. The US government was aware of the various usages to which Confederates put Black POWs and hoped to put a stop to Black troops' execution and enslavement. Confederates would not admit to executions, fearing that like punishment would be committed against Confederate POWs in US hands, but readily defended the principle of enslaving Black POWs that had been recaptured. Writing to Union army general Ulysses S. Grant on June 27, 1863, Major General Taylor denied that any atrocities had taken place following the Battle of Milliken's Bend. He referenced General Order 111, stating that "officers of the Confederate States Army are required, by an order emanating from the General Government, to turn over all such to the civil authorities, to be dealt with according to the laws of the State wherein they were captured."[83] Several weeks later, Confederate commanders likewise denied a massacre of POWs captured from the Seventy-Third USCI in Louisiana when questioned by US authorities.[84] Following these "embarrassments," Seddon and Davis deemed it best to try to avoid further complications by enslaving and imprisoning the majority of Black POWs instead.

Seddon further clarified his position in August 1864, when he sanctioned enslaving southern Black POWs and imprisoning northern Black POWs. On June 24, 1864, Governor Bonham had written to Seddon that he had seen two notices in Richmond newspapers stating "that certain slaves recently captured from the enemy by our troops will be delivered to their owners upon [slaveholders'] application to certain officers who have [the slaves in their] charge." This was *reclamation*, the process by which private enslavers identified and reclaimed enslaved men who had found freedom. Bonham, not having seen any proposed laws or resolutions regarding this practice, asked whether any had been passed that "have escaped my notice."[85] On August 31, Seddon wrote that "it has been considered best . . . to make a distinction between negroes . . . who can be recognized, or identified as slaves and those who were free inhabitants of the Federal States." Seddon told Bonham that a statute passed by the Confederate Congress on October 13, 1862, was to be applied to formerly enslaved men, "which makes arrangement for their return to the owners establishing title."[86] This was an explicit description of postliminy in practice, if not by name.

Formerly enslaved individuals would thus be returned to private enslavers where practicable. Seddon noted that Black POWs' return to enslavers "will not free them from the liability to criminal proceeding in the hands of owners . . . while at the same time it recognizes and secures the property of the owner." Seddon expressly linked private enslavers' property rights over Black POWs to the process of postliminy. Northern freemen, on the other hand, "are held in strict confinement and not as yet formally recognized in any official dealings with the enemy as prisoners of war," Seddon noted. Except "in some trivial particulars indicative of inferior consideration," he said, they "are treated very much in the same manner as our other captives," meaning white POWs. Northern freemen, like those of the Fifty-Fourth and Fifty-Fifth Massachusetts, were thus held in military prisons and less likely to be used as enslaved labor beyond prison walls, which was the common fate for formerly enslaved Black POWs from the South. "The decision as to [the freemen's] ultimate disposition," Seddon said, "will probably be referred to Congress, and . . . it is probable they will be recognized in some form as prisoners of war." Seddon then advised Bonham that southern Black POWs "as are identified as slave" be delivered to "their owners," and "those discovered to have been originally free to the Confederate authorities."[87] Thus, by mid-1864, and in the wake of repeated dealings with the United States over Black POWs' executions after capture, the Confederacy adopted a distinction between Black POWs based on prior status. Formerly enslaved men from the Southern states, however, would continue to be liable to treatment as recovered property under postliminy.

Confederates took steps to enable Black POWs' reclamation by former enslavers on numerous occasions. Long lists that named captured Black soldiers and their alleged enslavers appeared in several newspapers in 1864 in and around Richmond and in Mobile, Alabama. Governor Bonham of South Carolina noted on June 24 that he had seen two notices in Richmond newspapers stating "that certain slaves recently captured from the enemy by our troops will be delivered to their owners upon application to certain officers who have them in charge."[88] Two months later, an article entitled "Local Matters" appeared on the front page of the *Richmond Dispatch*, providing a list of eighty-one Black POWs by first name only (with the exception of one alleged freeman, Henry Lynch), all of them captured at the Battle of the Crater, near Petersburg, Virginia, on July 31. The article noted that these prisoners were being housed at Castle Thunder Prison in Richmond but did not clarify whether enslavers could claim the POWs upon providing sufficient proof of ownership.[89] Provost marshal of Richmond, Major Isaac H. Carrington, issued numerous special orders to return Black POWs from Virginia and Maryland and held in Richmond prisons to slavery by sale or reclamation. Special Order 60, on August 25, 1864, ordered that Private Peter Austin of the Twenty-Third USCI be delivered from Castle Thunder to R. L. Gordon of Orange, Virginia.[90] Special Orders 138 and 140 returned Private Levi Green of the Seventh USCI and Private Samuel Green of the Twenty-Third USCI from Castle Thunder to their former enslavers in Maryland and Virginia, respectively.[91] In the fall of 1864, at least 1,421 Black soldiers from the 44th, 106th, 110th, and 111th USCI surrendered or were captured en masse by Generals John Bell Hood and Nathan Bedford Forrest.[92] Hood facilitated the return of as many as 250 men of the 44th USCI to their former enslavers at Gadsden, Alabama.[93] The men of the 106th, 110th, and 111th USCI, meanwhile, were sent to Mobile to work as laborers for the Engineer Department. Their names were advertised in circulars in October 1864 and January 1865 so that their enslavers could receive compensation for their labors for the military.[94]

Though reclamation was Confederates' preferred outcome for Black POWs, Confederate politicians recognized the benefits of empowering soldiers with the right to claim Black POWs as war booty. In February 1863, Representative Thomas D. S. McDowell of North Carolina proposed that the Committee on the Judiciary "inquire into the expediency of reporting a bill providing for the sale of all negroes taken in arms against the Confederate states." The proceeds of the sales would then "be divided among the troops engaged in their capture." Should the resolution pass, McDowell noted, "our soldiers may have an opportunity to make the war profitable to themselves." Representative McDowell was himself a large planter, with his plantation, Purdie, having been valued at $65,000 and worked by fifty-seven enslaved people in 1860. He well understood the means by which white people could be incentivized to keep valuable Black soldiers alive. McDowell's resolution specified that "unless they be fugitive slaves," Black soldiers would "become the property of their captors, and shall thereafter be held and considered as slaves."[95] McDowell thus suggested that *all* Black soldiers, not simply southerners, were liable to be enslaved. The resolution was adopted, though whether it became a law is unclear.

Additional resolutions throughout 1863 expanded on this idea to allow white people to claim Black POWs as war booty. Eight days after McDowell's proposal, Representative Charles F. Collier of Virginia introduced a resolution in the House that proposed that "the Committee on the Judiciary inquire into the expediency of providing by law that all negroes captured whilst . . . in the service of the United States *ipso facto*, unless they be fugitive slaves, shall become the property of the captors, and shall thereafter be held and considered in all respects as slaves."[96] Months later, on December 10, Representative Henry S. Foote of Tennessee offered a resolution calling for the Committee on the Judiciary to "inquire into the expediency of amending the law now existing in regard to prisoners of war of the African race, in order to distinguish those who enlisted in the service of the United States as freemen and those who were slaves according to the laws of the Confederate States at the time of their enlistment, and who, therefore, when they shall fall into our hands by the chances of war, are subject, according to the recognized principles of international law, to be returned at once to their original condition of servitude."[97] The resolution was adopted, but whether it became a law is not clear. These politicians likely viewed treating Black POWs as booty as an extension of the idea that all white people had a role to play in controlling Black people.[98]

Soldiers did claim Black POWs as war booty more than once during the war, and certain commanders' communications on the subject made a clear argument for keeping Black POWs alive to benefit from their status as recaptured slaves. Following the Battle of Milliken's Bend in June 1863, in which more than fifty Black soldiers were taken prisoner, Brigadier General McCulloch (who had stepped in to save these Black POWs from execution by his subordinates) stated that "these negroes had doubtless been in possession of the enemy, and would be a clear loss to their owners but for Captain [George T.] Marold [of the Sixteenth Texas Infantry]." Should they be "forfeited to the Confederate States or returned to their owners," wrote McCulloch, "I would regard it nothing but fair to give Captain Marold one or two of the best of them." McCulloch also recommended the same for a young German-born soldier who helped facilitate the capture: "if such things are admissible, I think [Private Albert Schultz] should have a choice boy from among these fellows to cook and wash for him and his mess during the war, and to work for him as long as the negro lives." McCulloch likewise recommended that "as the horse of Dr. [William J.] Cocke [of the Seventh Texas Infantry] was lost in the praiseworthy effort to procure water for our wounded, another of these fellows might be well and properly turned over to him to compensate for his loss."[99] The service records for several Black POWs also note that various Confederate officers claimed them as enslaved workers and servants, indicating that treating Black POWs as spoils of war was perhaps a common practice.[100]

Confederate politicians likewise tried to ensure that enlisted men would benefit from Black POWs' survival by allowing soldiers and regiments to sell off unclaimed Black POWs to enrich themselves and their outfits. Though evidence remains to be found on whether sales resulted in profits for the captors of Black POWs, sales did indeed take place, and the proceeds went somewhere. In March 1864, Colonel W. Pinkney Shingler of the Seventh South Carolina Cavalry recommended that the best course of action regarding four "negro soldiers" captured near Williamsburg, Virginia, "was to sell them and give the proceeds to the command capturing them," as per discussions with General Arnold Elzey, commanding the Department of Richmond, some months prior.[101] Colonel E. B. Montague of the Thirty-Second Virginia Infantry, however, forwarded the prisoners to Elzey rather than approving the POWs' sale without proper authority. Whether the men were ultimately sold remains unclear.

In October 1864, General Robert E. Lee, the commander of the Army of Northern Virginia, gave clear voice to the Confederate government's policy of treating Black soldiers as recaptured property under postliminy. He did so to refute the US claim that the Confederacy had violated the laws of war in its treatment of Black combatants. Lee wrote to General Grant several weeks after the mass captures of the 106th, 110th, 111th, and 44th USCI in Georgia in September and October 1864, and amid successful reclamations of Black Virginian and Marylander POWs in Richmond prisons by their former enslavers.[102] Grant had demanded information regarding reports that Black POWs had been placed at work on Confederate fortifications while still in their blue uniforms and exposed to US fire.[103] "Before stating the facts with reference to the negroes alluded to," Lee responded, "I beg to explain the policy pursued by the Confederate Government towards this class of persons, when captured by its forces." Lee noted he had been "instructed" to tell Grant "that all such slaves when properly identified as belonging to citizens of the Confederate States, or to persons enjoying the protection of their laws, will be restored, like other recaptured private property, to those entitled to them." Though Lee did not use the term *postliminy*, he summarized its definition under Confederate law. Lee confirmed that at least fifty-nine Black POWs currently at work on Confederate fortifications had been identified as formerly enslaved to Confederate citizens.

They were, he stated, simply at work on fortifications until they could be reclaimed. Lee asserted that the "legal right of the owner to reclaim" recaptured enslaved people was as strong in the present cases as in past wars, such as the Revolutionary War and the War of 1812.[104]

Lee elided discussion of how his army's raids in Pennsylvania in June and July 1863 to capture and kidnap formerly enslaved and free Black people fit with this policy, but by the time he communicated with Grant on this issue, the Confederate policy had slightly changed. Historian David G. Smith notes that like Black POWs, these noncombatants from Pennsylvania had been murdered, sold, reclaimed, and "forced to labor in Confederate prisons or on military projects." Many of the people targeted by the Pennsylvania slave raids were allegedly refugees from slavery.[105] The raids reflected a policy laid out by President Davis in a speech to the Confederate Congress on January 5, 1863, in which Davis had declared that "on and after February 22, 1863, all free negroes within the limits of the Southern Confederacy shall be placed on the slave status, and be deemed to be chattels, they and their issue forever." This proclamation thumbed its nose at the Emancipation Proclamation by terming *all* Black people within the Confederacy slaves. Davis further declared that all Black people, even in states where slavery did not exist, were, should they be captured by the Confederacy "in the progress of our arms," ipso facto slaves. Should the Confederacy invade and occupy or conquer any of the free states, "the respective normal conditions of the white and black races may be placed on a permanent basis, so as to prevent the public peace from being thereafter endangered."[106] When Lee and his men invaded Pennsylvania and captured as many as one thousand people for the purpose of enslaving them, the soldiers upheld Davis's proclamation. However, following the issues of the summer of 1863 regarding execution, enslavement, and retaliation, Confederate military slave raids did not take place in US territory again. Confederate policy likewise adapted following the 1863 raids to make distinctions between northern freemen and formerly enslaved southerners captured in arms.

Confederate policy therefore declared that under postliminy, enslaved people's escape to the United States did not terminate their obligation of lifetime servitude to their enslavers. Formerly enslaved Black POWs, Lee claimed in his letter to Grant, continued to "owe service or labor to citizens or residents of the Confederate States." Even if enslavers did not come forward to reclaim Black POWs, the prisoners still owed a lifetime of labor. Furthermore, Lee referenced a previous communication regarding the recent policy toward Black POWs "who are not identified as property of citizens or residents of any of the Confederate States." These Black POWs (freemen from free states) were not subject to the requirements of postliminy because they did not owe any enslavers their labor. Northern freemen would henceforth be "regarded as prisoners of war, being held to be proper subjects of exchange, as I recently had the honor to inform you. No labor is exacted from such prisoners by the Confederate authorities." As such, Lee declared, the Black POWs placed at work could not have been exposed to fire except as a violation of orders—endangering enslaved laborers was, quite simply, against the policy and interests of the Confederacy.[107]

In a report to Congress on November 3, 1864, Seddon specifically cited postliminy as the Confederate policy toward Black POWs. The "principle of the *jus post liminium* in regard to persons such as slaves," noted Seddon, "has been uniformly applied on the continent of Europe." Prior to the Civil War, the United States "has determined that slavery and the slave trade are not contrary to the law of nations, and that the voluntary removal of slaves by a master to a State where slavery does not exist, does not prevent the renewal of the relation between master and slave upon their return to the State of their origin or domicil [*sic*]." Additionally, Seddon continued, the "diplomatic correspondence and the solemn treaties of the United States show reclamations for escaping slaves, abducted in time of war and of peace, and the recognition of those claims by a foreign power, and the payment of indemnity for the use of the masters, to the Federal Government." Seddon noted that at the time of his writing, "the Constitution of the United States contains a stipulation for the return of slaves escaping to one State, from their owner in another State, upon his claim." He stated that "the principle that a slave withdrawn from his master in war or peace, by desertion, capture, or other act not sanctioned by the law of the State, or the will of the master, *does not change [the slave's] condition within the State to which he belongs, or prevent the right of the master [to reclaim him] upon his recapture*."[108] Here Seddon clearly laid out the official policy of postliminy that had been applied, and would continue to be applied, to formerly enslaved men acting as enemy combatants.

The Confederacy's application of postliminy to Black soldiers demonstrates the cold logic at work in the refusal to recognize Black men as soldiers and as men based on racialized notions of personhood and masculinity. Over the course of the antebellum period, enslaved men increasingly lost access to the traits that white and Black Americans associated with manhood, such as earning a living, providing for a family, enjoying personal independence, and defending one's freedom through military service: the Civil War provided a chance for two hundred thousand Black men to lay claim to these privileges of citizenship and manhood.[109] Black men thus used military service during the war as a means to proclaim and exercise their independence and manhood. Confederates were right to fear them, and used existing practices and policies to try to prevent Black men from asserting their legitimacy as men through military service.

Black Civil War soldiers who survived capture posed legal and symbolic problems for the Confederacy because they became both captives and slaves in a nation not recognized as legitimate by the United States or international powers. To be recognized by international powers as a legitimate nation-state protected under the laws of war, the Confederacy had to act as a belligerent power obligated to conform to the laws of war.[110] The United States was already recognized as a legitimate, sovereign nation, and likewise conformed to European standards of acceptable conduct in warfare. This was not a multilateral set of international conventions at the time of the Civil War, but rather a set of customs and ideals that set the conditions for postconflict negotiations. The Confederacy thus attempted to adhere to the limitations of the laws of war in the hope of securing official recognition, and perhaps support, by foreign powers, while at the same time preserving its raison d'être of white supremacy and Black slavery.

The people of the Confederacy followed this logic and adapted it to the confusions and disruptions of war. The Confederacy required no new systems for handling Black soldiers, but rather adapted its extant slave codes and denial of Black manhood to the demands of warfare.[111] Jefferson Davis took the first major step when he formally denied Black soldiers' status as combatants by instead terming them "negro slaves captured in arms."[112] His phrasing was not mere semantic exercise or empty gesture; it was deliberately dehumanizing and emasculating, as well as enforced by positive law. Davis thus not only stripped Black POWs of the protections that were typically accorded enemy combatants under the laws of war (and which the Confederacy largely applied to white POWs for the entirety of the conflict), he also denied them treatment as people and men. Once Black soldiers began to fall into Confederate hands in greater numbers from 1863 onward, the Davis administration, state governments, military officials, and independent enslavers used familiar methods of control that served the interests of a white supremacist slave state. Black troops' murder, torture, imprisonment, and enslavement were thus all considered not only legal in the slave states throughout the war, but also necessary for maintaining white people's security and social status. Despite Confederates' best efforts, however, they could not stamp out the significance or the visibility of Black US soldiers' actions, which would ripple into the postwar era by recognizing Black men's legitimacy as men and as citizens.

5

Race and Region in Post–Civil War US Army Recruiting

KEVIN ADAMS

ALTHOUGH THE GILDED AGE MILITARY occupies an obscure corner of the American past for many professional historians, popular interest in African American soldiers—the famed Buffalo Soldiers—has persisted since the publication of William Leckie's *The Buffalo Soldiers: A Narrative of the Negro Cavalry in the West* in 1967. Leckie's study, a straightforward narrative description of the activities of the Ninth and Tenth Cavalry Regiments, had the good fortune to emerge at a moment when the profession was starting to take the challenge of studying the African American past of the United States seriously. In Leckie's wake have come a number of other scholarly overviews of the African American military experience in the trans-Mississippi West—most notably Arlen Fowler's *The Black Infantry in the West, 1869–1891* (1971), Charles L. Kenner's *Buffalo Soldiers and Officers of the Ninth Cavalry, 1867–1898: Black and White Together* (1999), William Dobak and Thomas Phillips's *The Black Regulars, 1866–1898* (2001), and Elizabeth Leonard's *Men of Color to Arms! Black Soldiers, Indian Wars, and the Quest for Equality* (2010).[1] When it comes to more focused studies that analyze, for example, the experiences of Black officers, the military histories of particular forts or regions where African American soldiers served, or the story of Black soldiers against the larger context of late nineteenth-century military life, the scholarly bounty is even richer.[2]

Despite the robust literature revolving around the story of Black soldiers in the West, research into these soldiers' origins has been haphazard. To be sure, the field still awaits a comprehensive analysis of white soldiers' origins in the post–Civil War period, but it is also true that descriptions of the social backgrounds of white enlisted men from the War of 1812 to the eve of World War I regularly appear in the monographic and article literature.[3] The same cannot be said for

African American soldiers: historians to date either have not been interested in African American enlisted men (preferring to focus on the handful of Black officers), have been stymied by the lack of primary sources these soldiers left behind, have shown less enthusiasm for social history methodologies, or have relied on vague and inconsistent reports on the recruitment of African American soldiers issued by the highest command levels of the US Army. Consequently, answers to basic questions about an African American man's decision to volunteer for service in the regular army in the decades after the Civil War remain unknown or glimpsed through a glass darkly. Simply put, where did the Buffalo Soldiers hail from, how did they manage to join the army, and how did the army try to recruit them?

One reason why we lack compelling answers to these questions is that chronological blinders define the scholarship published to date, as most of what we think we know about African American soldiers' backgrounds comes from studies focused on the immediate postwar period (1865–70) that investigate the creation of African American regiments in the regular army. Studies in this vein suggest—and *suggest* is the right word here—that many early African American recruits in the new units were veterans of US Colored Troops regiments who hailed from the Upper South, most notably Kentucky and Tennessee. Charles Kenner, for example, examined every death statement for the first few years of the Ninth Cavalry's existence (1866–69) and discovered that about 40 percent of men had prior military service, roughly in line with William Dobak and Thomas Phillips's claim that "about half of the black men who joined the regular army in the late 1860s had served during the Civil War." For those who did not list their occupation as soldier, Kenner found that the most common occupations given by Black troops were laborer or farmer. Because the regiment was founded there, Louisiana supplied a large number of recruits early in the Ninth's history. Toward the end of his dataset, however, Kenner found that most Black recruits hailed from Upper South locales like Tennessee or Virginia; only 5 percent had been born in prewar free states. Because a large number of recruits came from Kentucky, however, the total percentage of African American soldiers coming from Union states was over 40 percent. In contrast, the 1870 US Census reveals disparate origins for Black soldiers at Fort Duncan and Fort McKavett, Texas, with Robert Wooster noting that African American soldiers at the former post in that year were younger, reenlisted more often, and mostly came "from the rural South," while at Fort McKavett, as Edward M. Coffman notes, "a disproportionately larger number" of Black soldiers hailed from border states or the North. Another dataset of Kenner's, a sampling of enlistment records for six troops of the Ninth Cavalry between 1868 and 1877, reveals that 40 percent of recruits came from Kentucky, 33 percent were born in the Upper South, and only 17 percent traced their origins to the Deep South, which Kenner defines as all states east of Louisiana through South Carolina. Additionally, a small number of Black soldiers, between 1 and 2 percent, were foreign born, generally from Canada or the West Indies.[4]

A set of assumptions about the geographic reach of army recruiting has also limited our understand of who the Buffalo Soldiers were.[5] Dobak and Phillips provide some context for the army's recruitment of African Americans, for example, but also base their analysis on a series of geographic precepts: regimental recruiting parties were mostly sent to "Kentucky and Tennessee," army recruiting stations were "seldom south of the Ohio and Potomac rivers," and the army essentially failed to recruit in the South, "the largest source of black manpower." They then claim that the army's regular inability to enlist "enough black recruits to maintain segregated regiments . . . posed problems that would never quite be solved" and produced regular recruiting crises, particularly before 1880. None of these claims, it should be noted, is clearly underwritten with evidence, and Dobak and Phillips's analysis fails to consider that men who enlisted in Kentucky or Tennessee were not necessarily born there.[6]

These historiographical boundaries have been amplified by primary source deficiencies. Despite churning out a seemingly endless array of paper records, the Gilded Age US Army did not make life easy for future historians interested in analyzing its soldiers' backgrounds. Although some description of army recruiting activities and outcomes appears for each year between 1870 and 1890 in the adjutant general's report in the *Annual Report of the Secretary of War*, the quality of these reports varies significantly. For the immediate postwar period, the adjutant general's reports tend to not only be brief, but also lack statistical detail—not until the 1880s in fact do the adjutant general's reports reliably examine army recruiting in detail. Here, in the last years of the "frontier army," one can discern the influence of the professionalizing social sciences as the recruiting portion of the adjutant general's report runs for several dozen pages, complete with charts, tables, and statistical analysis of pressing issues in the main text. For all that, the more we know, the more we realize we don't know: while the army was taking some pains to count the number of foreigners serving in its ranks, it only broke enlistees down by ethnicity for three years between 1865 and 1890, and it paid no attention whatsoever to the birthplaces of native-born soldiers. In other words, we can speak with more confidence about the origins of foreign-born soldiers than we can about the birthplaces of native-born soldiers, Black or white.[7]

Given the inadequacies of the adjutant generals' reports, the other place to turn for information about enlisting or reenlisting soldiers is the contemporary Register of Enlistments, which was maintained by War Department clerks working in Washington, DC. Physically stored in the National Archives, the enlistment register possesses the advantage of being widely available on microfilm and through an online database.[8] Outside of Kenner's partial sample of the registers for a single African American regiment for nine years, however, no historians studying the Buffalo Soldiers have made use of this source, the best one we have regarding the backgrounds of individual enlisted men serving in the late nineteenth century. To be clear, this oversight is not limited to Black soldiers, as the registers remain an underutilized source for white soldiers as well. My own *Class and Race in the Frontier Army* (2009) tried to rectify this situation by analyzing a dataset derived from the registers. Since I wanted to eventually finish my book, I did this for only two years (1872 and 1878), years for which the skimpy adjutant general summaries told us very little about who joined the army. In brief, I found that roughly 30 percent of white soldiers were foreign born (the actual percentage varies, depending on whether the sample includes only first-time enlistees or also reenlistments), that the most common occupation given by enlistees was laborer (about 25 percent of all white soldiers testified that this was their occupation), and that over 60 percent of white soldiers hailed from just four states: New York, Pennsylvania, Ohio, and Massachusetts. White southerners were dramatically underrepresented in both years. For example, in 1872 more white enlistees were born in Rhode Island than in Alabama, Arkansas, Florida, Georgia, Louisiana, South Carolina, and Texas combined, while in 1878 more enlistees were "born at sea" than came from Alabama, Arkansas, Florida, and Mississippi. At the time, however, my interest in soldiers' backgrounds was directed toward discovering how many (white) soldiers were born abroad, and how many entered the army with no discernible skill. Just like for westerners, who were underrepresented because the new states and territories of the trans-Mississippi West were not old enough in many cases to have produced adults able to enlist, there seemed to be good reason for white southerners to have avoided military service after the Civil War, and so I noted these trends and moved on.[9] More to the point, I did no work on African American enlistees because *Class and Race in the Frontier Army* emerged from debates in the 1990s and early 2000s about whiteness and the racialization of European immigrants.

There is no reason, however, that one cannot repeat the above research for African American soldiers, since the enlistment registers contain the same information for all enlisted men. To wit, the enlistment registers list an enlistee's name, the place of enlistment, the officer who enlisted them, the recruit's birthplace, their occupation, their height, their hair and eye color, their regimental assignment, and their ultimate fate in the service (discharged, deserted, or died). These records do not identify race as such, but that can be discerned by looking at the regimental assignment, since there were only four static African American regiments after the consolidation of the US Army in the late 1860s: the Ninth and Tenth Cavalry, and Twenty-Fourth and Twenty-Fifth Infantry Regiments. Much like another valuable nineteenth-century source, the US Census, the post–Civil

War enlistment registers thus provide historians with a wealth of (self-reported) information about an ordinary person who might otherwise vanish from history. One should also keep in mind, however, that a single line in a vellum volume housed in an office in Washington, DC, represented the entirety of a soldier's personnel record in the Gilded Age army.

Since perhaps two hundred thousand men served in the US Army collectively in the twenty-five years after the Civil War ended, devising a sampling method before reading the registers is essential. Establishing chronological boundaries for the analysis is key: limiting our reading of the registers to the years between 1870 and 1890 not only gets us past expiring Civil War enlistments, but also allows us to center the years where the postwar army came into institutional focus. The fluidity that defined congressional debates and policy shifts concerning the postwar army's future had by the early 1870s settled into a consensus, whereby the army reverted to a largely frontier constabulary composed of twenty-five thousand men. This consensus matters for a study of recruiting because the army's yearly recruiting requirements should, in theory, remain the same, though real-world factors such as miserly congressional appropriations or unusually large numbers of desertions could shift said requirements a bit. Meanwhile, stopping in 1890 not only converges with the canonical "end of the frontier," but also bypasses a series of gradual transformations that hit the army in the 1890s, most notably the 1894 requirement that enlistees either be citizens or have filed their first papers (a declaration of intention to become a citizen).[10]

Once the chronological bounds of the sample have been determined, a few other factors have to be considered before sampling can begin in earnest. For example, although a cyclical pattern of enlistment characterized army recruiting (more men joined during the harsh grip of winter; fewer joined in spring, when the number of itinerant jobs in agriculture and construction began to increase), the register volumes are divided by last name, not by month. Within last names, enlistments are broken down by month, however, so it is possible to build a sample that includes all twelve months. To accomplish this, I tracked enlistments for each letter of the alphabet for a specific month for five random years between 1870 and 1890—for example, enlistees whose last name started with the letter *G* who enlisted in June 1874, 1876, 1881, 1883, and 1886. The number of soldiers captured by this method varied from the 419 *M*s who enlisted in five Septembers to the 4 *U*s who enlisted in five Augusts, with a grand total of 3,936 soldiers who enlisted in that twenty-one-year period, a few more than 200 per year, ending up in the sample. Figure 5.1 captures a big-picture view of US Army demographics based on this dataset.

A global view of enlisted men in the Gilded Age army reveals that native-born white men constituted the largest percentage of soldiers (52 percent, or 2,064 in the dataset) but represented only a bare majority of enlisted men, since

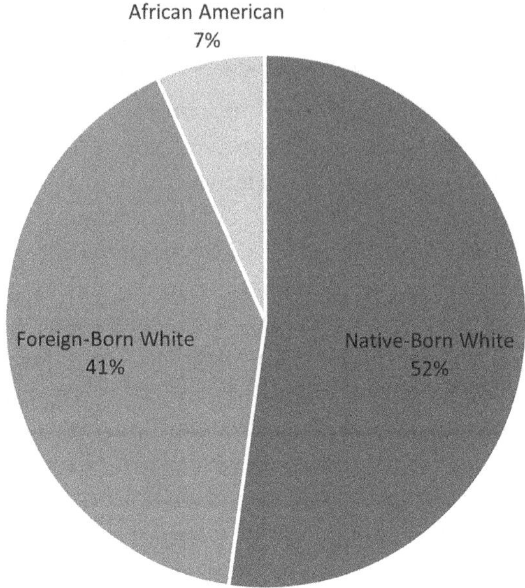

FIGURE 5.1. US Army demographics, 1870–90. Based on the study sample of 3,936 enlistments.

over 40 percent of enlistees or reenlistees were European immigrants. On first glance, African Americans seem to be underrepresented, since only 7 percent of enlistees were Black but 10 percent of line regiments were African American, but we should keep in mind that African Americans were prohibited from serving in the staff bureaus for much of this period. Further, African American soldiers' lower rates of desertion and higher rates of reenlistment meant that the army did not need to recruit large numbers of Black soldiers because their loss of manpower was lower.[11]

Little in the above portrait would surprise scholars who study the post–Civil War army. Recall, however, that the conclusions concerning African American enlisted men offered by historians have mostly relied on fragmentary data that rarely comes from the actual enlistment registers. Since the registers list place of birth for every man who entered the army, one can use this source to scrutinize previous claims concerning the origins of African American enlisted men. Drilling down into the data in this way not only provides new insight into the lives of the Black men who joined the army in the generation or so after the Civil War, but also allows us to draw some larger conclusions about the complicated relationship between American society, race, and region in army recruiting.

Let's start by returning to that deceptively simple question: where were African Americans who served in the US Army in the decades after the Civil War born? To date, we have learned that death records from three years in the late 1860s for the Ninth Cavalry, in conjunction with a study of enlistment records between 1868 and 1877 for a portion of that same regiment, indicate that new recruits mostly hailed from the margins of the South, including Kentucky, with only a smattering of men having been born in free states. Both datasets suggest that comparatively few African Americans born in the Deep South joined the regiment. Additionally, the 1870 US Census produced perhaps inconsistent results for two Texas forts, with one study suggesting that most Black enlisted men at Fort Duncan were born in the "rural South," and another indicating that most Black enlisted men at Fort McKavett had been born in the border South or the North. Despite this possible inconsistency—since "rural South" is not defined in the study in question, it could encompass a wide range of border states—the weight of the extant evidence points to Black men who served in the regular army having been mostly born on the fringes of the South, including in Kentucky.

When one expands the chronological boundaries of one's survey, however, and examines African American enlistments in all four African American regiments, the outlines of another story come into focus.[12] Significantly, in order to perceive this reality, one must adjust one's frame of analysis. Thus far conversations about the origins of the Buffalo Soldiers have sorted their places of birth into idiosyncratic geographic categories (e.g., Upper South, Deep South, border state, free state) that elide what was the salient geographic distinction of the era: Confederate versus Union. In other words, the laudable scholarly goal of adding nuance and refusing to treat regions as monoliths has caused us to miss the forest for the trees. Using the preeminent political distinction of the era to analyze soldiers' backgrounds not only improves our understanding of Black soldiers serving in the post–Civil War era, but exposes some much larger truths about southern society and American society in the wake of the Civil War.

Let's start by dividing the enlisted personnel of the regular army into men born in the former Confederacy (which we will use as our proxy for "the South"), men born in Union states, and men born abroad. Doing this enables the marginal status of southerners within the institution of the US Army to leap off the page (figure 5.2).

As with figure 5.1, the surface-level demographics appear abundantly clear: southerners of all races were a distinct minority in the post–Civil War army, only representing about one in fifteen soldiers (262 of 3,936 in the dataset). On the one hand, this makes sense. Given many white southerners' commitment to eliminating the revolutionary biracial democracies established by federal policymakers and sustained by federal power, it is hard to envision large numbers of white southern men, no matter how desperate, joining the US Army.[13] On the

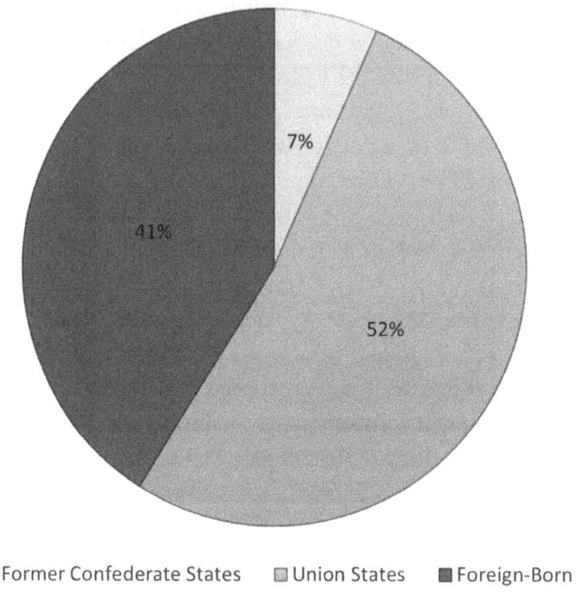

FIGURE 5.2. US Army demographics by nationality, 1870-90. Based on the study sample of 3,936 enlistments.

other hand, our tripartite division fails to shed much light on the patchwork of statistics found in earlier studies, since that literature revolves around categories like border state and Upper South, which can include states from both the Union and the Confederacy.

Real clarity comes when our sample accounts for race as well as region. Integrating race and region into our analysis reveals a postwar army recruiting system so influenced by the persistence of Civil War–era divisions that the Gilded Age army resembled an updated version of the Union army, with both forces relying on African Americans and northerners. At the same time, this demographic resemblance should not obscure a revelation heretofore unknown in the historiography: even though their numbers were limited by law and even though they constituted a minority of the southern population, more Black southerners (137) served in the post–Civil War US Army than did white southerners (125) (figure 5.3).

Put another way: 52 percent of all native-born Black soldiers (137 out of 263) were born in the states of the former Confederacy, a rate *nearly nine times* greater than the rate of white southerners among the native-born white soldier population (6 percent, or 125 out of 2,064). At the same time, this data exposes the limits of the extant literature's focus on the recruitment of African American

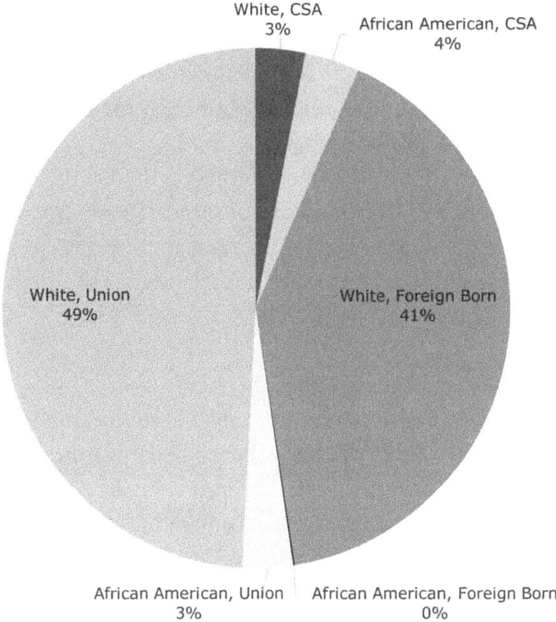

FIGURE 5.3. US Army soldiers by nationality and race, 1870–90. Based on the study sample of 3,936 enlistments.

soldiers from the Upper South, for nearly as many African American soldiers were born in Union states as were born in Confederate states (126 to 137).[14]

Of course, relying on data without considering context is a dangerous path to follow, so it is important to consider whether Gilded Age army recruiting's structural features might account for the vast racial disparities among the southerners who joined the institution. Here, one might note that the popular belief that the army withdrew from the South after 1877 is wrong twice over. Not only does one have to cleverly excise Texas from the South to maintain this position, but, more importantly, southern states contained federal military installations within their borders after Reconstruction. From the coastal forts guarding southern ports to scattered federal arsenals, to the major forts that were eventually established in the region (e.g., Fort McPherson in Atlanta, first garrisoned in 1885), federal troops remained in the South, albeit in sharply reduced numbers, during the latter stages of Reconstruction and beyond.

The presence of army garrisons in the Gilded Age South matters because an easy way to join the army in this period involved walking up to the main gate of a post and enlisting. Each fort had a recruiting officer detailed from its ranks of commissioned personnel, and the army actually preferred to get its soldiers this way, mainly because, as Adjutant General R. C. Drum wrote in 1885, this work could be conducted "without expense to the recruiting fund."[15] Still, since there were only a handful of federal military installations within the boundaries of the former Confederacy, it would not have been as easy for southerners to join the army this way as it was for northerners.

Two other paths to the army for southerners existed. One involved the army recruiting in the South; the second way consisted of southerners who migrated to other regions of the country joining the army in their new homes. In terms of the first path, it has long been suspected that the army did almost no recruiting in the South; not only do Dobak and Phillips assert this, but, in fact, one review of my book *Class and Race in the Frontier Army* stated this as an outright fact.[16] Yet if one reads the annual reports on army recruiting filed by a series of adjutant generals in the *Annual Report of the Secretary of War*, one discovers that in most years between 1870 and 1890 the US Army operated recruiting stations or sent recruiting rendezvous into the South. Occasionally, these recruiting forays are identified as attempts to find Black soldiers only; in 1888, for example, the adjutant general reported that the Charleston, South Carolina, recruiting station was closed at the end of March because the quota for African American soldiers had been met.[17] Most of the time, however, they are not described this way, and since the recruitment of Black soldiers was often curtailed in this period because of African Americans' low desertion rates and high rates of reenlistment, we can surmise that the continued operation of these stations indicates that recruiters were trying to attract white southerners.[18] In fact, the army operated recruiting stations in twelve years between 1870 and 1890 in the following cities in the former Confederacy: Atlanta and Augusta, Georgia; Charlotte, North Carolina; Charleston, South Carolina; Memphis and Nashville, Tennessee; Richmond, Virginia; and San Antonio, Texas. Moreover, by the late 1880s, army recruiters were using the main southern recruiting stations as bases of operations for rural recruiting efforts; in 1890, for instance, army recruiters moved through rural areas of Georgia and Virginia. "Whether or not any immediate results were accomplished in the way of enlistments," acting adjutant general Chauncey McKeever optimistically observed, "much prejudice against service in the army was removed by the dissemination of information concerning the nature and condition of military service and the inducements offered young men to serve in the Army." While there is no doubt that, as one army bureaucrat put it, its main recruiting efforts were carried out "in the principal northern and western cities," it is also apparent that white southerners could remain in their native region and find their way into the army if they so desired—the broader distribution of birthplaces found among white southern enlisted men compared to their Black peers provides supplemental evidence for this view (figures 5.4 and 5.5).[19] It would be even easier for white southerners who left the South to join the army.

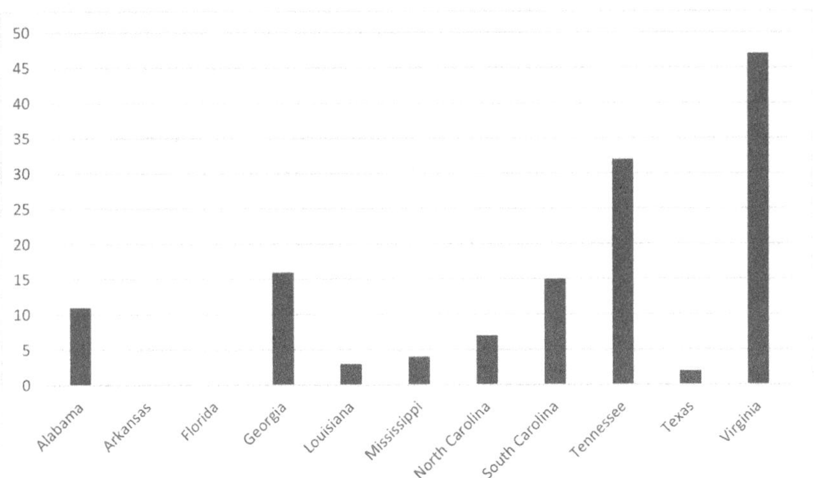

Figure 5.4. Number of African American soldiers born in each state of the former Confederacy, in the study's sample of 3,936 enlistments between 1870 and 1890.

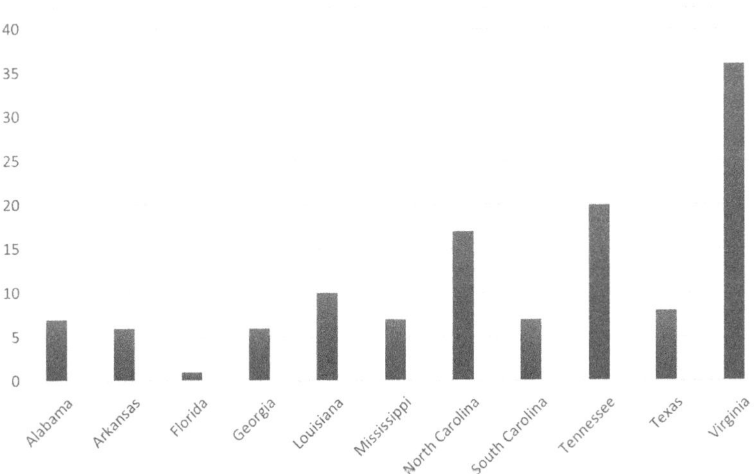

Figure 5.5. Number of white soldiers born in each state of the former Confederacy, in the study's sample of 3,936 enlistments between 1870 and 1890.

Far from being unable to join the army, in short, white southerners chose not to do so, a particularly interesting finding given the widespread (and long-standing) connection between white southern identity and military prowess apparent in American culture and repeated in a wide range of scholarly monographs. From Bell Irvin Wiley's descriptive account of white southerners' belief in their inherent military aptitude in *The Life of Johnny Reb* to Grady McWhiney and Perry Jamieson's reliance on "Celtic" culture as an explanation for high Confederate casualty rates to Jason Phillips's recent invocation of a Confederate culture of invincibility that persisted into Reconstruction (the war's actual outcome notwithstanding), the notion that southern white men reside within the confines of a martial culture unique in American history has legs.[20]

At the same time, however, this analysis of army enlistments suggests that we need to reframe the terms of the discussion and rethink our prevailing assumptions. The contours of white southern martial culture as invoked by both nineteenth-century actors and the historians who study them can seem frustratingly vague because both groups tend to employ *martial culture* as mere shorthand for "violent" or "violence," not as a window into a fully articulated cultural system. This has led our understanding of the complex relationship among masculinity, military service, and militarism in the nineteenth-century South astray in important ways.[21] Although the boundaries among them were certainly permeable, masculinity, martial behavior, militarism, and the military represented distinct cultural concepts with unique histories to which period Americans brought unique associations.[22] Rather than conflating white male southerners' propensity toward violence in the nineteenth century with military service or a military mindset, historians are better served by decoupling masculinity from the military and reconsidering the adjective *martial*. Far from representing the apogee of manhood and mastery, service in the US Army was more akin to its nadir in the eyes of most nineteenth-century Americans. From their loss of republican independence to their oppression by aristocratic officers to their lives of drudgery, enlisted men in the regular army were the objects of pity, scorn, and suspicion from an American public wary of standing armies. To fully realize their potential as *martial men* in the way that contemporary historians use the term, nineteenth-century men (North or South) more commonly unmoored themselves from formal military service in favor of private expeditions (e.g., filibustering or local Indian wars), temporary militia service, or the consistent application of personal violence. And, speaking of this last option, the violence unleashed by men in the nineteenth century was overwhelmingly directed at local (usually domestic) actors, served local interests, and exposed social marginalization or insecurity about social and cultural standards as much as it did mastery.

If we keep this in mind, our analysis of the recruitment and enlistment of soldiers in the US Army from 1870 to 1890 might lead us to consider whether we can speak of a martial South at all; given its paltry record of service in the military, the white South may well have been the *least* martial population in the United States. This position becomes clearer when one considers the home states listed on the enlistment papers of Black and white southerners. While Virginia and Tennessee were the most common places of birth for both groups, and while several states had five or fewer Black enlistees, the greater diversity of white southern birthplaces should not distract us from the fact that only 1.2 percent of white soldiers in this sample—a mere forty-four men—were born in the seven states of the Deep South (as defined by Coffman in his magisterial overview *The Old Army*). The comparable rate for Black soldiers was 18.3 percent (forty-nine individuals).[23] Here in perhaps the most southern part of the South, the vast disparity in white and Black enlistments demonstrates a major flaw connected to the notion of a martial white South: our commitment to depicting white southern men as uniquely martial has caused us to completely overlook the real martial southerners, African Americans. Although some barriers to southern enlistment did exist, neither they nor the racist practices that limited African American mobility in the South prevented members of this southern racial minority population from finding their way into the army at a much higher rate than the white majority (and in greater absolute numbers as well). This tells us something pretty revealing about the persistence of Civil War animosities in the postwar South and engages the larger discussion about the pace and extent of reconciliation in the postwar world.

To be sure, one could argue that the comparative absence of white southerners in the Gilded Age army should be read not as an indictment of martial manhood in the white South but simply as a reflection of lingering resentments from the war. Such an argument certainly matches the modern historiographical recognition that the political battles of Reconstruction continued into the 1890s.[24] At the same time, however, if we sever the connection between military service and martial masculinity and increase our field of vision a little, the South appears less an outlier than a regional variant of an unmartial *nation*.

Let us return to the demographics of enlistees. Useful as they are, the enlistment registers do not tell us where soldiers' parents were born, but a sample of over one thousand white soldiers drawn from the 1880 US Census (which did ask respondents to state where their parents were born) reveals that 62 percent of white enlisted men were either immigrants or the children of immigrants.[25] If we apply the same rate of foreign parentage to the white enlisted men in this sample, we find that nearly *two-thirds* of soldiers who enlisted or reenlisted between 1870 and 1890 were African American, were born abroad, or had at least one parent born outside of the United States. In other words, compared to the nation's population as a whole, *native-born white soldiers with native-born parents* constituted the real underrepresented group in the US Army—a description of nearly all the white southern population in this period to be sure, but also one applicable to wide swaths of the North. In essence, those with what one would presume would be the most established stake in society—native-born white soldiers with native-born parents—were massively underrepresented in the US Army. Those who stepped forward to fill the ranks in their stead tended to be the most marginal and vulnerable members of American society during a period of wrenching economic change: African Americans, the unskilled, and the foreign born. To cut to the chase, the United States in the Gilded Age relied on individuals who had seemingly the least stake in society to advance that society's interests through military service—just as the United States had done throughout the nineteenth century. The canonical "Old Army," in other words, was less a smaller version of the Union army than it was an updated version of the antebellum regular army, since race shaped the institutional military in a different fashion than it did before 1861.[26] And, we should keep in mind, during these years the military's role in advancing "society's interests" covered everything from the military component of its presumed mission to rule over the continent, to the suppression of striking workers, to the construction of roads and trails, to the protection of the new national parks, to the revolutionary attempt to build a biracial democracy on the back on a military occupation during congressional Reconstruction. Important work, it would seem.

That the Civil War cast a long shadow is perhaps a truism in the 2020s, but not everything covered by that shadow has been brought into the light. While not always discussed as such, that African Americans could and did serve in the US Army in the postwar years should represent two important legacies of the war for historians—even if the returns for Black soldiers themselves consisted of a few dollars' pay per month, duty stations in the desert wastes of the Southwest, and participation in the forcible subjugation of Native America. Teasing out exactly what African Americans' continuing commitment to federal military service meant to them and their communities in the wake of war and Reconstruction remains a blank spot on the historiographical map, and it is to be hoped that the rising generation of historians will do a better job of understanding the true protagonists in the story of African American military service.[27] Sometimes, however, one can catch a fleeting glimpse of this history: when the infamous lynching of Sam Hose took place in April 1899, a few thousand white people (men, women, and children) journeyed into rural Georgia on excursion trains so they could personally witness Hose's death amid a carnival atmosphere. Many of the spectators had embarked from Atlanta, and after Hose's death, they boarded return trains laden "with ghastly reminders of the affair," as the *Savannah Morning News* discreetly reported. Normally, this is where the story of Sam Hose ends, for few seem to have noticed newspaper accounts detailing how, as "one of the trains . . . passed through Fort McPherson, four miles out of Atlanta," the train "was stoned, presumably by negroes," breaking several windows and injuring two white passengers seriously. There were no African American soldiers stationed at Fort McPherson in the mid-1880s (it was hard enough to persuade northern and western cities to accept detachments of Black troops), but "negroes" could nevertheless make a statement on federal military ground.[28]

6

Robert Brown Elliott

Assistant Adjutant General, National Guard, South Carolina

GREGORY MIXON

THE CIVIL WAR AND RECONSTRUCTION transformed the United States. The war redefined the status of Black men and women, from enslaved persons to citizens. It also changed free Black status, from second-class noncitizen to a member of the community, even if only temporarily. White men were forced to accept or reject Black citizenship as a result of the conflict and postwar changes. War and its aftermath as well as Reconstruction in the United States realigned who among men had access to political participation, policymaking, and the power to shape long-term daily life in the mid- to late nineteenth century. The nation, especially the South, had to work through the problem of freedom. What to do with Black people plagued every emancipating western hemisphere nation-state during the age of revolution and civil wars. The problem of freedom forced white leaders of the nation-state to decide such questions as: Were Black people enslaved with no rights? Were they citizens with all the rights and privileges a nation offered, or were they to be shunned and excluded because white people assumed that Black people should not have access to the pantheon of governance? Nineteenth-century gender traditions reserved power for white men, especially elite white men. Before the Civil War, these white men controlled government, defined white male liberty, and served in the state militia. Government and its supporting institutions, especially the militia, operated to serve elite white men and empower them with the right to rule. That was the essence of white male liberty.

Post–Civil War South Carolina was one community facing these very questions about male gender dominance and racial inclusion. Elite white South Carolinians maintained their attachment to slavery after the war. They resisted Black freedom just as they had rejected the Black Civil War citizen-soldiers' presence as occupation troops. The white population sought to restore an antebellum status quo as they pursued policies intended to empower an all-white people's militia. The all-white militia was one structure white people hoped would help them reclaim control of South Carolina and make state government an exclusive, elite white male domain. They believed that only elite white men should govern the state and serve in the militia. The first two postwar years allowed the return of white male rule. Years three and four, however, brought about a sea change initiated by congressional Reconstruction and Black people, especially men. South Carolina's political composition was transformed by the Black man's right to vote and a Black demographic majority.

Further, postwar and Union-occupied South Carolina was a place where Black men could access economic, political, and leadership opportunities. The Civil War had provided Black citizen-soldiers with combat and leadership training. Black soldiers joined the Union war effort armed with the vision of ending slavery, freeing the race, and realizing the essence of full citizenship as they defended the Union. These goals came with Black troops who fought in and occupied such places as South Carolina from 1861 to 1866. Among those Black men who found combat and leadership training in war-torn South Carolina were two formerly enslaved South Carolina men—river pilot Robert Smalls and coachman and Union army sergeant Prince Rivers (of the Thirty-Third US Colored Troops, a unit created, organized, and based in the state)—and New Yorker and Fifty-Fourth Massachusetts Infantry officer Stephen A. Swails. These three men would be stationed in and around Beaufort, South Carolina, throughout the conflict, as both combatants and occupation troops.

Wartime leadership opportunities carried over for these three Black men into Reconstruction and the realization of Black political power within the Republican Party three years after the war. In the male-dominated domain of postwar politics, the three Civil War veterans would become Republican Party stalwarts in the state. Swails became mayor of Kingstree, a member of the legislature, and a militiaman. Rivers assisted in founding Aiken County, served in the legislature, and rose to major officer status in the South Carolina National Guard. He worked closely with two Black National Guard leaders: Assistant Adjutant General Robert Brown Elliott and Adjutant General Henry William Purvis. Smalls returned home to Beaufort to become one of the most politically powerful Black people in South Carolina. Smalls and Swails constructed vibrant political machines. Serving in the legislature and then Congress, Smalls, like Rivers, would earn general militia officer status under Elliott and Purvis in the 1870s. While these three men were Civil War combat leaders, their wartime experiences did not result in any of them becoming the administrative head of the South Carolina National Guard. They served under two Black men without combat and military experience after the war. The five Black men came together in the late 1860s, just as African American male political ascendancy became a reality. Elliott, born outside the United States, not only rose to lead the three combat veterans active in state politics, but became a chief architect of South Carolina Republican Party Reconstruction policymaking and party organization. This Atlantic World man also helped make the National Guard an institution Black men led during Reconstruction.

Robert Brown Elliott, South Carolina's Black assistant adjutant general, took his responsibilities and rank in the South Carolina National Guard seriously. According to one biographer, he "performed his duties . . . in a straight arrow fashion."[1] Yet, there was more. Elliott assumed that the opportunity to lead would be empowering. He combined leadership in the militia and Republican Party to acquire political power for himself, militia protégés, and Black South Carolinians. Elliott served as assistant adjutant general in 1869–70 and major general commanding the National Guard in 1870–77. His militia leadership coincided with his congressional career and time as a South Carolina Republican Party leader. These posts and the power that went with them allowed Elliott to help create a new institution, the National Guard. As a senior militia officer, Elliott challenged South Carolina governors, asserted his official authority to make militia policy, defined and defended his decisions, and commanded white and Black militiamen. In his capacity as a political and militia leader, Elliott insisted that white people respect both the office and his personhood.

Militia leadership marked Elliott's personal evolution and public rise to major political power in South Carolina's Reconstruction Republican Party and National Guard. He ascended from powerless obscurity in the African diaspora to his two militia leadership appointments. These appointments, combined with his success in gaining election to state and national offices, helped make Elliott a unique African-descended person, a Black man with real power leading two major political institutions. Few if any Black men wielded such authority during Reconstruction. His influence increased after his year as assistant adjutant general: he served two terms in the US House of Representatives (1871–74), held the state speakership (1874–76), and served as South Carolina's attorney general (1876–77). The significant political power he garnered enabled him to place his stamp on the South Carolina National Guard, the state's Reconstruction militia. Elliott's militia service illustrates how race and power defined the hopes of Black South Carolina at the dawn of Black freedom.

Robert Brown Elliott was a man of the African diaspora and Atlantic World who, like other nineteenth-century African-descended people, crossed multiple boundaries in search of opportunity and a chance to prove not only his personal worthiness, but that of the Black race. Early biographers reported his birth in Boston in 1842 to West Indian parents, followed by education in Massachusetts,

Jamaica, and London.[2] Elliott's most detailed biographer, however, argues that his early life was shrouded in mystery, perhaps because of slavery and the need to protect those who might have assisted his parents in escaping the peculiar institution. Yet even that argument appears problematic. Elliott's education, professional training, and maritime service suggest a childhood, adolescence, and early adulthood in the port city of Liverpool, England.[3]

This British port produced another African-descended individual who crossed the Atlantic around the same time, John Robert Bond, a British-born Irish African man—or, as his biographer and descendant Adele Logan Alexander classified him, a "*black* Anglo-Saxon Protestant."[4] Elliott, like Bond, appears to have been born in Liverpool and probably spent his early childhood and adolescence in that port city. The similarities do not end there. Bond and Elliott also apparently worked or served in the British naval/maritime services before separately disembarking in Massachusetts during the US Civil War. These Black men had murky early lives outside the United States, but each respectively contributed to Black freedom and institution-building, either as a Civil War combatant as Bond did or in Reconstruction-era policymaking as Elliott did. Each man viewed the Civil War as an opportunity to shape and advance Black freedom in the Americas.[5] The African diaspora and the movement of Black people throughout the Atlantic World made Elliott one of numerous African-descended people who migrated to the United States from Africa, Canada, or Europe seeking a direct hand in defining Black freedom. It was in Liverpool presumably that Elliott acquired his literacy, writing skills, and professional training as a printer/typesetter before he crossed the Atlantic.[6]

The nineteenth-century Atlantic World was a place of change and new institutions. White people engaged in independence wars, civil wars, and transcolonial and transnational conflicts in such places as Argentina, Uruguay, Paraguay, and the United States. White political leaders on all sides of these conflicts invited enslaved and free Black men to join them as soldiers and militiamen, as white people utilized Black bodies for military and combat services to secure white independence and initiate nation-state formation. These western hemisphere wars opened up opportunities for African-descended people to serve as a bridge between the white and Black communities in the Americas. One of these conduits between the races was the Black *letrado* or man of letters. The Black man of letters was generally an educated and military personage with defined ties to the Black community who also served as a translator of bureaucracy between Black people and the white community. He might also be an active leader in community and state politics.[7]

As a military person empowered with literacy, the Black man of letters additionally helped usher in what one scholar has described as "a new and diasporic 'black' consciousness"—that of Black people seeking autonomy within the communities where they lived.[8] This meant being able to utilize the space they occupied and sometimes the power they wielded for collective economic, social, and political action serving Black people. It also meant that Black people sought access to public space, where they could celebrate events that identified and verified their presence and announce their right to lives recognized by white members of the state. Such a utilization of space publicly declared that Black people were citizens who had earned the protection of the state because of their service and loyalty to it. Utilizing public space also allowed Black people to stretch the limits of white willingness to accept Black people into purported white space, and to test the boundaries that defined race relations locally.[9]

Writing about the Río de la Plata region of South America, Alex Borucki has explored how enslaved shipmates developed friendships during the transatlantic slave trade's Middle Passage. These relationships were maintained by enslaved people and soldiers in the Río de la Plata's Spanish and Portuguese colonies. Some of these enslaved men and their descendants served in the local militia and became military officers, trained to serve in the state military. These men of color utilized their acquired educations and leadership skills to serve the Black community as intermediaries with white policymakers, police, and local, colonial, and state governmental and political agencies. Some of these Black men also organized Black people politically as they helped found local Black political parties.[10] Elliott, similarly, was a Black man of letters who combined internal political party work and power with service as a significant postwar military leader. He appears to have been the foremost African-descended man to lead and shape a mid- to late nineteenth-century governmental institution, the South Carolina National Guard.

Elliott's pre-Reconstruction life has been hard to pin down for researchers, but there is concrete evidence of his political actions and life starting in 1867. That year, Elliott's credentials as a man of letters with political power can be accurately tracked. He moved in 1867 from an active civic life in Boston's Black communities to South Carolina, working as a typesetter in both settings and participating in their respective literary worlds. In South Carolina, Elliott became a conduit between the Black mass of newly emergent freedpeople and the world of post–Civil War southern politics, serving as associate editor of the Republican and Black- and white-owned newspaper *South Carolina Leader*. In this position—a newspaper man and community leader under the mentorship of the newspaper's owner and editor, the minister Richard H. Cain—Elliott was no longer an invisible working-class man lacking the ability to influence people, shape policy, and exert political power. In Charleston, he represented Black South Carolinians seeking to make the state a more open and inclusive place where free and formerly enslaved Black people might begin to redefine themselves as citizens with power and as active community participants.[11]

The power that Elliott and other Black South Carolinians exercised during Reconstruction reflected African-descended people's ongoing nineteenth-century efforts to stake a claim for Black people as citizens, productive community members to be respected by their white neighbors. Such citizens also took actions to secure a place for themselves individually and for the race collectively. Black leaders such as Elliott operated within the nation-building processes that defined postcolonial and postwar mid- and late nineteenth-century western hemisphere nationhood.[12] These African-descended people sought to exercise nineteenth-century Black power. Proponents of Black power shaped local public policy, defended Black rights, helped formulate and define what public rights were, and molded public institutions to serve and protect Black civil, political, and economic rights in a society transformed by war. The US Civil War and postwar society appeared open to their contributions as equal participants. Black power within these open spaces meant the endorsement, recognition, and acceptance of Black people's opinions and actions. This process included the search for Black self-determination, with economic and political autonomy as well as the freedom to make mistakes. But Black people also endeavored to belong as recognized citizens of South Carolina and the nation.[13]

Elliott made public statements to that effect, contending, "Before us lies our mighty future, with all its hopes and its aspirations. . . . That future is ours to shape. . . . Let us realize that upon each of us rest duties commensurate with our rights." Elliott became part of an effort by Black people to take freedom into their own hands as they began the process of shaping Black liberty, with all its opportunities, mistakes, and learning experiences, cultivating access to citizenship, and building the institutions that defined local and state government.[14] This was nineteenth-century Black power. Elliott was among those people exercising power within institutions previously closed to African-descended people throughout the Americas, especially in postwar South Carolina.

Elite white South Carolinians did not and could not envision a post–Civil War world where the formerly enslaved, free Black people, and working-class white people exercised power and decision-making. The Postwar era transformed South Carolina, providing Black people and working-class white men with access to institutions that upper-class white people controlled and had long assumed the sole right to rule. Black laborers and the jobs they had performed prior to the war reinforced postwar white assumptions that African Americans regardless of achievement were inherently inferior. Additionally, white elites believed that Black people should own nothing and lacked the ability to lead, govern, or rule.[15] Further, the "slaves of South Carolina having been [solely] emancipated by the action of the United States authorities," according to the 1866 Constitution, had been freed not by state authority, but by the federal government and Union army. Elite white South Carolinians as a result claimed no connection to ending slavery. They defined Black liberty as another reason to disqualify Black men from the right to rule or govern. The all-white General Assembly Committee on the Military also claimed that Black people had "become so largely contaminated with false notions as to their rights" that they were infected "with feelings of hostility towards the whites." In that context, white elites claimed that their class alone possessed the leadership skills needed to lead, govern, and make decisions for South Carolina's postwar future. According to white elites, only "the people"—that is, the white elite—were qualified to vote, govern, serve in the militia, and make policy. They alone were the governing class. Black people did not belong in the exclusive leadership circle.[16]

Race, class, and gender defined who had the right to exercise power, to belong. Postwar white elites pursued multiple avenues to ensure that they—"the best men," "the right men," and "the people"—ruled South Carolina.[17] They also hoped that skin color would unite white men across class boundaries under white superiority. Whiteness, these men argued, transcended class and the sectional boundaries that had caused the Civil War.[18] Whiteness stressed maleness, individuality, productivity, racialized unity, aristocracy, self-improvement, and, above all, self-governance, all traits defined as solely white. White supremacy, whiteness, and maleness guaranteed access to power, governance, and belonging. White status determined who belonged and who did not. White immigrants were welcomed by these white men because the infusion of whiteness expanded white voting power. Immigration also offered a way to erode emergent Black political power, with the goal of severing Black men from the power they were beginning to amass.[19] White elite South Carolina men, with post–Civil War provisional governor Benjamin Franklin Perry's endorsement, set the immediate postwar standard for belonging. Perry defined the ideal white elite man as "a free white man . . . not a pauper, nor a non-commissioned officer or private soldier of the army, nor a seaman or marine of the navy of the United States." The free white man, as Governor Perry publicly conceived it, was an elite white male who possessed an aristocratic loyalty to "this State."[20] Belonging was exclusively white.

Although over four hundred thousand African-descended people could claim South Carolina as home in 1865 and 1866, elite white people defined them as a foreign threat that existed outside the boundaries of belonging. Black people were automatically inferior, unworthy, and incapable, lacking the refinement that had marked the aristocratic antebellum white elite South. Postbellum white people hoped to reserve the right to belong and rule.[21] By 1867, the twenty-seven-year-old Elliott had come a long way from his transatlantic Liverpool roots. He arrived in South Carolina armed with a classical education and some fluency in English, French, and Spanish. These qualities made him, according to an 1871 Massachusetts newspaper, "the ablest colored man in the South," a claim that might also have gone to Mohammed Ali Nicholas Sa'id, former Fifty-Fifth

Massachusetts Colored Infantry medic. Sa'id had come to South Carolina armed with a global profile enhanced by Civil War combat service. A teacher in Charleston from 1865 to 1867, and a member of the Berkeley District Board of Registration, Sa'id registered Black voters in 1867. Sa'id was born free into a West African military family. The death of his father in war and military defeat were followed by Sa'id's enslavement and later employment as valet to a white military officer and nobleman. These jobs and experiences took Sa'id on a global journey through eastern Europe, western Asia, Russia, western Europe, and the Caribbean. His life in Africa, Asia, Europe, and the Americas equipped him with language fluency in "Kanouri, Mandra, Arabic, Turkish, Russian, German, Italian . . . French," and English.[22]

Both Elliott and Sa'id came to South Carolina with Atlantic World experiences that prepared them to explore leadership, policymaking, decision-making, and power. Elliott accessed belonging experiences that had been reserved for white men before the Civil War. He worked his way into positions of trust within Black and white South Carolina as a Republican Party stalwart and power broker, high-ranking militia officer, and cofounder of an all-Black law firm. In contrast, Sa'id was less successful in his attempt to acquire political clout and belonging in South Carolina. He did not reside there long, departing either at the end of the 1860s or beginning of the 1870s on a journey across the US South.[23]

Nevertheless, both Sa'id and Elliott, having migrated to the United States in search of opportunity, joined postwar Black South Carolinians attempting to redefine Black people in South Carolina, the South, the nation, and the hemisphere. These Black men and the people they sought to represent endeavored to redefine themselves as a people with dignity, humanity, and self-rule. The formerly enslaved, free people, and members of the African diaspora entered Reconstruction in the United States not as the foreign "mob" of crazed savages that white elites imagined, but as self-directed, capable, and visionary people. Black leaders also wanted a partnership with white people in local and state governance. African-descended people, especially men of letters, accessed the world of power, politics, policymaking, and governance, seeking to redefine belonging as a much broader concept that included them. That was Black power in the nineteenth century. Elliott was one of those African-descended men of letters who belonged in the community and who laid claim to the right to help govern postwar South Carolina.[24]

Elliott did multiple things that connected him to South Carolina's Black community. In 1867 he helped print and edit the *South Carolina Leader*. By 1868 he had studied for and passed the bar, becoming a lawyer with his own Charleston-based law firm. Elliott partnered with two other Black men: the northern-educated lawyer and Michigan-based Civil War infantryman and future militia officer William J. Whipper, and antebellum legal pioneer Macon

B. Allen. Elliott also married a young woman from Columbia, Grace Lee. Each of these acts solidified his commitment to life in South Carolina.[25] He joined a population of 400,000 Black men transforming South Carolina. These men had a 125,000-person majority over the 275,000 white men. Further, 84,393 of these Black men were eligible to vote, an advantage of almost 19,000 voters over the 65,610 registered white men.[26] Black people by 1868 had begun exercising their demographic and political majorities, using the Republican Party to establish their vision of freedom. They began as delegates to the 1868 constitutional convention. Black and white delegates crafted a more inclusive state constitution. It included a provision for a multiracial militia. Their vision countered the white-only people's militia authorized three years earlier by an all-white constitutional convention. Elliott would rise within the 1868 counternarrative constructed by Black and white people, which included a new vision of belonging. The political power Elliott acquired between 1868 and 1870 enabled him to climb the heights of power within the Republican Party. He became an influential presence within the party and the South Carolina National Guard, holding top-level leadership roles in both institutions. Elliott was one of several Black people in South Carolina who created new spaces for Black South Carolinians to belong and exercise power as he endeavored to be an "eloquent spokesman for his race."[27]

Black and white South Carolinians adopted a new state constitution on April 16, 1868. It made all able-bodied men in the state between the ages of eighteen and forty-five years old subject to two years of military duty for the state.[28] Less than a year later, the 1869 creation of the South Carolina National Guard was an attempt by Black people, white people, and Republican Party members of both races to install new leadership systems, recognizing that Black people had power, liberty, freedom, and a seat at the table of governance.[29] Speaker of the South Carolina House of Representatives (and future adjutant general of the National Guard) Franklin J. Moses Jr. acknowledged as much in fall 1869 when he addressed the Black majority in the House, with Representative Elliott present.[30]

South Carolina, Moses observed, existed "in a condition where lawlessness was the rule," and certain forces "preferred that ruin should prevail" over "political and material prosperity." Yet, he joined Black and white South Carolinians in the House as they collectively engaged in making "our political experiment," a "new and novel order of . . . administration." Emancipation was a part of that process, but it also meant the "enfranchisement of a race hitherto enslaved, reared to manhood without the advantages of education, and trained to . . . unquestioning obedience to the will of a dominant people, wealthy, educated, and powerful." The "startling experiment" in liberty, freedom, and African American leadership also meant Black "advancement to equality of rights and privileges before the world, and [elevation] to positions of power and high responsibility." The "power to rule" within the context of a "great social and political revolution" was becoming a reality in South Carolina. The Black "gentlemen of the House, who formerly belonged to that enslaved race," had been delivered from slavery by the Civil War. They were in 1869 controlling "the destinies of the entire State."[31]

Moses also paternalistically warned, however, that slavery and "your political subordination [were] ordained of Heaven." The Black experience paralleled the bondage endured by "the [biblical] children of Israel," as both Black people and the Israelites had "bowed in quietness and submission, patiently enduring their burden [and] . . . the heavy exactions of their powerful taskmasters. But their hour of deliverance came," secured by "those who have aided in your deliverance from servitude and who have join[ed] with you in the salvation of your beloved State." As a result, Black South Carolinians had been elevated by their Union benefactors "to positions of honor and of authority." Blacks had also "been willing, in *their* power, to forget the past . . . wrongs and its cruelties . . . to mete out evenhanded justice." Moses argued that trust in the rule of law would additionally yield "the protection of the citizens," with Black and white South Carolinians residing "in harmony and happiness, sharing equally in the administration of public affairs, and sharing equally in the protection which the law affords." The man who would embody these hopes, dreams, promises of protection, and desires for a safer as well as more prosperous South Carolina would be Civil War general and Freedmen's Bureau official Robert K. Scott. Scott became governor, Moses announced, because "*His* purpose and aims are yours—the welfare of the whole people who constitute the citizenship of the State."[32]

Representative Elliott was an active legislator. He served Barnwell County as one of its five commissioners, the sole African American, at the same time that he was training as a lawyer and securing admission to the South Carolina Bar. He embraced his role and responsibilities, proposing bills to regulate, prosecute, and prevent concealed weapons abuses. Elliott attempted to address land use and internal improvements. Publicly, Elliott spoke firmly for Black people, promoting African American access to public accommodations.[33]

Elliott's political work led to more political influence and helped facilitate access to political institutions for African American and working-class white people. By September 1868, Elliott had earned one of eight informal leadership positions in charge of South Carolina's Radical Reconstruction.[34] Near the end of February 1869, Adjutant General Moses sent Governor Scott a letter seeking guidance on how to organize South Carolina's state militia, thereby creating the South Carolina National Guard. On March 25, Governor Scott appointed Elliott as assistant adjutant general. Scott and Moses apparently defined the National Guard as a political institution. These two leading white Republican men did not seek Black citizen-soldiers who had led Black men and fought in the Civil War for the post of assistant adjutant general. They appointed an articulate political operative, one who exercised political leadership on the same level as white men within the Republican Party. The governor and adjutant general also rejected at least one white Civil War combat veteran expressing interest in being Moses's deputy. This post placed Elliott in a position to build a new institution.[35] He went to work perhaps realizing that "in any democratic state military defense is a political issue." This was particularly true in violent postwar South Carolina, a state where anti-Black political terror was defined by political assassinations and white paramilitary organizing, all aimed at dismantling emergent Black political power.[36]

As assistant adjutant general, Elliott wrote 90 percent of the adjutant general's militia correspondence. Even though Governor Scott appointed Moses as the National Guard's primary official (that is, as adjutant general), Elliott used the assistant adjutant general's responsibilities and policymaking opportunities to put his imprint on the South Carolina National Guard. The appointment of a Black man to militia leadership in Reconstruction South Carolina marked a major transition in defining the militia in the United States. Since the eighteenth century, white men had used the colonial and antebellum militia to defend white liberty, property, freedom, and power, which meant that white men alone were intended to lead and serve as the community's defense force. Prior to the Civil War, only white men had the right to bear arms. Fear, protection, liberty, worthiness, and control also defined the militia's existence. In colonial South Carolina, all white men were eligible to serve as the colony's policing and military defense forces. It was white men's antebellum duty to patrol the countryside, monitoring behavior and movement of the enslaved while defending against slave insurrections and Native American incursions.

Colonial militia service was generally denied to Black men, but colonial governments did sometimes offer freedom to enslaved Black people and land to free Black populations when the colony faced manpower shortages and needed additional military defense against external threats. Nevertheless, Black militia membership threatened white people's position as the sole arbiters of freedom, liberty, and status; as a potential route to Black freedom and participation in colonial society, it raised the fear of Black people killing white people (in defense of the colony) in exchange for freedom. Colonial South Carolina's government wrestled with this issue. The colony resolved the problem by amending militia regulations "so that a slave who killed or captured one of the enemy received not his freedom but a cash reward."[37] The patrol system, John Hope Franklin noted, merged with the militia in the American South. Patrolling also reinforced the colony and state's military defense system, uniting regular military white servicemen and local white militiamen. Together, these men were called on to control the enslaved and provide the white community with protection against European invasion and Native American attacks.[38]

The 1792 Militia Act made militias exclusively white, certifying citizenship as white only. White citizen-soldiers served in each state's voluntary military force and in the union's professional army. US regulars, however, were tainted in the national mindset as a standing army threatening individual white male liberty. Americans had held this image of military occupation since the British army occupation and the American Revolution. American fear of occupation carried over into the antebellum era. The state militia, an organization of local white citizen-soldiers, was projected locally, regionally, and nationally as the epitome of freedom because volunteer citizen-soldiers did not look like a professional military, the standing army of occupation. The militia never lived up to its mythological billing as "the bulwark of the nation," the great defender of individual liberty and personal freedom, but it did provide individual white men with a social outlet, status in the community, and an opportunity for leadership and manhood training.

Antebellum white people also continued to view the militia as their defender against people of color. Specifically, the militia was a police force controlling the enslaved and preventing slave insurrections. The militia was also a public institution envisioned as the nation's preferred defense force that made white liberty a reality. Antebellum national leaders, however, failed to construct the crucial financial and bureaucratic structures to ensure institutional permanence; political will and federal military planning never came together to make the militia a national institution. From 1856 to 1861, white southerners believed that the militia was their last line of defense against slave insurrection and northern intrusion into southern affairs. As a result, white southern political leaders pursued national military resources to build up their state militia units in preparation for war. Southern white fears of insurrection and centralized government, northern resistance to slavery's expansion, and John Brown's 1859 raid to liberate the enslaved in Harpers Ferry, West Virginia, also caused white southerners to increasingly look to the state militias and the citizen-soldier as the only forces protecting white life, property, and liberty. In 1861, southern state military forces served the Confederacy.[39]

The Civil War and white Union leadership invited the enslaved to become citizen-soldiers defending the nation against the rebelling white Confederate military.[40] Black Union troops defined the conflict as a war of liberation, with the aim of ending slavery and making all Black Americans, enslaved and free, citizens of the nation. After the war, Black occupation troops in South Carolina—including the Fifty-Fourth and Fifty-Fifth Massachusetts Infantry Regiments, the Thirty-Third US Colored Troops (from South Carolina), and the Thirty-Fifth US Colored Troops (from North Carolina)—urged local Black people to organize to defend freedoms won during the Civil War by Black Union troops. These units also arbitrated Black-white postwar relations.[41] The post–Civil War vision of Black citizenship thus included militia service. The militia was directly tied to Black efforts to define freedom, autonomy, citizenship, and belonging after the war.[42]

The key question for Elliott in contrast to white South Carolina Republican Party leaders was: why did the militia exist? The vision shared by Governor Scott and Adjutant General Moses conflicted with Elliott's. Both white men envisioned the South Carolina National Guard as their personal tool. Scott wanted the National Guard to be a coercive force in his reelection campaign apparatus. Moses viewed the state militia as an enriching vehicle that secured him financial kickbacks from arms purchases that coincided with organizing and arming the National Guard.[43]

Elliot's vision, on the other hand, was to have an honest, professional, and functional institution respected by the public. The predominantly Black South Carolina National Guard Elliott led was an institution defining the public image of Black people. He insisted that militia officers control their enlisted men. Further, Elliott wanted the militia to operate free of political favoritism and steer clear of any interference in the election process. His early militia correspondence as assistant adjutant general in 1869–70 reflected his commitment to "the character of the service and good order of society." He did not want to embarrass or besmirch the race as an administrator or superior officer. Elliott demanded that militia units maintain public images of efficiency and propriety. As a result, he insisted that militiamen and even his bosses, the governor and adjutant general, behave in the "interest of the service." As his power over the militia increased in 1872, when he became major general commanding the National Guard, Elliott promoted his protégé, African American H. W. Purvis, to brigadier general and his chief of staff (in January 1872). He also celebrated Purvis's election as adjutant general in December 1872. That year also marked Elliott's involvement in reorganizing the National Guard, a process that engaged Elliott into the mid-1870s. In 1873, Elliott insisted that militia officers secure the proper uniform for a July 4 celebration and inspection, where he too would wear a full-dress uniform, acknowledging his rank as major general commanding the militia.[44]

South Carolina's National Guard had its share of internal structural challenges. Elliott "had difficulties maintaining order among his men," according to J. Brent Morris, a problem reflective of the transition from white to Black political power and the evolution of the militia as an American institution from its antebellum white-only social club tradition to the post–Civil War organizing of southern Black militiamen. This transition also heralded new militia traditions, with the appointment of a Black man to an important militia leadership position (Black militia leadership at any level had not been the norm before 1869). Leading and arming a biracial but racially segregated militia posed persistent challenges. Only half the National Guard had functional weapons, a problem Adjutant General Moses sought to remedy while also profiting from purchasing arms. The National Guard was also predominantely Black, which made it difficult but not impossible to recruit white members. Further, the 95,856-member militia, which would be dismantled eight years after its creation, was viewed by white elites as "an organization existing merely on paper," as reported by E. W. Moise, who would serve as adjutant general in the late 1870s. White people also condemned Governor Scott and the US secretary of war during Scott's governorship for first "arming the negroes" and indebting South Carolina to the tune of "nearly a half million dollars [in weaponry] for a militia which was not worth anything." Finally, white people were upset that Scott "issued [those arms] to colored people exclusively," intending "to retain the control of the white people."[45]

These burdens—corrupt white Republican leadership, anti-Black opposition, limited access to weapons, and a racially segregated militia membership—all combined to erode the National Guard's effectiveness. Collectively, these challenges undercut Elliott's vision for the National Guard and democracy for Black people, yet there were some white people in South Carolina, "though not disposed to recommend Colored Militia," who noted that the predominantly Black National Guard was a deterrent against white violence. Union army captain Felix H. Forbell observed "that no Ku Kluxing is done in the county [Union County] in the vicinity of the Armed Militia."[46] So the National Guard when armed could and did prevent white violence and intimidation. Elliott would persist in seeking to make the South Carolina National Guard a viable institution not only during his solitary year as assistant adjutant general but for much of his time as a powerful South Carolina political leader.

Scholars examining Elliott's South Carolina political career have suggested that he defined the South Carolina National Guard first as an institution "vital to the maintenance of democracy"; second, as a clear deterrent to ongoing Ku Klux Klan terrorism; and third, as a peacekeeping force. Peacekeepers, according to Elliott, were not "an offensive militia." The militia as he envisioned it would appear nonthreatening to South Carolina's white elite.[47] Elliott's militia correspondence helps us refine and rethink some of these assertions. More specifically, Elliott directed local militia leaders to monitor and control rank-and-file behavior, defend state government, and perhaps safeguard Black political and economic rights.

Captain Rivers received Elliott's orders to that effect on July 22, 1869. Governor Scott, Elliott noted, appointed Rivers as "Captain of a Company [of] the Special Armed Force of the State" for Hamburg, Edgefield County. Elliott, nevertheless, put his stamp on Scott's directives to Rivers. The assistant adjutant general informed Rivers that he should "promptly take proper steps in order to have your company enrolled, drilled, and ready for action whenever it may become necessary to act." Further, Rivers should "exercise great care in the selection of your men," while devoting "great energy in the enforcement of discipline." Elliott called for a disciplined force because he did not want Rivers or his command "to act on the aggressive."[48] Elliott, according to this letter, envisioned an orderly, self-controlled, and vigilant but defensive militia that did not attract negative public attention.

Black and white National Guardsmen, he hoped, would not initiate violent confrontations. Elliott, the highly literate assistant adjutant general, directed Rivers, the formerly enslaved man, Civil War noncommissioned officer, and combat veteran who led men in war and now in peace, that disciplined ranks made a successful militia. The prime directive was: "Should any of your men commit any act of violence, perpetrate any outrage, or be guilty of any unbecoming act of insubordination, you will immediately cause such offender to be placed under arrest and report your action together with the causes to these Headquarters without delay."[49]

Elliott with this correspondence conceived a concrete idea about how the South Carolina National Guard might interact with South Carolina citizens. He understood South Carolina's tense, violent, and racialized atmosphere, but he wanted Black people to succeed as active political participants. Further, the position of assistant adjutant general empowered Elliott. It enhanced his growing political influence, providing him with "tremendous power" and a chance to build an institution from the ground floor.[50] Elliott imagined that a disciplined Black and white militia controlled by attentive officers might succeed, allowing African Americans to define freedom as an inclusive component of state government. The militia became an important part of Black power in South Carolina at the dawn of freedom.

Given his superiors' differing visions and the internal limitations that defined the South Carolina National Guard, it may not be surprising that Elliott resigned twice in 1870. His work between the resignations involved writing correspondence between the adjutant general's office and South Carolina National Guard units, officers, and citizens. More importantly, Elliott continued to serve the office and Governor Scott as a troubleshooter, with several trips to Abbeville, Laurens, and Charleston. Beginning in early March 1870, Elliott traveled multiple times to Charleston seeking to resolve ownership and custodianship of two properties: the muster ground and Military Hall. The muster ground appeared to be in possession of private individuals, even though Elliott concluded that the state government really owned the land, transformed by Civil War deprivation into garden plots. Military Hall, however, generated a multiyear, racially charged debate, beginning with the question of whether the building was owned by the federal government or the South Carolina state government. Once South Carolina eventually repossessed the building, disputes arose within the militia over upkeep, control, and use of the facility. It appears that under National Guard jurisdiction, Military Hall served as a place where Black people assembled for political discussion and rallies. White militiamen insisted in 1877, when the state military returned to being predominantly white, on banning political meetings, declaring the building to be for militia use only. Elliott first visited Charleston on March 3, 1870. He found the building controlled by Freedmen's Bureau agent L. L. Bennett. Elliott, exercising his authority as the governor's authorized representative, "personally took possession [of Military Hall] in the name of the State," while demanding that Bennett relinquish the building's keys to him. A month later, Elliott reported to the governor that he had used "the power delegated to me by Your Excellency" to compel Bennett to do a title search to definitively establish Military Hall's ownership as federal, state, or municipal.[51]

In July, Elliott returned to Charleston and Military Hall. His visit was intended to investigate an officer's refusal to assemble his command in the summer heat for a scheduled July 4 parade. Elliott interviewed the commanding officer, with the goal of "draft[ing] a proper course of procedure." Then he requested that the officer assemble his company "for inspection in order to afford all parties concerned an opportunity of presenting their side of the case in a proper manner." Meeting the company in Military Hall, Elliott was annoyed that the company's captain was absent without leave (AWOL). Elliott inspected the unit's arms and equipment and found them "well kept." He then shifted his attention to "the cause of difference" between the commanding officer and the officers of Company C. Elliott listened to each complaint and came "to but one just and fair conclusion": the AWOL captain was the center of the problem. Captain William H. Mishaw had been "wanton[ly] insubordinate" and mutinous with superior officers. Mishaw had also "instill[ed] in . . . his command the spirit of Mutiny" by telling militiamen "they were or could become an independent organization," transcending the governor's authority. Mishaw further argued about the governor that the "Commander-in-Chief had not the power to disband the command or take away their arms now in their possession." Elliott concluded his report by "ask[ing] for the immediate revocation" of Mishaw's commission.[52]

Elliott added to his report some comments concerning his work, position, and self-identity in South Carolina's National Guard. He felt, to say the least, "disrespect[ed]" by Mishaw's failure to report with his company for inspection. Mishaw's absence, however, meant more. It was personal. Elliott wrote, "the absence of Capt. Mishaw from his Company inspection when ordered to present himself is strong presumptive evidence of disrespect to your humble servant who is at present the Heart of the Department as well as to your Excellency whose representative I am." With this phrase, Elliott declared his importance to the National Guard. Despite his May 1870 "resignation" for unclear reasons, he considered himself to be at the core of the organization. Even more significantly, Elliott declared that he was the heart of the department before he acknowledged that he served at the pleasure of the governor.[53]

In May 1870, Elliott sent orders to recently promoted captain J. A. Green, a directive "to go to Abbeville immediately [for the] purpose of organizing the Militia of said county." In June, Elliott visited Abbeville "to dismiss from the State Guard" three militiamen and to address the "many occasions" when National Guardsmen had been "used as stump-speakers and distributors of books" as active political actors. Before the assembled militia unit, Elliott told the militiamen that they could not involve themselves in public political functions when on duty as National Guardsmen. At the same time, every militiaman "had a full and perfect right to the enjoyment of their individual opinions." They possessed the right to "attend public meetings" as South Carolina citizens, but not as militiamen. These individualized political rights were only possible when militiamen "obtained [a] leave of absence" from their commanding officer, Colonel E. L. Mann. Yet the colonel "then and there took issue with" Elliott. Mann "declared that no one had the right to so restrict the men, and as for himself he should pursue first such a course in political matters as he saw fit." The assembled National Guardsmen were "emboldened" by Mann's direct challenge to Elliott's authority and arguments concerning appropriate National Guardsmen's private, public, and official behavior. Guardsmen took their commander's lead and responded to Elliott's position and authority with insolence and insubordination. Elliott, rising to the challenge, threatened to "discharge them," but after a private discussion with Mann, Elliott "dropped the matter."[54]

Mann and Elliott then engaged another ongoing militia personnel issue, the payroll, but their work was disturbed by the three men Elliott would eventually discharge from the National Guard. These three militiamen apparently continued the debate concerning three issues: militiamen's participation in local politics, Colonel Mann's authority, and Elliott's policy declarations and ultimate authority. According to Elliott, the three militiamen made it clear that they had no respect for Elliott because "they did not care a d---n for any n——r." Their allegiance went to "Col. M. and no one else." Expecting Mann to maintain respect for Elliott's rank and authority, Elliott assumed that the three would be dismissed or discharged on the spot. Mann, however, "did not say one word" and refused to "do one single thing to stop such proceedings." He instead reinforced his personal authority after Elliott departed, telling his command and the three men specifically "that he," Colonel Mann, "had full power" because "he had more influence" with Governor Scott.[55] Given these connections, Mann told his unit that he would not let Elliott dismiss the insubordinate National Guardsmen.

While Mann made these declarations in Elliott's absence, his claims, Elliott charged, "render[ed Elliott's authority] contemptible in the sight of the men." Elliott's own personal network of "persons regarded by me as being quite reliable" informed Elliott of Mann's assumptions and targeted denigration of Elliott's authority. In response, Elliott (who was at the time both assistant adjutant general and inspector general) decided "to assert my prerogative as an officer of this State—being as such, entitled to the respect of all in subordination to myself. I therefore discharged them and filled the vacancies caused thereby." Mann objected, employing a surrogate to allege misconduct and abuse of power by Elliott. The assistant adjutant general challenged Mann and his supporters by using the power of his position, urging those antagonists to recognize that while they had equal rank, Elliott's position gave him the "prerogative as an officer of higher grade."[56]

By late September 1870, Elliott sent Mann correspondence requesting "that you will recommend the names of suitable persons to fill positions of Capt. & Lieuts. of the six companies allotted to Abbeville County." Seven days later, in early October, Elliott informed Mann that National Guard headquarters had sent Abbeville ninety-six "Breech loading Rifles" for select squads of "reliable and efficient men." Mann had the freedom to send these men "whenever in your judgement they are most needed," but he also was directed to "give charge of one squad to L. L. Griffin, Esq." Griffin's mission was to "best exercise the keeping of the place," Abbeville Court House, and execute "Militia instructions necessary to the skillful use and promotion of the arms." Mann also received one hundred Winchester rifles and permission to request more arms and men to maintain Abbeville's electoral peace.[57] These orders appear to have given Mann the power to use the militia to reinforce the electoral process, though Elliott had reprimanded individual militiamen for doing do.

Yet keeping the peace and protecting public buildings were important roles for the South Carolina National Guard. Also in October 1870, Charles L. Anderson was promoted to major general commanding the National Guard, the rank and position that Elliott would hold later that year. Two days later, Elliott penned correspondence to Major General Anderson, "assign[ing him] to duty as commander of the Militia of this State," with orders to report to Governor Scott, who noted that "a bad state of things exist[ed] in Laurens." The same day, October 31, Elliott drafted Special Order 38, directing Anderson to Laurens Court House to "demand from the Sheriff of Laurens County, all the arms, equipment, ammunition, etc" that the sheriff had allegedly taken by order of a South Carolina circuit judge. Elliott added his own personal regards for Anderson, offering, "my earnest prayer for your safety, as well as success, coupled with my heartfelt emotions of friendship and esteem," in recognition of how dangerous this assignment was projected to be for Anderson. In Laurens County, Anderson joined forces with the US military to restore order.[58]

In October 1870, Laurens County was a political hot spot, alongside Union and York Counties, places where the Ku Klux Klan had mobilized, terrorizing Black and white residents. The Klan hoped to disrupt the upcoming November state elections. Anderson reported that "terrible murders" had occurred in Laurens County. The Eighteenth US Infantry captain G. A. Estes with sixty infantrymen was sent to assist local authorities. Estes developed a plan to restore order and peace by getting leading local men to stand with Laurens County sheriff B. F. Jones to calm the community. Governor Scott also sent Elliott to Edgefield Court House to execute a similar plan. First, Elliott was to "take personal charge of the arms" and "get reliable men to protect both citizens and arms against a repetition of the outrages perpetrated at Laurens." Further, the violence in Laurens had attracted the attention of the US president, who was "fully aware of the State of things existing here." Scott expected US forces to assist with protecting life and property. Before departing for Edgefield, Elliott informed Rivers of his promotion from captain to lieutenant colonel in the South Carolina National Guard.[59]

On December 3, 1870, Elliott resigned his post for good. In a highly illegible document, ruined by the corrosion of time, Elliott let Governor Scott know that their relationship appeared to be broken. The fracture centered on Scott's abusive utilization of National Guard resources to build a political machine for the governor's personal use and reelection. Elliott prefaced his resignation with a self-assessment: "I have earnestly endeavored to perform faithfully and satisfactorily the duties assigned me." Elliott, however, charged that for at least eighteen months, persons outside of the adjutant general's office had been permitted to receive funds "from this Department for work they never performed" for the militia. Further, Elliott charged that it "was well known to you [the governor] . . . that they have never performed" any work for the office. These questionable activities had transformed the militia into "a Department which has for its basis unjust discrimination" and an "unfair . . . controlling favoritism."[60]

Despite this second resignation at the end of 1870, the summer of that year cemented Elliott as a major power in the Republican Party, first chairing the nomination convention and then winning election to the US Congress that fall. Throughout 1871, while Elliott represented the third congressional district, Moses and Anderson administered the South Carolina National Guard, serving under Governor Scott. In 1872, Moses, then still adjutant general, launched a successful run for governor. Elliott resumed his involvement with the National Guard as Scott's governorship came to an end with the November election. Elliott became commanding major general with Purvis as his chief of staff in January 1872. Purvis would serve as adjutant general from 1872 to 1876 while Elliott commanded the National Guard. Elliott's involvement, including the issuance of an invitation to Anderson to attend a "Military Council" in the adjutant general's office to consider the "best measures" for reorganizing the National Guard, announced Elliott's return and a partnership with Moses. Individual letters also went to African American militia generals Swails, Smalls, and Rivers, along with white militia administrative stalwart James Kennedy, whom Elliott included on his staff as major general and who had served with Elliott, Moses, and Purvis.[61]

Elliott's service to the South Carolina National Guard lasted until the National Guard's 1877 dismantling and reduction. Adjutant General Moise disarmed and purged the predominantly Black National Guard in 1877 and 1878 while pledging that "a better class of colored men can join it" and populate what remained of the Black militia service for the rest of the nineteenth century. He also installed a predominantly white militia, the State Volunteers, under former Confederate general and South Carolina governor Wade Hampton III.[62] Elliott nevertheless maintained a significant relationship with the National Guard from 1870 to 1877. His active involvement with the militia coincided with his rise to power as a US congressman, political boss, Speaker of the South Carolina House, state attorney general, and Republican Party leader.

On July 30, 1870, South Carolina Republicans nominated Elliott to run for US Congress in the state's third congressional district. On August 1 of that year, before Elliott's second resignation as assistant adjutant general, Governor Scott commissioned him as major general commanding the National Guard of South Carolina. Elected to Congress in December 1870, Elliott took up his Washington, DC, congressional duties in March 1871, but he maintained direct connections to events in South Carolina. He entered Congress essentially as the head of the Republican Party, having risen in importance by way of his statewide work organizing the South Carolina National Guard and his continuous promotion of the Republican brand across the state.

By 1873 Elliott led a National Guard staff of fourteen that included Purvis as adjutant general and inspector general of South Carolina, and Kennedy as assistant adjutant general. Moses, the former adjutant general, was governor and commander in chief of the South Carolina National Guard. Overall, it was a significant leadership group. Yet, South Carolina legislators "neglected" the National Guard between 1870 and 1873. While the National Guard had "a peculiar and higher value to the sovereign citizens of this free Republic," institutions including the General Assembly and state educational bodies did not comprehend the need for the militia. According to Purvis, the "main reason for the non-appreciation of a perfect militia system is that the necessity of the military branch of the government is not so constantly manifest." Further, while "the military power . . . gives to the government its strength," the militia was prominent in the public mind "only in time of emergency, and in the meantime relaxes into a mere useless branch of government, which leads the popular mind into the depreciation and neglect of its importance." Nevertheless, Purvis contended, "we must sustain a military force. The general government demands it, our own protection and interests require it." At the same time Purvis conceded that the National Guard existed in a "disorganized state" and badly needed reorganization and a reduction in size.[63]

In 1874, with South Carolina suffering from a "depressed state of business" in the wake of the national 1873 economic panic, it was difficult to drill and review the National Guard. The internal organizational problems had also persisted. Governor Moses appointed "a Board of Commissioners" with the mandate to "perfect a re-organization" of the National Guard. The board was headed by Elliott, Rivers, and Colonel E. W. M. Mackey of the Fifteenth Regiment, with Kennedy as clerk.[64] Elliott and Rivers had been militia officers at the founding of the South Carolina National Guard in 1869, colonel and captain respectively. They had evolved together as significant members of the South Carolina National Guard. Both Black men had risen within the Republican Party between 1869 and 1874, becoming by 1874 elected state officials and party leaders. Their National Guard service had come full circle by 1874, as they led a second effort to reorganize the militia two years after Elliott had called National Guard leadership for a meeting in Moses's office. Elliott in 1874 combined his influence as a member of Congress, general officer in the National Guard, South Carolina Republican Party leader, and major Black voice for South Carolinians. He had achieved what no other southern Black militiaman during Reconstruction did: he earned the opportunity to lead, mold, set policy for, discipline, and reorganize a state's National Guard. He made these decisions without the Civil War combat experience that Swails, Smalls, and Rivers possessed. Robert Brown Elliott, the lawyer, politician, militia administrator, and man of letters—but not a combat veteran of the bloody Civil War—received appointments as assistant adjutant general and major general commanding the National Guard. Elliott had secured a position of power, demanding respect from those above and below him as he attempted to exercise Black power for Black people.

7

"A Class of People Far Superior"

White Soldiers, Civilians, and Perceptions of Race and Class in the Spanish-American War

Kari L. Boyd-Weisenberger

On May 19, 1898, Harry M. Crawford boarded a train for Tampa, Florida. It was not a business trip, but he would be working. It was not a pleasure trip, but he went in "glorious spirits."[1] With him were over one thousand other young Michiganders all with the same purpose: to serve Uncle Sam. Mustered in as a private in the Thirty-Second Michigan Volunteer Infantry only five days prior, Crawford was now embarking on a journey that would take him far from his corner of the world, the small but growing city of Pontiac and its surrounding farmlands, dropping him outside the growing industrial city of Tampa. Crawford wrote over one hundred letters and postcards home to family and friends, documenting almost daily his thoughts and actions. These letters, along with the dozens sent to him that Crawford saved, offer historians an opportunity to witness how one young man experienced military service and the changes it brought to his life. Between descriptions of camp and guard duty, Crawford offered considerable commentary on the South, its people, and the places he got to see as a result of his service.

Despite the Spanish-American War officially lasting a mere eighty-three days, the disruption it caused to the lives of the men who volunteered to fight in it offers historians an opportunity to understand how ordinary white Americans perceived the world around them.[2] Over two hundred thousand men volunteered to liberate Cuba and, in the process, wrote thousands of letters home detailing their experiences in the service. But in their discussions of empire and in-depth analyses of the Rough Riders, many historians have overlooked a great deal of what the volunteers experienced. The majority of these men, particularly those who never left the States, appear only in the aggregate in much of the historiography of the Spanish-American War, if they even appear at all.[3] Their letters, however, reveal a rich commentary about perceptions of race, region, and respectability from people that in times of peace are frequently absent from the historical record. Service during the Spanish-American War took tens of thousands of men from their relatively isolated hometowns in the North and Midwest and moved them southward, exposing them to new people and places. In their letters, these soldiers shed light on how regular Americans at the turn of the century conceived of Civil War reconciliation, the effects of segregation, and the viability of white Anglo-Saxon superiority.

There has been a considerable amount of scholarly work examining the experiences of Black soldiers in the period between the American Civil War and World War I, and rightfully so. The experiences of Black soldiers serving in state militias, in the regular army fighting against Native nations in the American West, in their charge up San Juan Hill (where they rescued the more famous Rough Riders), and in the Philippines can teach historians a great deal about race, racism, and masculinity at the end of the nineteenth and start of the twentieth century.[4] The Twenty-Fourth and Twenty-Fifth Infantry and the Ninth and Tenth Cavalry all saw action in Cuba, with the soldiers of the Ninth and Tenth receiving considerable praise in contemporary newspapers for their bravery and the essential role they played in the Battle of San Juan Hill. In the Philippines, African American troops were among the longest tenured US soldiers, and their role in American imperialism and racial policies toward Filipinos has piqued the interest of historians in recent examinations of American empire building.[5] There were also six Black state volunteer regiments formed in 1898, with an additional four Black US volunteer regiments proposed. Though many Black volunteers had similar reasons to their white counterparts for joining the service, their experiences with the systemic racial discrimination confirmed by *Plessy v. Ferguson* (1896), particularly in the South, created a unique experience for them, as has been deftly covered by other historians.[6]

The illustrious Rough Riders with their enigmatic personalities have often served as surrogates in the pantheon of American military units for the whole of the white volunteers. A mishmash of Ivy League athletes and western cowpokes, they cut a dashing picture, but their combat service in the First US Volunteer Cavalry separates them from the majority of the volunteers.[7] Most volunteers never left the States, let alone saw the enemy. Furthermore, the Rough Riders' diverse makeup belies the fact that most volunteer units were comparatively homogeneous. They were often composed of men from the same area or city and usually shared similar ethnic and socioeconomic backgrounds. Though the relative diversity of the Rough Riders allows historians to examine the interactions of people from different backgrounds in the intimate setting of shared tents and combat, the intentional way in which the First US Volunteer Cavalry was recruited makes it an outlier among the volunteers.

Far more typical were units like the Thirty-Second Michigan and the Sixty-Ninth New York, composed of young white men that mostly shared a common ethnic, religious, social, and even political background. For some of these units, especially those from the Midwest, the war exposed them to people different from them for long periods of time, so much so that even interactions with white southerners proved novel and noteworthy. By diving into the sources left behind by these unassuming volunteers, historians can see some of the less obvious ways that white supremacy and the lingering tensions of the Civil War permeated the fabric of American life, and how military service could simultaneously challenge and reinforce internalized prejudices.[8] Additionally, it is important to read these letters within the context of military service and war. These are not letters written by tourists. And when their dreams of combat came up against the reality that most of them would never "see the elephant," their sense of disuse was sometimes projected onto those around them. The dehumanizing effect of warfare extended farther from the front line than one might think during a war that cost few American lives.[9] If nothing else, the sicker and more stationary the men were, the worse the physical and emotional condition of the volunteers became.

"ALL EAGER FOR THE FRAY"

High morale in late April and May 1898 among the volunteers often rested on the excitement and sense of purpose the volunteers felt upon enlisting.[10] With calls to "Remember the Maine—To Hell with Spain" ringing in their ears, men flocked to recruitment centers clamoring to serve their country. "All day yesterday there was a steady stream of applicants at the local recruiting office," the *Detroit Free Press* reported. "As early as 8 o'clock yesterday morning a large crowd assembled in front of the recruiting station at 6 Monroe avenue, eager to gain admittance."[11] Though the Midwest and Northeast outpaced other regions in recruitment, men eagerly offered their service all over the nation. Even in South Dakota, "more than 10,000 men have offered their service and a number of companies will be formed," reports promised.[12] Motivated mostly by patriotism, a strong sense of duty, a fear of being left behind, and a desire to punish the Spanish for their treatment of the Cubans, the recruits in April and May believed they had enlisted in the service to fight.[13]

After the heady atmosphere of the recruitment station had lured them into the service, recruits still had to pass a physical inspection before mustering in at the state guard camp. Doctors and surgeons subjected recruits to a series of physical examinations to determine whether they met the basic physical fitness requirements for military service. In New York, recruits stripped and passed before "a line of well-dressed medical inquisitors to join a group of naked enlistees who were jumping up and down as if practicing to stamp the Spaniards to death. This was a scientific test to see if our hearts were in the right place."[14] Upward of 20 percent of the men who signed up failed to pass these examinations and were sent home, though some continued to try to enlist elsewhere or found creative ways to slip through the process. Andrew Wadsworth of the First Nebraska Volunteers was so popular in his unit that the medical board passed him, despite his being underweight for his height. His father claimed that Wadsworth's shooting skills contributed to his not being sent home.[15] Bernard Lichtig of Illinois had a friend in the local government send a telegraph to the secretary of war to ask him "to order by telegraph my enlistment which he did bad leg & all."[16] Compelled by patriotism and a sense of duty, the volunteers of 1898 had high hopes for their service and were often willing to try anything to ensure they had a shot at glory.

Eagerness to serve kept morale high as the new recruits trained in state guard camps, often in cold, rainy conditions and with inadequate supplies. The Illinois National Guard arrived at the state fairgrounds in Springfield in late April and spent several nights sleeping in tents on the muddy horse track or in pig stalls lined with hay. Despite these less than appealing accommodations, the men adapted to the conditions with "little concern and real good humor."[17] As the volunteers settled into the rhythms of military life and learned the basics of drill and guard duty, they became aware of the dearth of supplies available to them in state volunteer units. Though the government had hoped to send the state guard units to the army's assembly camps in the South fully outfitted, many volunteers lacked tents, full mess kits, and uniforms when they boarded southbound trains.[18] Worse, and perhaps foreshadowing the futility of their service, the weapons offered to the volunteers were often the outdated 1873 Springfield rifle. Charles Butters of the Third Illinois Infantry received his Springfield rifle reluctantly, calling it a "leftover from the Civil War," Charles Wood of the First Arkansas Infantry remarked that the Springfields "knocked hell" when fired, and Harry Crawford reported that most of the rifles the Thirty-Second Michigan had were unserviceable and had to be sent back.[19] Even unarmed and missing key supplies, the volunteers left their home states full of optimism that they would soon meet the enemy in battle.

Until boarding the train for a national assembly camp, most volunteers interacted with other men quite similar, demographically, to themselves. Harry Crawford's tentmates were all Detroiters, and though Crawford came from the smaller town of Pontiac, they were "very obliging" to their new comrade. Will, John, and Ross Frederick of Sault Ste. Marie, Michigan, frequently ran into other men from their hometown while at Camp Eaton. Karl Kraemer was even able to reunite with old friends while at his state camp: "All the boys were very much surprised to see me. I have seen most of them I knew. All of them were tickled to see me."[20] Experiences with inadequate shelter, drills in camp, and unsavory army food only strengthened the bonds between the volunteers and did little to diminish their zeal to see the enemy. As long as combat remained a possibility, almost everything could be viewed through a positive light.

"I DON'T THINK WE WILL STAY HERE VERY LONG"

High morale and the volunteers' belief that they were getting one step closer to meeting the enemy in battle made the long trips south or westward feel more like a vacation despite the cramped conditions and poor food on the train.[21] For some volunteers, the thrill of seeing new places and people had them glued to the train windows. This journey was frequently the first time they had left their home state. The mountains and valleys of Kentucky fascinated the soldiers from Michigan, who wondered how people got in and out of the isolated gorges. The southern pines and magnolia blooms that greeted them in Georgia and Florida reminded them they were in a far different landscape then the one they had left behind.[22] The First Nebraska's long trip from Camp Saunders to San Francisco took its men across the Great Plains and through the Rocky Mountains. "Every mother's son of us had a neck a several inches longer from looking at the sights of which we had read and heard and never expected to see much less be paid for seeing them," Andrew Wadsworth wrote. "The scenery beats anything I ever thought of."[23] The eagerness expressed by Crawford, Wadsworth, and others, however, was about to come up against the reality of military service. They were no longer near the doting public of their home states, and most still lacked the basic supplies needed for camp or combat.[24]

The journey south was also often the first time many northern and midwestern volunteers had any sustained encounters with southerners, white or Black. With little else to do on the train, many of them wrote home about their impressions of the region and its people and the ways it differed from their own. Between descriptions of cheering crowds and young ladies pining for brass buttons, Crawford wrote, "In Kentucky we found more hills and valleys for some miles. Great many negroes. They live in little frame cottages with brick or stone chimneys."[25] Given that the Black population of the Detroit area hovered around 2 percent of the total population, in all likelihood this was the first time Crawford had seen large African American communities.[26] John Frederick was even more blunt about what the men of the Thirty-Third Michigan witnessed on their way to Camp Alger, Virginia: "we ran along the New River for a good many miles and saw old fashioned n——r houses and slime wheeler boats, there are more colored people here than white people."[27] The novelty of seeing large numbers of Black people would continue for some time for many volunteers, especially as they witnessed the effects of segregation and white supremacy in the South.

It would not take long for many of these white northern volunteers to witness racism and segregation after their arrival. John Frederick, on his first full day in

Falls Church, Virginia, saw several white officers refuse to salute the Black officers of a segregated regiment nearby. "The Colonel of the regiment," Frederick wrote, "got off his horse and made the white Colonel apologize for it."[28] As the Thirty-Second Michigan wound its way through Georgia, Crawford noted that "every one down here has negro servants. It makes no difference how poor a man is. The black are a very demoralized set."[29] Upon interacting with the Second Georgia after arriving in Tampa, Crawford was introduced to the racial prejudices of white southerners. "Made acquaintance of some Georgia soldiers. They are encamped near us. My, how they hate the blacks. We have a black man in our company. They could not understand how we would allow it."[30] It is unclear whether Crawford was sympathizing with the poverty of Black Americans in the Deep South or whether he held a more critical view of their stark existence. Crawford's comments reflect in some ways the combination of surprise many northerners felt when confronted by the realities of white racism and segregation in the South. Many middle- and upper-class northern reformers in the 1890s saw the South as a region that presented various political, social, and economic problems that needed to be solved.[31]

In some regards, Crawford's initial reactions toward white southerners were far less descriptive and much more critical. It is clear that at the time of his arrival in the South, Crawford believed, to some degree, that southerners were inferior. This feeling for the most part would only be reinforced by his experiences over the course of the four months he spent in Florida. He believed that northern white people were "far more intelligent than the whites of Georgia," many of whom he called "poor white trash."[32] In letters written after Crawford and his tentmates got a chance to venture out into Tampa a few days after settling into Camp DeSoto, Crawford's bias becomes even clearer. Crawford mentioned that there were some fine residences in the city, which was likely a great winter resort. His tentmate Gaston's relative let them inside the Tampa Bay Hotel, a place Crawford described as "finer than anything I ever saw before."[33] He added that the hotel was mostly a winter hotel for northern people of wealth. Crawford's comments concerning the Tampa Bay Hotel and several other mentions of northerners reveal that he perceived finery and quality as distinctly northern qualities. He was not alone. The perception that the South was "caught in a premodern and preindustrial era" led many white northerners to see the South as a distinct place untouched by modernity, where northerners could relax in leisure and peace.[34]

A measure of this prejudice came from lingering tensions in the aftermath of the Civil War and emancipation. Many volunteers were the sons and nephews of Civil War veterans, raised on stories of courage under fire, and eager to match or exceed the martial achievements of their forebears.[35] They held high hopes and expectations that their military service would bring themselves personal glory and make their families proud.[36] They were well versed in the exploits of the war generation, both inspired and burdened by their fathers' glory, glory constantly renewed by campaign speeches, Grand Army of the Republic parades, and the flurry of Civil War memoirs and regimental histories published in the 1870s and 1880s.[37] Harry Crawford's uncle Walter had served with secretary of war Russell A. Alger during the Civil War and wrote to Harry often with advice on how to survive battle: "A pile of sand the size of a man's head has saved many a man's life in the last war."[38] Walter also advised his nephew to always keep some water with him, cook food whenever possible, and save grease whenever he could so he could add flavor to his hardtack ration. Henry and Julian Buckbee's father was a Civil War veteran of the First Michigan who saw action not far from where his sons were stationed at Camp Thomas, Georgia. It was close enough that he promised to send them the name of, presumably, the prostitute he frequented in Chattanooga, Tennessee.[39]

The volunteers were aware that they were doing more than simply following in the footsteps of their elders. They would be among the first northern soldiers outfitted for war in the South since Reconstruction, a fact almost every American from the president on down was acutely aware of. The only city, according to Crawford, that did not shower the men of the Thirty-Second Michigan with praise on their way to Florida was Atlanta, where they were greeted with "no cheers, no flags, no enthusiasm."[40] The last time a long column of soldiers in blue had marched through Atlanta the entire city burned—thirty-three years was not enough time to mend the trauma caused by the Civil War. The account in the *Atlanta Constitution* of the Thirty-Second's visit to Atlanta counters Crawford's claim, but it is likely that the paper was interested in promoting reconciliation. The animosity Crawford sensed might have been a result of the Michiganders whistling "Sherman's March to the Sea" while in the city, though Crawford's cousin Mabel felt that the feelings were unfounded: "It seems strange that the Southerners are still so bitter against the North and especially that they would show it at a time like this." Crawford's observations reveal that the rifts caused by the Civil War had not healed everywhere to the extent the government wished.[41]

Perhaps the most bizarre example of how the volunteers interacted with relics from the Civil War involved grave desecration in Virginia. On August 6, 1898, soldiers in the Twenty-Second Kansas found themselves encamped outside Union Mill, Virginia, with several thousand other troops waiting for orders at Camp Alger. Like most volunteers, the men of the Twenty-Second Kansas were anxious to return home, since the rumors around camp were that a cease-fire was soon to be signed, ending the war and with it their chances of meeting the enemy in combat. Morbid curiosity, boredom, and a general lack of discipline prompted an unknown number of men to participate in the desecration of Confederate graves in the search for rebel bones.[42] The incident sparked outrage in the local community, forcing the army to conduct a massive investigation into the incident and leading to the courts-martial of three members of the Twenty-Second Kansas that fall. The trials of Captain Louis C. Duncan, Lieutenant Guy W. Morgan, and Private Prince Albert Weisse reveal both the considerable effort the army and the American government were putting into the reconciliation process during the Spanish-American War and the practical limits that reconciliation project had. Amid a very different war, the memory of the Civil War and its combatants remained contested.[43] The response from locals in Northern Virginia to northern soldiers digging up the graves of long-dead Confederates also shows that many white southerners still felt like second-class citizens within the United States: "And yet the South-haters of Ohio, and the whole North, say the animosity of the Southern people for those of the North is such that the latter cannot get justice here." When two of the three men put on trial for grave desecration in 1898 were acquitted, the *Alexandria Gazette* argued that the clemency toward the officers "indicates that Southern leniency to a northern offender has been produced entirely too far."[44]

For Crawford, the longer he remained in the South the more critical he became of white southerners. In July, after two full months in Tampa, he wrote home explaining, "the northern fellows all do well here—in fact they do the greatest part of business. This is not because the country is rich—it isn't: but because no one else knows how to do business."[45] The Thirty-Second's transfer to Fernandina, Florida later that month hardened Crawford's belief in the unsophisticated nature of southerners. Unlike Camp DeSoto, which had become disease ridden and was populated by African Americans and Cubans, Fernandina reminded Crawford and his company of a northern town. Healthful, clean, and technologically advanced compared to Camp DeSoto, Fernandina was populated "by a class of people far superior to those at Tampa. They are mostly Northerners."[46] For Crawford and many of his comrades, there was a direct correlation between white northerners and healthy, profitable living.

In addition to exposing white northerners to southern white people, military service in the South brought many northern volunteers into more sustained contact with large numbers of African Americans and legal segregation, often for the first time. In a letter to his youngest sister, Eva, Crawford described a conversation he had with a young African American boy: "He said we went to school to a colored school Ma'am." Crawford recalled, "He told me that white boys and girls and black boys and girls did not go to the same school."[47] Crawford's conversation about segregated schools with the young Black boy and his interactions with other people of color in the South reveal how segregation held a certain intrigue to some northern volunteers who had never encountered it face-to-face.

Even though many of Crawford's interactions with individual African Americans seemingly challenged his preconceived views of them, Crawford's prejudice toward people of color surfaced as he came to realize that the Thirty-Second would remain in the States and his frustration with the service grew. Early on in his time in Florida, with foreign service in Cuba still a possibility, Crawford wrote more positively of his interactions with the Cuban and African American individuals around Camp DeSoto. "I got acquainted with a poor Cuban lemonade seller who runs a stand near this seat. He told me much about Cuba—its climate, people etc.," Crawford wrote. "He has a mother and sister whom he thinks are living near Matangas. Also has a brother in Cuban Army. I am not trying to draw a sentimental picture, but tell the exact truth when I say the poor fellows eyes were full of tears and his hand shook with emotion when he handed me my glass."[48] In a separate encounter while eating breakfast in the home of an elderly Black woman outside of Camp DeSoto, Crawford "was surprised by the neatness of everything. These blacks are generally very dirty. She finally brought me the best cup of coffee I ever tasted."[49] In these incidents Crawford's face-to-face interactions with people of color around Tampa challenged some of his presupposed ideas about them.

The long stay in Tampa and the realization that combat duty was unlikely had one more effect on men like Crawford, especially those volunteers from small towns and farms in the Midwest and North. Military service in the South broadly, and Florida specifically, meant interactions with large numbers of African Americans and Cuban Americans, as well as encounters with legal segregation. Crawford found this last impossible to ignore: "There is one thing noticeable here—every saloon, every rail-road station has two entrances, one plainly labeled 'colored entrance.'"[50] Crawford's first foray into Tampa included a trolley ride through Ybor City, the home of most of Tampa's Black and Cuban poor. "This is [a] rough town," Crawford explained to his father. "Negro dives, saloons, and gambling dives. There is no law or order."[51] As time wore on and the Thirty-Second's frustration with being left in Tampa grew, Crawford's commentary about Tampa became more vehemently racialized. After the Thirty-Second got transferred to Fernandina, he wrote home that "it was a relief to get away from those chattering Cubans and mongrel whelps at Tampa."[52] Crawford blamed the poor conditions in Tampa on the Black and Cuban populations that lived there, rather than the government that had so thoroughly failed to properly supply its volunteer units. Upon moving to Fernandina, Crawford praised the town's modern plumbing and clean water, saying, "It does us good to see clean well dressed, intelligent looking American again after ten weeks of Spanish, Cuban, Negro, + Negro-Cuban gab."[53] Rather than see the connection between the state of Ybor City and the segregation of public places in the South, Crawford pinned the condition of the town partly on Black and Cuban inferiority. He held preconceived notions of class and race that influenced how he viewed the nonwhite civilian populations around him. Crawford's remarks about Tampa reveal not only some of the persistent racial prejudices of the time, but also the way that one volunteer processed his disappointment concerning his military service.[54]

Starting the evening of July 13, Crawford made his final venture into Ybor City while on provost guard. "This is a bad town," he wrote, "and a strong guard is stationed upon the streets, in the saloons and in the govt storehouses."[55] To a degree, Crawford was right. Ybor City had been the scene of rioting during the night of June 9, when, the *Baltimore Sun* reported, a company of Ohio men seized a Black toddler by the feet and held the child upside down while another soldier shot at it. A bullet grazed the child's arm before the soldiers let the child return to its mother.[56] Black soldiers from the Twenty-Fourth and Twenty-Fifth US Infantry Regiments, already fed up with local racial customs, raided a saloon, stole all the alcohol, and ransacked nearby businesses, particularly those that had refused to serve them.[57] Several white soldiers, including an officer, were shot by Black privates. When Company H of the Second Massachusetts failed to suppress the riot into its second night, an unidentified company of "Southern white volunteers" (later revealed to be the Second Georgia Volunteers) arrived and attacked the rioters, killing four Black soldiers. Reports from Black soldiers in the army hospital in Atlanta after the riot claimed that over forty of their comrades had been killed.[58] Newspapers denounced the behavior of the soldiers as a disgrace to the country. The behavior of the Ohioans and the willingness of southern soldiers to fight the Black regulars demonstrate that though white supremacy was easier to spot in the segregation of southern life, it was alive and well in some northern troops as well.

Personal interactions between northerners and African Americans occurred in other camps as well and show some other ways that internalized white supremacy manifested during mobilization. Calvin Mixter of the Fifth Massachusetts Volunteer Infantry wrote home about his interactions with various African Americans working in and around Camp Meade in Pennsylvania. His generally positive first impressions with these people contradicted some of his preconceived notions of white supremacy. In September 1898, with the men tired of bad cooking by inexperienced volunteers on kitchen duty, the Fifth hoped to hire an African American man as its cook. The Fifth first tried to lure the Black man employed by the Second Tennessee to cook for its soldiers, but the Second increased his pay and the man decided to stay with the Tennesseans.[59] By October, after a few weeks of searching, the Fifth managed to secure two Black men to attend to the cooking. "We have succeeded to getting a cook," Mixter wrote, "and although he is of dark and shady complexion, he is all right and is neat and understands his business."[60] The excitement the Fifth's soldiers felt at finally having a qualified cook in the mess belied the prejudice many of the men harbored toward the various African Americans that filtered through camp on a daily basis. Most viewed the Black laundresses with suspicion, considering their work subpar and hearing rumors that uniforms taken in were not always returned.[61] Ultimately, the Fifth's excitement ended up being short lived. Just three days after the new cooks were hired, Mixter reported that one of them had been discharged for taking supplies from the mess home to his family.[62] Though Mixter had little prior exposure to people of color and had high hopes for the hired men, the limited experience Mixter and the Fifth Massachusetts had in Camp Meade with African American civilians ultimately seemed to reinforce the men's preconceived notion that people of color could not be trusted.

"THE THRILL WE HAD COME FOR"

Not every volunteer remained stateside, stuck in camp with no promise of combat.[63] Observations of race and cleanliness in Cuba by Albert Gudatt of the Second US Volunteers reveal that disease in Cuba, and its association with dark skin, quickly eroded the morale of soldiers sent overseas. Gudatt's diary documents the Second's journey to Cuba in August 1898, where the men garrisoned in the recently captured city of Santiago de Cuba. They encamped on the Alameda, a once-popular city park now overrun by soldiers, horses, and military equipment. Dead bodies choked the city streets, Gudatt wrote, and the Alameda was one of the least healthy pieces of ground in Cuba. Refuse deposits from the dry season had been churned into a thick, foul-smelling muck by horses and the rain. The harbor's stagnant water carried an unimaginable stench. The situation for the people of Santiago de Cuba was desperate, Gudatt recorded, and people died by the hundreds every day, lowering morale among the men. In early August, Gudatt wrote:

> It was pitiable to see women and children stand around our kitchens—which were put up near the wall, the boys using the wall for a table. At every meal there would be several hundred women and children outside of the walls watching every mouthful one took with a greediness that can be amagined, very few men can eat under the circumstances, and a very few did eat, though it cost them an effort to do so, most of our food went over the wall to the little ones—and women.[64]

For over a month, Gudatt and the Second remained at the Alameda, the only American unit in a city quarantined for yellow fever, typhoid, and malaria outbreaks. In forty-five days, the Second lost over thirty men to disease. Morale plummeted as even the company doctors took to alcohol to deal with the situation.[65] Even a move to Songa, thought to be a health resort by army officials, did little to improve conditions. Gudatt remarked that Songa, choked by mud and inhabited by poor Cubans, offered little to the men but dress parades, drills, and the "occasional funeral thrown in."[66] Gudatt's dissatisfaction with the Cubans as expressed in his diary often seems to be a result of waging war in the rainy season, reinforcing an equivalency in Gudatt's mind between sickness and poor, dark-skinned Cubans.

In January 1899, after five months in the sickly cities of Santiago de Cuba and Songa and the occasional escort mission through the jungles, Gudatt's company arrived in Gibara, a city on the Caribbean Sea. Unlike Santiago de Cuba and Songa, Gibara was "the paradise of Cuba—no cleaner or healthier spot could be found, the rainy season was almost over, and the men recuperated fast. The inhabitants numbered about forty-five thousand—mostly Spanish and Spanish-Cubans, the majority were refined and cultivated—and wealthy." The women there, Gudatt wrote, had "a complexion as fair as can be found anywhere in the United States or the Continent."[67] Whatever Gudatt's prewar thoughts on the relationship between race and disease, his time in Cuba and experiences heavily reinforced a connection between dark skin and disease and between healthfulness and fair skin. Rather than see the disease and decay in Santiago de Cuba as a result of three years of civil war, which created food shortages among those too poor to flee the city, Gudatt saw the healthfulness of Gibara as a product of the inherent superiority of wealth and white skin.

Gudatt carried this equivalency from Cuba to the Philippines after reenlisting, this time in the Thirty-Third US Infantry, in August 1899. While on the way to the Philippines, the Thirty-Third passed through Honolulu, where conditions in the city continued to solidify Gudatt's perceptions of race and disease: "The Chinese and Japanese were in the majority and living as they did—crowded in the small huts, which were all more or less filthy, health had not much room in these places, here is where the bubonic plague broke out later, and the whole water front was destroyed by fire in trying to burn an infected hut."[68] The Thirty-Third arrived in the Philippines and immediately engaged the enemy. Gudatt generally saw the Filipino people as untrustworthy, a symptom of the complicated political allegiances of the various villages on the island and a general belief that the people of the Philippines were less civilized than the American soldiers stationed there. In February 1901, after fifteen months in the Philippines, Gudatt's unit moved from the area around Manila to San Fernando and Tondo. By this point, Gudatt and his comrades' impressions of the Filipino people were declining with each passing week. Gudatt recorded the horrible sanitary conditions the Thirty-Third encountered, claiming that the stench arising from the ditches and backyards of the town was horrid enough to knock someone out. Tondo was, Gudatt wrote, a district composed of bamboo huts, inhabited by the poorer class of people, mostly "thieves and murderers."[69] Unable to see or acknowledge the effect of years of warfare and centuries of colonial oppression by the Spanish, Gudatt attributed some of the sordid conditions in Tondo and the Philippines to the race of the people living there. Despite this, Gudatt's attitude toward the Filipino people was far more positive and less racialized than that held by other volunteers, particularly those who saw sustained action in the early part of the war.

Some volunteers who saw combat in the Philippines had longer, more sustained contact with new people and places during the war. Andrew Wadsworth of the First Nebraska went to war brimming with optimism and ready for adventure as he narrated his journey from Beatrice, Nebraska, to Manila from July 1898 to February 1899. The First Nebraska remained in and around Manila, living in proximity to the people of the Philippines, as the United States and Spain worked out the future of the islands without much input from its native peoples. His first comments about the native Filipinos in July described them as "bright and intelligent as the average run of people," but by mid-August his descriptions took on a more critical tone, as he repeatedly called the Filipinos lazy and addicted to smoking.[70] The initial war against the Spanish had ended after the First Nebraska's arrival in Manila, before the soldiers had managed to see combat. However, Wadsworth and the volunteers would not be going home yet. The First Nebraska would remain in Manila for several more months, after the Spanish left and before the Filipino insurrection against American rule began. The longer Wadsworth was there, the more racist and reliant on racial stereotypes his descriptions of the Filipinos and others became. Chinese residents of the Philippines, at least the people Wadsworth identified as "chinamen," drew the least flattering descriptions: "I might send you a chinaman to split the wood and draw water but I don't think you would appreciate the gift. I didn't ever like a negro but they are pretty good people after seeing the nabobs that live here."[71] Wadsworth reveals quite a few racial perceptions of the time: that the Chinese were only fit for physical labor, that African Americans were inferior but not as much as people of Asian descent, and that racial epithets could be used interchangeably.[72]

Wadsworth's experience of the war, unlike that of many other volunteers, did not end with the disappointment of missing out on combat. The First Nebraska was there in February 1899, when the tense relationship between the Americans and their erstwhile Filipino insurgent allies devolved into the Philippine-American War. But this war was not what Wadsworth and his comrades thought it was. "We feel that every man of ours that's lost is worth more than the whole darned island but what can we do about it. We don't know what we are fighting for hardly."[73] This was a different sort of disappointment. Wadsworth did not see the point in the loss of American life; the Filipinos "armed with bows and arrows" were not the enemy he had signed up to fight. This war had the First Nebraska "chasing n——rs" through the jungle, skirmishing against an enemy able to appear and disappear in the forest at will.[74] What followed were weeks of sleeping in the field under threat of enemy attack, which only ended with his wounding in action on April 23, at the hands of "a bunch of n——rs."[75] It is only after the outbreak of combat that Wadsworth's already racialized language devolved further. To Wadsworth, the Filipinos were barely human. They lived uncivilized lives at odds with how white people lived. He said so rather directly: "what a relief last night was the first time I have slept like a white man should for six weeks."[76] The dehumanizing effects of combat simply deepened the existing prejudices Wadsworth had, in part because combat was not what Wadsworth had expected. It seemed pointless and uncivilized, with no glory to be had, and the Filipino people, at least for Wadsworth, were to blame for all of it.

"A HAPPY LOT OF BOYS"

Andrew Wadsworth held quite the distinction among the volunteers. He was combat wounded in April 1899, something that relatively few of the zealous volunteers of 1898, even those sent overseas, could lay claim to. From his hospital bed, he told his family of the First Nebraska's withdrawal from the front lines and the men's imminent return home: "The Regiment is in quarters now and a happy lot of boys I tell you as they had been put up against the n——rs for three months and had about 200 killed or wounded and in Officers alone 3 killed and 15 wounded shows we were up against them plenty but we did our duty and that's satisfaction for me." His anger toward the enemy and the army only grew as he lay there waiting for a ship to take him home: "[They] left us here to sweat and fume over a piece of land that in my estimation hadn't ought to be on the map."[77] Harry Crawford, too, welcomed his trip home. The Thirty-Second Michigan spent two weeks winding its way through the South, going from Fernandina to Huntsville, Alabama, to Chattanooga, and finally heading back to Michigan. Crawford remarked only on the beauty of the landscape in these letters, making no further remarks on the people of the South.[78]

What the volunteers of 1898 offer historians is an opportunity to understand the myriad effects of war on the psyche of those that serve. In addition to getting a glimpse into the average American's understanding of reconciliation, race, and white supremacy at the end of the nineteenth century, historians can also see how the dehumanizing effects of warfare extend well past the front lines. Men like Crawford, Gudatt, and Wadsworth would have likely never recorded many of their thoughts about segregation, southerners, Filipinos, or Cubans had it not been for the Spanish-American War. But it is important to read their insights within the context of that war: the Spanish-American War was for many volunteers a war of unfulfilled expectations and one with no clear purpose once Spain signed the cease-fire. Their primary enemies became disease, boredom, and insufficient supplies. Those feelings of misuse, of futility, both uncovered the underlying prejudices these men held and made them more likely to express those prejudices to others. Their letters and diary entries chronicle how ordinary men saw the people and places the war introduced them to and how their experience of war both challenged and reinforced those views. Ultimately, they offer historians an opportunity to create a more complete picture of American racial attitudes at the dawn of the twentieth century.

8

The Problem with Wolves

American Servicemen's Sexuality across the Two World Wars

MICHELE CURRAN CORNELL

IN *THE WOLF*, A WORLD War II cartoon drawn by US Army sergeant Leonard Sansone and printed in military newspapers across the world, an American serviceman, depicted with the body of a man and the head of a wolf, lounges in his hospital bed. Obvious in his sexual desires, the Wolf stares hopefully at a female nurse with an accentuated womanly figure. While the nurse times the Wolf's pulse and takes his temperature, she observes aloud, "My, what big eyes you have!" (figure 8.1).[1] The nurse's familiar line is drawn from the classic children's fairy tale *Little Red Riding Hood*. In the story, when the Wolf meets Red, "a little country girl, the prettiest creature that ever was seen," he becomes ravenous with hunger for her. She innocently shares her destination with him, and he races ahead to Red's grandmother's house. After devouring Red's bedridden grandmother, the Wolf hides himself under her bedcovers. When Red arrives, the Wolf acts as her grandmother and instructs her to "lie down" with him. Naively, Red "undressed herself and went into bed, where she was much surprised to see how her grandmother looked." "Grandmamma, what great eyes you have got!" is Red's last observation before she notices the Wolf's fangs and falls prey to him. The story ends: "this wicked Wolf fell upon Little Red Riding-hood, and ate her all up."[2]

The Big Bad Wolf became a legendary villain in French Mother Goose nursery rhymes, the German Grimm brothers' fairy tales, English fables, and Russian symphonies, later being adapted into American children's stories.[3] These cautionary tales prepared children to enter a dangerous world and taught them basic morals about trust, deception, safety, danger, and good and evil. Specifically, *Little Red Riding Hood* warned young girls that speaking to strangers could culminate in physical danger. Informed by this narrative, Sansone's *The Wolf* turned a childhood villain into a humorous sexual predator. But how did the American

FIGURE 8.1. Leonard Sansone, "My, what big eyes you have!," in *The Wolf* (New York: United, 1945), n.p.

serviceman come to be characterized as the Wolf, and what did the existence of this character reveal about America's wartime mission?

This essay surveys the heteronormative soldiering sexuality established by white American servicemen across the two world wars.[4] It considers how American servicemen constructed and viewed their own sexual identity, and how this identity exemplified American power in the global arena. While the following sections evaluate military sex policy to measure the social climate, military newspapers authored by servicemen themselves serve as the foundation of this study because they offer a useful lens to explore how servicemen viewed themselves, their comrades, their enemies, and civilians—both foreign and domestic.[5] In other words, the behavior of individual soldiers served as a symbolic reflection for critiquing America's wartime mission. The manner in which military newspapers illustrated and discussed soldierly behavior, and the broader meaning of their interactions collectively, revealed the cultural pulse of the service members producing, reproducing, and consuming the material. Military newspapers, then, mirrored established service culture.[6]

This essay further explores the military's effort during World War I to shelter the American public by hiding and repressing servicemen's sexual habits, which officials believed were a consequence of the hypermasculine identity they expected men to adopt for war fighting. Constructing America's Great War mission as paternal within *Stars and Stripes*, a military newspaper published in Paris for the troops serving in Europe, the doughboys also shaped their collective identity as protective and actively defended their reputations against rumors of promiscuity.[7] Today, these idealizations appear somewhat hollow in light of venereal disease (VD) infection rates among the doughboys. Nonetheless, these images serve as a point of comparison to show that after a generation of changed social standards, a more understanding American public granted World War II servicemen freer sexual license. So even while World War II military policies continued protecting white servicemen's reputations, military newspapers transformed into spaces humorously riddled with references to sex. As authors and illustrators, servicemen used humor to express aggressive sexuality as a keystone of their collective identity. As readers, servicemen embraced depictions of themselves and their comrades as sexual aggressors. Specifically, in *The Wolf*, American servicemen sought sexual conquest over American and foreign women. To enjoy the spoils of war then, American servicemen traded projections of themselves as protectors on the home front and liberators abroad to become sexual predators on both fronts, which complicated ideas about America's wartime mission.

COMBATING VENEREAL DISEASE DURING THE FIRST WORLD WAR

During World War I, the manpower and money lost to treating VD infections in doughboys placed a heavy burden on the war effort. Of the over two million men in the American Expeditionary Forces fighting abroad, approximately eighteen thousand (9 percent) were hospitalized each day due to VD infections. On the home front, the problem grew even more severe, as over the course of the war medical workers diagnosed 12.7 percent of soldiers stationed in the United States with VD. At home and abroad, this equated to the loss of seven million days of active duty. To treat one soldier, it cost the federal government seven dollars per day for approximately thirty-three days of treatment. Therefore, VD not only robbed the military of significant manpower, it also cost the federal government almost $50 million to ensure that infected soldiers received the care they needed.[8]

To protect military men against VD during World War I, two groups came at the problem differently. According to historian Elizabeth Alice Clement, most military men believed that "sexual conquests and excessive sexual appetites were clearly linked" in their "vision of their identity as fighting men." Military leaders feared that repressing the sexuality of soldiers would "feminize troops and decrease their capacity to fight." Clement terms this hypersexual soldiering behavior—the championing of servicemen who pursued sex and "conquered" female bodies to demonstrate their manliness—as "sexually aggressive masculinity."[9] Those who shared these views rationalized that to control VD, the military needed to regulate prostitution and regularly distribute condoms to troops. On the other hand, according to Clement, social purity activists believed in the "basic virtue, strength, and innocence of American manhood" and worked to repress prostitution while encouraging the "moral education" of the troops.[10] The concept of protective masculinity rose to leverage familial relationships and repress the sexuality of American servicemen. This discourse urged men to be deserving of selfless mothers and expected each man to treat eligible women with the same respect they would demand of their sister's suitors. Thus, protective men acted paternally as guardians of women's sexuality and behaved morally and chivalrously by repressing their own sexual desires, acting on them only with their wives for procreation. Officials hoped that by promoting protective masculinity, they could separate violence and sexuality in the masculine identities of American soldiers, so that men would "fight fiercely," but resist the temptation to have sex with promiscuous women.[11]

During World War I, the military appeared to side with social purity activists, by supporting abstinence, discontinuing the distribution of condoms to troops, and attempting to distance the military from prostitution, leaving the repression of prostitution mostly to nonmilitary governmental organizations and civilians.[12] However, official military policies sent a more contradictory message. The commander of the American Expeditionary Forces, General John J. Pershing, issued general orders for officers to promote continence by providing diversionary recreational activities and educating their units on the dangers of VD (though not directly forbidding soldiers to have sex out of wedlock). Next, Pershing's orders worked to prevent major outbreaks of VD. Camps set up prophylaxis stations and required soldiers to use them if they engaged in sex. Officers also conducted mandatory bimonthly medical inspections for all personnel. Unlike with any other military training or regulation, military leaders expected initial and secondary sex policies to fail. The implementation of safeguards suggests that military leaders *planned* for the men in their ranks to disregard training and disobey orders relating to sex. To discipline careless soldiers and to prevent others from going astray, possible punishments for an individual soldier contracting VD included court-martial, forfeiture of pay, denial of privileges, supervision, daily inspection, manual labor, quarantine, denial of promotion, delayed return to the United States, detention, restriction to segregated camps, and denial of discharge until cured. Additionally, the military held officers accountable for the physical condition of the men under their command, and review boards used VD rates to determine an officer's suitability for command. Pershing's final line of defense against VD provided for medical treatment to restore the health of servicemen known to have contracted the disease.[13] While the orders regarding continence and punishment seemed to reinforce protective masculinity, the safeguards pertaining to prevention and treatment acknowledged that sexually aggressive servicemen would have sex regardless of the consequences.

CLEANSING THE IMAGE OF DOUGHBOYS AND ESTABLISHING MORAL SUPERIORITY

The occurrence of VD infections among servicemen, as well as the military's effort to control the spread, served as evidence of sexual promiscuity among American troops during World War I. Many Americans tightly married their perceptions about the nation's cause for war with valuations of the servicemen carrying out the mission. Therefore, negative views of the cause or the troops threatened to destabilize public support for the war.

Despite being a soldier's newspaper, *Stars and Stripes* projected the official wartime agenda of the US armed forces. Therefore, depicting an ideal image of American servicemen for themselves and the American public played a large role in its purpose.[14] On February 8, 1918, the first issue of *Stars and Stripes* pledged to its uniformed readers, it's "your paper," "for you and for those of your friends and relatives to whom you will care to send it."[15] Thus, the newspaper made its intentions clear that content designed by and for servicemen would reach the American public. *Stars and Stripes*, therefore, acted as a vehicle to help conceal the sexual habits of the doughboys abroad and cleanse the image of deployed troops for audiences on the home front.

In the first issue of *Stars and Stripes*, the editors and writers denied mass promiscuity among the troops overseas and conveyed a protectively masculine image of themselves as servicemen. A page-four piece called "To the Folks Back Home" denied the "alarming" and "sensational" stories that had been relayed about the conduct of the troops in France. "Our first inclination is to laugh," admitted the writers, because, they claimed, the rumors were "so far from the truth." Conversationally, the article attributed the rumors to "reckless and irresponsible people." The authors discredited the mythmakers as war profiteers, who "probably" "asked you to contribute money to their worthy cause, haven't they?" To defend the reputation of servicemen, the writers cited a 0.3 percent VD rate among the troops abroad, describing it as "the smallest percentage on record for any army, or any civil population, in the world's history." It is unclear how the writers calculated this statistic, but with it, they conveyed the image of a "sober," "well-behaved," and "clean" army to readers. The article also quoted a Protestant chaplain who found the "moral conditions most satisfactory" due to military authorities who vigilantly removed temptation. Lastly, the servicemen's "severest critic," their commanding officer, shared that he had never known an army garrison with "so good a record." To wrap up their defense, the writers guaranteed that servicemen would "come home to you clean in body, exalted in mind and heart, and with the record behind us of a man's size job manfully done."[16]

To further solidify the image of doughboys as protectively masculine servicemen, *Stars and Stripes* filled the top right corner of the page with Charles Dana Gibson's illustration "On Their Way" (figure 8.2). The republication of this *Life* magazine illustration in the first issue of *Stars and Stripes* signified that servicemen desired to be perceived as the virtuous heroes conveyed by Gibson's art. "On Their Way" features a masculine white American soldier, prominently recognizable by his Montana Peak hat.[17] The doughboy marches forth across the foreground with purpose, leading Victory in escort. A commonly used allegorical figure in European art, Victory represents Western humanity through the feminine beauty of a woman, whose purity radiates from her porcelain-white complexion, her large angelic wings, and the halo of light atop her crown, which is engraved with "Victory."[18] Her flowing robes hint at the ancient Greek and Roman roots of democracy, while the palm branch she grasps symbolizes the triumph that promises prosperity in peace.[19] As binaries, Victory's femininity perfectly contrasts with the masculinity of her doughboy escort. Her body mirrors his motion as her bare foot equally matches the step of his boot. Yet, she is *his* companion. He leads her into the future. Emotionally, she appears uneasy and distracted, yet calm and peaceful. Her facial expression reveals the urgency of the present with faith in the future, and she confidently trusts the doughboy with her fate.

"On Their Way" presented readers with a convincing visual of doughboys as protectively masculine servicemen. *Stars and Stripes* writers also contrasted themselves with their foes by reporting on enemy atrocities against European women. "German Brands Young Mother with Iron" screamed a headline in the first issue of *Stars and Stripes*. An American army officer in training, who formerly served in the British Army at Cambria, witnessed French refugees fleeing their liberated frontline town, which had been under German occupation for three years. He recalled that the Germans marked "scores of women and girls," "all about to become mothers," "on the breast by a cross in red paint." This symbol indicated that the unborn babies had German fathers and, therefore, would "belong to the German Government." A German officer had "forced" one girl, "not more than seventeen years old," "to accede" to him and then ordered her to be "branded with a hot iron to mark her for life" when he had no further use for her.[20]

FIGURE 8.2. Charles Dana Gibson, "On Their Way," in *Stars and Stripes*, February 8, 1918, 4.

Collectively, the women portrayed in the article shared stories of savage German brutality, and *Stars and Stripes* framed their experience as the "prostitution of womanhood which the Kaiser is forcing in order to repopulate the German Empire." The article stated that before retreating, Germany usually deported civilian populations living in occupied towns, an act that threatened reproductive slavery. The article concluded with the witness professing, "Thank God, America, by coming into the war, will help to stamp out this beastly 'kultur' from the world and make it a safe, clean place to live in for your womenfolk and mine—our mothers, our sweethearts, our wives, and our daughters."[21] Here as elsewhere the doughboys and nation stood as paragons of protective masculinity. The protective language, however, also extended the men's ownership over the bodies of women, effectively granting American servicemen rights to women's sexual and reproductive capacities as well. While American propaganda swapped brutality for benevolence, the women remained property under both regimes. In other words, the war would reinforce patriarchy and subject domestic, liberated, and conquered women to the victor's sexual mastery.[22]

MODERN THINKING AND NEW POLICY

In the years between the two world wars, the sexual revolution of the 1920s and unsettling family effects of the Great Depression altered American constructions of sexuality, allowing for more openness. For example, out-of-wedlock sex became more socially acceptable, and many Americans came to view sex as an entitlement for masculine servicemen.[23] New Deal funding for public health amped up the anti-VD campaign, normalizing prevention and treatment efforts, which continued into the 1940s.[24] Still, the fear that VD would financially burden the American war effort and weaken manpower, as it did during World War I, inspired World War II policymakers to act hastily to combat VD with more liberal, preventative policies that reflected a socially changed nation. After 1943, newly available penicillin made VD more easily and affordably treated.[25] As a collective result of these constructions and medical advances, images of sexually aggressive servicemen rivaled the ideal of protectively masculine soldiers in American culture, and military sexual policy reflected this shift. In 1944, US Congress repealed the pay penalty for servicemen undergoing VD treatment, suggesting "an acceptance of servicemen's sexual activity."[26]

The 1942 pamphlet *Sex Hygiene and Venereal Disease* conveyed the military's sexual expectations of servicemen. On September 30, 1943, secretary of war George C. Marshall ordered the military to furnish each newly enlisted recruit with a copy. The pamphlet directly related heterosexual sex to manliness and masculine soldering identity, stating: "Sex is one of the most important things in your life, for it makes you a man. It's something to be proud of. But, like everything else you prize, it must be well cared for." Similar to World War I policy, the pamphlet promoted abstinence to ensure health and encouraged men to save sex for the sanctity of marriage.[27] However, the War Department recognized that young servicemen would likely seek sexual adventures during their service, and so punishment for contracting VD became much less pervasive. Instead, the pamphlet coached men to use provided condoms, chemical prophylaxis, and cleaning stations if they engaged in sexual relations. If a man caught VD, the pamphlet assured him that with proper treatment, he could be cured. Additionally, the military resorted to surgically altering male bodies en masse through circumcision as a method of preventing sexually transmitted diseases. A 1944 US Navy medical bulletin stated that military doctors performed circumcision more frequently than trauma surgery.[28] Clearly indifferent to the variety of sexual mores and experiences of individual men, military officials lumped servicemen together, assuming that most would exert their martial masculinity through sex.

Military officials and lawmakers designed measures to protect the health of soldiers, and World War II VD rates declined thirtyfold from World War I rates. The average incidence rate of VD for the duration of World War II hovered around 37 per 1,000 men, with an average of nearly 600 servicemen incapacitated from VD each day.[29] However, the incidence rate of venereal infection varied from year to year and fluctuated in severity according to location. For example, the US Army reported a spike in the VD infection rates in the first half of 1941 to 42 per 1,000 men, a ratio that medical officers considered high at the time.[30] Outbreaks in specific locations, moreover, could easily develop into public health crises. At Fort Huachuca, Arizona, during 1943, VD rates reached a height of 368 per 1,000 soldiers. In August 1942, just one month after American forces arrived on West African shores, VD cases among American servicemen stationed in Liberia soared to 580 per 1,000 soldiers. In France, between September and December 1944, VD rates jumped 200 percent.[31] Still, education, preventative measures, and medical advances helped limit the overall impact of VD on American troops. However, this effort also reinforced the practice of sexually aggressive masculinity, which fused violence and sex together as traits that defined war fighting.

The sexual entitlements white servicemen enjoyed had negative ramifications for Black servicemen, American women, and foreign peoples. Military leaders and doctors, informed by racism, often blamed Black servicemen for high VD rates because they failed to recognize that discriminatory prevention efforts and inadequate medical treatment neglected the health of Black men.[32] Sex could also be dangerous for Black servicemen, as interactions and intercourse with white women could lead to rape allegations, courts-martial, and public hangings. In other words, Black servicemen did not enjoy the same sexual license as white servicemen. Nor did women. While the government and military largely left the sexual policing of women to nongovernmental organizations and local authorities, women in the United States could be jailed for promiscuous behavior. Abroad, the military's refusal to help regulate prostitution for the benefit of American servicemen and foreign peoples led to VD epidemics and major public health crises for other nations. In other words, the US military granted white American servicemen sexual entitlements, at the expense of Black people, women, and public health.[33]

Historians have observed that sexual fantasies passed down from World War I doughboys motivated World War II soldiers to "get off the boat and fight" in France. According to historian Mary Louise Roberts, such fantasies inspired a "tsunami of male lust," and American GIs became renowned for their promiscuity. In French cities, white American servicemen cast aside the norms of civilized decency to fulfill their sexual desires in public spaces. Despite soldiers' behavior, US military authorities worked to shelter the US public from their promiscuity while upholding the "myth of the GI as a traditional family man, disciplined and self-controlled."[34] As a result, images of the sexually aggressive servicemen shared space with persistent depictions of protectively masculine servicemen in both mainstream American culture and wartime propaganda.[35] Yet in military newspapers, the image of the sexually aggressive white serviceman became a morale-boosting symbol that championed the virility of the fighting American man.

THE PROBLEM WITH WOLVES

Amusing depictions of sexually aggressive servicemen became a standard in military newspapers during World War II. In 1942, the US Army began the Army News Service to inform servicemen around the world of daily events. The Army News Service staff summarized, rewrote, and updated news from the Associated Press and other commercial services before transmitting it nightly to locations far and wide. On June 15, 1943, the Army News Service established the Camp Newspaper Service, whose writers authored original content. Initially the Camp Newspaper Service sent material to four hundred army newspapers, but by the end of the war, it had expanded its reach to four thousand military newspapers. Its most popular product was a weekly clipsheet with feature stories, photos, comic strips, cartoons, and maps. One survey indicated a readership of ten million service members, and the US Army found that Army News Service material in overseas papers helped servicemen "battle isolation, boredom and loneliness and brought a bit of home to GIs overseas."[36]

Leonard Sansone, a corporal and later sergeant with the US Army, began working at the Camp Newspaper Service after his recurring cartoon, *The Wolf*, became a favorite in *Duck Board*, the camp newspaper at Fort Belvoir, Virginia. Servicemen referred to men with a special talent for luring women into bed as "wolves," in recognition of their predatory skill. Sansone's cartoons became famous for depicting the everyday sexual encounters of the GI Wolf. During the height of its reign, *The Wolf* appeared in three thousand military newspapers each week.[37]

During World War I, *Stars and Stripes* had conveyed a romantic image of US soldiers engaged in protective masculinity; during World War II, in contrast, American military newspapers offered bawdier and more sexualized depictions of US servicemen. World War II ribaldry in service culture increased the polarization of images of servicemen as either protectively masculine or sexually aggressive. Lewd humor laid bare a fierce contradiction: American servicemen fought for the protection of women as their fathers, husbands, and brothers, yet at the same time verbally assaulted female bodies through humor or physical conquest to demonstrate their masculinity.[38] While the protectively masculine serviceman represented a cultural ideal, the popularity of lewd sexual humor among American troops proved perhaps more real to them. Not all servicemen behaved as wolves, but many fantasized about sex, and some sought female companionship with sexual motives.[39] Sansone's *The Wolf* displayed the pride that sexually aggressive servicemen gained from their sexual prowess, while capturing the humor that others found in it. These jokes reflected how some servicemen viewed their own sexual identity and how others perceived the sexual identities of their comrades.

In 1945, United Publishers celebrated *The Wolf*'s wartime success by producing a book of Sansone's best work. In the book's foreword, popular cartoonist Milton Caniff noted that most servicemen admired the prowess of the company Casanova and also thought of themselves as a "pretty hot deal, capable of endless conquests over female hearts." However, Caniff admitted that the cartoon Wolf's "blundering moments" often reminded servicemen of themselves or of Wolf pals, especially when an illustration of "an unwilling Dollie" sent the cartoon Wolf "spiraling."[40] *The Wolf* not only provided fair ladies for sporting servicemen to gaze at, but also poked fun at the many wartime exploits, tensions, and problems the Wolf's excessive sexual desire caused.

Sansone provided a humorous outlet for venting the frustrations caused by the rivalry between men and the competing priorities of soldiering and satisfying sexual desire. While perpetuating the notion that a healthy sexual appetite went hand in hand with good soldiering, *The Wolf* captured instances when the pursuit of women distracted men from their wartime responsibilities during training. One segment of *The Wolf* depicted the Wolf hiding from his first sergeant in an exhaust pipe on the deck of a ship, as other sailors participate in their morning physical training. The Wolf has lipstick kisses all over his face. When the Sergeant discovers the Wolf, he yells, "Whaddya mean ya don't care t' join us right now!" Capturing the same sentiment, another illustration depicts the Wolf yawning and stretching on a cot, just rising for the day (figure 8.3). The barrack walls surrounding his cot are plastered with pinup girls. A private first class (PFC), recognizable by the stripe on his coat, observes the Wolf waking and comments,

"If you spent less time in bed and 'n' more time studyin', you'd make PFC too!" While the language frames the Wolf's sexual escapades as a damaging distraction that prevents his promotion while in training, the visual cues suggest that the Wolf is physically more prepared for battle than the PFC. Dressed only in his skivvies, the Wolf has a thin waist and a broad chest, with the tidy chest hair of a mature man beneath his dog tags. His physique projects a masculine ideal. In contrast, the baby-faced PFC appears scrawny and duckfooted. The PFC's comment reeks of self-congratulation at his modest accomplishment and jealousy about the Wolf's romantic skills.

FIGURE 8.3. Leonard Sansone, "If you spent less time in bed and 'n' more time studyin', you'd make PFC too!," in *The Wolf* (New York: United, 1945), n.p.

The Wolf's sex drive nearly always got him into trouble, but his charisma and antics also made him a popular friend as well as a ladies' man. In the barracks, ship berths, far-off staging areas, and war zones of Sansone's cartoons, servicemen flocked to the Wolf to hear stories of women and, when possible, share in his talent for a good time. Sansone frequently depicted the Wolf as the focal point of every group and the pal of choice for scraping up a double date. Although the cartoons often poked fun at the Wolf's failed sexual conquests, they also romanticized his pursuits and applauded his successes. One illustration featured a group of three servicemen and two women gathered around a piano where the Wolf plays Frank Sinatra's 1943 hit "All or Nothing at All." Captivated by his performance, a woman comments, "He has a wondering touch, hasn't he?" while her friend gazes at the Wolf as if assessing her next move. The Wolf returns her look, as if asking whether she would give him all or nothing at all. The illustration captured the Wolf's charm and skillful prowl as he lured in his willing prey.

While *The Wolf* showcased the pride and humor servicemen found in sexual prowess, Sansone flamboyantly depicted women as sexual prey, demonstrating that servicemen felt entitled to visual and physical access to women's bodies as a reward for their service. The majority of the illustrations depict women in voluptuous glory, with accentuated breasts, thin waists, long exposed legs, and hair that cascaded past their shoulders. The women's lovely faces all feature dark lips, small noses, big eyes, and long eyelashes. In other words, the standardized beauty characteristics stripped each woman of her individuality and collectively objectified women for servicemen's pleasure.

In the illustrations, only the women's clothing differentiates them as civilian women or servicewomen. The civilian women wear short, fitted dresses or skirts with tight blouses of varying necklines, while the servicewomen appear in standardized uniforms, such as khaki knee-length skirts and blazers with ties and hats, or the occasional jumpsuit. Regardless, women's service granted them no special privilege in *The Wolf*, but rather provided servicemen with access to women in military spaces. For example, one cartoon features a military cargo plane where the Wolf sits, sipping coffee and holding a doughnut, focused intently on a blonde who sits across from him, one knee crossed over the other, in her Red Cross uniform (figure 8.4). The woman innocently suggests to him, "Time'll go much faster if you know of any games we two can play." The punch line encourages the Wolf's sexual imagination. In another illustration, a first sergeant appears to be escorting two servicewomen through base. One looks fearfully at the men who gawk at her from the second story of a barracks, while the other observes the first sergeant scowling at the Wolf, who is dressed in fatigues and raking trash, apparently cleaning up the barracks with two comrades. The first sergeant knowingly stares at the Wolf and asks, "Well, well!—Th' foist robin!

Who whistled?" Expecting to be disciplined, the Wolf stares back at the first sergeant glumly. In such cartoons, *The Wolf* reduced servicewomen to sexualized female bodies, suggesting that sexually aggressive servicemen saw servicewomen not as equals in the war effort, but as fair game in military spaces.[41]

FIGURE 8.4. Leonard Sansone, "Time'll go much faster if you know of any games we two can play," in *The Wolf* (New York: United, 1945), n.p.

Despite the different clothing for the women featured as the Wolf's prey, Sansone drew all the women as white. To be clear, *The Wolf* shows no racial diversity among women, whether in depictions of small-town America, French towns, Australian parks, Pacific Northwest snowscapes, Jamaican expressways, tropical beaches, or Indian markets. But aside from those women who were serving in the military or participating in religious missions, few white women inhabited the Pacific, Asia, North Africa, or the Middle East. So why, then, did Sansone fail to depict nonwhite women? Historian Melissa McEuen has observed that skin complexion played a large role in constructions of eroticism and sexual desirability during the war. American beauty standards rendered dark-complected women as undesirable and unworthy of white servicemen, while anti-miscegenation laws created a legal barrier to racial mixing.[42] Furthermore, historian Lary May argues, the conformity of military service, women's wartime independence, and consumerism contributed to white men's fears that they were losing gendered and racial power in society. White men, therefore, looked to home for a place where their freedom and authority remained unchallenged. Wartime images of white women, then, helped construct white male authority through heterosexuality.[43] By depicting no women of color in *The Wolf*, Sansone contributed to the escapism that worked to culturally sanctify white male power.

In a powerful cross-cultural depiction, Sansone sketched an Indian market where the Wolf and his sailor pal stalk two Indian women, making plans to pair off with them (figure 8.5). The sailor questions the Wolf: "What d'ya mean—'*mine* don't look so good'?" The two Indian women both wear ghoonghat veils and sarees, fully covering their bodies and faces apart from the area around their eyes, which appear white. The Indian woman in front of the Wolf has a perfect hourglass figure, tidy eyebrows, and long eyelashes, and she wears small shoes and bangle bracelets. In contrast, the Indian woman in front of the sailor bears thicker curves, fuller hands, untidy eyebrows, shorter eyelashes, and wider shoes. The drawing implies that the veiling custom does not hide women's sexual appeal from wolves, but rather adds to their mystery. Historically, the veiling practice in India symbolized modesty, shielding women from the male gaze and offering respect to elders. However, it later became more rigorously enforced to ward off the abductions of local women, who could have been taken as "prizes of war" by medieval invaders.[44] After the threat diminished, the veil continued to allow men more patriarchal control over women's bodies. *The Wolf*'s depiction of the veiled women as prizes of war shows that while patriarchy is universal, local customs designed to shield women from invaders will not deter the Wolf from his present sexual conquest. Thus, in this worldly illustration, the Wolf represents the virility of white American men in a war that would expand their power abroad.

"**Whad d'ya mean—'mine don't look so good'?**"

FIGURE 8.5. Leonard Sansone, "Whad d'ya mean—'*mine* don't look so good'?," in *The Wolf* (New York: United, 1945), n.p.

In many ways *The Wolf* reflected the power dynamics that saturated American military culture. First, as a private the Wolf ranked near the bottom of the military command structure. He would be the beast of burden in the military and the one carrying out commands in the thick of battle. The Wolf's animalistic depiction owed to his predatorial skills as both a warrior and a hunter. In other words, his abilities provided a source of pride, even as he coped with his low-ranking stature with a facetious attitude. As a pack animal, the Wolf served as an appropriate tribute to the military brotherhood, solidified through common service. Racial segregation in the military, however, divided the brotherhood and elevated white servicemen in status over Black servicemen. Constructed as a white man, the Wolf enjoyed the white privilege that awarded him a superior place in American perceptions of the global racial hierarchy. Universal whiteness in *The Wolf* backgrounded racial divisions, and instead highlighted men's common, heterosexual interest in women. *The Wolf* occasionally poked fun at effeminate men, whom Sansone would depict as geeky, young, and immature, but homosexuality never made an appearance. Instead, through the cartoon's focus on men and women as binaries and sexual counterparts, the character of the Wolf became a symbolic reinforcement of the patriarchal gender hierarchy.

Much like the war itself, the conquest of women's bodies was fraught with violence. In different segments of the cartoon, Sansone depicted the Wolf in various physical pursuits with violent overtones. One illustration shows a beautiful woman leaving a room while refastening her earring (figure 8.6). Glaring at the staring onlookers, she clearly feels judged. Behind her, the Wolf sits happily, folding a checkerboard and smoking a cigarette. The woman's earring and the Wolf's cigarette both serve as cultural indicators of sex. In addition, the chair across from the Wolf has been overturned, and checkers are strewn across the floor. The caption states, "Unless the rules have changed, he plays a pretty rough game of checkers!" The disheveled room indicates that in his lust, the Wolf attacked the woman, though it is unclear whether she reciprocated his desire. A different drawing shows the Wolf actively ransacking a living room as he pursues a woman. When within reach, she attempts to hold him off with a stiff arm to his face. Another illustration depicts the Wolf as a hospital patient as he uses his menacing hands to grope assisting nurses while he pretends to be unconscious. The Wolf physically chasing women who run to escape his grasp is a common theme in the cartoons as well. In one segment, a military police officer snags the Wolf's shirt to halt his vigorous pursuit of a woman. To escape the Wolf's clutches, she has broken through a fence, leaving a hole of her silhouette in the wooden panels. These illustrations show that when the Wolf's charm failed, he used his physical strength to overpower women to achieve his means.

While the Wolf is usually shown as an avid hunter, one cartoon depicts him as a trapper who casually leans against the telephone pole to which he has chained a metal foothold trap. When triggered, the trap would violently seize his prey's ankle and hold her captive. In another sketch, the Wolf hides beneath a park bench and, from his concealed position, grabs the ankle of a woman passing by. A different illustration shows the Wolf with a woman's wrist handcuffed to his own; he is trying to drag her away with him, despite her angry face and physical resistance. Thus, in the place of his charm or physical strength, the Wolf also used alternative methods like traps, restraints, and surprise attacks to secure his prize.

"Unless the rules have changed, he plays a pretty rough game of checkers!"

FIGURE 8.6. Leonard Sansone, "Unless the rules have changed, he plays a pretty rough game of checkers!," in The Wolf (New York: United, 1945), n.p.

Figure 8.7. Leonard Sansone, "Victory Marks," in The Wolf (New York: United, 1945), n.p.

Together, the Wolf's methods cast humor on the topics of physical assault and female consent. In the Wolf's darkest moments, he threatened the safety and assaulted the women that he, as a serviceman, was supposed to protect. It seems that the "all is fair in love and war" mentality extended the violence of the war to women's bodies. In the wartime battle of the sexes, women became the spoils of war at home and abroad at the hands of American servicemen.[45] Capturing this sentiment, Sansone drew a North American B-25 Mitchell bomber on a tarmac (figure 8.7). Beneath the cockpit, the crew has proudly painted victory marks, also known as kill marks, celebrating their successes, including thirteen bombing missions, two German aircraft kills, two fighter sweeps, one destroyed train, and what appears to be three German soldiers.[46] The Wolf walks casually in front of the plane, lighting a cigarette. Like the B-25, the Wolf also sports victory marks, but instead of decals representing war targets, the sleeve of the Wolf's jacket displays six marks featuring the side profile of a woman's head. The marks represent the Wolf's successful sexual conquests. The parallel symbols of sex and violence celebrated in wartime fashion paint women, just like the enemy, as fallen victims in the serviceman's path.

Much like the enemy in war, many women depicted by Sansone aggressively resisted the Wolf. For example, one leaves him collapsed in the street, seeing stars. One breaks a vase over his head. Two women in a European village throw snowballs to deter him. Another woman, labeled by the caption as a "guerilla," uses only a single hand to pick him up and bash his head on the ground. One segment shows the Wolf standing with three large welts on his head, while a woman stands in front of him, leering, a hammer in each hand behind her back, as the Wolf stubbornly tries to "guess the empty hand to win a kiss." On rare occasion, Sansone even flipped the narrative, depicting girls looking for a good time and taking advantage of the Wolf's frivolous spending in exchange for sexual favors. Thus, resisting women and good time girls, much like those mentioned earlier who succumbed to him as willing prey, conveyed women's agency, despite their subordinate place on the gender hierarchy and the threat of violence that accompanied the Wolf's pursuit.

Sansone occasionally, however, captured the moments of fear that preceded the act of resisting or succumbing. For example, on a bus full of passengers, a woman looks worriedly at the Wolf, who welcomingly taps the vacant seat next to him. In another depiction of an ordinary outing, a serviceman holds the Wolf back as he lunges, teeth bared, toward a woman who fearfully bites her nails, while her friend looks on in concern. Thus, Sansone's illustrations of the Wolf constructed the battle of the sexes amid ever-shifting power dynamics. Although women had power over the Wolf as sexual beings, it seems that within the violent context of the cartoon's history, should the Wolf's prowess fail during his conquest, he would resort to physically assaulting women's bodies, despite women's resistance.

Sansone drew *The Wolf* as a figure of humor to entertain and uplift servicemen perusing the pages of military newspapers. In their lives, the cartoon likely drew momentary reactions ranging from an appalled head shake to a hearty laugh. Though the cartoons peddled escapism and levity, they represented scenarios that reflected real wartime power dynamics between white American men and women around the world. Even more so, considering that 25 percent of the American male population born between 1918 and 1927 served in the military during World War II, humor among servicemen may have also reflected larger national sentiments.[47] Side by side in wartime culture, *The Wolf* and still-flourishing images of protectively masculine servicemen perhaps capture the tension between misogyny and chivalry in American wartime society while also illuminating the universality and familiarity of white patriarchy and the culture behind it.

CONCLUSION

During World War I and World War II dual images of American servicemen's sexuality manifested as protective and aggressive. While policies and images generated by servicemen during World War I mostly projected a protectively masculine serviceman, high rates of VD and necessary medical treatments for the infected provide evidence of promiscuity among the troops. A cultural shift and medical advances leading up to World War II enabled a change in policy that reflected the greater social acceptance of servicemen's sexual entitlements. As a result, images of sexually aggressive servicemen became more prominent in American culture. Leonard Sansone's *The Wolf* cartoons captured servicemen's general pride in successful sexual conquests, but also the many problems the Wolf's sexual appetite caused. The cartoons both celebrated and mocked the Wolf's brand of sexual prerogative with boys-will-be-boys nonchalance. As a product of its time, *The Wolf* symbolized tensions and power struggles between military leaders and grunts, men and women, the victors and the conquered, and home fronts and war zones. Furthermore, its silence on race and homosexuality contributed to the cultural normalization of the power and privilege of the white heterosexual American man. In other words, while images of protective servicemen reflected American paternalism during World War I, *The Wolf*'s rise to prominence in World War II service culture symbolized the expanded power that white servicemen enjoyed to express their sexual prerogative openly. With sexual aggression as a metaphor for conquest, perhaps images of wolves in American culture also alluded to the rapid expansion of America's sphere of influence abroad during World War II and the Cold War to come.

9

Gender, Sexual Orientation, and the US Military

Heather Marie Stur

It could have been a fraternity party, and Paula Coughlin found herself amid a hazing. On the third floor of the Las Vegas Hilton in September 1991, navy and marine corps aviators fondled Coughlin's breasts and tried to pull down her pants as they passed her down "the gauntlet" they had formed along the hallway. When Coughlin had first entered the hallway, it hadn't occurred to her that she should be afraid. She was a thirty-year-old navy lieutenant and a pilot. She was one of them, she thought. But then they began to assault her, and she wondered whether she would be gang-raped by her comrades that night.[1]

At this year's Tailhook Association convention in Las Vegas, navy and marine corps aviators sexually assaulted eighty-three women and seven men. Tailhook, a private organization composed of active and retired pilots, independent defense contractors, and others associated with the navy and marines, had been holding a yearly convention since 1956, and it was known for its debauchery. Its alcohol-fueled parties typically featured strippers, nudity, and sex acts of varying degrees of lewdness.[2] A few months after Tailhook 1991, Lieutenant Coughlin reported that she had been sexually assaulted at the convention, and her complaint launched an investigation that revealed the degree to which aggressive sexual behavior was part of the event. In the aftermath, secretary of the navy H. Lawrence Garrett III resigned, and naval officials issued a zero-tolerance policy regarding sexual assault.[3]

A female navy commander linked the excesses of Tailhook 1991 to men's anger over the presence of servicewomen in the Persian Gulf War and the ongoing debates about women in combat: "This was the woman that was making you, you know, change your ways," she said. "This was the woman that was threatening your livelihood. This was the woman that wanted to take your spot in that combat aircraft."[4] Journalist and cultural critic Susan Faludi observed that those who were disciplined were charged with violations such as "indecent exposure" and "conduct unbecoming an officer," not sexual assault. It was a boys-will-be-boys slap on the wrist administered with a wink and an eye roll in the direction of feminists who had spoken out against the military culture that instigated the Tailhook assaults, Faludi argued. The message that the navy sent was that it would punish the accused for their immaturity, not for their sexually violent behavior.[5]

The fraternity party vibe and the use of the term *gantlet* to describe the hallway of sexual assault link the civilian and military worlds and power, sexuality, and punishment. The drinking, partying, and sexual depravity that mark fraternities in image if not in reality characterized the Tailhook scandal. *Gantlet* once referred to a form of military punishment in which the penitent ran between two rows of men who beat him as he hurried down the line. The woman navy commander who reflected on Tailhook noted that anger at women's presence in the navy motivated men's behavior. If men saw women as competitors for the positions they wanted on combat ships or aircraft, they might take their anger out on women by punishing them. The sexual dimension of Tailhook's gauntlet reminded the female aviators that they weren't just competitors, they were women, and because of that, they didn't belong.

Tailhook occurred within the context of a broader US military that had been in transformation since the end of the Vietnam War. After the Vietnam-era draft ended, the US armed services became a volunteer force, and one of the results of the shift was an increased focus on recruiting women. By the late 1970s, Congress had abolished the women's sections, such as the Women's Army Corps, and the service academies had begun admitting women. Yet the presence of more women in arms did not change military culture. It remained steeped in ideas about masculinity and soldiering, and those concepts made it difficult, if not dangerous, for women to serve alongside their male counterparts. The Tailhook scandal revealed the volatile nature of military culture, in which attitudes regarding who belongs had not kept pace with personnel changes. In a broader historical context, the Tailhook scandal coincided with Anita Hill's decision to reveal that Supreme Court nominee Clarence Thomas had sexually harassed her for years when she worked for him in the US Department of Education and the Equal Employment Opportunity Commission. Taken together, Tailhook and Anita Hill's testimony illustrate the tension between the expansion of military and career opportunities for women and a deep-seated culture of separate spheres that crossed the military-civilian divide. Laws opening military jobs and civil employment opportunities to women could not force opponents of gender equality to change their minds. Women flying navy aircraft and working as lawyers in federal offices challenged conventional wisdom about what men and women do. They also confronted the assumption that sexual lasciviousness, in word and deed, was simply normal male behavior. Once women were in the picture as equals, old sexual stereotypes collapsed, stereotypes that formed the basis of everything from jokes to some heterosexual men's sense of themselves. In responding to the perceived threat of lost identity, some men attacked women rather than attack the culture that had so narrowly defined what it meant to be a man.

In 1991, the US military fought as a gender-integrated force in Operation Desert Storm, and in 1992, Congress authorized servicewomen to fly combat aircraft. In 1993, President Bill Clinton signed into law "Don't Ask, Don't Tell," which allowed gay and lesbian service personnel to remain in the military so long as they kept their sexuality to themselves. Efforts to integrate women and openly gay or lesbian individuals into the military in the 1990s met with angry opposition in both military and civilian contexts, with sex and privacy as main concerns. Public responses revealed how deeply committed American civilians were to the image of the US soldier as a heterosexual man, and to traditional ideas about gender, sexuality, and power. In the 1990s, heterosexual women, gay men, and lesbians challenged that image as they sought opportunities for more service roles and the chance to serve openly.

The 1990s brought concerns about social inequality to the public conversation in the civilian world, including issues of gender and sexual orientation. The AIDS crisis dealt a devastating blow to public health in the gay community, and federal silence as the epidemic raged motivated activists to take to the streets and demand attention be paid to the illness and to sexual health more broadly. Organizations such as the AIDS Coalition to Unleash Power (ACT UP), a grassroots AIDS awareness group that formed in New York City in 1987, staged demonstrations and guerrilla theater performances to highlight the impact of AIDS on public health and push for policies aimed at making treatments such as the antiviral drug AZT more affordable. The deaths of high-profile entertainers, including Liberace and Freddie Mercury, from AIDS in the late 1980s and early 1990s, also kept the virus in the public mind. Attention to gay and lesbian issues continued into the 1990s, centering not just on AIDS but also on equality in areas such as marriage and military service.

Women's equality was also at the center of civil rights discussions in the early 1990s. Hillary Clinton's speech at the 1995 UN women's conference in Beijing, in which she asserted that "women's rights are human rights," vocalized the assertions of the international women's movement. Clinton herself, as First Lady during Bill Clinton's presidency, tried to symbolize an equal partnership in work and marriage as she wrote health-care policy and worked closely with her husband on that and other policy issues. Anita Hill's testimony in Clarence Thomas's Supreme Court confirmation hearings in 1991 brought the issue of sexual harassment in the workplace to network television. Hill recounted how Thomas had used vulgar language and talked vividly about sex when he supervised her at the US Department of Education and the Equal Employment Opportunity Commission. Hill's statements raised the issue of workplace sexual harassment, which, in the late 1980s, the Supreme Court had determined to be a violation of Title VII of the 1964 Civil Rights Act. The topics of gender discrimination and sexual harassment were also central to debates over the expansion of women's military service.

Just as the 1990s saw women's and gay rights come more fully into the national spotlight, the decade was one of change for female and gay military service. Before the 1990s, women had served in the US military in various official and unofficial ways. During World War II, the branches of the US armed forces established women's auxiliaries to mobilize womanpower for clerical and other desk jobs to free up men for combat. The largest of these was the Women's Army Auxiliary Corps, later renamed the Women's Army Corps, founded in 1942. Civilian opponents of women's military service argued that women did not belong. War was too dangerous, they asserted, and only women chasing men—or other women—saw military service as attractive. Yet personnel needs during World War II and the Cold War motivated the forces to make women's sections permanent in the armed services. In the 1960s and 1970s, women served in the Vietnam War, mostly in the Army Nurse Corps.

The integration of women into the armed services coincided with military racial integration. World War II manpower needs saw the army and marine corps experiment with racially integrated units, even before official desegregation occurred in 1948. In the navy, more than twelve thousand African Americans served as Seabees in both the European and Pacific theaters during World War II. They built bases, warehouses, railroads, and landing strips that were vital to Allied war efforts. By 1944, approximately one hundred thousand African American men were serving in the navy. Two postwar studies, *The American Soldier*, published by Princeton University in 1943, and *Project Clear*, which was commissioned by the Department of Defense in 1951, revealed a significant improvement in white troops' attitudes toward Black service personnel as a result of integration. Taken together, the studies showed that the more interactions white soldiers had with Black troops, the more white people came to support integration. Among white people surveyed in 1943, 84 percent opposed integration, but by 1951, that number had dropped to 44 percent. Among Black soldiers, 36 percent of those surveyed in 1943 opposed integration, but by 1951, only 4 percent of those surveyed preferred segregated units.[6]

Yet integration did not end racial tension. Racial attitudes among white soldiers and officers generally mirrored those in the civilian world in the 1950s and 1960s. Racial unrest came to a head during the Vietnam War era. For example, in 1972, racial clashes on the USS *Kitty Hawk* and USS *Constellation* brought to public attention the issue of racial tension in the military. Secretary of defense Melvin Laird and other Pentagon officials took note and were also thinking ahead to the end of the draft and the implementation of the all-volunteer force. They worried that continued racism would prevent African Americans from enlisting. Leaders of each of the service branches implemented racial and cultural awareness training and developed campaigns aimed at recruiting and retaining Black service members. Admiral Elmo R. Zumwalt Jr., chief of naval operations, took a particular interest in transforming the navy's racial culture. He met with Black navy officers and enlisted men and their wives to learn about their experiences in the service. Black navy families still had trouble finding housing due to housing discrimination, even though President Lyndon B. Johnson had signed into law the Fair Housing Act in 1968. Navy exchanges lacked beauty and health products that African American personnel and their dependents needed. Black barbers and beauticians were in short supply on ships and near bases.

It was only after talking with Black sailors and their wives that Zumwalt realized the subtle and overt discrimination African Americans in the navy faced. To address the issues, Zumwalt ordered that communication with minority personnel and empathy for their experiences be priorities for naval leadership. He ordered that all commanders appoint a minority group liaison and that shore-based commanders appoint a minority wife to the navy wives' ombudsman group. In 1974, the navy published its first equal opportunity manual. Two years later, navy leaders released the first navy affirmative action plan. The other service branches also examined racial issues within their ranks and the ways that racism would impede recruitment. With the all-volunteer force on the horizon, recruitment and retention became critical for the military to meet personnel needs.

Military leaders also targeted women with their recruitment campaigns. In addition, Congress in 1975 authorized the opening of US service academies to women, and in 1980, the first women graduated from West Point. In 1978, President Jimmy Carter signed an order dissolving the women's sections of the military and integrating women into the regular forces. Newspaper headlines reflected the debates in the military and the public about what the full integration of women into the service academies would do to the character of the military. Media coverage voiced Americans' anxieties about how servicemen and women would interact with one another, whether women had the physical and mental stamina to handle military service, how this change might affect unit cohesion, and, most importantly, whether the integration of women into the military would lead to women serving in combat. It was the idea of women in combat, more than anything else, that challenged Americans' beliefs about who should serve in the military and in what roles.[7] Tailhook brought this tension into sharp relief.

Debates about women in the military reflected arguments on the legality of using gender to apply laws differently to men and women. They revealed tensions within the feminist movement over war and militarization and about how far feminists were willing to go to demand gender equality. They illuminated American cultural attitudes about gender and sexuality, and they illustrated the influence that culture often has on politics. As historian D'Ann Campbell has argued, discussions of women in combat emphasize law, psychology, and biology but rarely examine the history of women's roles in militaries and wartime. Rather than being based on empirical evidence regarding women's suitability for combat service, restrictions on women in combat have been the result of political decisions that reflected public opinion and congressional attitudes.[8] The expansion of women's military opportunities in the 1970s coincided with efforts to ratify the Equal Rights Amendment, with one point of contention being whether it would subject women to the draft. Gender roles and the stability of the family were central to arguments both for and against the expansion of women's military roles. Opponents argued that the trauma of separation from a parent was more difficult for a child to bear when the parent deploying was the mother. Those in favor of the gender integration of the military suggested that the deployment of wives and mothers would contribute to a reshaping of gender roles within the family, leading to a more equitable sharing of childcare and other domestic duties.

The National Organization for Women (NOW) had pushed Congress to set an effective date for the integration of the service academies in 1975, after Congress authorized their integration. Speaking specifically about the integration of West Point, Betty Friedan, founder of NOW, asserted that rather than threatening masculinity, the admission of women brought "the possibility of a new model of what it is to be a man, a new kind of male hero in America, as men begin to share the care of the children and home with their wives, as women share the burdens and responsibilities of earning—even the hardships and dangers and glories of military careers." Friedan added that attending West Point did not turn women into men; they maintained their femininity while proving their competence.[9] It was not women or femininity that needed to change, Friedan suggested, but men and masculinity, and that was happening as the military was opening more fully to women.

When the Equal Rights Amendment was making its way through state legislatures, the issue of whether it would require women to be drafted into the military and serve in combat units caused conflict among feminists. The debate became especially heated in 1980, when President Carter reinstated the Selective Service System in response to the Soviet invasion of Afghanistan and called for both men and women to register. Public debate and congressional hearings on the issue eventually led to the 1981 case of *Rostker v. Goldberg*, in which the

US Supreme Court ruled that the draft exists primarily to fill combat positions, and since women were at the time excluded from combat, it was legal to exclude women from selective service and the draft. In response to the *Rostker* ruling, NOW, along with the League of Women Voters and the National Federation of Business and Professional Women's Clubs, filed briefs with the Supreme Court arguing that drafting men but not women violated women's constitutional rights and privileges of citizenship. NOW spokespeople argued that women should have the same right as men to use military service as a means through which to prove their leadership skills.[10]

The outbreak of the first Gulf War in 1991 threw these issues into sharp relief. About forty thousand servicewomen served in Operation Desert Shield and Operation Desert Storm, and fifteen were killed: five in battle and the rest in noncombat incidents. "The Persian Gulf helped collapse the whole chivalrous notion that women could be kept out of danger in a war," said Representative Patricia Schroeder, a Colorado Democrat who was an advocate of rescinding all rules excluding women from combat. "We saw that the theater of operations had no strict combat zone, that Scud missiles were not gender-specific—they could hit both sexes and, unfortunately, did," Schroeder said.[11]

Captain Carol Barkalow, who served with the army in the war and was a member of West Point's class of 1980, said: "Until the Persian Gulf, the American people didn't understand the modern battlefield. Even in noncombat roles, women have been exposed to risk for some time." She continued: "As the military downsizes in the coming years, there will be a need to keep the best and the brightest, and women will need to be convinced they have the chance for future advancement. And that means combat arms cannot be closed to them." Such change required that male officers think differently about female personnel, she said, and servicewomen's performance in the Persian Gulf was a start. "Many of the guys of my generation have had that experience, but the senior military ranks have never worked with women as peers," she said. "Someone 20 years my senior and a general still sees women as a mother, wife, girlfriend or daughter. They know how to deal with guys but may not know what to do with women. It makes them uncomfortable."[12]

Opponents of the opening of combat positions to women blamed career servicewomen for pushing combat service opportunities for women. Certain promotions require combat service, and without it, servicewomen did not have the same advancement pathways as their male counterparts. Writing in the *National Review* in November 1991, Phyllis Schlafly protégé Elaine Donnelly, founder of the Coalition for Military Readiness, which opposed the gender integration of the military, likened the expansion of military jobs to seeing men and women as interchangeable parts without physiological or psychological differences. Donnelly argued that the military was not primarily an institution to provide education, job training, and career advancement; it existed for national security purposes, and only an all-male military could protect American interests.[13] The Presidential Commission on the Assignment of Women in the Armed Forces, of which Donnelly was a member, made this same argument in its recommendations in November 1992. The commission concluded that women should not be allowed to serve in combat. Members also recommended that additional limitations on women's service be implemented to prevent the appearance that servicewomen were near or in any way involved in combat. Commissioners referred to the 1976 case of *Craig v. Boren*, which determined that separate laws for men and women are unconstitutional unless there is a clear government interest to be served by such laws. Commissioners argued that the government interest in national security mandated a law limiting women's military service.[14]

In the 1980s and 1990s, studies of women's military service sought to determine whether concerns about a gender-integrated military bore out. Civilian and military critics of women's service argued that the presence of women in uniform hindered unit cohesion, lethality, and military readiness. In a report to the Presidential Commission on the Assignment of Women in the Armed Forces based on a fact-finding tour she had taken of Fort Bragg, North Carolina, and Parris Island, South Carolina, Donnelly asserted that were women to be integrated more fully into the military, including gaining access to combat jobs, standards would have to be lowered to accommodate women's physical limitations. If one set of troops were held to a lower standard than others, that would harm readiness. She also referred to a conversation she'd had with some enlisted men who worried about privacy matters if men and women trained together, such as having to share the communal showers at the infantry school.[15] The notion that women in combat would damage military effectiveness and cohesion was a mainstream view in the 1990s. One commentator said, "the presence of women inhibits male bonding, corrupts allegiance to the hierarchy, and diminishes the desire of men to compete for anything but the attentions of women."[16] The underlying concern driving opposition to women's equal participation in the military was the desire to enforce traditional gender roles. Americans had long considered the military, and war more broadly, as a means through which boys became men. Embedded in that understanding of military service was the idea that male soldiers protected women on the home front. If women were allowed to serve in combat, it would upset the gender divisions that opponents of women's military service considered natural.

A 2012 survey of the impact of gender stereotypes on women marines found that derogatory gender stereotypes, not the presence of women themselves, negatively affected morale and unit cohesion. The stereotype that a woman who joins the military is a "bitch," "dyke," or "whore" is grounded in home front/civilian gender beliefs about men as the protectors and women as the protected. Those who oppose women's military service see servicewomen as deviant because they operate outside traditional gender roles. The survey suggested that gender stereotypes "contribute to a reduced sense of camaraderie and mentorship, a reduced sense of shared mission and ultimately poorer performance."[17] Illustrating the connection between personal beliefs about gender roles and attitudes toward women's military service, a 1974 study asked male and female army personnel stationed on three stateside bases to answer whether their gender beliefs were "traditional" or "contemporary" while also answering survey questions about women in combat. Male soldiers were asked, "Is the job 'rifle-carrying infantry foot soldier' an appropriate job for women?" Thirty percent of respondents who indicated that they had "contemporary" gender beliefs responded yes. Of those who identified themselves as having "traditional" gender attitudes, only 12 percent responded yes.[18]

Despite the cultural objections to women's military service, a RAND Corporation study of the military's history of integrating minority populations revealed that even those military personnel who had initially opposed integration grew to accept, if not welcome, the presence of these groups. In the era of the all-volunteer military, as the armed services have expanded recruitment campaigns aimed at women to fill their ranks, defense leaders have attempted to define "risk" in ways that limit the specialties open to women. In 1988, a Department of Defense task force proposed a "risk rule which excluded women from noncombat units or missions if the risks of exposure to direct combat, hostile fire, or capture were equal to or greater than the risk in the combat units they supported." After the Gulf War, the Department of Defense abolished the risk rule, concluding that "the rule no longer applied since, based on the experiences during Desert Storm, everyone in the theater of operation was at risk."[19] This decision increased positions available to women in the navy and marines by about 30 percent. By 1997, more than 80 percent of positions in the military were open to women.

In December 2015, secretary of defense Ash Carter announced that the military would open up combat positions to women, one of the last hurdles on the path to women's equality in the services. One primary reason for the decision was that women personnel in Iraq and Afghanistan already served in combat. According to that same RAND Corporation report, "women made up approximately 15 percent of the U.S. armed forces in the decade of 2000s. Given the fact that there are no front lines in counterinsurgency campaigns, and that armed forces personnel in combat support and combat service support positions (where women soldiers and marines were concentrated) often came into contact with adversary forces, women service members took part in many firefights and close combat that characterized the campaigns in Iraq and Afghanistan."[20] By 2015, before the official prohibition on women in combat ended, women military personnel had earned more than ten thousand combat badges and Bronze Stars.[21]

Many military leaders ultimately concluded that "assertions that women do not possess the leadership capability or that they will destroy unit cohesion are overbroad generalizations, and are disproved by the actual successful combat performance of mixed-gender combat support units."[22]

Gay men and lesbians also faced discrimination in the military through the twentieth century and into the twenty-first. In the first half of the twentieth century, the military criminalized homosexuality by making sodomy illegal, as it was in the civilian world, according to state laws throughout the United States. Article 125 of the Uniform Code of Military Justice banned "unnatural carnal copulation" with "another person of the same or opposite sex or with an animal."[23] Although it applied to heterosexual contact as well as same-sex engagements, it criminalized all homosexual encounters. The military focused on behavior rather than identity, and while heterosexual individuals could also be discharged for committing sodomy, the act was associated with gay men, and by implication, the policy outlawed homosexuality.

During World War II, the military changed its thinking about homosexuality to conform with the prevailing belief in American society that homosexuality was a mental illness. This policy shift meant that gay service members could be discharged for their identity, regardless of whether they engaged in criminalized behavior such as sodomy. Although the military made homosexuality a crime, historian John D'Emilio has shown how World War II created the conditions for the start of the gay rights movement of the late twentieth century.[24] Wartime mobilization took young people away from their small towns and the watchful eyes of parents, teachers, and neighbors, and concentrated them on military bases. With so many young men at their disposal, military leaders instituted strict qualification standards and screening processes to exclude minorities, including African Americans, women, and gay individuals. Military authorities used the same reasoning for excluding all three groups: they would not be able to handle combat, they would threaten unit cohesion, and their integration would sacrifice military readiness in order to turn the military into a social laboratory.

During World War II, the military recognized homosexuality in three categories that had three different punishment schemes. One category included men who committed sodomy by force; they were subject to court-martial and, if convicted, a prison sentence and a dishonorable discharge. At the other end of the military's classification was the "casual homosexual," who had engaged in homosexual contact out of curiosity or drunkenness. A soldier in that category was to be treated and returned to duty, reflecting the belief that homosexuality was a medical, and thus "curable," disorder. In between these two ends of the spectrum was the "true pervert," a nebulous category that generally referred to a soldier who engaged in homosexual acts or had homosexual desires. A soldier classified in the middle category was to receive an undesirable or "blue" discharge. Some advocates of the undesirable discharge asserted that it was a kinder way than a court-martial to remove gay men from the military, where they allegedly did not belong. But blue discharges were not subject to the same scrutiny and evidence requirements as courts-martial, and so they offered a method for the military to quickly discharge soldiers suspected of being gay.

Gay men and lesbians met and developed networks that grew after the war ended. Many gay and lesbian groups went underground in the 1950s as a result of the Lavender Scare of the Joseph McCarthy era. The Federal Bureau of Investigation and other law enforcement agencies targeted gay individuals in the Department of State and other government agencies as security risks due to the mental disorder of homosexuality. Gay Americans faced ostracism, firing, and violence during the McCarthy era. This context contributed to the military's solidifying its policy of excluding gay men and lesbians entirely. Movements for gender and sexual equality in the 1960s, as well as the counterculture's challenge to traditional social norms, converged with US military mobilization for the Vietnam War. With military personnel needs in mind, defense authorities gave officers the discretion to ignore homosexuality among their troops if the servicemen in question were good soldiers. Throughout the decade, gay rights organizations held demonstrations in major cities such as Washington, DC, and Philadelphia, and the Stonewall uprising in New York City in 1969 garnered nationwide attention for the gay rights movement.

Gay and lesbian service personnel challenged the military's stance through various court cases arguing that the military's approach to homosexuality violated equal protection rights. In 1975, US Air Force sergeant Leonard Matlovich came out as gay and filed a lawsuit against the Department of Defense for its ban on gay men in the military. Matlovich and his lawyers fought for five years, arguing that the military's ban on gay servicemen was a violation of due process and equal protection, just as the limiting of African Americans' service opportunities had been. Upon hearing Matlovich's case, Judge Gerhard A. Gesell declared, "No one . . . who has studied the civil rights movement and the striving of blacks for opportunity will ever fail to recognize that the Armed Forces, more than any branch of the government and far ahead of the private sector in this country, led to erasing the stigma of race discrimination. . . . Here, another opportunity is presented."[25] Yet Gesell decided to leave the fate of gay servicemen to Pentagon officials, and in 1980, Matlovich gave up his fight, accepting a settlement and an honorable discharge. Despite the efforts of the gay rights movement to make the case for equality in the civilian world, the fight was long from finished. The 1980s saw a devastating stigma attached to gay men as the AIDS crisis raged, and the military affirmed its exclusion of gay men and lesbians from the services.

A year after Matlovich left the air force, US Army staff sergeant Perry Watkins challenged the army's discrimination against gay servicemen. Watkins had joined the military in 1967, at the height of US military escalation in Vietnam, when he was nineteen years old. He was openly gay and told an army psychiatrist about his sexuality when he was drafted, but he was inducted anyway. After Watkins's tour of duty ended in 1970, he reenlisted, still open about his sexuality, which did not prevent the army from reaccepting him. Watkins continued to serve with distinction for a decade, until the army revoked his security clearance in 1980 due to his homosexuality. In February 1981, Watkins went to court in Tacoma, Washington, where he was stationed, to appeal the army's removal of his clearance, and his case made its way through the courts for two years. A district court judge ruled that the army couldn't use Watkins's homosexuality against him now after allowing him to serve for years while knowing he was gay. But judges of the Ninth Circuit Court of Appeals overturned the lower court's decision, ruling that a court could not force the army to defy its own rules unless the court found the rules themselves unconstitutional.[26]

Watkins's experience illustrates the military's shifting attitude toward homosexuality, depending on personnel needs. During the Vietnam War, the army accepted Watkins's enlistment and reenlistment despite knowing he was gay. Unofficial Department of Defense policy during the Vietnam War allowed officers to ignore a serviceman's homosexuality if he performed well as a soldier. The services needed manpower, and that need trumped the idea that gay men were not equipped to be good soldiers. Yet in 1980, when the United States no longer was heavily committed to a ground war, the army rescinded Watkins's security clearance due to his homosexuality. The armed forces had treated homosexuality similarly during World War II and the Korean War, and they would do the same during Operation Desert Storm. Personnel needs outweighed opposition to gay military service, and homosexual discharges decreased while the United States fought in those conflicts. Upon return to peacetime, the military returned to its homosexual purges. The navy discharged 533 sailors for homosexuality in 1951 but more than twice that in 1953, when the Korean War ended. The next time navy discharges for homosexuality dropped below 500 was in 1970, during the Vietnam War.[27]

In the early 1980s, the military revised its policy again to assert that homosexuality was grounds for discharge. In 1982, the Department of Defense issued a policy statement declaring that homosexuality was "incompatible with military service." Defense officials believed that gay and lesbian service members hindered "the ability of the Armed Forces to maintain discipline, good order, and morale" and "to foster mutual trust and confidence among the members." The language mirrored the wording in statements opposing the integration of African Americans and women into the services. The statement also mentioned privacy concerns, noting that personnel "frequently must live and work under close conditions affording minimal privacy." Reflecting a holdover from the McCarthy-era

Lavender Scare, the Department of Defense statement also asserted that gay and lesbian service members could commit "breaches of security."[28] Although the statement did not elaborate on the ways gay soldiers posed a security threat, the idea that they were weak minded, susceptible to bribery, and untrustworthy remained part of an old and tired caricature of them, despite the decorated service of Matlovich and others.

When Bill Clinton, then governor of Arkansas, ran for president in 1992, he declared that he would "do for gays what Harry Truman did for blacks in 1948—eliminate the military's discriminatory policies by executive order."[29] Clinton attempted to follow through on his campaign promise shortly after his inauguration, and he ordered the Department of Defense to draft a new inclusion policy eliminating discrimination based on sexual orientation. Facing considerable resistance in Congress and among military leadership, Clinton proposed "Don't Ask, Don't Tell" (DADT) as a compromise. It prohibited military officials from asking about a soldier's sexual orientation, but if service members revealed their homosexuality, the military could discharge them. DADT went into effect in 1993 as part of the National Defense Authorization Act for Fiscal Year 1994 and remained in place until President Barack Obama repealed it in 2010.

DADT differentiated between "homosexuality," which the military would no longer ban, and "homosexual conduct," which it could. Because of the thin line between the two, some critics of DADT argued that the policy did not constitute a departure from the military's previous stance on homosexuality. In the 2008 case of *Witt v. Department of the Air Force*, a district court ruled that the service of Major Margaret Witt, a lesbian, did not harm unit cohesion or military preparedness, thus rejecting one argument commonly used to justify the ban on openly gay service members in the armed forces. Witt had enlisted in the air force in 1987 and was outed in 2004. This led the air force to discharge her in 2006 on the grounds of her sexual orientation. In 2011, after the repeal of DADT, the air force removed the less-than-honorable discharge from her record, allowing her to receive full veteran benefits in her retirement.[30]

In August 2012, the marine corps commandant said in a speech at the National Press Club that by then, he was hearing little if any conversation about the repeal of DADT, suggesting that it was of minimal concern to marines. Secretary of defense Leon Panetta said at a Pride event in June 2012 that the repeal of DADT demonstrated that the US military, in its diversity, is "the greatest military force in the world."[31] Politicians and others who called for the repeal of DADT argued that the policy led to the discharge of service members who had mission-critical skills, such as language fluency to work as interpreters. General Colin Powell, who had opposed gay and lesbian military service in the 1990s, had changed his stance by 2010, noting the greater "acceptance of gays and lesbians in society" and the experiences of a large number of other countries that already allowed such soldiers to serve openly.[32] The absence of any adverse effect on unit cohesion by the open service of gay men and lesbians was confirmed in 2010, when RAND conducted twenty-two focus groups on ten military posts concerning DADT. Nearly all participants indicated that they served with gay personnel, despite the de jure ban on open service. Results of the focus groups indicated "virtually no hostility toward gay people." To the contrary, most participants expressed respect for their gay and lesbian comrades and did not believe they should be discharged.[33]

Efforts to integrate women and gay service members into the US military required members of the armed forces to face deeply rooted cultural ideals about the archetypal American soldier. Even when military leaders made pragmatic decisions to open the services to the most qualified personnel, some civilians and soldiers protested the inclusion of anyone who wasn't a heterosexual man. Opponents argued that the presence of women and gay service members would disrupt unit cohesion, military readiness, and lethality. Yet in the years following the integration of both groups, Pentagon studies of military units indicated that those fears did not come to pass. In some ways, integration even changed the minds of opponents of women and gay service members in the military. The results of such studies indicate progress, but the military now must shift its attention to the persistent problem of sexual assault among its troops.

Thirty years ago, the Tailhook incident revealed the toxic masculinity and sexuality that permeated military culture. This toxic culture has not gone away, despite the advancements servicewomen have made up the ranks. The murder of Private First Class Vanessa Guillén at Fort Hood, Texas, in April 2020 is an example of the danger servicewomen still face, not in war zones but on stateside posts. According to authorities, Specialist Aaron David Robinson bludgeoned Guillén to death with a hammer in the armory, where she worked repairing small arms and artillery. Guillén had told her family that a fellow soldier had sexually harassed her, and a lawyer for the family said that Guillén intended to file a harassment complaint against Robinson. An enraged Robinson allegedly attacked and killed Guillén, and then he and a girlfriend dismembered her body and buried it in a shallow grave near the Leon River in Bell County, where Fort Hood (now Fort Cavazos) is located. When law enforcement officers attempted to arrest Robinson, he shot and killed himself.[34]

In December 2020, secretary of the army Ryan McCarthy announced the suspension and firing of fourteen officers at Fort Hood, following an investigation that found "a pattern of sexual assault, harassment, suicides, and murder" at the post in Killeen, Texas. The dismissals were the result of an investigation McCarthy had launched in July, a few months after the murder of Guillén. In an interview with *CBS News*, McCarthy said that the murder of Guillén "shocked our conscience and brought attention to deeper problems" in the army regarding sexual assault, harassment, and violence.[35] Yet Guillén was not the first servicewoman to die at the hand of a comrade. In 1995, twenty-five years before Guillén's murder, US Army veteran and former Ranger Louis Jones Jr. kidnapped nineteen-year-old private Tracie McBride on Goodfellow Air Force Base in San Angelo, Texas. Jones drove McBride to his home, raped her, and beat her to death. Twenty-five years before McBride's death, in 1970, US Army investigators implicated GI Gregory Kozlowski in the murder of Red Cross "donut dolly" Virginia "Ginny" Kirsch on the Twenty-Fifth Infantry Division's base in Củ Chi, Vietnam.[36] Although Kirsch was not in the military, her Red Cross program was in Vietnam at Department of Defense request. Within those twenty-five-year intervals, incidents of sexual harassment and assault that did *not* result in murder have shown the danger servicewomen face on the military posts and bases where they are stationed.

Pentagon authorities are aware of the problem. In 2004, they established the Sexual Assault Prevention and Response Office. The army has its Sexual Harassment/Assault Response and Prevention program, and the navy created the Sexual Assault Prevention and Response program. A 2012 Pentagon investigation revealed twenty-six thousand sexual assaults in that year, although only about three thousand victims filed reports.[37] A 2019 Department of Defense study found that sexual assault cases increased from about fifteen thousand in 2016 to more than twenty thousand in 2018 across all branches of the US military.[38] The thousands of sexual violence cases that the 2012 and 2019 studies revealed should have shocked military leaders into action *before* Guillén's death. For officials to have not seen it coming, they had to have been looking the other way.

McCarthy's study concluded that that's exactly what leaders at Fort Hood did. They created a toxic command climate that allowed sexual harassment and assault to occur by dismissing reports of incidents. Neither the existence of the Sexual Harassment/Assault Response and Prevention program nor the Pentagon's evidence of sexual violence in the military motivated Fort Hood's commanders to take the problem seriously. The army's decision to discipline the post's top authorities is a bold move, but past experience shows that the removal of leaders does not necessarily change a culture. In the wake of the Tailhook affair, secretary of the navy Lawrence Garrett resigned, and chief of naval operations Frank Kelso took early retirement after victims complained about his mishandling of the scandal. Yet sexual harassment and assault have not disappeared. In 2019, nearly 1,700 alleged victims filed assault claims with the navy.[39] The US armed services have made significant progress in diversifying the ranks and have, at times, opened up employment and advancement opportunities for minorities that did not exist in the civilian world. Cultural changes have been much slower to occur, which shows how deeply rooted traditional ideas about gender and sexuality are within perceptions of military identity.

Epilogue

African Americans, World War I, and the Boundaries of Military History

Chad L. Williams

The debate over just what constitutes American history, what narratives should be emphasized, and how they should be taught is not new. In an era of increased political polarization, misinformation, and backlash to demands for racial and gender equality, history has served as a proxy battlefield. Whether in state legislatures, on social media, at school board meetings, or in newspaper op-eds, the fights over history are really about America itself—what America is, who matters, and what the historian's responsibility is in telling the story of America's past.

A dustup on Twitter in early 2019 offers a perfect example of this ongoing fight and reinforces why gatherings like the one that produced this volume, and its centering of race and gender in the study of war, are so important. On February 20, 2019, Max Boot, a regular columnist for the *Washington Post*, published an opinion piece titled "Americans' Ignorance of History Is a National Scandal."[1]

So, first, who is Max Boot, and why does he even matter? Max Boot, as his *Washington Post* bio reads, is a historian, best-selling author, and foreign policy analyst who has been called one of the "world's leading authorities on armed conflict" by the International Institute for Strategic Studies. Boot holds a bachelor's degree in history, with high honors, from the University of California, Berkeley, and a master's degree in history from Yale University. He was a senior policy adviser to the presidential campaigns of John McCain, Mitt Romney, and Marco Rubio, and served as an adviser to US commanders in Iraq and Afghanistan.[2] He has lectured on behalf of the US Department of State and at many military institutions, including the US Army, US Naval, and Air War Colleges, the Australian Defence College, the John F. Kennedy Special Warfare Center and School, West Point, and the Naval Academy. So, it is safe to say that Mr. Boot would proudly proclaim himself to be, perhaps first and foremost, a military historian.

His op-ed, on the one hand, could be read as well intentioned. He mourned the decline in the number of history majors and the general lack of knowledge that Americans have about history. "You simply can't understand the present if you don't understand the past," he wrote, adding that "there is no more alarming case study of the consequences of historical ignorance than President Trump." So far so good. But then things went astray:

> Historians may not want to admit it, but they bear some blame for the increasing irrelevance of their discipline. As historians Hal Brands and Francis Gavin argue in *War on the Rocks*, since the 1960s, history professors have retreated from public debate into their own esoteric pursuits. The push to emphasize "cultural, social and gender history," and to pay "greater attention to the experiences of underrepresented and oppressed groups," they write, has been a welcome corrective to an older historiography that focused almost entirely on powerful white men. But like many revolutions, this one has gone too far, leading to the neglect of political, diplomatic and military history—subjects that students need to study and, as enrollment figures indicate, students want to study but that universities perversely neglect. Historian Jill Lepore notes that we have ditched an outdated national narrative without creating a new one to take its place, leaving a vacuum to be filled by tribalists.[3]

Needless to say, the clapback was fierce. The argument that historians have shied away from engaging with the public is ridiculous, and to say that the focus on women and nonwhite people was in part to blame is downright offensive. Boot was skewered mercilessly, and rightfully so. "Max Boot is simply wrong about this," retorted Jim Grossman, executive director of the American Historical Association. "Nope. Historians are in newspapers, on TV, podcasts, all over social media, blogs, Twitter, and Facebook engaging in debates with one another and non-historians," Annette Gordon-Reed responded. "I have to join the chorus of historians who disagree—strongly," tweeted Joanne Freeman. "We're in the public sphere and political history is thriving," Kevin Kruse chimed in. "I see some folks are peddling the same old 'historians do not engage the public' narrative," Keisha N. Blain sighed. "It's tired. It's inaccurate."[4]

As these responses, and many, many more made perfectly clear, historians engage with the public in a multitude of ways. And some of the best work in political, diplomatic, and, especially, military history doesn't just incorporate but centers race, along with cultural, gender, and social history.

But, despite his Twitter flogging, Boot held his ground. He offered a retort in a brief February 26 response, essentially saying that the hyperdefensiveness of his critics proved his point. He named Ron Chernow, Doris Kearns Goodwin, Walter Isaacson, and a few others as examples of writers whose "popular history" successfully reached larger audiences. He doubled down, albeit gingerly, on the most inflammatory part of his original argument, writing, "Recent decades have seen a welcome focus on many facets of history—and in particular on many disadvantaged groups—lamentably absent from older scholarship. But they have also seen an unfortunate decrease in that kind of public engagement, along with a decrease in the academic attention devoted to subjects unfairly derided as the preserve of 'dead white men.'" He also bemoaned the absence of historians from "the halls of power."[5]

So what was really going on here? Of all the various responses to Boot's original article, the Johns Hopkins historian Martha S. Jones perhaps best got to the crux of the issue in her response: "The heart of the matter is not whether we engage in public debate. Of course we do. It is not whether we attend to political, diplomatic and military history. Of course we do. This is a debate over who sets the terms of the nation's history and from what point of view we tell it."[6] What Jones spoke to here, and what Boot himself perhaps unwittingly revealed, is the issue of power: the function of power, inextricably connected to race and gender, in determining what history is, whose stories matter, and ultimately what the identity of the nation is. To bring this down to a more concrete level, this debate is about disciplinary fields, the ways they are defined and policed, and the contested nature of historiography.

As all these tweets and op-eds flew back and forth, I could not help but think about my own scholarly journey and engagement with military history through the experiences of African American soldiers in World War I.

When I was a graduate student, eager to make a name for myself, and even when I was an early-career professor, one of the most frequent questions I would get from people in conversations about my work was this: are you a military historian? This question would always give me pause, because I knew that it was not a benign question. It was loaded, depending on who was doing the asking, with a series of assumptions—or a series of investments in what military history was and what it should be. What type of historian did I see myself as, and where did I fit within the disciplinary spectrum and, most vexing, the ideological spectrum? More specifically, was my type of military history a challenge to the "older scholarship," to use Boot's wording, or was I one of the "new" historians looking to transform a field that had long been seen as foundational for the study of US history?

Luckily, I had some backup. I was fortunate to write my dissertation and publish my first book in the early 2000s, a time when the study of African Americans and World War I was experiencing a remarkable renaissance. Scholars like Adriane Lentz-Smith, Jennifer Keene, John Morrow Jr., Jeffrey Sammons, Mark Whalan, Nikki Brown, and a host of others were looking at the experiences of African Americans in World War I from a variety of perspectives. This critical historiographical intervention would not have been possible without the continued evolution of "cultural, social and gender" history, and I would add to this the study of diaspora. These fields moved from the periphery to the center, in the process transforming the very notions of military, political, and diplomatic history.

And make no mistake, this was and still remains a threat, as Boot's insecurity revealed. The centering of race and gender challenges both structures of power within history and disciplinary identities. I am reminded of a quote from James Baldwin, who in his 1976 book *The Devil Finds Work* wrote, "An identity is questioned only when it is menaced, as when the mighty begin to fall, or when the wretched begin to rise, or when the stranger enters the gates, never, thereafter, to be a stranger."[7]

It is necessary that we enter the gates and insist that our work not be treated as strangers. In 2010, I published my book *Torchbearers of Democracy*.[8] Of the recognitions it received, one was the Distinguished Book Award from the Society for Military History. It was, I believe, the first book devoted exclusively to the experiences of Black soldiers to win this award. I say this to offer an example of how centering the stories of one particularly "underrepresented and oppressed" group, and adopting race and gender as methodological frameworks, can menace old identities, challenge the status quo, and push a field like military history in new directions.

So I would like to make the case for my particular area of study, the history of African American soldiers in World War I, as the perfect opportunity to push the boundaries of military history. Some 380,000 Black soldiers fought and labored in the US Army. Over 200,000 Black servicemen traveled to France. Two all-Black divisions fought on the front lines; thousands of Black troops received medals of commendation. After the war, African American veterans, both physically and symbolically, shaped what would come to be known as the New Negro movement. The experiences of African American soldiers, and what they represented, allow us to develop a deeper understanding of how the war fundamentally shaped the social, cultural, and political terrain of Black life during the World War I era, as well as the broader history of the United States and the world. Moreover, the history of Black soldiers and veterans reminds us of the possibilities that come with the study of war and military history and of the need for our work to be bold, insurgent, and fundamentally challenging to how we tell the story of America.

This work is not new. If I could point to one scholar and historical figure who lived this approach in his life and work it would be W. E. B. Du Bois. A founding figure of the modern civil rights movement and arguably the greatest Black intellectual in American history, Du Bois, the embodiment of interdisciplinarity, was many things: sociologist, philosopher, political scientist, novelist, poet, and more. But he was at his core a historian and, very few scholars acknowledge, a damn good military historian. He is certainly well known for writing about the

Civil War and Reconstruction eras, but less acknowledged is his central place in the history and legacy of World War I for African Americans. He not only lived through the war, recognizing it as a defining moment in his political and intellectual career, but also spent decades writing about the war and grappling with its troubling and at times confounding memory.

One question that Du Bois asked, and one that historians continue to wrestle with and debate, is what the First World War was about. Just what were the causes of this maelstrom, which would ultimately lead to over seventeen million deaths? From the moment the gunfire erupted in August 1914, Du Bois made the explicit connection between the world war and the African diaspora. In his first musings about the conflict, a November 1914 *Crisis* editorial titled "World War and the Color Line," Du Bois warned his readers against "supposing that the present war is far removed from the color problem of America." He went further to argue that the cause of the war lay in "the wild quest for Imperial expansion among colored races" between the rival European nations, and the "theory of the inferiority of the darker peoples" that legitimized their actions.[9] Du Bois expanded and put a fine point on this argument in the essay "The African Roots of War," appearing in the May 1915 issue of *Atlantic Monthly*. "Yet in a very real sense Africa is a prime cause of this terrible overturning of civilization which we have lived to see," Du Bois presciently wrote.[10] He could point to the use of African colonial subjects as both laborers and, in the case of France, soldiers on the western front as prime evidence of his claim.

While Du Bois understood the democratic meaning of the war in the broader context of Africa and its diaspora, most African Americans remained principally concerned with the crisis of democracy facing Black people in the United States. Indeed, it is crucial not to forget just how divorced democracy had become from the lives of most African Americans on the eve of World War I, a time of Jim Crow segregation, disenfranchisement, debt peonage, convict lease, and racial violence. This was the nadir, as the pioneering African American historian—and World War I veteran—Rayford W. Logan noted.[11] In April 1917, Black people were, in effect, citizens in name only.

But the ideal of democracy continued to resonate for African Americans. It remained a powerful aspiration, one rooted in a history of struggle dating back to the antebellum period. That spark of democratic hope, that Black people could one day be seen and treated as full American citizens and equal participants in American democracy, remained very much alive.

So Woodrow Wilson would have been wise to think a little more carefully about his words on the evening of April 2, 1917, as he spoke before the US Congress and issued a declaration of war against Germany. In his thirty-six-minute speech, Wilson gave a memorable performance, solidifying America's role in the war and its larger political vision when he proclaimed, "The world must be made safe for democracy. . . . We are but one of the champions of the rights of mankind. We shall be satisfied when those rights have been made as secure as the faith and the freedom of nations can make them."[12]

Perhaps more than any other group, African Americans seized on the blatant hypocrisy of Wilson's pledge and appropriated democracy as a rhetorical and ideological weapon in the cause of racial equality. But fighting for African American civil rights while at the same time declaring the patriotic loyalty of the race was a challenge, one made even more painful by incidents like the July 1917 East Saint Louis Massacre, a two-day pogrom in Illinois during which white mobs lynched, shot, stabbed, and burned Black people at will, leaving well over one hundred dead and thousands homeless. Du Bois captured this dilemma when he penned a controversial editorial in the July 1918 issue of the *Crisis*, the NAACP's journal of news and opinion, which he edited, titled "Close Ranks."[13] The controversy that ensued around "Close Ranks" spoke to the fact that the warring ideals of being Black and being American that defined Du Bois's understanding of the double consciousness of African American identity would not be easily reconciled.

Nevertheless, the majority of African Americans knew that democracy would have to be fought for. Racial progress would require Black people to place their lives on the line. For this reason, military service, as the highest form of patriotism and civic obligation, and the role of African American soldiers, dominated public and private debates about Black participation in the war.

And this is why memory is so important. Debates regarding the use of African American soldiers in the war revolved around competing historical memories of the meaning of Black military service. Black soldiers were powerful symbols of freedom, manhood, citizenship, and power. African Americans drew from the inspiring memories of Black sacrifice in the American Revolution and especially the heroism of Black soldiers in the Civil War. Conversely, many white Americans, particularly from the South, feared the potential use of Black soldiers in the war, based on historical memories of Black troops as threats to white supremacy.

The worst nightmares of southern white people became a reality on the night of August 24, 1917, in Houston, Texas. After enduring weeks of racial abuse from racist white citizens and police officers, a battalion of Black soldiers of the Twenty-Fourth Infantry stationed at Camp Logan, on the outskirts of the city, struck back. Determined to enact retribution for weeks of racial discrimination and abuse, over one hundred soldiers procured weapons, deserted camp, and, with guns drawn, marched into downtown Houston. For three hours, Black soldiers ignited the streets of Houston in a fury of gunfire. When the smoke cleared, two Black soldiers and fifteen white men lay dead, including four police officers. Military officials promptly placed the entire battalion under arrest and subsequently court-martialed the soldiers for their actions. After the first of three trials, in which a total of 110 men were found guilty of mutiny, law enforcement hastily executed thirteen soldiers, denying them the opportunity to appeal their judgment. A total of nineteen Black servicemen were ultimately hanged, with sixty-three receiving life sentences in federal prison.

So these competing views of Black soldiers clashed from the outset of American involvement in the war. Questions swirled as to whether African Americans would be able to serve in the war and, if so, in what capacity. The War Department realized it did not have the luxury of simply excluding African Americans from service or severely complicating training procedures by restricting Black soldiers from southern camps. Despite southern opposition, the enlistment and mobilization of Black soldiers proceeded with the passage of the Selective Service Act in May 1917.

But this did not mean that Black servicemen would be treated equally. From the initial implementation of the draft, military officials and local administrators of the Selective Service System envisioned African Americans serving almost exclusively as laborers. Approximately 80 percent of all Black men in the wartime army served as labor troops. One official bluntly described Black troops as "laborers in uniform."[14] Of the 200,000 African American soldiers who served overseas in France, approximately 140,000 labored in the Services of Supply, loading and unloading ships, laying railroad track, digging ditches, salvaging battlefields, and burying the dead. If they had to serve, so reasoned racist military officials, it would be in a capacity suited to the natural abilities of Black men and in a role where they could be controlled.

The fact that the vast majority of Black soldiers carried shovels instead of rifles has been an important factor in the dismissal of the historical contributions and legacy of Black soldiers in the war, leaving them unknown, lost, or forgotten. But not all Black soldiers served in this capacity. The army established two Black combat divisions: the Ninety-Second and Ninety-Third Infantry Divisions.

The Ninety-Second Infantry Division, composed of draftees, was born out of political pressure from Black leaders who realized the importance of African American soldiers proving their worth on the battlefield to the larger cause of Black civil rights. Although commanded by white men, many of whom were committed racists, the Ninety-Second did contain Black officers. The War Department, seeking to placate Black critics, agreed to a Black officers' camp, which opened on June 15, 1917, in Des Moines, Iowa. Although segregated, to which many African Americans objected, the Des Moines camp represented an important moment in the history of the war and African American military history more broadly.

The Ninety-Second Infantry Division, what Du Bois would later characterize as "the storm center" of Black combat troops, had a trying experience.[15] The various regiments of the division trained at separate facilities in the United States, preventing cohesiveness and a sense of collective identity. In France, Black officers were targeted by efficiency boards, demeaned by their superiors, and plagued by rumors of habitual rape. The Ninety-Second actually became known among white racists in the American Expeditionary Forces as the "raping division."[16]

These Black troops' experience would have undoubtedly been even worse were it not for the support of Black women. The war created opportunities for Black women, at home and abroad, to demonstrate their leadership and demand their inclusion in the nation's democracy. They contributed to the war effort in a variety of ways, staffing YWCA hostess houses, serving as Red Cross nurses, and, in the case of YMCA secretaries Addie Hunton and Kathryn Johnson, providing services to Black soldiers in France. As they confronted the daily virulence of white supremacy, African Americans troops, especially those in the Ninety-Second Infantry Division, relished the kindness and racial motherhood of Hunton and Johnson.

The second Black fighting division, the Ninety-Third, was composed mostly of National Guard units from New York, Illinois, Washington, DC, Ohio, and Maryland. The Ninety-Third saw extensive combat duty in France. This was primarily due to the fact that it served with the French army as a result of the US military not knowing how to use this particular collection of soldiers. Soldiers of the Ninety-Third Infantry Division had a markedly different military and social experience than other American soldiers, Black or white. Despite being essentially discarded by the US military, members of the Ninety-Third were highly decorated and garnered widespread praise from their French comrades, many of whom preferred them over white American soldiers.

The most famous regiment of the Ninety-Third Infantry Division, and arguably the most famous regiment of Black soldiers in the entire war, was the 369th Infantry Regiment (the former Fifteenth New York National Guard), which after the war became known as the Harlem Hellfighters. The first African American combat unit to reach France, the 369th served for 191 consecutive days on the front, without losing any ground to the German army. The 369th's band, led by the renowned ragtime conductor James Reese Europe, contributed to the regiment's popularity and helped introduce France to jazz music.

The 369th was also popular for the remarkable heroics of two of its soldiers, Needham Roberts and Henry Johnson, who routed a twenty-four-man German raiding party on the night of May 13, 1918. Johnson, using a combination of grenades, his bolo knife, and the butt of his rifle, single-handedly killed four Germans and wounded another dozen. "The Battle of Henry Johnson" became front-page news in the United States. The two men were the first American soldiers to receive the French Croix de Guerre with Palm. African Americans at home, hungrily waiting for just such a moment, celebrated Johnson and Roberts as racial symbols. This was the perfect incident to shape a historical memory of Black participation in the war around the themes of bravery, manhood, and sacrifice. How could anyone deny that, as epitomized by Johnson and Roberts, African Americans were not only heroic but also worthy of first-class citizenship?

It would not be this simple. Memories of the 369th and other combat heroes engaged in a struggle with an alternative memory of the alleged failure of Black combat soldiers and officers. The Ninety-Second Infantry Division and its Black officers were the main targets of racist white military officials. The division's own white commanders labeled their Black officers "worthless," "inefficient," "untrustworthy," and "cowardly," among other insults. General Robert Lee Bullard, commander of the Second Army, American Expeditionary Forces, wrote off the division as a misguided experiment, writing in his postwar memoir, "The negro division seems in a fair way to be a failure." He went on to state that "altogether my memories of the 92nd Negro Division are a nightmare. . . . If you need combat soldiers, and especially if you need them in a hurry, don't put your time upon Negroes."[17] As his comment reflects, the accusations leveled by hostile white officers quickly became indictments not just of particular units, but of all Black combat soldiers and officers.

These charges had their effect, and in fact continue to inform assessments of Black soldiers by some historians to this day. An assumption still exists that African Americans didn't care about their history or the attacks on the legacy of their soldiers.

This was simply not true. African Americans, soldiers and civilians, engaged in a vigorous effort not only to redeem the memory of Black service in France, but to shape it on their own terms. This process began immediately after the November 1918 armistice. Black communities welcomed their soldiers home with parades and festivities throughout the country, ranging from small local gatherings to massive processions that took place in New York and Chicago. The Black press and political leaders hailed the service of Black troops as an unqualified success and eagerly anticipated the postwar era becoming a new "Reconstruction," akin to the momentous transformations in the social, political, and economic status of African Americans following the Civil War. A host of Black novelists, playwrights, and poets of the Harlem Renaissance produced a broad range of works that invoked the recent war or had Black servicemen as central characters. Several Black intellectuals, most notably Du Bois, also attempted to enshrine the contributions of Black soldiers into "official" written history. And a handful of African American veterans published memoirs of their individual and regimental exploits, testaments to their historical awareness and self-conscious desire to both preserve and share their experiences. Together, these acts created a triumphant communal public memory of Black service in the war that would be passed down from generation to generation.

But other memories existed as well, not all of them positive. African Americans also remembered the virulence of white supremacy and the racial discrimination endured by Black soldiers—the hypocrisy of American democracy. One disgruntled veteran wrote in a letter following the war, "We were treated like dogs. I mean worse than German prisoners. I would die before I would undertake to go through what I have gone through."[18]

Moreover, historical memories of Black military service were shaped as much by events of the postwar period as by the war itself. Black soldiers returned home from one war and entered another. Du Bois was being literal when he penned his May 1919 *Crisis* editorial "Returning Soldiers," declaring, "We *return*. We *return from fighting*. We *return fighting*. Make way for Democracy! We saved it in France, and by the Great Jehovah, we will save it in the United States, or know the reason why."[19]

But this turned out not to be the case. And it was by necessity, because white racists were ready to fight as well. Racial violence exploded throughout the country in 1919, much of it involving African American veterans and white people resistant to any changes, real or perceived, in the racial status quo. In the South, the number of Black people lynched skyrocketed to seventy-six. At least eleven returned Black servicemen lost their lives to southern vigilante justice. Race riots erupted in cities large and small, the most explosive taking place in Washington, DC, Chicago, and Elaine, Arkansas. Thirty-eight people died in the Chicago riot, where Black people, led by returned soldiers, gave as good as they took. Black people fought back, speaking to a new spirit of resistance and self-confidence inspired by the war. But the "Red Summer," as characterized by James Weldon Johnson, left a deep scar on the psyche of many African Americans and shaped their memory of the war as one of dashed expectations. As a Black veteran of the Ninety-Third wrote in a letter after the Chicago riot, "Try to imagine the smouldering hatred within the breast of an overseas veteran who is set upon and mercilessly beaten by a gang of young hoodlums simply because he is colored."[20]

Many African Americans translated this "smouldering hatred" and the raw memories of democracy denied into organized protest. African American veterans, both physically and symbolically, shaped the upsurge in Black radicalism and racial militancy that came to be known as the New Negro movement. Organizations such as the African Blood Brotherhood, the Universal Negro Improvement Association (led by Marcus Garvey), and lesser known groups like the veteran-led League for Democracy provided highly politicized former soldiers with vehicles to translate their frustrations into movements of national and international change.

So what do we make of this history? What do we make of the legacy of the war for African Americans and the larger world? By the late 1920s, as racial conditions in the United States and beyond showed no signs of improving, Du Bois would adopt a harsh view of the war, going so far as to describe it as "a Scourge, an Evil, a retrogression to Barbarism, a waste, a wholesale murder."[21] And perhaps it was. But he also acknowledged that the war and the experiences of Black soldiers marked a crucial moment in a longer history of the struggle for racial justice.

Historians of African Americans and World War I have built on this argument to shift our understanding of the periodization of the modern civil rights movement. The civil rights movement did not begin in World War II and its aftermath, but truly expanded during World War I and with men such as Charles Hamilton Houston, who served as an officer in the First World War, emerged from his experience highly embittered, and fought against racial segregation and discrimination in the military during the Second World War so that his struggles would not be repeated. The First World War was a pivotal moment when Black people began to confront the meaning of modern American democracy and their place in the nation as full and equal citizens.

So this is not just about telling the story of an underrepresented or oppressed group, although that is important. The Black experience in World War I informs the way we think about history, our approach to history, and ultimately our approach to America itself. What does democracy mean? We are at a critical moment, with white supremacy ascendant, blatantly false representations of the nation's past propagated, and fact-based truth dismissed as "fake history." The battle over the meaning and boundaries of history, military history included, is a battle for the identity of the nation and over what type of democracy we truly are. African Americans fought this battle some one hundred years ago. And a century later, through our scholarship, teaching, and ethical commitments, and through gatherings like the one that produced this volume, we have an important role to play in this battle as well.

Notes

Introduction

1. The literature on race, gender, and war is enormous and growing bigger all the time. Rather than attempt to list a representative sampling of that scholarship, we would point readers to the further reading section at the end of this volume for relevant works related to the chapters. For recent and broad historiographical overviews, readers should also consult *War and Society* 42, no. 1 (February 2023), and two essays in particular: Beth Bailey, "Race and the History of the Modern US Military," 12–19; and Kara Dixon Vuic, "Grand Narratives and Gendered Wars and Societies," 82–89.

Chapter 1

1. *Anglo-Texan* refers to English-speaking white colonists in Mexican and independent Texas, distinguishing them from both US citizens and culturally Mexican Tejanos.

2. Austin to Linn, May 4, 1836, in *The Papers of the Texas Revolution* (*PTR*), ed. John H. Jenkins (Austin, TX: Presidial Press, 1973), 6:160.

3. Austin to Linn, 6:160–61; see also Sam W. Haynes, "'Imitating the Example of Our Forefathers': The Texas Revolution as Historical Reenactment," in *Contested Empire: Rethinking the Texas Revolution*, ed. Sam W. Haynes and Gerald Saxon (College Station: Texas A&M University Press, 2015), 43–78.

4. See esp. Robert Parkinson, *The Common Cause: Creating Race and Nation in the American Revolution* (Chapel Hill: University of North Carolina Press, 2016); Carroll Smith-Rosenberg, *This Violent Empire: The Birth of an American National Identity* (Chapel Hill: University of North Carolina Press, 2010); Peter Silver, *Our Savage Neighbors: How Indian War Transformed Early America* (New York: W. W. Norton, 2007).

5. See, e.g., Andrew J. Torget, *Seeds of Empire: Cotton, Slavery, and the Transformation of the Texas Borderlands, 1800–1850* (Chapel Hill: University of North Carolina Press, 2015); Alice L. Baumgartner, *South to Freedom: Runaway Slaves to Mexico and the Road to the Civil War* (New York: Basic Books, 2020); Sam W. Haynes, *Unsettled Land: From Revolution to Republic, the Struggle for Texas* (New York: Basic Books, 2022); for coverage in a more traditional account, see Paul D. Lack, *The Texas Revolutionary Experience: A Political and Social History, 1835–1836* (College Station: Texas A&M University Press, 1992), 238–52.

6. Numerous historians have explored similar familial nationalist rhetoric in other American wars. See, e.g., Stephen Berry, *All That Makes a Man: Love and Ambition in the Civil War South* (New York: Oxford University Press, 2003); Aaron Sheehan-Dean, *Why Confederates Fought: Family and Nation in Civil War Virginia* (Chapel Hill: University of North Carolina Press, 2009); Kristin L. Hoganson, *Fighting for American Manhood: How Gender*

Politics Provoked the Spanish-American and Philippine-American Wars (New Haven, CT: Yale University Press, 1998); Andrew J. Huebner, *Love and Death in the Great War* (New York: Oxford University Press, 2018). Across these numerous iterations, familial nationalist rhetoric recycled many core elements, including the promise of reenacting past generations' heroism and the portrayal of military enlistment as an act of chivalric defense or rescue. They also proved consistently effective for bridging factionalism and linking national or international politics with more intimate motivations. Despite their continuities, however, these discourses remained highly contextual, reflecting contemporary social, cultural, and political circumstances. The Texas rebellion's distinctly Jacksonian version invoked a familial American nationhood that joined independent patriarchal households less through shared allegiance to a particular government or homeland than through a combination of race, revolutionary heritage, and loosely defined political and cultural values. As recent scholars have argued, Jacksonian-era Americans often consciously moved beyond US borders to pursue landownership and economic independence—quintessentially "American" ideals that seemed to grow ever more elusive in the United States. Such emigrants only became straightforward agents of US expansionism in hindsight. See, e.g., Thomas Richards Jr., *Breakaway Americas: The Unmanifest Future of the Jacksonian United States* (Baltimore, MD: Johns Hopkins University Press, 2020), 7–20; Sarah K. M. Rodriguez, "'The Greatest Nation on Earth': The Politics and Patriotism of the First Anglo American Immigrants to Mexican Texas, 1820–1824," *Pacific Historical Review* 86, no. 1 (February 2017): 57–63; Eric R. Schlereth, "Privileges of Locomotion: Expatriation and the Politics of Southwestern Border Crossing," *Journal of American History* 100, no. 4 (March 2014): 995–97. However, the nationalism of the Texas rebellion reveals an important countervailing force. If opportunity and ambition drove Anglo families beyond US borders, ties of kinship both real and fictive tethered them to a much more flexible "American" nation. Those same frameworks of familial obligation and honor also provided a road map for navigating and narrating the practice of this peculiarly unbounded nationhood. Appeals combining gender, race, and national kinship could thus catalyze nationalist thought and action in ways that transcended or even circumvented US national sovereignty.

7. Haynes, *Unsettled Land*, 83–130; Lack, *The Texas Revolutionary Experience*, 17–18, 24, 29.

8. Williamson address, June 22, 1835, *PTR* 1:198–201.

9. Milam to Johnson, July 5, 1835, *PTR* 1:207.

10. Columbia meeting, *PTR* 1:169–70; Mina resolutions, July 9, 1835, *PTR* 1:223–24; see also *PTR* 1:75–77, 1:135–37.

11. Gritten to Ugartechea, July 5 and 6, 1835, *PTR* 1:203–5, 1:208–9 (qtd.); see also Cós to political chief, July 7, 1835, *PTR* 1:212–13; *PTR* 1:217–18, 1:245–46, 1:278–79, 1:438–39.

12. Miller to Smith, July 25, 1835, *PTR* 1:274; see also "Miller, James B.," *Handbook of Texas Online*, updated May 13, 2022.

13. Literature on antebellum Anglo-American masculinity is vast; see esp. Jimmy L. Bryan, *The American Elsewhere: Adventure and Manliness in the Age of Expansion* (Lawrence: University Press of Kansas, 2017); Kenneth S. Greenberg, *Honor and Slavery: Lies, Duels, Noses, Masks, Dressing as a Woman, Gifts, Strangers, Humanitarianism, Death, Slave Rebellions, the Proslavery Argument, Baseball, Hunting, and Gambling in the Old South* (Princeton, NJ: Princeton University Press, 1996); Amy S. Greenberg, *Manifest Manhood and the Antebellum*

American Empire (New York: Cambridge University Press, 2005); John Hope Franklin, *The Militant South, 1800–1861* (Cambridge, MA: Harvard University Press, 1956). On Travis, see Archie P. McDonald, "Travis, William Barret," *Handbook of Texas Online*, updated March 24, 2017. In his diary, Travis wrote: "Chingaba una mujer, que es cinquenta y seis en mi vida" (I was fucking a woman, who is fifty-six in my life). William Barret Travis, *Diary, August 30, 1833–June 26, 1834* (Waco, TX: Texian Press, 1966), 15.

14. Travis to Burnet, April 11, 1835, *PTR* 1:63–64; Travis to Smith, July 6, 1835, *PTR* 1:209–10; Travis to Briscoe, August 31, 1835, *PTR* 1:380–81. Anglo-American culture consistently portrayed expansionist violence as a regenerative force; see Richard Slotkin, *Regeneration through Violence: The Mythology of the American Frontier, 1600–1860* (1973; repr., Norman: University of Oklahoma Press, 2000).

15. Zavala to Austin, September 17, 1835, *PTR* 1:453.

16. Austin circular, September 18, 1835, *PTR* 1:456; Archer to public, September 20, 1835, *PTR* 1:467–69.

17. Miller to public, c. September 1835, *PTR* 1:517.

18. David Weber, *The Mexican Frontier, 1821–1846: The American Southwest under Mexico* (Albuquerque: University of New Mexico Press, 1989), 177; Andrés Reséndez, *Changing National Identities at the Frontier: Texas and New Mexico, 1800–1850* (New York: Cambridge University Press, 2005), 22; Raúl A. Ramos, *Beyond the Alamo: Forging Mexican Ethnicity in San Antonio, 1821–1861* (Chapel Hill: University of North Carolina Press, 2008), 69–72.

19. Reséndez, *Changing National Identities at the Frontier*, 208; Lack, *The Texas Revolutionary Experience*, 133; Torget, *Seeds of Empire*.

20. Kaplan drew the original phrase from US Supreme Court justice Edward Douglas White's 1901 opinion in *Downes v. Bidwell*, where he used it to describe the legal status of Puerto Rico. Amy Kaplan, *The Anarchy of Empire in the Making of U.S. Culture* (Cambridge: Harvard University Press, 2002), 1–4.

21. Wilson to Travis, May 13, 1835, *PTR* 1:108; Harris [*sic*] address, December 22, 1835, *PTR* 3:290; see also *PTR* 9:240–41; Republic of Texas Const. of 1836, gen. prov., § 9; Bonnell to Gaines, April 20, 1836, *PTR* 5:507–8.

22. Walter Johnson, *River of Dark Dreams: Slavery and Empire in the Cotton Kingdom*, (Cambridge, MA: Belknap Press of Harvard University Press, 2013), 46–72; Torget, *Seeds of Empire*, 137–76.

23. Gary Clayton Anderson, *The Conquest of Texas: Ethnic Cleansing in the Promised Land, 1820–1875* (Norman: University of Oklahoma Press, 2005), 97–107.

24. Haynes, *Unsettled Land*, 139.

25. Smith to Austin et al., December 8, 1835, *PTR* 3:124; Houston to Parker, October 5, 1835, *PTR* 2:46–47; Burnet proclamation, April 3, 1836, *PTR* 5:305–6.

26. DeGreve to Houston, October 31, 1835, *PTR* 2:270–71.

27. Royall to public, October 26, 1835, *PTR* 2:225–26; Natchitoches meeting, October 7, 1835, *PTR* 2:62; Ward et al. to Fannin, December 23, 1835, *PTR* 3:305; see also *PTR* 2:174, 2:424, 3:118, 3:322–23.

28. On the creation myth, see Brian DeLay, *War of a Thousand Deserts: Indian Raids and the U.S.-Mexican War* (New Haven, CT: Yale University Press, 2008), 227–31; see, e.g., Chambers to ——, c. March 1836, *PTR* 5:260–67; *PTR* 3:153–54.

29. John E. Roller, "Capt. John Sowers Brooks," *Quarterly of the Texas State Historical*

Association 9, no. 3 (1906): 160, 165, 162–64, 186–89; see also Phillip T. Tucker, "Motivations of United States Volunteers during the Texas Revolution, 1835–36," *East Texas Historical Journal* 29, no. 1 (March 1991): 25–34.

30. Autry to Autry, December 7, 1835, *PTR* 3:105; Autry to Autry, January 13, 1836, *PTR* 3:503–4; Tucker, "Motivations of United States Volunteers during the Texas Revolution," 30; see also *PTR* 4:334.

31. Green to McCall, March 30, 1836, *PTR* 5:241–42; Green to public, April 5, 1836, *PTR* 5:327–29.

32. Edwards statement, February 6, 1836, *PTR* 4:271–73; Wharton to Smith, February 13, 1836, *PTR* 4:329; Wharton to Houston, February 16, 1836, *PTR* 4:369; Austin to Holley, February 16, 1836, *PTR* 4:349.

33. Wharton to Houston, February 16, 1836, *PTR* 4:369; see also *PTR* 4:42, 4:43, 4:51–53; Lack, *The Texas Revolutionary Experience*, 84–85, 137, 149–51; Texas Declaration of Independence, March 2, 1836, *PTR* 4:495.

34. Borden to voters, January 19, 1836, *PTR* 4:71; see also Lack, *The Texas Revolutionary Experience*, 78, 183–208.

35. Greenberg, *Honor and Slavery*, 88, 92, 98.

36. Bowie to Smith, February 2, 1836, *PTR* 4:238; Travis to Smith, February 12, 1836, *PTR* 4:317–18; Travis to Grimes, March 3, 1836, *PTR* 4:505; Smithers to public, February 24, 1836, *PTR* 4:422; Travis to public, February 24, 1836, *PTR* 4:423; Stephen Hardin, *Texian Iliad: A Military History of the Texas Revolution* (Austin: University of Texas Press, 1994), 156.

37. Goodrich to Goodrich, March 15, 1836, *PTR* 5:81–82.

38. Houston to Fannin, March 11, 1836, *PTR* 5:52–53; Parker to editor, April 29, 1836, *PTR* 6:121–22; "Latest from Texas [from *New Orleans Bulletin*, April 11, 1836]," *Portland Advertiser* (Maine), May 3, 1836, in *An Altar for Their Sons: The Alamo and the Texas Revolution in Contemporary Newspaper Accounts*, by Gary Zaboly (Buffalo Gap, TX: State House Press, 2011), 233.

39. Morris to Fannin, February 6, 1836, *PTR* 4:274–76; Fannin to Robinson, February 7, 1836, *PTR* 4:279–80; *Telegraph and Texas Register* (San Felipe), February 20, 1836.

40. Hardin, *Texian Iliad*, 127–31, 163–68.

41. Lack, *The Texas Revolutionary Experience*, 53–55, 111, 123, 133; the 50.3 percent statistic comes from adding Lack's US volunteer and "<1 year" categories (40.2 percent and 10.1 percent, respectively). Of the 3,685 total soldiers who served in the Texas army, length-of-residence data exists for 2,399 (65 percent). Of those, 964 (40.2 percent) were verifiably US volunteers arriving after October 1835, while the other 1,435 immigrated earlier. The remaining 1,286 soldiers' arrival dates are unknown. Therefore, US volunteer participation may have been as high as 2,250 individuals, or 61.1 percent of all Texas forces. Lack's length-of-residence data for Béxar and Goliad is far more complete than for the army overall—86 percent versus 65 percent.

42. Brazoria meeting, March 17, 1836, *PTR* 5:98–99; White to committee, March 22, 1836, *PTR* 5:165; Morgan to ——, March 24, 1836, *PTR* 5:182; Gaines to governors, April 8, 1836, *PTR* 5:375.

43. Sesma to Santa Anna, March 15, 1836, *PTR* 5:85; for the likely proclamation, see Santa Anna to citizens, March 7, 1836, *PTR* 5:20–21; José Enrique de la Peña and Carmen

Perry, *With Santa Anna in Texas: A Personal Narrative of the Revolution* (College Station: Texas A&M University Press, 1997), 112, 119–20.

44. Houston to the people, March 31, 1836, *PTR* 5:253; Houston to Martin, April 2, 1836, *PTR* 5:294; Tornel to Santa Anna, December 30, 1835, *PTR* 3:379–80; Santa Anna to Tornel, February 16, 1836, *PTR* 4:356–57; Santa Anna to citizens, March 7, 1836, *PTR* 5:20–21; Noriega to Santa Anna, February 29, 1836, *PTR* 4:466.

45. Lack, *The Texas Revolutionary Experience*, 40; Burnet address, March 17, 1836, *PTR* 5:101–2; Burnet proclamation, March 18, 1836, *PTR* 5:126; Burnet to citizens, c. March 1836, *PTR* 5:259; Rusk to public, April 13, 1836, *PTR* 5:460–61; see also *PTR* 5:398, 5:453, 5:504.

46. Burnet to public, April 6, 1836, *PTR* 5:342; Burnet proclamation, April 9, 1836, *PTR* 5:399.

47. Dilue Harris, "The Reminiscences of Mrs. Dilue Harris II," *Quarterly of the Texas State Historical Association* 4, no. 3 (1901): 159–60, 162 (qtd.), 166–67.

Chapter 2

1. Lucinda Davis, oral history, in *The WPA Oklahoma Slave Narratives*, ed. T. Lindsay Baker and Julie P. Baker (Norman: University of Oklahoma Press, 1996), 108, 113.

2. See, e.g., Scott Nelson and Carol Sheriff, *A People at War: Civilians and Soldiers in America's Civil War, 1854–1877* (New York: Oxford University Press, 2008), chap. 7; James M. McPherson, *Battle Cry of Freedom: The Civil War Era* (New York: Oxford University Press, 2003); Anne J. Bailey, *Invisible Southerners: Ethnicity in the Civil War* (Athens: University of Georgia Press, 2006); Susannah J. Ural, ed., *Civil War Citizens: Race, Ethnicity, and Identity in America's Bloodiest Conflict* (New York: New York University Press, 2010), 7.

3. See Clarissa W. Confer, *The Cherokee Nation in the Civil War* (Norman: University of Oklahoma Press, 2007); W. Craig Gaines, *The Confederate Cherokees* (Baton Rouge: Louisiana State University Press, 1989); Wilfred Knight, *Red Fox: Stand Waite and the Confederate Indian Nations during the Civil War Years in Indian Territory* (Glendale, CA: Arthur H. Clark, 1988). See also W. David Baird, ed., *A Creek Warrior for the Confederacy: The Autobiography of Chief G. W. Grayson* (Norman: University of Oklahoma Press, 1988).

4. Mary Jane Warde, *When the Wolf Came: The Civil War in Indian Territory* (Fayetteville: University of Arkansas Press, 2013); Bradley R. Clampitt, ed., *The Civil War and Reconstruction in Indian Territory* (Lincoln: University of Nebraska Press, 2015); Megan Kate Nelson, *The Three-Cornered War: The Union, the Confederacy, and Native Peoples in the Fight for the West* (New York: Scribner, 2020).

5. See Annie Heloise Abel, *The American Indian as Slaveholder and Secessionist* (Cleveland, OH: Arthur H. Clark, 1915; repr., Lincoln: University of Nebraska Press, 1991) and *The American Indian as Participant in the Civil War, 1862–1865* (Cleveland, OH: Arthur H. Clark, 1919), which are part of her three-volume series *The Slaveholding Indians*.

6. Fay A. Yarbrough, *Choctaw Confederates: The American Civil War in Indian Country* (Chapel Hill: University of North Carolina Press, 2021).

7. See Compiled Service Records of Confederate Soldiers Who Served in Organizations Raised Directly by the Confederate Government, microcopy no. 258, rolls 81–85 and 91, available through the National Archives, Washington, DC, and at Bizzell Memorial Library,

University of Oklahoma, Norman. I have compiled information from these service records into a database that includes name, rank, company, age, date of enlistment, remarks, receipt of clothing commutation, term of service, and information about reenlistment. Monty Olsen, *Indices of Choctaw and Chickasaw Confederate Soldiers* (Calera, OK: Bryan County Heritage Association, 1996), also contains a distillation of these records. Hereafter, except where otherwise cited, I refer to information obtained from the database.

8. Choctaw National Records microfilm series, roll CTN 16, doc. no. 18302, 254–56, Oklahoma Historical Society, Oklahoma City.

9. Iti Fabvssa, "Choctaw Nation and the American Civil War," October 2011, Chahta Anumpa Aiikhvna School of Choctaw Language (website).

10. Edward Elmer Prag, "The Confederate Diplomacy with the Five Civilized Tribes" (MA thesis, University of Oklahoma, 1966), 65.

11. Population estimates from "Civil War Facts: 1861–1865," National Park Service (website), last updated October 27, 2021. The caveat is, of course, that the numbers for Confederate enlistments are less accurate.

12. For Choctaw Nation and Chickasaw Nation population estimates in 1860, see Abel, *The American Indian as Slaveholder and Secessionist*, 211. William Loren Katz, *Black Indians: A Hidden Heritage* (New York: Atheneum, 1986), 135, describes the Choctaw population of 1860 as 14 percent enslaved. For additional population estimates for Native nations in the Indian Territory, see Warde, *When the Wolf Came*, 264; *The Confederate States Almanac and Repository of Useful Knowledge, for the Year 1863* (Augusta, GA: H. C. Clarke, 1863), 35, Sabin Americana.

13. Colonel Douglas H. Cooper to Jefferson Davis, July 25, 1861, quoted in Abel, *The American Indian as Slaveholder and Secessionist*, 211.

14. James M. McPherson, *For Cause and Comrades: Why Men Fought in the Civil War* (New York: Oxford University Press, 1997), viii.

15. See Lesley Gordon, *A Broken Regiment: The 16th Connecticut's Civil War* (Baton Rouge: Louisiana State University Press, 2014), esp. chap. 1; Mark H. Dunkelman, *Brothers One and All: Esprit de Corps in a Civil War Regiment* (Baton Rouge: Louisiana State University Press, 2004), chap. 1.

16. See, e.g., Compiled Service Records, microcopy no. 258, roll 82, records for Abelauli, Abitishteya, Ahtuklowtubbi, and Alfred. See the pamphlet *Compiled Records Showing Service of Military Units in Confederate Organizations* (Washington, DC: National Archives and Records Service, 1973) for examples of unit names from Southern states.

17. Cyrus Byington, *A Dictionary of the Choctaw Language*, ed. John R. Swanton and Henry S. Halbert (Washington, DC: Government Printing Office, 1915), 281, 328, 561.

18. Oklahoma and Indian Territory, Dawes Census Cards for Five Civilized Tribes, 1898–1914 (database), Ancestry.com, Dawes enrollment no. 4938, census card no. 1745; Enrollment Cards for the Five Civilized Tribes, 1898–1914, National Archives at Fort Worth, TX, NAI no. 251747.

19. Over 2,000 of the 3,126 records include date and location of muster.

20. Articles of Confederation Entered into between Muscogees, Seminoles, Choctaws, and Chickasaws and the Confederate States of America, July 1, 1861, Choctaw Nation of Oklahoma (website).

21. See Abel, *The American Indian as Slaveholder and Secessionist*, 207.

22. Prag, "The Confederate Diplomacy with the Five Civilized Tribes," 47. See also "Resolutions Expressing the Feelings and Sentiments of the General Council of the Choctaw Nation in Reference to the Political Disagreement Existing between the Northern and Southern States of the American Union," February 7, 1861, in *The War of the Rebellion: A Compilation of the Official Records of the Union and Confederate Armies*, ser. 1, vol. 1 (Washington, DC: Government Printing Office, 1880), 682.

23. William W. Freehling, *The Road to Disunion: Secessionists Triumphant, 1854–1861* (Oxford: Oxford University Press, 2007), 503.

24. Abel, *The American Indian as Slaveholder and Secessionist*, 207.

25. Clara Sue Kidwell, *The Choctaws in Oklahoma: From Tribe to Nation, 1855–1970* (Norman: University of Oklahoma Press, 2007), 57.

26. Henry I. Falconer and Ida L. Falconer, interview by Gomer Gower, July 15, 1937, Indian Pioneer Histories, vol. 64, 107, Oklahoma Historical Society.

27. Grant Foreman, ed., *A Traveler in Indian Territory: The Journal of Ethan Allen Hitchcock* (1930; Norman: University of Oklahoma Press, 1996), 148. Hitchcock mentions receiving a gift and message from Opothleyahola's wife, sent through her "negress."

28. Phoebe Banks, oral history, in Baker and Baker, *The WPA Oklahoma Slave Narratives*, 31.

29. See Warde, *When the Wolf Came*, 64–87, for a detailed account of the pursuit of Opothleyahola to Kansas.

30. Warde, 70, 90–91.

31. Quoted in Warde, 90.

32. Warde, 123–25; LeRoy H. Fischer, *The Civil War Era in Indian Territory* (Los Angeles: Lorrin L. Morrison, 1974), 79–80.

33. Albert Burton Moore, *Conscription and Conflict in the Confederacy* (New York: MacMillan, 1924), 12–14.

34. Ella Lonn, *Desertion during the Civil War* (Lincoln: University of Nebraska Press, 1998), 6.

35. "Proclamation by the Principal Chief of the Choctaw Nation," June 14, 1861, in *The War of the Rebellion: A Compilation of the Official Records of the Union and Confederate Armies*, ser. 1, vol. 3 (Washington, DC: Government Printing Office, 1881), 593–94.

36. Abel, *The American Indian as Slaveholder and Secessionist*, 156.

37. "Message of P. P. Pitchlynn, Principal Chief of the Choctaw Nation, Delivered before the Choctaw Council, in Extra Session," January 9, 1865, Confederate Imprints, microfilm 615, reel 72, item 2391, 4, University of Oklahoma Libraries.

38. Moore, *Conscription and Conflict in the Confederacy*, 334.

39. Peter P. Pitchlynn to William Cass, January 16, 1862, Western History Collection, box 3, folder 98, University of Oklahoma Archives.

40. Among those who did not were Private Henry Gibson, Joseph Harkin, and Cyrus Holly.

41. "An Act Ratifying the Compact Entered into between the Creeks, Seminoles, Choctaws and Chickasaws at North Fork Village, Creek Nation, on the First Day of July 1861," Acts and Resolutions Passed by the General Council of the Choctaw Nation in October 1861, box 7, folder 7, Peter Perkins Pitchlynn Collection, Western History Collections, University of Oklahoma Libraries, Norman.

42. Moore, *Conscription and Conflict in the Confederacy*, 7–8.

43. *Southern Confederacy* (Atlanta), February 13, 1862, Digital Library of Georgia.

44. Choctaw National Records microfilm series, roll CTN 8, vol. 295, 17, Oklahoma Historical Society, Oklahoma City.

45. Quoted in McPherson, *For Cause and Comrades*, 13.

46. Captain David Perkins to General D. H. Cooper, December 17, 1863, Compiled Service Records, microcopy no. 258, roll 85, 198–99.

47. Historian Claudio Saunt points out that federal officials were unsure whether the Thirteenth Amendment applied to Indian Territory; see Saunt, "The Paradox of Freedom: Tribal Sovereignty and Emancipation during the Reconstruction of Indian Territory," *Journal of Southern History* 70, no. 1 (February 2004): 63–94.

48. Charlotte Johnson White, oral history, in Baker and Baker, *The WPA Oklahoma Slave Narratives*, 466.

49. Warde, *When the Wolf Came*, 137.

50. In the larger Confederacy, the threat of the emancipation of enslaved people in the form of Abraham Lincoln's proclamation firmed the resolve of many. See Gary W. Gallagher and Joan Waugh, *The American War: A History of the Civil War Era* (State College, PA: Flip Learning, 2015), 125.

51. Whit Edwards, *The Prairie Was on Fire: Eyewitness Accounts of the Civil War in the Indian Territory* (Oklahoma City: Oklahoma Historical Society, 2001), 60.

52. Warde, *When the Wolf Came*, 156–59. See also "Cabin Creek Battlefield," Oklahoma Historical Society (website), accessed October 1, 2023.

53. Quoted in Edwards, *The Prairie Was on Fire*, 59–60.

54. Mark A. Lause, *Race and Radicalism in the Union Army* (Urbana: University of Illinois Press, 2009), 2.

55. See "Honey Springs Battlefield," Oklahoma Historical Society (website), accessed October 1, 2023.

56. Quoted in Warde, *When the Wolf Came*, 166.

57. Quoted in Edwards, *The Prairie Was on Fire*, 63.

58. Quoted in Edwards, 67.

59. Edwards, 66; Knight, *Red Fox*, 170; Fred Hood, "Twilight of the Confederacy in Indian Territory," *Chronicles of Oklahoma* 41, no. 4 (Winter 1963–64): 425–26.

60. See "Honey Springs Battlefield," Oklahoma Historical Society (website), accessed October 1, 2023; Warde, *When the Wolf Came*, 169.

61. Quoted in Edwards, *The Prairie Was on Fire*, 67.

62. Edwards, 68.

63. Henry Clay, oral history, in Baker and Baker, *The WPA Oklahoma Slave Narratives*, 83.

64. Lucinda Davis, oral history, in Baker and Baker, 113.

65. Quoted in Edwards, *The Prairie Was on Fire*, 67–68.

66. Phoebe Banks, oral history, in Baker and Baker, *The WPA Oklahoma Slave Narratives*, 32.

67. Quoted in Edwards, *The Prairie Was on Fire*, 69.

68. Knight, *Red Fox*, 166, 173 (qtd.).

69. Edwards, *The Prairie Was on Fire*, 71.

70. Edwards, 71. Of 173 cases in this unit, 170 occurred in 1863.

71. On May as a planting time among the Choctaw, see Iti Fabvssa, "Traditional Choctaw Agriculture," 2 parts, 2011, Chahta Anumpa Aiikhvna School of Choctaw Language (website).

72. Compiled Service Records, microcopy no. 258, roll 84, 1729.

73. Compiled Service Records, microcopy no. 258, roll 84, 1735.

74. William McKean (Van Buren, AR) to Peter P. Pitchlynn, May 21, 1857, and Lycurgus Pitchlynn to Peter P. Pitchlynn, April 28, 1857, both letters in Western History Collection, box 2, folder 92, University of Oklahoma Archives.

75. Ann DeFrange, "Goodland Home Will Mark 150th Anniversary Today," *Oklahoman*, April 15, 2000.

76. Compiled Service Records, microcopy no. 258, roll 84, 1730.

77. Choctaw National Records microfilm series, roll CTN 16, file 1, doc. no. 18302, 322, Oklahoma Historical Society, Oklahoma City.

Chapter 3

1. Brakkton Booker, "Lloyd Austin Confirmed as Defense Secretary, Becomes 1st Black Pentagon Chief," National Public Radio, January 22, 2021.

2. Lloyd Austin (@SecDef), "It's an honor and a privilege . . . ," Twitter, January 22, 2021, 10:07 a.m.

3. Helene Cooper, "African-Americans Are Highly Visible in the Military, but Almost Invisible at the Top," *New York Times*, May 25, 2020.

4. Cooper; George M. Reynolds and Amanda Shendruk, "Demographics of the U.S. Military," Council on Foreign Relations (website), updated April 24, 2018.

5. Aaron O'Neill, "Black and Slave Population in the United States 1790–1800," Statista (website), posted June 21, 2022.

6. Brian Taylor argues that during the Jim Crow era of the late nineteenth century, many African Americans did not possess a "sense of acceptance within American society . . . only derive[d] from a feeling of equal standing, and this feeling would only come when black Americans possessed the same array of rights as white Americans." Taylor, *Fighting for Citizenship: Black Northerners and the Debate over Military Service in the Civil War* (Chapel Hill: University of North Carolina Press, 2020), 11.

7. Antislavery advocate William Yates contended in 1838 that military service was connected to citizenship; see his *Rights of Colored Men to Suffrage, Citizenship and Trial by Jury* (Philadelphia: Merrihew and Gunn, 1838), cited in Martha S. Jones, *Birthright Citizens: A History of Race and Rights in Antebellum America* (Cambridge: Cambridge University Press, 2018), 2–3. According to Stephen David Kantrowitz, the "linkage of political rights to military service" frustrated some female suffragists during the nineteenth century. In this historical context, women were excluded from conversations about citizenship. See Kantrowitz, *More Than Freedom: Fighting for Citizenship in a White Republic, 1829–1889* (New York: Penguin Books, 2013), 361–62.

8. David W. Blight, *Frederick Douglass: Prophet of Freedom* (New York: Simon and Schuster, 2018), 343.

9. Blight, 345; Frederick Douglass, *Narrative of the Life of Frederick Douglass* (Boston: Anti-Slavery Office, 1845), 1.

10. Frederick Douglass, *Life and Times of Frederick Douglass* (Boston: De Wolfe and Fiske, 1892), 410–11.

11. Blight, *Frederick Douglass*, 385; Frederick Douglass, "Men of Color, to Arms!," broadside, Rochester, March 21, 1863, University of Rochester Frederick Douglass Project.

12. Blight, *Frederick Douglass*, 385.

13. John David Smith, *Lincoln and the U.S. Colored Troops* (Carbondale: Southern Illinois University Press, 2013), 61–62.

14. Gerrit Smith, "Denying Suffrage Even to Soldiers," *Liberator*, May 1, 1863, 3.

15. John David Smith, "Let Us All Be Grateful That We Have Colored Troops That Will Fight," in *Black Soldiers in Blue: African American Troops in the Civil War Era*, ed. John David Smith (Chapel Hill: University of North Carolina Press, 2002), 49.

16. William P. Woodlin, "Diary of an African American Soldier in 8th Regiment United States Colored Troops, Company G," May 6 and 7, 1864, Gilder Lehrman Collection no. GLC06599, New York.

17. "Soldier's Pay," *Harper's Weekly*, January 9, 1864, 18.

18. Smith, "Let Us All Be Grateful That We Have Colored Troops That Will Fight," 51.

19. An Act Making Appropriations for the Support of the Army for the Year Ending the Thirtieth June, Eighteen Hundred and Sixty-Five, and for Other Purposes, 13 Stat. 129 (1864).

20. *Autobiography of James L. Smith, Including, Also, Reminiscences of Slave Life, Recollections of the War, Education of Freedmen, Causes of the Exodus, etc.* (Norwich, CT: Press of the Bulletin, 1881), ix.

21. "Observer," Twenty-Second US Colored Infantry, Chapel Point, MD, May 13, 1865, *Christian Recorder*, May 27, 1865, in *A Grand Army of Black Men: Letters from African-American Soldiers in the Union Army, 1861–1865*, ed. Edwin S. Redkey (Cambridge: Cambridge University Press, 1992), 264–65.

22. "Observer," 265.

23. Elsie Freeman, Wynell Burroughs Schamel, and Jean West, "The Fight for Equal Rights: A Recruiting Poster for Black Soldiers in the Civil War," *Social Education* 56, no. 2 (February 1992): 118–20.

24. Chulhee Lee, "Socioeconomic Differences in the Health of Black Union Soldiers during the American Civil War," *Social Science History* 33, no. 4 (2009): 430.

25. J. David Hacker, "Recounting the Dead," *New York Times*, September 20, 2011.

26. Private Richard McDaniel, Co. G, Eleventh US Colored Heavy Artillery, Donaldsonville, LA, June 25, 1865, *Weekly Anglo-African*, July 26, 1865, in Redkey, *A Grand Army of Black Men*, 268.

27. Trevor K. Plante, "Buffalo Soldiers and Black Infantrymen," *Prologue Magazine* 33, no. 1 (2001).

28. See Holly A. Pinheiro Jr., *The Families' Civil War* (Athens: University of Georgia Press, 2022).

29. Sergeant Richard Etheridge and Wm Benson to General Howard, c. May or June 1865, Office of the Assistant Commissioner of North Carolina, letters received, record group 105, series 2453, microfilm 843, reel 16, National Archives, Washington, DC.

30. Gregory P. Downs, *After Appomattox: Military Occupation and the Ends of War* (Cambridge, MA: Harvard University Press, 2015), 143.

31. William A. Dobak, *Freedom by the Sword: The U.S. Colored Troops, 1862–1867* (New York: Skyhorse, 2013), 464.

32. Andrew F. Lang, *In the Wake of War: Military Occupation, Emancipation, and Civil War America* (Baton Rouge: Louisiana State University Press, 2017), 199.

33. Gabriel J. Chin, "The 'Voting Rights Act of 1867': The Constitutionality of Federal Regulation of Suffrage during Reconstruction," *North Carolina Law Review* 82, no. 5 (2004): 1582.

34. Downs, *After Appomattox*, 216–17.

35. "Robert Smalls," American Battlefield Trust (website), accessed October 5, 2023.

36. Laura M. Towne, diary entry, November 6, 1878, in *Letters and Diary of Laura M. Towne*, ed. Rupert Sargent Holland (Cambridge, MA: Riverside Press, 1912), 289.

37. Towne, 290, 291.

38. Downs, *After Appomattox*, 242.

39. Plante, "Buffalo Soldiers and Black Infantrymen"; James N. Leiker, "Black Soldiers at Fort Hays, Kansas, 1867–1869: A Study in Civilian and Military Violence," *Great Plains Quarterly* 17, no. 1 (1997): 5.

40. Leiker, "Black Soldiers at Fort Hays," 4.

41. Plante, "Buffalo Soldiers and Black Infantrymen."

42. Final statement and pay voucher for Abraham Hill, Tenth Cavalry, September 12, 1872, Gilder Lehrman Collection no. GLC07334.01, New York; Leiker, "Black Soldiers at Fort Hays," 7.

43. Dobak, *Freedom by the Sword*, 504; Andre Fleche, "United States Colored Troops, The," *Encyclopedia Virginia* (online), posted December 7, 2020.

44. "Diary for 1868 of Samuel K. Thompson," July 20, 1868, Gilder Lehrman Collection no. GLC09357.02.

45. W. Thornton Parker, "The Evolution of the Colored Soldier," *North American Review* 168, no. 507 (1899): 223–24.

46. Frank N. Schubert, "Black Soldiers on the White Frontier: Some Factors Influencing Race Relation," *Phylon* 32, no. 4 (1971): 412.

47. John F. Guilfoyle, first lieutenant, Ninth Cavalry, orders no. 1, in *Voices of the Buffalo Soldier: Records, Reports, and Recollections of Military Life and Service in the West*, by Frank N. Schubert (Albuquerque: University of New Mexico Press, 2003), 164.

48. Schubert, 36, 139, 164.

49. Sergeant Emanuel Stance, Co. F, Ninth Cavalry, to adjutant general of the US Army, July 24, 1870, in Schubert, 38.

50. Parker, "The Evolution of the Colored Soldier," 228.

51. "USS *Maine* Memorial (Mast of the Maine)," Arlington National Cemetery (website), accessed October 5, 2023.

52. For examples of editorials in the Black press from 1898, see "Buffalo Soldiers and the Spanish-American War," National Park Service (website), last updated February 9, 2022.

53. Frank W. Pullen Jr., "'A Perfect Hailstorm of Bullets': A Black Sergeant Remembers the Battle of San Juan Hill in 1899," *History Matters: The U.S. Survey Course on the Web*, George Mason University (website), accessed October 5, 2023.

54. David Omahen, "Black Americans in the US Military from the American Revolution

to the Korean War: The Spanish American War and the Philippine Insurgency," New York State Military Museum and Veterans Research Center (website), accessed October 5, 2023.

55. Sherri Charleston, "Black Soldiers in Cuba and Puerto Rico," in *The New Encyclopedia of Southern Culture*, vol. 24, *Race*, ed. Thomas C. Holt and Laurie B. Green (Chapel Hill: University of North Carolina Press, 2013), 191.

56. "Buffalo Soldiers and the Spanish-American War," National Park Service (website), last updated February 9, 2022.

57. Edward A. Johnson, *History of Negro Soldiers in the Spanish-American War, and Other Items of Interest* (Raleigh, NC: Capital Printing, 1899).

58. Treaty of Peace between the United States and Spain, December 10, 1898, available online through the Avalon Project, Yale Law School, Lillian Goldman Law Library.

59. Charleston, "Black Soldiers in Cuba and Puerto Rico," 192.

60. Thomas J. Morgan, "Epaulets or Chevrons?," *Independent* 50, no. 2587 (1898): 6.

61. "The Negro at the Front," *Philadelphia Press*, reprinted in *News and Citizen*, August 10, 1898, 2.

62. "The Hard Fate of the Negro," *Zion's Herald* 76, no. 44 (November 1898): 1387.

63. Colored National League, open letter to President McKinley, 1899, cited in Frank Putnam, "The Negro's Part in New National Problems," *Colored American*, June 1900, repr. in *African American Political Thought*, vol. 3, *Capitalism vs. Collectivism: The Colonial Era to 1945*, ed. Marcus D. Pohlmann (Milton Park, Abingdon: Taylor and Francis, 2003), 33.

64. "A Black Man Now Heads the Air Force. It's Progress, but Military Brass Remains Starkly White," editorial, *Washington Post*, June 13, 2020.

65. "Notable & Quotable: Gen. Charles Q. Brown," *Wall Street Journal*, June 9, 2020.

Chapter 4

Many thanks are due to the editors of this volume, Lesley J. Gordon and Andrew J. Huebner, for the opportunity to participate in the 2019 University of Alabama military history symposium, "Race and Gender Explorations: War and Military Service in 19th and 20th Century America," which led to the creation of this chapter, and for their expert and helpful feedback throughout its completion. This symposium led me to develop one of my major arguments regarding my research findings and sent me in new directions that continue to shape my work. I also wish to thank W. Fitzhugh Brundage, Joseph T. Glatthaar, William Barney, Caroline Janney, and Thavolia Glymph for their feedback and support, particularly during the COVID-19 pandemic, as I developed this argument. Lastly, I wish to thank Paul Quigley, Melanie Kiechle, Rachel Midura, Holly A. Pinheiro Jr., Lorien Foote, and Jaime Amanda Martinez for their support, friendship, and guidance over the last several years. I am forever grateful for and awed by their generosity.

1. C. C. Washburn to N. B. Forrest, June 19, 1864, in *The War of the Rebellion: A Compilation of the Official Records of the Union and Confederate Armies*, ser. 1, vol. 23, pt. 1 (Washington, DC: Government Printing Office, 1899), 588. The chapter epigraph is reproduced from the Compiled Military Service Records (CMSR), Records of the Adjutant General's Office, 1780s–1917, record group 94, National Archives, Washington, DC.

2. C. C. Washburn to S. D. Lee, June 17, 1864, in *The War of the Rebellion*, ser. 1, vol. 32, pt. 1 (1891), 587.

3. N. B. Forrest to C. C. Washburn, June 23, 1864, in *The War of the Rebellion*, ser. 1, vol. 32, pt. 1, 590–91 (emphasis added); see also Eleventh US Colored Infantry, CMSR; William F. Fox, *Regimental Losses in the American Civil War, 1861–1865: A Treatise on the Extent and Nature of the Mortuary Losses in the Union Regiments, with Full and Exhaustive Statistics Compiled from the Official Records on File in the State Military Bureaus and at Washington* (Albany, NY: Albany, 1898), 54; John Cimprich and Robert C. Mainfort Jr., "The Fort Pillow Massacre: A Statistical Note," *Journal of American History* 76, no. 3 (December 1989): 836.

4. Joan E. Cashin, "Trophies of War: Material Culture in the Civil War Era," *Journal of the Civil War Era* 1, no. 2 (September 2011): 341.

5. Mark Grimsley, *The Hard Hand of War: Union Military Policy toward Southern Civilians* (New York: Cambridge University Press, 1995), 120–44.

6. *Laws for the Army and Navy of the Confederate States* (Richmond, VA: Ritchie and Dunnavant, 1861); *Regulations for the Army of the Confederate States and for the Quartermaster's Department and Pay Department* (Richmond, VA: Ritchie and Dunnavant, 1861); Cashin, "Trophies of War," 341.

7. Edward Baptist, "The Absent Subject: African American Masculinity and Forced Migration to the Antebellum Plantation Frontier," in *Southern Manhood: Perspectives on Masculinity in the Old South* (Athens: University of Georgia Press, 2004), 139. Baptist notes that "resistance" has often "served as a code word for manhood" in discussions of antebellum Black manhood.

8. LeeAnn Whites, *Gender Matters: Civil War, Reconstruction, and the Making of the New South* (New York: Palgrave MacMillan, 2005), 21.

9. Daniel P. Black, *Dismantling Black Manhood: An Historical and Literary Analysis of the Legacy of Slavery* (New York: Routledge, 1997), 3; Sergio Lussana, "To See Who Was Best on the Plantation: Enslaved Fighting Contests and Masculinity in the Antebellum Plantation South," *Journal of Southern History* 76, no. 4 (November 2010): 901–22; Joseph Armengol, *Masculinities in Black and White: Manliness (and Whiteness) in African American Literature* (New York: Palgrave Macmillan, 2014), 5; Edward Baptist, *The Half Has Never Been Told: Slavery and the Making of American Capitalism* (New York: Basic Books, 2014), 217.

10. Baptist, "The Absent Subject," 137.

11. Emer de Vattel, *The Law of Nations, or Principles of the Law of Nature, Applied to the Conduct and Affairs of Nations and Sovereigns*, 7th ed., trans. Joseph Chitty (Philadelphia: T. and J. W. Johnson, 1849), 392. Vattel originally wrote this work in 1758; it was published in English for the first time in 1760 and went through several English editions throughout the eighteenth and nineteenth centuries.

12. This number comes from my research into USCT compiled military service records, accessed via Fold3. I identified Black POWs by searching through the individual compiled military service record for every soldier from fifty-one USCT regiments. Seven of these regiments had no confirmed POWs, while forty-four regiments had at least one POW. I also included two adolescents who served as body servants in a white regiment (the Forty-Fourth Massachusetts Volunteer Infantry), and several US sailors who were captured in early 1863 and imprisoned in Charleston, South Carolina, until the end of the war. See Caroline Wood Newhall, "'Under the Rebel Lash': Black Prisoners of War in the Confederate South" (PhD diss., University of North Carolina at Chapel Hill, 2020).

13. N. B. Forrest to C. C. Washburn, June 23, 1864, in *The War of the Rebellion*, ser. 1, vol. 32, pt. 1, 591.

14. Robert C. Ould, "The Exchange of Prisoners," in *The Annals of the War Written by Leading Participants, North and South* (Philadelphia: Times, 1879), 43.

15. J. A. Seddon to R. C. Ould, June 24, 1863, in *The War of the Rebellion*, ser. 2, vol. 6 (1899), 44–45.

16. *Journal of the Congress of the Confederate States of America, 1861–1865*, vol. 6 (Washington, DC: Government Printing Office, 1904–5), 103, 129, 517; "Congress on Saturday," *Weekly Raleigh Register*, February 25, 1863.

17. Armengol, *Masculinities in Black and White*, 7.

18. Joshua R. Giddings, *Payment for Slaves: Speech of Mr. J. R. Giddings, of Ohio, on the Bill to Pay the Heirs of Antonio Pacheco for a Slave Sent West of the Mississippi with the Seminole Indians in 1838. Made in the House of Representatives, Dec. 28, 1848, and Jan. 6, 1849* (Washington, DC: Buell and Blanchard, 1849), 3–4.

19. Jacob D. Wheeler, *A Practical Treatise on the Laws of Slavery* (New York: Allan Pollock Jr., 1837), 233; R. J. M. Blackett, *The Captive's Quest for Freedom: Fugitive Slaves, the 1850 Fugitive Slave Law, and the Politics of Slavery* (New York: Cambridge University Press, 2018), 3–41.

20. John Hope Franklin and Loren Schweninger, *Runaway Slaves: Rebels on the Plantation* (New York: Oxford University Press, 1999), 149; Laura F. Edwards, *A Legal History of the Civil War and Reconstruction: A Nation of Rights* (New York: Cambridge University Press, 2015), 3. Northern states passed personal liberty laws throughout the antebellum period that sought to virtually annul the Fugitive Slave Acts through "positive defiance," an assertion of state sovereignty akin to nullification as enumerated in the Kentucky Resolution of 1799. See Thomas D. Morris, *Free Men All: The Personal Liberty Laws of the North, 1780–1861* (Baltimore, MD: Johns Hopkins University Press, 1974), 179–80. Though the Supreme Court effectively upheld the constitutionality of the Fugitive Slave Act of 1793 in the 1842 case *Prigg v. Pennsylvania*—and that of the Fugitive Slave Act of 1850 in the 1859 case *Ableman v. Booth*—free states continued to fight back against the rulings. See Leon Litwack, *North of Slavery: The Negro in the Free States, 1790–1860* (Chicago: University of Chicago Press, 1961), 250; Morris, *Free Men All*, 127, 179–80; Thomas D. Morris, *Southern Slavery and the Law, 1619–1860* (Chapel Hill: University of North Carolina Press, 1996), 340; Paul Finkelman, ed., *Slavery & the Law* (Madison, WI: Madison House, 1997), 147–48. Indeed, proslavery politicians cited northern states' attempts to circumvent the Fugitive Slave Acts as a primary reason for secession. See Morris, *Free Men All*, 1.

21. James A. Seddon, *Report of the Secretary of War, Richmond, November 3, 1864* (Richmond, VA: Confederate States of America War Department, 1864), 7. Lorien Foote argues that the Civil War was itself a "crisis of civilization" in which the United States and the Confederacy sought to portray the other as savage and itself as civilized. Key to this process were the ways in which both sides exhibited restraint and used retaliation in the wake of alleged atrocities. Confederates, for example, declared the mere presence of Black US soldiers on fields of combat to be an atrocity. White Americans generally presumed that Black people "did not possess self-control and restraint, which were essential characteristics of civilized war," a stereotype that Confederates wielded to accuse the United States of violating accepted principles of warfare by arming Black men and giving them sanction to kill white people. Foote's

work covers many of the examples laid out in this essay, but her focus is on US policy in anticipation of and response to Confederates' actions in South Carolina, Georgia, and Florida, while my focus is on Confederate policy throughout the entirety of the territory claimed by the Confederacy. See Lorien Foote, *Rites of Retaliation: Civilization, Soldiers, and Campaigns in the American Civil War* (Chapel Hill: University of North Carolina Press, 2021), 4, 44.

22. J. A. Seddon to R. C. Ould, June 24, 1863, in *The War of the Rebellion*, ser. 2, vol. 6, 43.

23. Wayne E. Lee, *Barbarians and Brothers: Anglo-American Warfare, 1500–1865* (New York: Oxford University Press, 2011), 233.

24. Lee, 233. West Point, the US Military Academy, was established in 1802 and "modeled its curriculum on the French École Polytechnique, stressing professionalism . . . engineering, and honor. . . . West Point's culture inculcated a certain formality in its students that would later manifest itself in the larger Civil War surrender ceremonies . . . war ought to be fought according to civilized and orderly principles." David Silkenat, *Raising the White Flag: How Surrender Defined the American Civil War* (Chapel Hill: University of North Carolina Press, 2019), 9; see also Michael Howard, George J. Andreopoulos, and Mark R. Shulman, eds., *The Laws of War: Constraints on Warfare in the Western World* (New Haven, CT: Yale University Press, 1994); John Grenier, *The First Way of War: American War Making on the Frontier, 1607–1814* (Cambridge: Cambridge University Press, 2005).

25. Lee, *Barbarians and Brothers*, 4. A reprisal is a limited and deliberate violation of international laws to punish another sovereign state that has already broken them. See Foote, *Rites of Retaliation*, 4, 6, 11, 13, 70.

26. Vattel, *The Law of Nations*, 153–54, 346–57.

27. US Department of State, *Message from the President of the United States, Transmitting Documents Relative to the Execution of the First Article of the Late Treaty between the United States and Great Britain* (Washington, DC: William A. Davis, 1817); Benjamin Quarles, *The Negro in the American Revolution* (Chapel Hill: University of North Carolina Press, 1961), 90, 138, 157, 169, 171; Don E. Fehrenbacher, *The Slaveholding Republic: An Account of the United States Government's Relations to Slavery* (New York: Oxford University Press, 2001), 216, 231–32; Alan Taylor, *The Internal Enemy: Slavery and War in Virginia, 1772–1832* (New York: W. W. Norton, 2013), 28, 429–35; Giddings, *Payment for Slaves*.

28. Vattel, *The Law of Nations*, 394–95.

29. The nineteenth-century jurist Henry Wheaton discussed slavery in his works, notably *History of the Law of Nations*, but confined his discussion to issues of the slave trade and the people enforcing slavery. Enslaved people themselves did not figure into his analysis of the main issues surrounding diplomacy on the high seas and in courts of law. Enslaved people were objects, not subjects. See Wheaton, *History of the Law of Nations in Europe and America* (New York: Gould, Banks, 1845), 45, 92, 490; Wheaton, *Elements of International Law* (Philadelphia: Lea and Blanchard, 1846), 653. See also John K. Thornton, "African Dimensions of the Stono Rebellion," *American Historical Review* 96, no. 4 (October 1991): 1101–13; Manuel Barcia, *West African Warfare in Bahia and Cuba: Soldier Slaves in the Atlantic World, 1807–1844* (New York: Oxford University Press, 2016); Vincent Brown, *Tacky's Revolt: The Story of an Atlantic Slave War* (Cambridge, MA: Harvard University Press, 2020).

30. According to Geoffrey Parker, in Europe "the combined pressure of continued church censure, the spread of Roman law, and the growing power of the state gradually" led Europeans to define wars by the sixteenth century as "only deemed just when waged by a legitimate

government." Parker, "Early Modern Europe," in Howard, Andreopoulos, and Shulman, *The Laws of War*, 42.

31. Foreign powers such as Britain also expressed concern over American Black men's entry into the war. Confederate ambassadors appealed to British officials' shared concerns of the potential for racial atrocities committed by enslaved Black men against white people in hopes of gaining international support. It almost worked; emissaries nearly convinced the British prime minister, Lord Palmerston, to recognize the Confederacy and intervene in the war in the fall of 1862, based on mutual anxieties and interests in the cotton and wheat trades. Palmerston and others worried that a "servile war" could upset Britain's entire commercial relationship with the United States. Furthermore, in late summer 1862, the United States' repeated defeats at the hands of the Confederacy seemed to indicate that the war would soon conclude in the Confederacy's favor. British observers thus interpreted the 1863 Emancipation Proclamation as a desperate last resort to stave off defeat by introducing a vicious race war. See Joseph T. Glatthaar, *Forged in Battle: The Civil War Alliance of Black Soldiers and White Officers* (New York: Free Press, 1990), 201; Howard Jones, "History and Mythology: The Crisis over British Intervention in the Civil War," in *The Union, the Confederacy, and the Atlantic Rim*, ed. Robert E. May (Gainesville: University Press of Florida, 2014), 50–52.

32. James Oakes, *Freedom National: The Destruction of Slavery in the United States, 1861–1865* (New York: W. W. Norton, 2013), 138–43.

33. Grimsley, *The Hard Hand of War*, 121–27.

34. *Biographical Souvenir of the States of Georgia and Florida: Containing Biographical Sketches of the Representative Public, and Many Early Settled Families in These States* (Chicago: F. A. Battey, 1889), 75–76; Barry Sheehy, Vaughnette Goode-Walker, and Cindy Wallace, *Savannah, Immortal City* (Austin, TX: Emerald Book, 2011), 51, 66, 154–55, 230.

35. I have been unable to identify Manuel, but he may have been a formerly enslaved man on Jacob Waldburg's plantations on Saint Catherines Island, off the coast of Georgia, who was recruited, uniformed, and armed by the US Navy during its operations in the area in spring 1862. See Clarence Mohr, "Before Sherman: Georgia Blacks and the Union War Effort, 1861–1864," *Journal of Southern History* 45, no. 3 (August 1979): 342–43; Russell Duncan, *Freedom's Shore: Tunis Campbell and the Georgia Freemen* (Athens: University of Georgia Press, 1986), 4.

36. H. W. Mercer to T. Jordan, November 14, 1862, in *The War of the Rebellion*, ser. 2, vol. 4 (1899), 945–46.

37. J. A. Seddon to J. Davis, n.d., in *The War of the Rebellion*, ser. 2, vol. 4, 946.

38. P. G. T. Beauregard to J. A. Seddon, November 17, 1862, in *The War of the Rebellion*, ser. 2, vol. 4, 946.

39. J. A. Seddon to P. G. T. Beauregard, November 30, 1862, in *The War of the Rebellion*, ser. 2, vol. 4, 954.

40. James Hamilton, *Negro Plot: An Account of the Late Intended Insurrection among a Portion of the Blacks of the City of Charleston, South Carolina* (Boston: Joseph W. Ingraham, 1822), 50; Thomas Doughty Condy, *A Digest of the Laws of the United States & the State of South-Carolina Now of Force, Relating to the Militia* [. . .] *the Laws of the Government of Slaves and Free Persons of Colour* [. . .] (Charleston, SC: A. E. Miller, 1830), 162; Virginia Writer's Project, *Virginia: A Guide to the Old Dominion* (New York: Oxford University Press, 1992), 78; Walter Johnson, *River of Dark Dreams: Slavery and Empire in the Cotton Kingdom*

(Cambridge, MA: Belknap Press of Harvard University Press, 2013), 240–43; Patrick H. Breen, *The Land Shall Be Deluged in Blood: A New History of the Nat Turner Revolt* (New York: Oxford University Press, 2015), 94.

41. Ariela Gross, "Slavery, Anti-Slavery, and the Coming of the Civil War," in *The Cambridge History of Law in America*, vol. 2, *The Long Nineteenth Century (1789–1920)*, ed. Michael Grossberg and Christopher Tomlins (Cambridge: Cambridge University Press, 2008), 292.

42. William Goodell, *The American Slave Code in Theory and Practice: Its Distinctive Features Shown by Its Statutes, Judicial Decisions, and Illustrative Facts* (New York: American and Foreign Anti-Slavery Society, 1853), 36–37, 39, 309.

43. J. A. Seddon to P. G. T. Beauregard, November 30, 1862, in *The War of the Rebellion*, ser. 2, vol. 4, 954; see also Daniel J. Flanigan, "Criminal Procedure in Slave Trials in the Antebellum South," *Journal of Southern History* 40, no. 4 (November 1974): 537–64.

44. Guerrillas—irregular combatants who did not operate in uniforms that marked them as combatants and who did not observe the rules of engagement—were not subject to the protection of the laws of war and could therefore be summarily executed without retaliation or reprisal. They could not become POWs, and thus were not subject to protections accorded enemy combatants. Disagreements over whether people were guerrillas could sow seeds of conflict, however. See General Orders, no. 100, 1863, art. 82–85; Daniel E. Sutherland, *A Savage Conflict: The Decisive Role of Guerrillas in the Civil War* (Chapel Hill: University of North Carolina Press, 2009), 33, 64; Joseph M. Belein Jr. and Matthew Hulbert, *The Civil War Guerrilla: Unfolding the Black Flag in History, Memory, and Myth* (Lexington: University Press of Kentucky, 2015), 23–24, 31.

45. Jones, "History and Mythology," 46–56.

46. J. A. Seddon to P. G. T. Beauregard, November 30, 1862, in *The War of the Rebellion*, ser. 2, vol. 4, 954.

47. J. A. Seddon to J. H. Forney, December 13, 1862, in *The War of the Rebellion*, ser. 2, vol. 4, 954; Colin E. Woodward, *Marching Masters: Slavery, Race, and the Confederate Army during the Civil War* (Charlottesville: University of Virginia Press, 2014), 133–34; George C. Burkhardt, *Confederate Rage, Yankee Wrath: No Quarter in the Civil War* (Carbondale: Southern Illinois University Press, 2007), 46. On November 8, 1862, Alabama colonel John F. Tattnall had consulted his commanding officer, Captain S. Croom, on what to do with Black men captured in arms alongside white US troops. Croom passed the inquiry on to Forney, who held ultimate military authority in that department. Forney's response has been interpreted as a blanket approval for giving no quarter to Black soldiers: he recommended hanging captured Black soldiers rather than shooting them, "a punishment he apparently deemed more appropriate for traitors and spies." Forney included a caveat, however, that guilt needed to be determined first, and that "when force has been used to make a captured negro" serve as a guide in any way, "the same guilt is not involved." Forney thus made allowances for some process of determining coercion that could prevent indiscriminate killings. Seddon's instructions to Forney and Beauregard only a few weeks later emphasized similar practices of discretion. See Ira Berlin, Joseph P. Reidy, and Leslie S. Rowland, eds., *The Black Military Experience* (Cambridge: Cambridge University Press, 1982), 570–71.

48. Jones, "History and Mythology," 50–52; Foote, *Rites of Retaliation*, 5–6, 72, 97–98.

49. General Orders, no. 100, 1863, art. 42–43 (emphasis added).

50. General Orders, no. 100, 1863, art. 43; see also Foote, *Rites of Retaliation*, 70–71. President Lincoln initially rejected Major General Benjamin Butler's 1861 treatment of refugees from slavery as contraband of war, given the implications of treating the Confederacy as a legitimate entity. Though the United States treated Confederate soldiers, for all intents and purposes, as legitimate combatants in consideration of postwar conflict resolution, it never recognized the Confederacy in any way other than as an insurrectionary power violating the Constitution. See Grimsley, *The Hard Hand of War*, 8–11.

51. Seventy-eight percent of the 180,000 US Colored Troops hailed from slave states. See Frederick H. Dyer, *A Compendium of the War of the Rebellion* (Des Moines, IA: Dyer, 1908), 11.

52. General Orders (CSA), no. 111, 1862, art. 3, in *The War of the Rebellion*, ser. 2, vol. 5 (1899), 797 (emphasis added). Davis's proclamation not only addressed the issue of Black soldiers, but also declared Major General Butler (then commanding the Union forces occupying New Orleans) and his officers to be criminals rather than combatants. These white soldiers would, like Black soldiers, be subjected to criminal processes and face execution rather than military imprisonment.

53. Aaron Sheehan-Dean, *The Calculus of Violence: How Americans Fought the Civil War* (Cambridge, MA: Harvard University Press, 2018), 4. For examples of historians' interpretations of General Order no. 111 as a directive designed to encourage executions, see Lonnie Speer, *Portals to Hell: Military Prisons of the Civil War* (Mechanicsburg, PA: Stackpole Books, 1997), 107–18; Howard Westwood, "Captive Black Union Soldiers in Charleston: What to Do?," in *Black Flag over Dixie: Racial Atrocities and Reprisals in the Civil War*, ed. Gregory J. W. Urwin (Carbondale: Southern Illinois University Press, 2005), 35–36; Burkhardt, *Confederate Rage, Yankee Wrath*, 41, 46–47, 205.

54. Burkhardt, *Confederate Rage, Yankee Wrath*, 46–47.

55. Indeed, Davis's order did not explicitly or implicitly recommend execution for Black soldiers, doing so only for certain white soldiers. Davis targeted Major General Butler and the white commissioned officers under his command for inciting slave insurrection and, as such, called for them to be treated as "robbers and criminals deserving death." Similarly, any white officers found leading "armed slaves in insurrection" were to be executed. "Armed slaves," on the other hand, were to be captured and delivered to state authorities. Davis thus provided an official statement that denied Black soldiers' status as legitimate combatants, rendered them property, and placed them under states' control, but did not explicitly recommend execution as he did for certain white officers. General Orders (CSA), no. 111, 1862, art. 1 and 4, in *The War of the Rebellion*, ser. 2, vol. 5, 797.

56. Section 9 of the Fugitive Slave Act of 1850 states that "it shall be the duty of the officer making the arrest to retain such fugitive in his custody, and to remove him to the State whence he fled, and there to deliver him to said claimant, his agent, or attorney."

57. C. Miller to G. Welles, March 13, 1864, in *The War of the Rebellion*, ser. 2, vol. 7 (1899), 93. One of Miller's fellow POWs smuggled out this note.

58. See, in *The War of the Rebellion*, W. Ludlow to R. Ould, July 15, 1863, ser. 2, vol. 6, 121; E. M. Stanton to E. A. Hitchcock, August 8, 1863, ser. 2, vol. 6, 188; W. Ludlow to L. Thomas, May 30, 1863, ser. 2, vol. 5, 721; see also report of S. P. Lee to G. Welles, February 21, 1863, in *Official Records of the Union and Confederate Navies in the War of the Rebellion*, ser. 1, vol. 8 (Washington, DC: Government Printing Office, 1899), 543; S. P. Lee to G. Welles, January 31, 1863, in *Official Records of the Union and Confederate Navies*, ser. 1, vol. 13 (1901), 563.

59. On January 5, 1863, following on the heels of the official Emancipation Proclamation, Davis declared that "on and after February 22, 1863, all free negroes within the limits of the Southern Confederacy shall be placed on the slave status, and be deemed to be chattels, they and their issue forever." Free Black people captured in the free states would also be rendered slaves under the laws of the Confederacy. As demonstrated by General Lee's forces in Pennsylvania leading up to the Gettysburg campaign in July 1863, the Confederacy sought to return all Black people to a state of racialized chattel slavery. See Erwin L. Jordan, *Black Confederates and Afro-Yankees in Civil War Virginia* (Charlottesville: University of Virginia Press, 1995), 320.

60. J. L. Barbour to A. Lincoln, April 11, 1863, in *The War of the Rebellion*, ser. 2, vol. 5, 469–70. See also, in the same volume, C. B. Burrell to E. W. Quincy, March 2, 1863, 455; E. A. Hitchcock to E. M. Stanton, April 14, 1863, 484.

61. See, in *The War of the Rebellion*, H. Ware to A. G. Browne, April 8, 1863, ser. 2, vol. 5, 455; J. Barbour to A. Lincoln, April 11, 1863, ser. 2, vol. 5, 469; E. R. S. Canby to J. A. Andrew, April 15, 1863, ser. 2, vol. 5, 484; E. A. Hitchcock to J. A. Andrew, May 31, 1865, ser. 2, vol. 8 (1899), 586–87; H. Ware to E. A. Hitchcock, June 2, 1865, ser. 2, vol. 8, 633–34; E. A. Hitchcock to E. R. S. Canby, June 5, 1865, ser. 2, vol. 8, 640; H. Ware to E. A. Hitchcock, June 7, 1865, ser. 2, vol. 8, 646.

62. Linda Barnickel, *Milliken's Bend: A Civil War Battle in History and Memory* (Baton Rouge: Louisiana State University Press, 2013), 111.

63. Historian William A. Dobak asserts that eighty enlisted men from the Forty-Sixth USCI were captured at Mound Plantation on June 30. He finds that eight escaped, eight died in captivity, and twenty-two returned to the regiment. The remaining forty-two did not return; see Dobak, *Freedom by the Sword: The U.S. Colored Troops, 1862–1867* (Washington, DC: Center of Military History, 2011), 187–88. I have identified 103 men from the Forty-Sixth USCI who appear to have survived capture long enough to be noted as POWs, which aligns with the claim that perhaps a dozen of 113 men from the Forty-Sixth perished shortly after capture. Historian Linda Barnickel dedicates an entire chapter to parsing out the fates of POWs from the Forty-Sixth and Forty-Ninth USCI after their captures, and suggests that as many as 128 men were captured on June 30. See Barnickel, *Milliken's Bend*, 124.

64. Barnickel, *Milliken's Bend*, 123.

65. Soldier's certificate (SC) 1.071.808, Private Daniel Govan (a.k.a. Robinson), Co. E, Forty-Sixth USCI, Case Files of Approved Veterans Who Served in the Army and Navy in the Civil War and the War with Spain, 1861–1934 (CFAV), Records of the Veterans Administration, record group 15, National Archives, Washington, DC.

66. SC 413.772, Private Cy Taylor, Co. I, Forty-Ninth USCI, CFAV (emphasis added).

67. J. A. Seddon to M. L. Bonham, August 31, 1864, in *The War of the Rebellion*, ser. 2, vol. 7, 703–4.

68. M. L. Bonham to P. G. T. Beauregard, July 22, 1863, in *The War of the Rebellion*, ser. 2, vol. 6, 139.

69. General Orders (CSA), no. 111, 1862, art. 3, in *The War of the Rebellion*, ser. 2, vol. 5, 797 (emphasis added). For an in-depth examination of this correspondence, see Westwood, "Captive Black Union Soldiers in Charleston," 34–50.

70. M. L. Bonham to P. G. T. Beauregard, July 22, 1863, in *The War of the Rebellion*, ser. 2, vol. 6, 139–40.

71. See, in *The War of the Rebellion*, M. L. Bonham to J. A. Seddon, July 23, 1863, ser. 2, vol. 6, 145; M. L. Bonham to J. A. Seddon, August 10, 1863, ser. 2, vol. 6, 193; J. A. Seddon to J. Davis, August 14, 1863, ser. 2, vol. 6, 193.

72. J. A. Seddon to J. Davis, August 23, 1863, in *The War of the Rebellion*, ser. 2, vol. 6, 194.

73. On May 1, 1863, the Confederate Congress adopted a joint resolution signed by Davis that upheld Davis's initial proclamation of December 1862 and clarified how to handle issues of prewar status among Black POWs and which state authorities should have authority over them. The resolution declared that "all negroes and mulattoes who shall be engaged in war or be taken in arms against the Confederate States . . . shall when captured . . . be delivered to the authorities of the State or States in which they shall be captured to be dealt with according to the present or future law of said States." See *The War of the Rebellion*, ser. 2, vol. 5, 940. Interestingly, the Congress inadvertently associated Black soldiers' actions with legitimate warfare by using the phrase "engaged in war . . . against the Confederate States." I have not found any other instances thus far in which Black soldiers' actions are described in this way.

74. J. Davis to J. A. Seddon, August 25, 1863, in *The War of the Rebellion*, ser. 2, vol. 6, 194 (emphasis added).

75. Westwood, "Captive Black Union Soldiers in Charleston," 40; see also, in *The War of the Rebellion*, J. A. Seddon to M. L. Bonham, August 31, 1864, ser. 2, vol. 7, 703–4; General Orders, no. 111, 1862, ser. 2, vol. 5, 797; M. L. Bonham to P. G. T. Beauregard, July 22, 1863, ser. 2, vol. 6, 139–40; M. L. Bonham to J. A. Seddon, July 23, 1863, ser. 2, vol. 6, 145; M. L. Bonham to J. A. Seddon, August 10, 1863, ser. 2, vol. 6, 193; J. A. Seddon to J. Davis, August 14, 1863, ser. 2, vol. 6, 193; J. A. Seddon to J. Davis, August 23, 1863, ser. 2, vol. 6, 194; J. Davis to J. A. Seddon, August 25, 1863, ser. 2, vol. 6, 194; J. A. Seddon to M. L. Bonham, September 1, 1863, ser. 2, vol. 6, 246.

76. J. A. Seddon to M. L. Bonham, September 1, 1863, in *The War of the Rebellion*, ser. 2, vol. 6, 246 (emphasis added).

77. Westwood, "Captive Black Union Soldiers in Charleston," 41–46.

78. E. K. Smith to R. Taylor, June 13, 1863, in *The War of the Rebellion*, ser. 2, vol. 6, 21–22. Per Seddon's instructions of November 30, 1862, Smith was the military authority entrusted with deciding Black troops' fate in battle, as the commander of the geographic department in which Taylor operated. Although Taylor had on June 8 informed Smith's chief of staff, Brigadier General William R. Boggs, that Taylor's men had "unfortunately" captured fifty Black troops and two officers, it seems that this report (and request for instructions) failed to reach Smith before June 13. The fundamental issue Smith laid out for Taylor was not that Taylor had taken Black POWs alive (though Smith was certainly frustrated by that outcome), but rather that Taylor was still holding them under his authority nearly a week after the battle. Smith had been confronted by Governor Thomas O. Moore about Taylor's Black POWs. The governor, as the executive authority of the state of Louisiana (where the Black soldiers were taken captive), demanded that Taylor immediately remit any Black POWs in his possession to the attorney general to begin the process of prosecuting them under civil law. It appears that Taylor's seeming failure to inform Smith about the capture of the Black POWs had embarrassed Smith in front of the governor. Smith appears to have been reprimanding Taylor for keeping Black POWs under military authority rather than forwarding them to the Louisiana governor.

79. H. L. Clay to E. K. Smith, July 13, 1863, in *The War of the Rebellion*, ser. 2, vol. 6, 115.

80. J. A. Seddon to E. K. Smith, August 12, 1863, in *The War of the Rebellion*, ser. 1, vol.

22, pt. 2 (1888), 965 (emphasis added). For further discussion of the treatment of white officers of Black regiments, see James G. Hollandsworth, "The Execution of White Officers from Black Units by Confederate Forces during the Civil War," *Louisiana History* 35, no. 4 (Autumn 1994): 475–89. Despite Seddon's argument regarding white officers of Black regiments, nearly every white USCT officer positively identified as a POW survived captivity and was paroled and exchanged. Out of twenty-seven USCT regiments surveyed for white officer mortality, twenty-five had survival rates of 100 percent among white POWs.

81. See, in *The War of the Rebellion*, E. K. Owen to D. Porter, June 16, 1863, ser. 1, vol. 24, pt. 3, 425; R. Taylor to U. S. Grant, June 27, 1863, ser. 1, vol. 24, pt. 3, 443; U. S. Grant to R. Taylor, July 4, 1863, ser. 1, vol. 24, pt. 3, 469; G. Andrews to J. Logan, August 5, 1863, ser. 2, vol. 6, 177; see also Westwood, "Captive Black Union Soldiers in Charleston," 36. Why Seddon felt that executing white USCT officers would not invite retaliation was not made clear.

82. General Orders, no. 252, 1863, in *The War of the Rebellion*, ser. 2, vol. 6, 163. As early as August 8, 1863, US officials placed Confederate POWs in conditions like those of Black POWs whose treatment had been communicated to them, including placing three men in close confinement as a response to the imprisonment of the three Black sailors from the *Isaac Smith*. See E. M. Stanton to E. A. Hitchcock, August 8, 1863, in *The War of the Rebellion*, ser. 2, vol. 6, 187–88. Major General Butler placed Confederate soldiers into hard labor in October 1864 as retaliation for reports that Black soldiers were laboring on Confederate fortifications in their uniforms and while under threat of fire from the United States. See B. Butler to R. Ould, October 12, 1864, in *The War of the Rebellion*, ser. 2, vol. 7, 876. Lorien Foote argues, however, that the retaliatory order was only as forceful as the Lincoln administration's willingness to implement it, and that the administration's "inaction" in the wake of atrocities against Black soldiers in February and April 1864 "contributed to the subsequent escalation of violence between white Confederate soldiers and Black Union soldiers and their officers." Ultimately, Foote argues, the war "became more brutal because Black Union soldiers and white Confederates were no longer willing to surrender to each other." See Foote, *Rites of Retaliation*, 138.

83. See, in *The War of the Rebellion*, U. S. Grant to R. Taylor, June 22, 1863, ser. 1, vol. 24, pt. 3, 425; R. Taylor to U. S. Grant, June 27, 1863, ser. 1, vol. 24, pt. 3, 443–44; U. S. Grant to R. Taylor, July 4, 1863, ser. 1, vol. 24, pt. 3, 469.

84. See, in *The War of the Rebellion*, J. Logan to B. S. Ewell, September 3, 1863, ser. 2, vol. 6, 258; N. Warren to J. Griffith, September 2, 1863, ser. 2, vol. 6, 258–59; J. E. Johnston to S. D. Lee, August 31, 1863, ser. 1, vol. 30, pt. 4 (1890), 573.

85. M. L. Bonham to J. A. Seddon, June 24, 1864, in *The War of the Rebellion*, ser. 2, vol. 7, 409.

86. J. A. Seddon to M. L. Bonham, August 31, 1864, in *The War of the Rebellion*, ser. 2, vol. 7, 703–4. The Confederate Congress passed the statute in question "to protect the rights of owners of slaves taken by or employed in the army." The act enumerated a system of five depots for each Confederate state wherein (re)captured enslaved people would be housed, and from which they could be reclaimed by their enslavers. Long-standing practices for reclaiming escaped enslaved people were to be used. Descriptions and names of the enslaved people were to be "advertised in each State, in one or more newspapers of general circulation." Furthermore, Congress allowed the military to use the people held at these depots as a labor pool until enslavers arrived to reclaim them. While "such slaves are in depot, they may be employed,

under proper guard, on public works" if they remained in the depot for a month after first advertised without being reclaimed. An Act to Protect the Rights of Owners of Slaves Taken by or Employed in the Army, 1862, c. 62 (CSA). These slave depots were used throughout the war to house and distribute recaptured enslaved people, including several Black POWs, though they were not originally intended to house Black combatants. General Orders (CSA), no. 25, 1863, in *The War of the Rebellion*, ser. 2, vol. 5, 844. The depots were established in Richmond, Petersburg, and Dublin Station, Virginia; Raleigh, North Carolina; Columbia, South Carolina; Macon and Decatur, Georgia; Notasulga and Talladega, Alabama; Tallahassee, Florida; Brookhaven and Enterprise, Mississippi; Monroe, Camp Moore, and New Iberia, Louisiana; Houston, Texas; Knoxville and McMinnville, Tennessee; and Little Rock, Arkansas. The McMinnville depot was later moved to Chattanooga. See B. Bragg to S. Cooper, May 24, 1863, in *The War of the Rebellion*, ser. 1, vol. 23, pt. 2 (1889), 850.

87. J. A. Seddon to M. L. Bonham, August 31, 1864, in *The War of the Rebellion*, ser. 2, vol. 7, 703–4. Lorien Foote argues that Confederate policy toward Black prisoners became "an inconsistent mess . . . once the government veered away from its plans of state trials for all of them" and that the "presence of Black soldiers at Andersonville" beginning in February 1864 "legitimized them as combatants" on both sides of the war. Foote, *Rites of Retaliation*, 132–33.

88. M. L. Bonham to J. A. Seddon, June 24, 1864, in *The War of the Rebellion*, ser. 2, vol. 7, 409. I was unable to locate any editions of Richmond newspapers that contained these notices.

89. "Local Matters," *Richmond Dispatch*, August 27, 1864. Butler also cited a notice found in the *Richmond Examiner*, October 11, 1864, that listed at least two Black POWs from the Twenty-Third USCI among a group of Black men liable for reclamation; B. Butler to R. Ould, October 12, 1864, in *The War of the Rebellion*, ser. 2, vol. 7, 970.

90. Private Peter Austin, Co. C, Twenty-Third USCI, CMSR. Reuben L. Gordon of Orange was a farmer who held twenty-two enslaved people in bondage in 1860. The son of General William Fitzhugh Gordon, a veteran of the War of 1812 and former member of the US House of Representatives, Reuben had inherited his wealth in land and slaves. In December 1863, however, Gordon's house was burned down by General George Meade's forces. See the entry for Reuben L. Gordon in the 1860 US Census, Orange County, Virginia, slave schedule, p. 6, US National Archives and Records Administration microfilm M653, roll 1395; "Ravages of the Enemy When Last This Side of the Rapidan," *Richmond Dispatch*, December 11, 1863.

91. Private Levi Green, Co. G, Seventh USCI, CMSR; Private Samuel Green, Co. I, Twenty-Third USCI, CMSR. Though enslavers from border slave states were compensated by the US Army for their enslaved men's service, and Lincoln took considerable care to avoid infringing on slavery within the US slave states for as long as possible, many border enslavers joined the Confederate war effort and enslaved men along the border sometimes escaped to join the US Army. Enslaver J. H. Forbes of Saint Mary's, Maryland, may have reclaimed Levi Green from Castle Thunder, or the Confederate military may have delivered Levi to Forbes directly. The POW memorandum slip in Levi's service record notes him as "delivered," suggesting that some enslavers in Maryland were willing and able to reclaim their enslaved property from Confederate authorities, despite residing within the borders of the United States. Several other Maryland and Washington, DC, enslavers successfully reclaimed Black POWs from Richmond throughout 1864.

92. Forty-Fourth, 106th, 110th, and 111th USCI, CMSR; Roger Pickenpaugh, *Captives*

in Blue: The Civil War Prisons of the Confederacy (Tuscaloosa: University of Alabama Press, 2013), 190; Burkhardt, *Confederate Rage, Yankee Wrath*, 175.

93. See, in *The War of the Rebellion*, L. Johnson to L. Thomas, February 3, 1865, ser. 2, vol. 8, 175; J. S. Leach to L. Johnson, February 3, 1865, ser. 2, vol. 8, 175; J. Buckner to L. Johnson, February 3, 1865, ser. 2, vol. 8, 175; see also SC 934.122, Private Abram Ralls, Forty-Fourth USCI, CFAV.

94. See, in *The War of the Rebellion*, statement of Private Joseph Howard, January 30, 1865, ser. 2, vol. 8, 153; O. O. Poppleton to B. Butler, January 5, 1865, ser. 2, vol. 8, 26–27; O. O. Poppleton to B. Butler, January 21, 1865, ser. 2, vol. 8, 109. On October 15, 1864, a circular in the *Mobile Advertiser and Register* named between 569 and 575 of the 1,488 Black POWs taken prisoner in September 1864. The circular was forwarded by Lieutenant O. O. Poppleton, 111th USCI, to Major General Butler, but a copy was not provided in *The War of the Rebellion*. Poppleton also referred to a second, later circular containing a list of about 300 additional names, bringing the total number of Black POWs held in the city to roughly 900. This second list of 309 men was printed on October 16, 1864, and includes men from the 106th, 110th, and 111th USCI, as well as several men from unidentified Tennessee cavalry units. It is possible that those men were laborers in a white cavalry regiment. Unfortunately, I have thus far been unable to locate a physical copy of these circulars. A transcribed copy of the list of 309 names, provided by historian and genealogist Peggy Allen Towns, however, includes the signature of Major General Dabney H. Maury, commander of the Department of the Gulf. He authorized these two circulars notifying owners as to the large presence of captured POWs under his control. See Towns, *Duty Driven: The Plight of North Alabama African Americans during the Civil War* (Bloomington, IN: AuthorHouse, 2012), 88. Many thanks to Chris Rein for bringing Towns's work to my attention.

95. *Journal of the Congress of the Confederate States of America, 1861–1865*, vol. 6, 103.

96. *Journal of the Congress of the Confederate States of America, 1861–1865*, vol. 6, 129.

97. *Journal of the Congress of the Confederate States of America, 1861–1865*, vol. 6, 517.

98. Aaron Sheehan-Dean, *Why Confederates Fought: Family and Nation in Civil War Virginia* (Chapel Hill: University of North Carolina Press, 2007), 113.

99. H. E. McCulloch to R. P. Maclay, June 8, 1863, in *The War of the Rebellion*, ser. 1, vol. 24, pt. 2, 467–70.

100. See Private Henry Jordan, Co. C, Seventh USCI, CMSR; Private James Oddaway, Co. A, 111th USCI, CMSR; Private Spencer Sloss, Co. B, 111th USCI, CMSR.

101. W. P. Shingler to Hunton, March 6, 1864, in *The War of the Rebellion*, ser. 2, vol. 6, 1022–23. These "negro soldiers" were likely men from the Sixth USCI, but what happened to them is unknown.

102. See note 94.

103. Grant was referencing a communication from Major General Butler wherein Butler stated that he had heard that Confederates placed uniformed Black POWs under fire while laboring on fortifications. Butler declared that he would retaliate by placing a like number of captured Confederate soldiers into hard labor under fire in the Dutch Gap Canal. See B. Butler to U. S. Grant, October 12, 1864, in *The War of the Rebellion*, ser. 2, vol. 7, 966.

104. "Correspondence between Generals Lee and Grant, Relative to the Treatment of Negro Soldiers and the Retaliation Measure of Gen. Butler," *Daily Confederate*, November 2, 1864.

105. David G. Smith, "Race and Retaliation: The Capture of African Americans during the Gettysburg Campaign," in *Virginia's Civil War*, ed. Peter Wallenstein and Bertram Wyatt-Brown (Charlottesville: University of Virginia Press, 2005), 138.

106. Quoted in Jordan, *Black Confederates*, 319–20.

107. "Correspondence between Generals Lee and Grant," *Daily Confederate*.

108. Seddon, *Report of the Secretary of War*, 16–17 (emphasis added).

109. Goodell, *The American Slave Code in Theory and Practice*, 96–97; Black, *Dismantling Black Manhood*, 142; Lorien Foote, *The Gentlemen and the Roughs: Violence, Honor, and Manhood in the Union Army* (New York: New York University Press, 2016), 3.

110. Joseph T. Glatthaar, "Black Glory: The African-American Role in Union Victory," in *Why the Confederacy Lost*, ed. Gabor Boritt (New York: Oxford University Press, 1993), 149–50.

111. Henry Cleveland, *Alexander H. Stephens, in Public and Private: With Letters and Speeches, before, during, and since the War* (Philadelphia: National, 1886), 717–29.

112. George Washington Williams, *A History of the Negro Troops in the War of the Rebellion, 1861–1865* (New York: Fordham University Press, 2012), 220.

Chapter 5

1. William Leckie, *The Buffalo Soldiers: A Narrative of the Negro Cavalry in the West* (Norman: University of Oklahoma Press, 1967); Arlen Fowler, *The Black Infantry in the West, 1869–1891* (Westport, CT: Greenwood Press, 1971; repr., Norman: University of Oklahoma Press, 1996), 118; Charles L. Kenner, *Buffalo Soldiers and Officers of the Ninth Cavalry, 1867–1898: Black and White Together* (Norman: University of Oklahoma Press, 1999); William Dobak and Thomas Phillips, *The Black Regulars, 1866–1898* (Norman: University of Oklahoma Press, 2001); Elizabeth Leonard, *Men of Color to Arms! Black Soldiers, Indian Wars, and the Quest for Equality* (New York: W. W. Norton, 2010). Readers interested in following the story of Black soldiers into the twentieth century should consult Marvin Fletcher's *The Black Soldier and Officer in the United States Army, 1891–1917* (Columbia: University of Missouri Press, 1974).

2. Charles M. Robinson III, *The Court-Martial of Lieutenant Henry Flipper* (El Paso: Texas Western Press, 1994); Charles M. Robinson III, *The Fall of a Black Army Officer: Racism and the Myth of Henry O. Flipper* (Norman: University of Oklahoma Press, 2008); Frank Schubert, *Buffalo Soldiers, Braves, and the Brass: The Story of Fort Robinson, Nebraska* (Shippensburg, PA: White Mane, 1993); James Leiker, *Racial Borders: Black Soldiers along the Rio Grande* (College Station: Texas A&M University Press, 2002); Kevin Adams, *Class and Race in the Frontier Army: Military Life in the West, 1870–1890* (Norman: University of Oklahoma Press, 2009); Douglas McChristian, *Regular Army O! Soldiering on the Western Frontier, 1865–1891* (Norman: University of Oklahoma Press, 2017); Jack Foner, *The United States Soldier between Two Wars: Army Life and Reforms, 1865–1898* (New York: Humanities Press, 1970).

3. J. C. A. Stagg, "Soldiers in War and Peace: Comparative Perspectives on the Recruitment of the U.S. Army, 1802–1815," *William and Mary Quarterly* 57, no. 1 (2000): 79–120; J. C. A. Stagg, "Enlisted Men in the United States Army, 1812–1815: A Preliminary Survey," *William and Mary Quarterly* 43, no. 4 (1986): 615–45; Durwood Ball, *Army Regulars on the Western Frontier, 1848–1861* (Norman: University of Oklahoma Press, 2001), 57–60; Adams, *Class and Race in the Frontier Army*, 23–28; Robert Utley, *Frontier Regulars: The United*

States Army and the Indian, 1866–1891 (New York: Macmillan, 1973), 22–23; Edward M. Coffman, *The Old Army: A Portrait of the American Army in Peacetime, 1784–1898* (New York: Oxford University Press, 1986), 137–41, 329–33; Robert Wooster, *The American Military Frontiers: The United States Army in the West, 1783–1900* (Albuquerque: University of New Mexico Press, 2009), 33, 67; McChristian, *Regular Army O!*, 16–21. For officers, see J. C. A. Stagg, "United States Army Officers in the War of 1812: A Statistical and Behavioral Portrait," *Journal of Military History* 76, no. 4 (2012): 1001–34; Mark Grandstaff, "Preserving the Habits and 'Usages of War': William Tecumseh Sherman, Professional Reform, and the U.S. Army Officer Corps, 1865–1881," *Journal of Military History* 62, no. 3 (1998): 521–45; Adams, *Class and Race in the Frontier Army*, 20–23.

4. Kenner, *Buffalo Soldiers and Officers of the Ninth Cavalry*, 11–13, 316n9; Wooster, *The American Military Frontiers*, 190–91; Coffman, *The Old Army*, 331–32; Dobak and Phillips, *The Black Regulars*, 24. Dobak and Phillips say that six times as many Black soldiers who joined in 1866 came from the South as from the North, but that by the end of 1867, more hailed from the North. Not only is it unclear not how they define each region, but there are no citations for these assertions. See Dobak and Phillips, *The Black Regulars*, 10.

5. Dobak and Phillips do discuss challenges in recruiting Black soldiers, a discussion that leads them to examine the various attempts to eliminate Black regiments in the postwar period. See Dobak and Phillips, *The Black Regulars*, 70–77.

6. Dobak and Phillips, 44–46, 53. Dobak and Phillips's reasoning that "the army had difficulty in attracting enough fit white recruits to keep the regular force near authorized strength without having to worry about four regiments with racial requirements" rests at the heart of their analysis of the recruitment of African American soldiers (53). It is important to note that while commanders did express anxieties about the quality of white enlistees in the decades after the Civil War (given the paltry pay and lack of benefits extended to enlisted men), the US Army never had trouble finding enough soldiers. In fact, the exact opposite was the case. Between 1880 and 1891, for example, only a little more than a quarter of the over three hundred thousand men who presented themselves for enlistment into the US Army were accepted by recruiting officers. See Adams, *Class and Race in the Frontier Army*, 23.

7. Other sources fill in some of the blanks concerning the ethnic backgrounds of soldiers. The first, a product of the House Committee on Military Affairs, breaks down the nationalities of all foreign-born individuals to enlist between January 1, 1865, and December 31, 1874. This chart can be supplemented with the adjutant general's tally of all enlisted men between 1880 and 1888, which counts the number of foreign-born and African American recruits. Additionally, I compiled a slightly longer dataset (1880–91) and recorded all enlistments in 1872 and 1878 for *Class and Race in the Frontier Army*. See H.R. Misc. Doc. 44-105, at 1–2 (1876); *Annual Report of the Secretary of War for the Year 1888*, vol. 1 (Washington, DC: Government Printing Office, 1888), 74; Adams, *Class and Race in the Frontier Army*, 25–28.

8. See the Fold3 database *US, Army Register of Enlistments, 1798–1914*.

9. My discussion of the demographic data can be found in Adams, *Class and Race in the Frontier Army*, 25–28.

10. Coffman, *The Old Army*, 331.

11. On segregation in the staff bureaus, see Foner, *The United States Soldier between Two Wars*, 141–42; Dobak and Phillips, *The Black Regulars*, 79–83. Not only was the comparative rarity of desertion among Black enlisted men "widely known" among parties interested in

postwar military life, but it served as an important leg of Republicans' argument that creating Black regiments would be economical. Statistics confirm the stereotype: between 1876 and 1891, desertion rates were 86 percent lower in Black infantry regiments than in white ones, and 70 percent lower in Black cavalry regiments than in white ones. Secretary of war Redfield Proctor, the most reform minded of the men who held that office in the last quarter of the nineteenth century, believed that the army's experience with African American soldiers proved that the solution to the army's desertion problem rested in making service in the army attractive. "It is an instructive fact," Proctor wrote, "that the soldiers in the colored regiments rarely desert, whereas the percentage of desertion in the rest of the army is so large. Their previous condition in civil life largely explains it. To the colored man, the service offers a career; to the white man too often only a refuge." *Annual Report of the Secretary of War for the Year 1889*, vol. 1 (Washington, DC: Government Printing Office, 1889), 9. Dobak and Phillips's contention that Black soldiers avoided desertion because they were more likely to be caught due to the paucity of African Americans in civilian communities surrounding forts in the trans-Mississippi West is plausible, but the size of the effect is a matter of conjecture. See Dobak and Phillips, *The Black Regulars*, xiii, 58, 62–63; Adams, *Class and Race in the Frontier Army*, 246n29.

12. My sample of nearly 4,000 soldiers includes 267 African American recruits or reenlistees.

13. The literature on the racial politics of Reconstruction is massive, but important aspects of the story may be traced in Dan T. Carter, *When the War Was Over: The Failure of Self-Reconstruction in the South, 1865–1867* (Baton Rouge: Louisiana State University Press, 1985); Joseph G. Dawson, *Army Generals and Reconstruction: Louisiana, 1862–1877* (Baton Rouge: Louisiana State University Press, 1982); Gregory Downs, *After Appomattox: Military Occupation and the Ends of War* (Cambridge, MA: Harvard University Press, 2015); James K. Hogue, *Uncivil War: Five New Orleans Street Battles and the Rise and Fall of Radical Reconstruction* (Baton Rouge: Louisiana State University Press, 2006); Leanna Keith, *The Colfax Massacre: The Untold Story of Black Power, White Terror, and the Death of Reconstruction* (New York: Oxford University Press, 2008); Elaine Frantz Parsons, *Ku-Klux: The Birth of the Klan during Reconstruction* (Chapel Hill: University of North Carolina Press, 2015); George C. Rable, *But There Was No Peace: The Role of Violence in the Politics of Reconstruction* (Athens: University of Georgia Press, 1984); Ted Tunnell, *Edge of the Sword: The Ordeal of Carpetbagger Marshall H. Twitchell in the Civil War and Reconstruction* (Baton Rouge: Louisiana State University Press, 2001); Richard Zuczek, *State of Rebellion: Reconstruction in South Carolina* (Columbia: University of South Carolina Press, 1996).

14. Four African American soldiers were foreign born, representing 0.1 percent of all soldiers in the sample and 1.5 percent of African American soldiers.

15. *Annual Report of the Secretary of War for the Year 1885*, vol. 1 (Washington, DC: Government Printing Office, 1885), 75.

16. Frank Schubert, review of *Class and Race in the Frontier Army: Military Life in the West, 1870–1890*, by Kevin Adams, *Journal of Military History* 73, no. 4 (2009): 1342–43.

17. *Annual Report of the Secretary of War for the Year 1888*, vol. 1, 74–75.

18. The lack of desertions among the Buffalo Soldiers, in conjunction with high enlistment rates, led to complaints among officers serving in African American regiments about their rarely being sent to cushy recruiting details in major cities. See Fowler, *The Black Infantry in the West*, 127.

19. *Annual Report of the Secretary of War for the Year 1890*, vol. 1 (Washington, DC: Government Printing Office, 1890), 67; *Annual Report of the Secretary of War for the Year 1872*, vol. 1 (Washington, DC: Government Printing Office, 1872), 120. My finding is based on a close reading of every recruiting report in those years; it should be noted that for most of the 1870s, no list of cities where recruiting efforts were carried out appears in said source.

20. Bell Irvin Wiley, *The Life of Johnny Reb: Common Soldier of the Confederacy* (Indianapolis, IN: Bobbs-Merrill, 1943); John Hope Franklin, *The Militant South, 1800–1861* (Cambridge, MA: Harvard University Press, 1956); Grady McWhiney and Perry Jamieson, *Attack and Die: Civil War Military Tactics and the Southern Heritage* (Tuscaloosa: University of Alabama Press, 1982); Jason Phillips, *Diehard Rebels: The Confederate Culture of Invincibility* (Athens: University of Georgia Press, 2007).

21. While I am skeptical about the use of a simplistic "martial manhood" as an explanatory device for the actions of men in both North and South, the nuanced *spectrum* of masculine behavior described by Amy Greenberg continues to merit serious attention from scholars. See Greenberg, *Manifest Manhood and Antebellum American Empire* (New York: Cambridge University Press, 2005).

22. For example, in a pattern evident since the Revolution, nineteenth-century Americans had divergent understandings of service in the standing military forces of the United States and service in volunteer militias. On this theme, see Charles Royster, *A Revolutionary People at War: The Continental Army and American Character, 1775–1783* (Chapel Hill: University of North Carolina Press, 1979); John Resch, *Suffering Soldiers: Revolutionary War Veterans, Moral Sentiment, and Political Culture in the Early Republic* (Amherst: University of Massachusetts Press, 1999); Paul Foos, *A Short Offhand Killing Affair: Soldiers and Social Conflict during the War with Mexico* (Chapel Hill: University of North Carolina Press, 2002); Andrew Lang, *In the Wake of War: Military Occupation, Emancipation, and Civil War America* (Baton Rouge: Louisiana State University Press, 2017).

23. Coffman's *The Old Army* contains a solitary sentence about the lack of enlisted men from the Deep South, which he defines as Alabama, Arkansas, Florida, Georgia, Louisiana, Mississippi, and South Carolina, but his data, drawn from the 1880 *Annual Report of the Secretary of War*, combines Black and white enlistments from the region. See Coffman, *The Old Army*, 330, 475n4.

24. Charles Calhoun, *From Bloody Shirt to Full Dinner Pail: The Transformation of Politics and Governance in the Gilded Age* (New York: Hill and Wang, 2010), provides the best overview here.

25. Adams, *Class and Race in the Frontier Army*, 24.

26. The basic shift here was from a regular army conditioned on the formal exclusion of African Americans from federal military service to one that permitted the partial integration of African Americans into the US Army. On this point see esp. Stagg, "Soldiers in War and Peace"; Stagg, "Enlisted Men in the United States Army"; Adams, *Class and Race in the Frontier Army*; Foos, *A Short Offhand Killing Affair*; Marcus Cunliffe, *Soldiers and Civilians: The Martial Spirit in America, 1775–1865* (Boston: Little, Brown, 1968).

27. Le'Trice D. Donaldson's recent study *Duty beyond the Battlefield* represents a valuable step in this direction, though its analysis of the "Old Army" is less detailed—and more reliant on the perspectives of Black officers—than its sections on the US Army in the 1890s and beyond. See Donaldson, *Duty beyond the Battlefield: African American Soldiers Fight for*

Racial Uplift, Citizenship, and Manhood, 1870–1920 (Carbondale: Southern Illinois University Press, 2020).

28. "Mutilated and Burned," *Savannah Morning News*, April 24, 1899. An important analysis of the Hose case in relation to larger patterns of white southern violence toward African Americans appears in Leon Litwack, *Trouble in Mind: Black Southerners in the Age of Jim Crow* (New York: Knopf, 1998), 280–325.

Chapter 6

1. Peggy Lamson, *The Glorious Failure: Black Congressman Robert Brown Elliott and the Reconstruction in South Carolina* (New York: W. W. Norton, 1973), 89.

2. "Honorable Robert Brown Elliott," in *Negro Legislators in South Carolina, 1868–1902*, preliminary report no. 4, ed. Lawrence C. Bryant, 1967, 3, South Carolina Department of Archives and History (SCDAH), Columbia. Peggy Lamson questions the legitimacy of this set of facts; see Lamson, *The Glorious Failure*, 23–31.

3. Lamson, *The Glorious Failure*, 25, 27.

4. Adele Logan Alexander, *Homelands and Waterways: The American Journey of the Bond Family, 1846–1926* (New York: Pantheon Books, 1999), 3–4.

5. Alexander, 4; Lamson, *The Glorious Failure*, 27–29, and see 21–27.

6. For Africa, see two accounts of Nicholas Sa'id, born in Africa and forced to migrate to Turkey, Russia, England, Haiti, and the United States: Douglas R. Egerton, *Thunder at the Gates: The Black Civil War Regiments That Redeemed America* (New York: Basic Books, 2016), 11–28; Paul E. Lovejoy, "Mohammed Ali Nicholas Sa'id: From Enslavement to American Civil War Veteran," *Millars: Espai i història* 42 (2017): 219–32. For Canada, see Richard M. Reid, *African Canadians in Union Blue: Volunteering for the Cause in the Civil War* (Kent, OH: Kent State University Press, 2015).

7. Alex Borucki, *From Shipmates to Soldiers: Emerging Black Identities in the Río de la Plata* (Albuquerque: University of New Mexico Press, 2015), 183–84, and see 147–228.

8. Borucki, 184, 190.

9. Borucki, 183–84. See also Gregory Mixon, *Show Thyself a Man: Georgia State Troops, Colored, 1865–1905* (Gainesville: University Press of Florida, 2016), 52–53, 65–70, 78–79, for the use of public space as a right of citizenship.

10. Borucki, *From Shipmates to Soldiers*, 192, 208–9, 218–20.

11. Lamson, *The Glorious Failure*, 21–23, 27.

12. Ronald R. Krebs, *Fighting for Rights: Military Service and the Politics of Citizenship* (Ithaca, NY: Cornell University Press, 2006), 3, 15, 17–19, 38, 116. See also Dexter B. Gordon, *Black Identity: Rhetoric, Ideology, and Nineteenth-Century Black Nationalism* (Carbondale: Southern Illinois University Press, 2003), xi.

13. For a similar assessment see Bradley D. Proctor, "'From the Cradle to the Grave': Jim Williams, Black Manhood, and Militia Activism in Reconstruction South Carolina," *American Nineteenth Century History* 19, no. 1 (2018): 47–79. See also *Christian Century*, September 16, 1970, quoted in James H. Cone, *Risks of Faith: The Emergence of a Black Theology of Liberation, 1968–1998* (Boston: Beacon Press, 2000), 1, for Black Power as self-definition. For counterarguments concerning the problem of freedom and the Black use and vision(s) of freedom, see William A. Link and James J. Broomall, eds., *Rethinking American Emancipation: Legacies of Slavery and the Quest for Black Freedom* (Cambridge: Cambridge University Press,

2016). In addition to Link and Broomall's introduction (1–14), see the following essays in this volume: Yael A. Sternhell, "Bodies in Motion and the Making of Emancipation," 15–41, esp. 32–33, 35; Gregory P. Downs, "Force, Freedom, and the Making of Emancipation," 42–68, esp. 45–47, 60–61, 63; Carole Emberton, "Axes of Empire: Race, Region, and the 'Greater Reconstruction' of Federal Authority after Emancipation," 119–45, esp. 127, 130–31, 140; Justin Behrend, "Fear of Reenslavement: Black Political Mobilization in Response to the Waning of Reconstruction," 146–66, esp. 148–49, 159. See also Jeffrey R. Kerr-Ritchie, *Freedom's Seekers: Essays on Comparative Emancipation* (Baton Rouge: Louisiana State University Press, 2014), 1–20, esp. 2, 4, 6–10, 15, and 101–25, esp. 117–21.

14. Lamson, *The Glorious Failure*, 39, 46 (qtd.), 62, 64, 67. For parallels, see Kerr-Ritchie, *Freedom's Seekers*, 101–25, esp. 117–21.

15. Carolyn Hall, "Poking King David in His Imperial Eye/'I': Woolson Takes on the White Man's Burden in the Postbellum United States," in *Witness to Reconstruction: Constance Fenimore Woolson and the Postbellum South, 1873–1894*, ed. Kathleen Diffley (Jackson: University Press of Mississippi, 2011), 180–81, 185.

16. S.C. Const. of 1866, art. I, § 13, art. IV, § 1, art. IX, § 11; "Report of the Agent of South Carolina Troops, Submitted at the Session of 1865," in *Reports and Resolutions of the General Assembly of the State of South Carolina, Passed at the Annual Session of 1865* (Columbia, SC: Julian A. Selby, 1866), 139, SCDAH. See also Anthony Szczesiul, "Reconstructing Hospitality," in Diffley, *Witness to Reconstruction*, 147–61, exploring the issue of belonging.

17. Martin T. Buinicki, "Imagining Sites of Memory in the Post–Civil War South: The National Cemetery in Woolson's 'Rodman the Keeper,'" in Diffley, *Witness to Reconstruction*, 167.

18. For the relationship between Black freedom and national imperialism, see Emberton, "Axes of Empire," 119–45.

19. Hall, "Poking King David in His Imperial Eye/'I,'" 187–89; Szczesiul, "Reconstructing Hospitality," 151–53; Henry Louis Gates Jr., *Stony the Road: Reconstruction, White Supremacy, and the Rise of Jim Crow* (New York: Penguin Press, 2019), 130–31.

20. S.C. Const. of 1866, art. IV, § 1; see also Szczesiul, "Reconstructing Hospitality," 151–54.

21. Szczesiul, "Reconstructing Hospitality," 153–54.

22. For Elliott's capabilities, see Lamson, *The Glorious Failure*, 27–28 (qtd.). See also Lovejoy, "Mohammed Ali Nicholas Sa'id"; *The Autobiography of Nicholas Said: A Native of Bornu, Eastern Soudan, Central Africa* (Memphis, TN: Shotwell, 1873), 226 (qtd.), and see 219–26. Sa'id moved on to Georgia, Alabama, and Tennessee in the 1870s and 1880s, teaching, lecturing, publishing his autobiography, marrying, and staying ahead of the Ku Klux Klan. My thanks to Paul E. Lovejoy for sharing these sources during my tenure as a Fulbright Scholar at York University, Toronto, January–June 2019.

23. Lamson, *The Glorious Failure*, 27–28; *The Autobiography of Nicholas Said*, 202–3.

24. Szczesiul, "Reconstructing Hospitality," 157–58.

25. Lamson, *The Glorious Failure*, 31–33, 50, 75–76.

26. Lamson, 44; Edward A. Miller Jr., *Gullah Statesman: Robert Smalls from Slavery to Congress, 1839–1915* (Columbia: University of South Carolina Press, 1995), 35. Both Lamson and Miller discount Black capabilities. For the white elite vision of governance, see Rod Andrew Jr., *Wade Hampton: Confederate Warrior to Southern Redeemer* (Chapel Hill: University of North Carolina Press, 2008), 49–498; Michael T. Bernath, "The Confederacy as a

Moment of Possibility," *Journal of Southern History* 79, no. 2 (May 2013): 299–338; Michael Perman, *Pursuit of Unity: A Political History of the American South* (Chapel Hill: University of North Carolina Press, 2009), 117–41.

27. Lamson, *The Glorious Failure*, 22–23. Lamson discusses Elliott's political power and political representation of Black people. She does explore Elliott's militia career, but not in depth.

28. An Act to Organize and Govern the Militia of the State of South Carolina, S.C. statute no. 143, § 1 (1868).

29. Lamson, *The Glorious Failure*, 39–42, 61; R. B. Elliott to Honl W. J. Lomax, May 3, 1869, Adjutant General Letter Books, 1869–70, SCDAH; see also Borucki, *From Shipmates to Soldiers*, 183–228; George Reid Andrews, *Afro-Latin America, 1800–2000* (New York: Oxford University Press, 2004), 85–116.

30. F. J. Moses Jr., address of November 23, 1869, in *Journal of the House of Representatives of the State of South Carolina, Being the Regular Session of 1869–70* (Columbia, SC: John W. Denny, 1870), 3–4.

31. Moses, 3–4.

32. Moses, 5–7.

33. Lamson, *The Glorious Failure*, 73–78.

34. Lamson, 74–75. The eight men were equally divided between white and Black Republicans. Rev. Richard Cain, lawyer William Whipper, and Black advocate Robert DeLarge joined Elliott as the four Black political leaders in the new legislature. Robert Scott, Daniel Chamberlain, David F. Corbin, and B. F. Whittemore rounded out the white leadership.

35. F. J. Moses Jr. to R. K. Scott, February 20, 1869, Adjutant General Letter Books, 1869–70, SCDAH; Richard Realf[?] to R. K. Scott, March 29, 1869, box 6, folder 23, Governor Robert K. Scott Papers, SCDAH; Lamson, *The Glorious Failure*, 80, 86.

36. Elbridge Colby, *The National Guard of the United States: A Half Century of Progress* (Manhattan, KS: Military Affairs and Aerospace Historian, 1977), 1; see also J. Brent Morris, "'No Peer in His Race': Robert Brown Elliott and the Politics of Reconstruction Era South Carolina," in *Before Obama: A Reappraisal of Black Reconstruction Era Politicians*, ed. Matthew Lynch, vol. 2 (Santa Barbara, CA: Praeger, 2012), 10–12; Gates, *Stony the Road*, 132.

37. Mixon, *Show Thyself a Man*, 28.

38. See Mixon, 13, 21, 28; John Hope Franklin, *The Militant South, 1800–1861* (Cambridge, MA: Belknap Press of Harvard University Press, 1956), 72–75.

39. Franklin, *The Militant South*, 170–243; Marcus Cunliffe, *Soldiers and Civilians: The Martial Spirit in America, 1775–1865* (Boston: Little, Brown, 1968), 31–32, 36, 38, 43–44, 180–240.

40. Tera W. Hunter, *Bound in Wedlock: Slave and Free Black Marriage in the Nineteenth Century* (Cambridge, MA: Belknap Press of Harvard University Press, 2017), 121–64.

41. Edythe Ann Quinn, *Freedom Journey: Black Civil War Soldiers and the Hills Community, Westchester County, New York* (Albany: State University of New York Press), 38–42; Egerton, *Thunder at the Gates*, 279–304; H. D. Dudley, "Mr. Editor, Emancipation Proclamation; President Lincoln; United States; Honey Hill," *South Carolina Leader*, March 31, 1866, 1. For the Thirty-Third US Colored Troops, see Lawrence T. McDonnell, "Killing Calvin Crozier: Honor, Myth, and Military Occupation after Appomattox," 2019, manuscript in possession of the author.

42. Mixon, *Show Thyself a Man*, 13–15, 21–22, 24.

43. Lamson, *The Glorious Failure*, 88–92.

44. See, in Adjutant General Letter Books, 1869–70, SCDAH: general order, August 25, 1870, signed by Robert Brown Elliott and Robert K. Scott; R. B. Elliott to P. R. Rivers, July 22, 1869. See, in General Orders Headquarters SC Military Department Letter Book, 1870–73, Special Orders, 1877–78, General Orders, 1877–81, SCDAH: R. B. Elliott to C. L. Anderson, January 22, 1872; R. B. Elliott to R. K. Scott, January 31, 1872; major general in command of the National Guard State of South Carolina (NGSSC) to F. J. Moses, December 30, 1872; R. B. Elliott to Devlin and Company, April 10, 1873; J. Kennedy to L. J. Lee, April 25, 1873; James Kennedy, NGSSC circular, June 10, 1873. See also James Kennedy, "Attention Invited to the Endorsement of Major General Robert Smalls Commanding 2nd Division NGSSC, by Command of Major General Elliott," November 26, 1875, Adjutant General Abstracts of Letters Received, 1870–82, SCDAH.

45. Morris, "No Peer in His Race," 12 (qtd.), and see 10–13; Lamson, *The Glorious Failure*, 88–92. See also "Report of the Adjutant and Inspector General of the State of South Carolina, November 1870," in *Reports and Resolutions of the General Assembly of the State of South Carolina at the Regular Session, 1870–71* (Columbia, SC: Republican, 1871), 521, SCDAH, for militia numbers where the militia was divided into "first class" (58,563) and "second class" (37,293) according to the age of the militiamen. And see "Report of the Adjutant General of the State of South Carolina to the General Assembly for the Fiscal Year Ending October 31, 1877," 735–36 (qtd.), 738, 742 (qtd.), General Assembly Reports and Resolutions, 1877, SCDAH, for comment by new adjutant general E. W. Moise and Governor Wade Hampton, two anti-Black and anti–National Guard Democratic Party members, after they took control of the South Carolina government and renamed the militia the State Volunteer Troops.

46. F. H. Forbell to W.[?] P. Clinton, December 3, 1870, box 13, folder 18, Governor Robert K. Scott Letters Received and Sent, October 26, 1870–January 8, 1871, SCDAH.

47. Morris, "No Peer in His Race," 12; Lamson, *The Glorious Failure*, 90.

48. R. B. Elliott to P. R. Rivers, July 22, 1869, Adjutant General Letter Books, 1869–70, SCDAH.

49. Lamson, *The Glorious Failure*, 90. For the entire letter to Rivers see R. B. Elliott to P. R. Rivers, July 22, 1869, Adjutant General Letter Books, 1869–70, SCDAH.

50. Lamson, *The Glorious Failure*, 80.

51. R. B. Elliott to R. K. Scott, March 11, 1870; R. B. Elliott to R. K. Scott, June 22, 1870; R. B. Elliott to R. K. Scott, April 5, 1870; all three letters in Adjutant General Letter Books, 1869–70, SCDAH.

52. R. B. Elliott to R. K. Scott, July 15, 1870; see also R. B. Elliott to R. K. Scott, August 15, 1870; both items in Adjutant General Letter Books, 1869–70, SCDAH. Mishaw's commanding officer submitted official charges for the revocation of his commission.

53. R. B. Elliott to R. K. Scott, July 15, 1870, Adjutant General Letter Books, 1869–70, SCDAH.

54. R. B. Elliott to J. A. Green, May 21, 1870; R. B. Elliott to R. K. Scott, August 8, 1870; both items in Adjutant General Letter Books, 1869–70, SCDAH.

55. R. B. Elliott to R. K. Scott, August 8, 1870, Adjutant General Letter Books, 1869–70, SCDAH. The elision in *d---n* is Elliott's.

56. Elliott to Scott.

57. R. B. Elliott to E. L. Mann, September 29, 1870; R. B. Elliott to E. L. Mann, October 6, 1870; R. B. Elliott to L. L. Griffin, October 6, 1870; all three letters in Adjutant General Letter Books, 1869–70, SCDAH.

58. J. B. Dennis to C. L. Anderson, October 29, 1870; General Orders, no. 3, R. B. Elliott to C. L. Anderson, October 31, 1870; Special Orders, no. 38, R. B. Elliott to C. L. Anderson, October 31, 1870; R. B. Elliott to sheriff of Laurens County, SC, October 31, 1870; R. B. Elliott to C. L. Anderson, November 2, 1870; all items in Adjutant General Letter Books, 1869–70, SCDAH.

59. Lamson, *The Glorious Failure,* 111–15, esp. 114; R. K. Scott to R. B. Elliott, October 26, 1870, Adjutant Inspector General's Office, Letters Received, 1869–79, SCDAH; R. B. Elliott to I. A. Belanger, October 22, 1870, Adjutant General Letter Books, 1869–70, SCDAH. See also, in General Orders Headquarters SC Military Department Letter Book, 1870–73, Special Orders, 1877–78, General Orders, 1877–81, SCDAH: B. S. Jones to R. K Scott, November 13, 1870; R. E. Richardson to C. L. Anderson, November 3, 1870; C. L. Anderson to G. A. Estes, November 3, 1870.

60. R. B. Elliott to R. K. Scott, December 3, 1870, Adjutant General Letter Books, 1869–70, SCDAH; see also Morris, "No Peer in His Race," 12.

61. See, in General Orders Headquarters SC Military Department Letter Book, 1870–73, Special Orders, 1877–78, General Orders, 1877–81, SCDAH: R. B. Elliott to C. L. Anderson, January 22, 1872; R. B. Elliott to R. K. Scott, January 29, 1872; R. B. Elliott to R. K. Scott, January 31, 1872; major general in command of the NGSSC to F. J. Moses, December 30, 1872. See, in Adjutant General Letters Sent, 1876–80, Letters Sent Penn Letter Book, SCDAH: J. Kennedy to R. B. Elliott, February 21, 1877; E. W. Moise to J. R. Cochran, August 4, 1878.

62. "Report of the Adjutant General of the State of South Carolina to the General Assembly for the Fiscal Year Ending October 31, 1877," 729–43, General Assembly Reports and Resolutions, 1877, SCDAH.

63. "Report of the Adjutant and Inspector General of the State of South Carolina to the General Assembly, for the Fiscal Year Ending October 31, 1873," in *Reports and Resolutions of the General Assembly of the State of South Carolina, at the Regular Session, 1873–74* (Columbia, SC: Republican, 1874), 531–32 (qtd.), and see 533–34, SCDAH; see also Lamson, *The Glorious Failure,* 91–98.

64. "Report of the Adjutant and Inspector General of the State of South Carolina to the General Assembly, for the Fiscal Year Ending October 31, 1874," in *Reports and Resolutions of the General Assembly of the State of South Carolina, at the Regular Session, 1874–75* (Columbia, SC: Republican, 1875), 631–32, SCDAH.

Chapter 7

1. Harry M. Crawford to father, May 19, 1898, Crawford Family Papers, Bentley Historical Library, University of Michigan, Ann Arbor.

2. By "ordinary white Americans," I mean that volunteers in 1898 were, with few exceptions, under the age of twenty-five, literate, and employed in blue-collar and entry-level white-collar jobs. Most of these men did not leave behind extensive historical records, and their letters and diaries have not informed much of the historical understanding of the period. An additional note about the use of "Spanish-American War" to refer to the conflict between the

United States and Spain in Cuba, Puerto Rico, and the Philippines in 1898: historians have been questioning the efficacy of this term for decades. The title excludes the role that Cuban revolutionaries played in the conflict and ignores the larger series of conflicts that surrounded the war in the 1890s and 1900s. Discussions about the term bring up valid criticism of the war's nomenclature but have yet to posit a phrase that has been widely accepted by scholars. As "Spanish-American War" remains the most recognizable term for the conflict of April–August 1898 between American and Spanish troops, it is the phrase I use, but I acknowledge its shortcomings. For a discussion of how "Spanish-American War" emerged as the conventional title in the historiography of the war and how it falls short, see Louis A. Pérez, *The War of 1898: The United States and Cuba in History and Historiography* (Chapel Hill: University of North Carolina Press, 1998).

3. There are a few published memoirs of the Spanish-American War. Charles Johnson Post's *The Little War of Private Post: The Spanish-American War Seen Up Close* (Lincoln, NE: Bison Books, 1999) follows Post through his time with the Seventy-First New York Volunteer Infantry. See also Stephen Bonsal, *The Fight for Santiago: The Story of the Soldier in the Cuban Campaign from Tampa to the Surrender* (London: British Library, 2011); Joseph McCallus, ed., *Gentlemen Soldier: John Clifford Brown & the Philippine-American War* (College Station: Texas A&M University Press, 2003). These works focus mostly on combat but can provide insight into the volunteer experience stateside and postwar as well.

4. Among the most in-depth studies in this historiography is Gregory Mixon's *Show Thyself a Man: Georgia State Troops, Colored, 1865–1905* (Gainesville: University Press of Florida, 2016), which demonstrates how Black Georgians competed for state militia sponsorship after the Civil War in order to gain access to politics, economic independence, and self-defense, despite the efforts of white Georgians to use the militia to reinforce white rule in the South. Mixon's book continues a long historiography concerning the service and significance of Black soldiers in the American military from the American Civil War until World War I. William A. Dobak and Thomas D. Phillips's *The Black Regulars, 1866–1898* (Norman: University of Oklahoma Press, 2001), which builds off of Arlen Fowler's *The Black Infantry in the West, 1869–1891* (Norman: University of Oklahoma Press, 1996) and William Leckie's *The Buffalo Soldiers: A Narrative of the Negro Cavalry in the West* (Norman: University of Oklahoma Press, 1981), is now considered an authority on the problems faced by the military and African American recruits after the Civil War. The complex role played by the US Colored Troops and Buffalo Soldiers in the American imperial project against Native Americans, Mexico, and Cuba, as well as in the Philippine-American War, is explored in James N. Leiker's *Racial Borders: Black Soldiers along the Rio Grande* (College Station: Texas A&M University Press, 2002). Elizabeth Leonard's *Men of Color to Arms! Black Soldiers, Indian Wars, and the Quest for Equality* (New York: W. W. Norton, 2010) builds on these works in an attempt to connect the Buffalo Soldiers to a larger discussion of late nineteenth-century civil rights and the relationship between citizens of the United States and the Native American people they encounter. Black Americans were often willing participants in the US wars in the West. For more on the experiences of the Buffalo Soldiers, see the works of Frank N. Schubert, including *Voices of the Buffalo Soldier: Records, Reports, and Recollections of Military Life and Service in the West* (Albuquerque: University of New Mexico Press, 2009) and *Black Valor: Buffalo Soldiers and the Medal of Honor, 1870–1898* (Lanham, MD: Rowman and Littlefield, 2009).

5. Published originally in 1899, Herschel V. Cashin's *Under Fire with the Tenth U.S.*

Cavalry (Niwot: University Press of Colorado, 1993) serves as the earliest comprehensive accounting of the exploits of African American soldiers in the Santiago campaign. Compiled by several leading African American men that witnessed the bravery of the soldiers and recorded some of their stories, *Under Fire* sought to combat accusations by the white press of Black cowardice and preserve the valor and heroism the men showed under fire. In the 1970s, historians like Jack Foner in *Blacks and the Military in American History: A New Perspective* (New York: Praeger, 1974) and Marvin Fletcher in *The Black Soldier and Officer in the United States Army, 1891–1917* (Columbia: University of Missouri Press, 1974) hoped to return the Black cavalry- and infantrymen to their rightful place in the pantheon of American heroes. Renewed interest in the role of African Americans in the military occurred in the 2000s with works like Gail Buckley's *American Patriots: The Story of Blacks in the Military from the Revolution to Desert Storm* (New York: Random House, 2001), Robert Edgerton's *Hidden Heroism: Black Soldiers in America's Wars* (Boulder, CO: Westview Press, 2001), and Gerald Astor's *The Right to Fight: A History of African Americans in the Military* (Novato, CA: Presidio Press, 1998).

6. As marginalized as the experience of Black regulars became in the decades following the Spanish-American War, the experiences of Black volunteers during the war were studied even less. Willard B. Gatewood Jr.'s *"Smoked Yankees" and the Struggle for Empire: Letters from Negro Soldiers, 1898–1902* (Little Rock: University of Arkansas Press, 1987) offers a glimpse into the motivations and daily life of Black volunteers. Bruce A. Glasrud's edited volume *Brothers to the Buffalo Soldiers: Perspectives on the African American Militia and Volunteers, 1865–1917* (Columbia: University of Missouri Press, 2011) offers insight into the motivations behind Black Americans' support for the war in 1898, the pride Black men had in wearing the uniform, and the way white supremacy attempted to deny Black Americans a place within state militias at the turn of the century. Though many southern states succeeded in preventing Black men from serving in the volunteers altogether, or from participating in postwar restructuring, some northern states experimented with mild integration and the advancement of Black officers.

7. There is an extensive historiography of the Rough Riders, and numerous memoirs or biographies of members of the First US Volunteer Cavalry. The Rough Riders were famous in their own time and have retained a prominent place in American presidential folklore. Though works on the Rough Riders have become more critical of the unit's role in the Battle of San Juan Hill, particularly in Theodore Roosevelt's leadership on the hill, few works on the Spanish-American War can resist featuring the Rough Riders as surrogates for the whole of the volunteer force in Cuba. See Virgil Carrington Jones, *Roosevelt's Rough Riders* (Garden City, NY: Doubleday, 1971); Mark Lee Gardner, *Rough Riders: Theodore Roosevelt, His Cowboy Regiment, and the Immortal Charge Up San Juan Hill* (New York: HarperCollins, 2016). Recently, Mark Sheftall has explored the perspectives of Native American Rough Riders and the important role Native Americans played in the creation of the myth of the Rough Riders; see his "Original Americans: Native Americans in Teddy Roosevelt's Rough Riders during the Spanish-American War" (lecture, US Army War College, Carlisle, PA, May 20, 2020).

8. Several historians have pointed to 1898 as a key moment in the sectional reconciliation of the United States, particularly because of the rhetoric of nationalism, imperialism, and white supremacy that framed the war and its aftermath. David Blight in *Race and Reunion: The Civil War in American Memory* (Cambridge, MA: Harvard University Press, 2001), Nina Silber in *The Romance of Reunion: Northerners and the South, 1865–1900* (Chapel Hill:

University of North Carolina Press, 1993), and Caroline Janney in *Remembering the Civil War: Reunion and the Limits of Reconciliation* (Chapel Hill: University of North Carolina Press, 2013) all identify the Spanish-American War as a key turning point in which the North and South reconciled their lingering animosities from the Civil War and Reconstruction. While it's clear that politicians, especially then-president William McKinley, had a vested interest in emphasizing the ending of sectional tension, discussions of the Spanish-American War's role in reconciliation often do not look at how average Americans viewed one another.

9. For a succinct overview of the dehumanizing effects of warfare on soldiers and society, see Stefan Vetter, "Understanding Human Behavior in Times of War," *Military Medicine* 172, no. S12 (2007): 7–10. Eric T. L. Love, in *Race over Empire*, does a deep dive into the ways policymakers' internalized and inherited ideas of race influenced their decisions concerning the American imperial project. Love calls this, affectionately, looking at the "wobbles" in the actions of policymakers. To some degree, that is what this work is intended to do for the volunteers: deepen our understanding of race and region at the turn of the century by looking at how the pressure of warfare reveals internalized prejudices that otherwise would have remained obscure to historians. See Eric T. L. Love, *Race over Empire: Racism and U.S. Imperialism, 1865–1900* (Chapel Hill: University of North Carolina Press, 2004), xiv–xvi. Chandra Manning explores the disappointment with war felt by soldiers in the Civil War. Much of the disappointment felt by Confederate soldiers came from the reality of the Confederacy having to fight the United States while it also fashioned its government and economy. Anger at deprivation and the assertiveness of enslaved persons and free people of color added to this growing rage. There is greater overlap between the experiences of US soldiers in the Civil War and northern soldiers in the Spanish-American War. The glory many US soldiers thought they would find in combat in the Civil War was lost between cycles of boredom and the terror of combat. In contrast, Spanish-American War volunteers' primary experience of military service was with boredom and disease, without the experience of combat. Chandra Manning, *What This Cruel War Was Over: Soldiers, Slavery, and the Civil War* (New York: Alfred Knopf, 2007).

10. The section title is quoted from "They Want to Fight," *Detroit Free Press*, April 27, 1898.

11. "Host of Volunteers," *Detroit Free Press*, April 22, 1898.

12. "War Spirit in South Dakota," *New York Times*, April 23, 1898. The only region that struggled to reach its quotas for volunteers was the South. Even with considerable southern support in Congress for war, circumstances in the South made recruitment more difficult than in the North. Many southern states, even those with majority Black populations, initially refused to enlist African Americans. These states also feared the specter of African American violence if able-bodied white men were away at war. See David C. Turpie, "A Voluntary War: The Spanish-American War, White Southern Manhood, and the Struggle to Recruit Volunteers in the South," *Journal of Southern History* 80, no. 4 (2014): 862–63. Beyond the racially motivated obstacles to recruitment was a sense in many southern communities that there was nothing for southerners to gain from the war. The ideas of American honor and *Cuba libre* (free Cuba) might have been enough for others, but some southerners did not deem it part of their duty as citizens to fight a war for reasons they did not see or understand. For South Carolina, and several other southern states, it was only when enlistment was opened to all men, regardless of color, that they met their quotas. Some states even imported volunteers

from other states. See Harris Moore Bailey Jr., "The Splendid Little Forgotten War: The Mobilization of South Carolina for the War with Spain," *South Carolina Historical Magazine* 92, no. 3 (July 1991): 196–97. The recruitment lists in states like Arkansas are riddled with volunteers coming from primarily northern and midwestern states that had already met their recruitment quotas. See roster of the Second Arkansas Volunteer Infantry, 1898, box 1, folder 15, Spanish-American War Veterans Survey Collection (SAWVSC), US Army Heritage and Education Center Archives, US Army War College, Carlisle, PA.

13. Reflecting on their service seventy years later, the surviving volunteers of 1898 recorded their motivations for enlisting, prompted to do so by the Spanish-American War Veterans Survey sent out by the US Army Heritage and Education Center starting in 1968. These memories are imperfect as time frequently glosses over the worst parts of the past. But consistent patterns in these records make utilizing them worthwhile, especially concerning why each man joined the service. It is clear from the surveys that many volunteers enlisted primarily for patriotic reasons. A third of them, like Albert Luettich of the First Illinois Infantry, listed their "patriotic duty to country" as their reason for enlisting. John Lindsay of the First Florida Infantry, similarly, viewed enlistment as his duty "as a citizen." He signed the rolls when a recruitment officer came through the small town of Sneads, Florida. See Albert Luettich, questionnaire, 1969, box 4, folder 19, SAWVSC; John Lindsey, questionnaire, 1969, box 3, folder 17, SAWVSC.

14. Post, *The Little War of Private Post*, 4.

15. S. W. Wadsworth to Jennie Wadsworth, May 16, 1898, Hussey-Wadsworth Family Papers, William L. Clements Library, University of Michigan, Ann Arbor.

16. Bernard Lichtig, questionnaire, 1969, box 4, folder 6, SAWVSC.

17. Horace J. Mellum, "The Centennial Kid, or All in a Lifetime: The Story of an Ordinary Chicago Boy in the Eighties and Nineties," unpublished manuscript, c. 1950s, chap. 11, p. 1, Chicago History Museum Archives.

18. The chief ordnance officer of the US Army expected the need to replace about a third of the state units' supplies, but as mid-May arrived it became exceedingly clear that almost all the state units would need most of their supplies replaced. Most states had obsolete and worn-out equipment, if they had sufficient supplies at all. Graham A. Cosmas, *An Army for Empire: The United States Army in the Spanish American War* (College Station: Texas A&M University Press, 1998), 120.

19. Charles Butters, questionnaire, 1968, box 4, folder 29, SAWVSC; Charles Wood, questionnaire, 1968–69, box 1, folder 14, SAWVSC; Harry Crawford to father, May 16, 1898, Crawford Family Papers.

20. Karl Kraemer to parents and all, June 21, 1898, box 1, folder 1, Karl Kraemer Papers, US Army Heritage and Education Center Archives. Gerald Linderman discusses how, despite the steady decline of the self-sufficient small town by 1898, the power of the locale remained in 1898 as a "measurable force in American Life." The local militia, he argues, was a source of pride for the old and a source of excitement for the young; the militia was a part of the community no matter where it went. Gerald Linderman, *The Mirror of War: American Society and the Spanish-American War* (Ann Arbor: University of Michigan Press, 1974), 64–66.

21. The section title is quoted from Harry M. Crawford to Eva Crawford, May 24, 1898, Crawford Family Papers.

22. Harry Crawford to father and mother, May 22, 1898, Crawford Family Papers.

23. Andrew Wadsworth to sister, May 25, 1898, Hussey-Wadsworth Family Papers.

24. Kari Boyd, "Disease, Disuse, and Disappointment: The Volunteer Experience and the Modernization of the American National Guard, 1898–1902" (PhD diss., University of Alabama, 2020), 51–53.

25. Harry Crawford to friends, May 20, 1898, Crawford Family Papers. In nearly every city Crawford passed through, the men were asked for the buttons off their uniforms by the young women and girls at the station. Some men arrived in Tampa with no buttons left to give.

26. Census data for Ann Arbor, Detroit, and Flint between 1890 and 1900 shows that between 96.7 and 98.6 of the population was white, with the remaining population African American, American Indian, or Asian. Campbell Gibson and Kay Jung, "Historical Census Statistics on Population Totals by Race, 1790 to 1990, and by Hispanic Origin, 1970 to 1990, for Large Cities and Other Urban Places in the United States" (working paper, US Census Bureau, Washington, DC, February 2005), table 23.

27. John Frederick to Margaret Frederick Barry, May 10, 1898, Margaret Sutherland Frederick Barry Papers, Bentley Historical Library. The Fredericks lived in Sault Ste. Marie, Michigan, on the eastern shore of Lake Superior.

28. Frederick to Barry. It is not clear which all-Black unit Frederick is referring to or whether the colonel was Black or white, but it was common for Black units and officers to experience slights like a failure to salute. See Foner, *Blacks and the Military in American History*, for more on the prejudice faced by Black units in the war.

29. Harry Crawford to Eva Crawford, May 22, 1898, Crawford Family Papers. Chandra Manning describes how US soldiers in the Civil War encountered and understood slavery. Many northern soldiers expressed a considerable amount of disgust at the institution of slavery and the effect it had on southerners, both white and Black, though this sentiment was often phrased within the highly racialized language of white supremacy. Manning, *What This Cruel War Was Over*, 75–79.

30. Harry Crawford to mother, May 24, 1898, Crawford Family Papers. I have spent a long time trying to uncover the identity and story behind the Black man Crawford reports as serving with the Thirty-Second Michigan. Beyond finding pictures of the unit and a few photo scrapbooks describing the presence of a few prominent Black Detroiters at Camp Eaton, I have yet to learn more. This demonstrates that there were some people of color present in and around southeast Michigan in 1898, though not in the sort of concentration and visibility as in the South.

31. Among the many scholars to assess the idea of the "New South" and particularly northern attitudes toward the region, Natalie J. Ring sheds considerable light on how frequently northern liberal reformers not only saw the South as a "problem" to be fixed but also failed to see how varied the people and places of the South were. Ring, *The Problem South: Region, Empire, and the New Liberal State, 1880–1930* (Athens: University of Georgia Press, 2012), 176–77.

32. Harry M. Crawford to F. A. and Eva Crawford, May 22, 1898, Crawford Family Papers; Harry M. Crawford to friends, May 20, 1898, Crawford Family Papers.

33. Harry M. Crawford to F. A. Crawford, May 26, 1898, Crawford Family Papers.

34. Silber, *The Romance of Reunion*, 178–79.

35. David Traxel, *1898: The Birth of the American Century* (New York: Vintage Books, 1998), xi–xii, 88–89; Matthew McCullough, *The Cross of War: Christian Nationalism and*

U.S. Expansion in the Spanish-American War (Madison: University of Wisconsin Press, 2014), 24–25.

36. Mellum, "The Centennial Kid," chap. 10.

37. Traxel, *1898*, 64. Linderman discusses how Theodore Roosevelt felt that the generation of young men reaching adulthood in the 1890s had been denied the sort of vigorous and spiritual experience that the Civil War was to the generation before. People had forgotten the waste and tragedy of the Civil War and only remembered how it had made them men. The Spanish-American War was one way to invigorate the young men of the nation and get them out from the shadow of their forebearers. Linderman, *The Mirror of War*, 92.

38. Walter Crawford to Harry M. Crawford, July 3, 1898, Crawford Family Papers.

39. The Buckbees were under strict orders from their father to mind their health and their morals, with a stern warning to "be a good boy don't hunt for too much tail—one a month will do—when you get to Chickamauga—will send you the name of my girl—in Chattanooga. She may be a little old, but good." J. A. B. to Julian Buckbee, April 28, 1898, Buckbee Family Papers, Bentley Historical Library. Many volunteers at Camp Thomas were acutely aware of the Civil War, since Camp Thomas was built on top of the Chickamauga battlefield and plenty of memorials were within walking distance of the camp. Mellum, "The Centennial Kid," chap. 12, p. 3.

40. Harry Crawford to father and mother, May 22, 1898, Crawford Family Papers.

41. Mabel J. Crawford to Harry M. Crawford, May 26, 1898, Crawford Family Papers; "Michigan Troops to the Front," *Atlanta Constitution*, May 22, 1898, 7.

42. Bradley S. Keefer, *Conflicting Memories of the River of Death: The Chickamauga Battlefield and the Spanish-American War, 1863–1933* (Kent, OH: Kent State University Press, 2013), 215.

43. Plea in bar of trial for Captain Louis Duncan, testimony of Captain Louis Duncan, and statements of witnesses, 1898, Kansas Volunteer Infantry—22nd Kansas, box 3, folder 16, Spanish-American War Document Collection (SAWDC), US Army Heritage and Education Center.

44. *Alexandria Gazette*, 1898, Kansas Volunteer Infantry—22nd Kansas, box 3, folder 16, SAWDC.

45. Harry Crawford to friends, July 1, 1898, Crawford Family Papers.

46. Harry Crawford to friends, July 24, 1898, Crawford Family Papers.

47. Harry Crawford to Eva, July 18, 1898, Crawford Family Papers.

48. Harry Crawford to friends, May 28, 1898, Crawford Family Papers.

49. Harry Crawford to father, July 15, 1898, Crawford Family Papers.

50. Harry Crawford to father, June 12, 1898, Crawford Family Papers.

51. Harry Crawford to father, May 26, 1898, Crawford Family Papers.

52. Harry Crawford to mother, July 22, 1898, Crawford Family Papers.

53. Harry Crawford to friends, July 24, 1898, Crawford Family Papers. Linderman mentions how seldom Americans in the nineteenth century had to think deeply about the nature of foreign peoples. Determining vice and virtue was relatively easy and was often entirely based on one or two characteristics, such as race, religion, or class. Few Americans had differentiated much before the Cuban Revolution in 1895 between the Spanish and Cubans—until they needed to portray the Cubans as good allies and the Spanish as evil enemies. But the Cubans that the US Army met were not the light-skinned professional soldiers the newspapers

depicted them as; rather, they were dirty, hungry, and sick. Linderman, *The Mirror of War*, 114–15, 144–45.

54. Boyd, "Disease, Disuse, and Disappointment," 82. Linderman chronicles the lengths some volunteers took to make it on board a ship to Cuba and discusses the disappointment felt by those volunteers that could not navigate the chaos in Tampa to make it to the ships or that did not have the political clout to get away with physically forcing themselves aboard a transport like Roosevelt had. Linderman, *The Mirror of War*, 99–100.

55. Harry M. Crawford to F. A. Crawford, July 15, 1898, Crawford Family Papers.

56. "A Disgrace to the Country," *Baltimore Sun*, June 20, 1898.

57. "Soldiers on the Rampage," *Washington Post*, June 11, 1898. William Gatewood covers the incident in detail in "Negro Troops in Florida, 1898," *Florida Historical Quarterly* 49, no. 1 (July 1970): 1–15. There is surprisingly little else about the riot mentioned in other scholarly works about the war or racial violence in the early years of Jim Crow.

58. "Colored Troops 'on a Tear,'" *Baltimore Sun*, June 10, 1898; "Declare 40 Were Killed: Negroes in the Hospital at Atlanta Tell a Different Story," *Chicago Daily Tribune*, June 21, 1898. There was a great deal of criticism concerning the behavior of the Ohioans, but many reports condemned the actions of the Black soldiers as brutish, some demanding that the Twenty-Fourth and Twenty-Fifth Infantries be sent back to Oklahoma rather than to Cuba, for fear they might murder the good white Cubans there. Gatewood, "Negro Troops in Florida," 9–10.

59. Camp Meade was built to house soldiers from Camp Alger, which had been completely devastated by disease. It seems that many of the African Americans who had worked in and around Camp Alger followed the army north into Pennsylvania. Calvin Mixter to family, October 7, 1898, Calvin Mixter Papers, William L. Clements Library.

60. Frank Harmon letter (recipient unknown), October 1898, Calvin Mixter Papers; Calvin Mixter to Estelle, October 13, 1898, Calvin Mixter Papers.

61. Calvin Mixter to Will, October 19, 1898, Calvin Mixter Papers.

62. Calvin Mixter to Estelle, October 16, 1898, Calvin Mixter Papers.

63. The section heading is quoted from Post, *The Little War of Private Post*, 123.

64. Albert Gudatt, August 4, 1898, Albert F. Gudatt Journal, 1898–1904, 12, William L. Clements Library.

65. Gudatt, September 1898, 14.

66. Gudatt, September 23, 1898, 15–16.

67. Gudatt, January 6, 1899, 17. Many scholars have discussed how American depictions of Cubans prior to 1898 tended to focus on lighter-skinned Cuban people (mostly descendants of Spanish Creoles). Americans were in many ways surprised to see just how "black" Cubans were and often treated dark-skinned Cubans similarly to African Americans in the United States. Discussions of race in Cuba resurged after the centennial; see, e.g., Ada Ferrer, "Cuba, 1898: Rethinking Race, Nation, and Empire," *Radical History Review*, no. 73 (Winter 1999): 22–46.

68. Albert Gudatt, October 8, 1899, Albert F. Gudatt Journal, 1898–1904, 29.

69. Gudatt, February 5, 1901, 91.

70. Andrew Wadsworth to sister, July 20, 1898, August 14, 1898, and September 11, 1898, Hussey-Wadsworth Family Papers.

71. Andrew Wadsworth to sister, October 14, 1898, Hussey-Wadsworth Family Papers.

72. *Nabob* was usually used to refer to Indian officials or princes, but seems to have been used as a pejorative for any person of Asian descent. John Camden Hotten, *The Slang Dictionary: Etymological, Historical, and Anecdotal* (London: Chatto and Windus, 1874), 251.

73. Andrew Wadsworth to sister, February 19, 1899, Hussey-Wadsworth Family Papers.

74. Andrew Wadsworth to aunt, March 8, 1899, Hussey-Wadsworth Family Papers.

75. Andrew Wadsworth to aunt, April 26, 1899, Hussey-Wadsworth Family Papers.

76. Andrew Wadsworth to sister, March 19, 1899, Hussey-Wadsworth Family Papers.

77. Andrew Wadsworth to his siblings, June 1, 1899, Hussey-Wadsworth Family Papers.

78. Harry Crawford to father, September 10, 1898, Crawford Family Papers.

Chapter 8

I am grateful to Lesley J. Gordon and Andrew J. Huebner for inviting me to contribute to this collection and for providing insights on my work. A special thanks to Sarah Patterson for her suggestions on this chapter. I appreciate the mentorship of Elizabeth Smith-Pryor, Kevin Adams, and Kenneth J. Bindas, whose suggestions helped develop my research. I thank my family members Jeff, Alivia, and Maverick, who supported me as I devoted my time and attention to this piece.

1. Sansone drew *The Wolf* when he was a corporal, but he later achieved the rank of sergeant. See Leonard Sansone, *The Wolf* (New York: United, 1945).

2. "Little Red Riding Hood," in *The Tales of Mother Goose: As First Collected by Charles Perrault in 1696*, trans. Charles Welsh, intro. M. V. O'Shea (Boston: D. C. Heath, 1901), 80–84.

3. See "Little Red Riding Hood," 80–84; "The Wolf and the Seven Little Kits" (1812), in *The Brothers Grimm: Fairy Tales* (New York: Alfred A. Knopf, 1992), 229–33; Joseph Jacobs, "The Story of the Three Little Pigs," in *English Fairy Tales* (London: David Nutt, 1890), 68–72; Sergei Prokofiev, *Peter and the Wolf* (1936), musical composition; *Little Red Riding Hood*, Laugh-o-Grams (Walt Disney, 1922), animated short; *The Big Bad Wolf*, Silly Symphony (Walt Disney, 1934), animated short.

4. Informed by historian Margot Canaday's study on the ways governmental policy in the twentieth century served as "a catalyst in the formation of homosexual identity," this study explores how military policy and images produced by servicemen projected a heterosexual soldiering identity for US troops collectively. See Margot Canaday, *The Straight State: Sexuality and Citizenship in Twentieth-Century America* (Princeton, NJ: Princeton University Press, 2009), 4; Allan Bérubé, *Coming Out under Fire: The History of Gay Men and Women in World War II* (Chapel Hill: University of North Carolina Press, 2010); Leisa D. Meyer, *Creating GI Jane: Sexuality and Power in the Women's Army Corps during World War II* (New York: Columbia University Press, 1998). Legal racial segregation and systemic racial discrimination in the United States normalized the largely exclusive whiteness of American national imagery and discourse. In the context of the two world wars, the cultural depictions of American servicemen cannot be separated from the power derived through their whiteness. While images of protective servicemen exemplified a white masculine ideal, images of sexually aggressive servicemen symbolized American racial and gendered power through their sexual conquests on the home front and abroad. See Richard Dryer, "The Matter of Whiteness," in *White Privilege: Essential Readings on the Other Side of Racism*, 2nd ed., ed. Paula Rothenburg (New York: Worth, 2005), 9–14; Jonathan Rosenberg, *How Far the Promised Land? World Affairs and the American Civil Rights Movement from the First World War to Vietnam* (Princeton,

NJ: Princeton University Press, 2006); Rawn James Jr., *The Double V: How Wars, Protest, and Harry Truman Desegregated American's Military* (New York: Bloomsbury, 2014); Mary Dudziak, *Cold War Civil Rights: Race and the Image of American Democracy* (Princeton, NJ: Princeton University Press, 2000); Thomas Borstelmann, *The Cold War and the Color Line: American Race Relations in the Global Arena* (Cambridge, MA: Harvard University Press, 2001).

5. On the world stage, men's collective actions toward women often serve as the focal point by which other societies judge a nation's aptitude for leadership. See Ann Towns, "The Status of Women as a Standard of 'Civilization,'" *European Journal of International Relations* 15, no. 4 (2009): 681–706; Louise Newman, "Women's Rights, Race, and Imperialism in U.S. History, 1870–1920," in *Race, Nation, and Empire in American History*, ed. James T. Campbell, Matthew Pratt Guterl, Robert G. Lee (Chapel Hill: University of North Carolina Press, 2007), 157–79; Kevin White, *The First Sexual Revolution: The Emergence of Male Heterosexuality in Modern America* (New York: New York University Press, 1992), 5. For a history of soldiering sexuality in modern American wars, see Judith Ann Giesberg, *Sex and the Civil War: Soldiers, Pornography, and the Making of American Morality* (Chapel Hill: University of North Carolina Press, 2017); Thomas P. Lowery, *The Story the Soldiers Wouldn't Tell: Sex and the Civil War* (Mechanicsburg, PA: Stackpole Books, 1994); Andrew J. Huebner, *Love and Death in the Great War* (New York: Oxford University Press, 2018), 1; Michele Curran Cornell, review of *Love and Death in the Great War*, by Andrew J. Huebner, *Journal of the Gilded Age and Progressive Era* 18, no. 2 (April 2019): 256–58; Allan M. Brandt, *No Magic Bullet: A Social History of Venereal Disease in the United States since 1880* (New York: Oxford University Press, 1985); John Costello, *Virtue under Fire: How World War II Changed Our Social and Sexual Attitudes* (Boston: Little, Brown, 1985); Marilyn E. Hegarty, *Victory Girls, Khaki-Wackies, and Patriotutes: The Regulation of Female Sexuality during World War II* (New York: New York University Press, 2008); Mary Louise Roberts, *What Soldiers Do: Sex and the American GI in World War II France* (Chicago: University of Chicago Press, 2013).

6. James W. Cook and Lawrence B. Glickman outline the way that many historians view culture as a discursive system, one that emphasizes "the constitutive power of words and symbols in shaping the very parameters of what could be thought, said, imagined, and experienced." Thus, "language and imagery became crucial springboards for exploring new kinds of collective identities." See James W. Cook and Lawrence B. Glickman, "Twelve Propositions for a History of U.S. Cultural History," in *The Cultural Turn in U.S. History: Past, Present, and Future*, ed. James W. Cook, Lawrence B. Glickman, and Michael O'Malley (Chicago: University of Chicago Press, 2008), 13.

7. The term *doughboy* originated prior to World War I, when US Army general John J. Pershing's Expeditionary Forces fought a southern border war against Mexican rebel Pancho Villa. Mounted troops referred to American foot soldiers as *adobes* or *dobies* because of the white adobe dust that covered their uniforms. The same Expeditionary Forces deployed to Europe, where the term affectionately evolved into the nickname *doughboys*. See "Doughboys and the Birth of the Modern American Army," National WWI Museum and Memorial (website), accessed October 10, 2023.

8. Brandt, *No Magic Bullet*, 115–16. For discussions on how sex policing affected women, see Brandt, 78, 168; Elizabeth Alice Clement, *Love for Sale: Courting, Treating, and Prostitution in New York City, 1900–1945* (Chapel Hill: University of North Carolina Press, 2006), 115; Hegarty, *Victory Girls, Khaki-Wackies, and Patriotutes*; Meyer, *Creating GI Jane*; Beth

Bailey and David Farber, *The First Strange Place: Race and Sex in World War II Hawaii* (Baltimore, MD: Johns Hopkins University Press, 1992); Meghan Winchell, *Good Girls, Good Food, Good Fun: The Story of USO Hostesses during World War II* (Chapel Hill: University of North Carolina Press, 2008).

9. Clement, *Love for Sale*, 118, 125, 153, 155. See also Bailey and Farber, *The First Strange Place*, 121.

10. Clement, *Love for Sale*, 116, 118, and see 125; see also Nancy Bristow, *Making Men Moral: Social Engineering during the Great War* (New York: New York University Press, 1996); Hegarty, *Victory Girls, Khaki-Wackies, and Patriotutes*, 85–109.

11. Clement, *Love for Sale*, 118, 125, 155; see also Huebner, *Love and Death in the Great War*; Michele Curran Cornell, "Romanticizing Patriarchy: Patriotic Romance and American Military Marriages during World War II" (PhD diss., Kent State University, 2018), 85, 88–89.

12. Clement, *Love for Sale*, 118, 125, 153, 155; see also Bailey and Farber, *The First Strange Place*, 121.

13. See, in *United States Army in the World War, 1917–1919*, vol. 16, *General Orders, GHQ, AEF* (1948; Washington, DC: Center of Military History, 1992), the following general orders: no. 6, 1917, 11–12; no. 34, 1917, 71; no. 77, 1917, 144–46; no. 32, 1919, 657; no. 6, 1918, 162; no. 215, 1918, 546; no. 230, 1918, 575. For a discussion of the evolution of these policies, see Brandt, *No Magic Bullet*, 65, 101–4, 111, 117–18, 168.

14. The image that servicemen projected of themselves in *Stars and Stripes* (which portrayed them as much better behaved than statistics or military sex policy would suggest) also represented how servicemen wished to be perceived—vice free. However, on occasion stories and jokes provided subtle evidence of servicemen's sexual desires. See "Enjoying Our Leaves," *Stars and Stripes*, February 22, 1918, 4; "Ah! Those French!," *Stars and Stripes*, February 8, 1918, 5; "Make Mine Pink," *Stars and Stripes*, March 8, 1918, 2; "Want a Wife? Buy Some Blubber Oil," *Stars and Stripes*, June 13, 1919, 1.

15. "To the Colors!," editorial, *Stars and Stripes*, February 8, 1918, 4.

16. "To the Folks Back Home," *Stars and Stripes*, February 8, 1918, 4.

17. The Montana Peak hat became military standard in 1911, when the US Army adopted it into the uniform. See David Cole, *Survey of U.S. Army Uniforms, Weapons and Accoutrements* (Washington, DC: US Army Center of Military History, 2007), 58–59.

18. Several influential works of art presenting the allegory of Victory include: a relief sculpture of the goddess Nike (n.d.), located in the ruins of the ancient Greek city of Ephesus, Turkey; the ancient Greek marble sculpture *The Winged Victory of Samothrace* (200–190 BCE), located in the Louvre, Paris; the Le Nain brothers' oil painting *Allegory of Victory* (1635), located in the Louvre; Augustus Saint-Gaudens's gilded bronze monument William Tecumseh Sherman (Sherman Memorial, 1902–3), located in Grand Army Plaza, New York; and Thomas Brock's gilded bronze monument Victoria Memorial (1901–24), located between the Mall and Buckingham Palace, London.

19. F. B. Tarbell, "The Palm of Victory," *Classical Philology* 3, no. 3 (July 1908): 264–72.

20. "German Brands Young Mother with an Iron," *Stars and Stripes*, February 8, 1918, 3.

21. "German Brands Young Mother with an Iron."

22. See also Roberts, *What Soldiers Do*; Wendy Kline, *Building a Better Race: Gender, Sexuality, and Eugenics from the Turn of the Century to the Baby Boom* (Berkeley: University of California Press, 2001).

23. See Richard Malkin, *Marriage, Morals and War* (New York: Arden Book, 1943), 11–16; Elaine Tyler May, *Homeward Bound: American Families in the Cold War Era*, 20th anniversary ed. (New York: Basic Books, 2008), 41; Jane Mersky Leder, *Thanks for the Memories: Love, Sex, and World War II* (Washington, DC: Potomac Books, 2009), 2–3; Beth Bailey, *From Front Porch to Back Seat: Courtship in Twentieth-Century America* (Baltimore, MD: Johns Hopkins University Press, 1989), 42.

24. Brandt, *No Magic Bullet*, 125–26, 131, 133, 147–49, 154.

25. Penicillin was discovered as an effective treatment for VD in 1943 but was not widely accessible until 1944. See Brandt, 161.

26. Christina S. Jarvis, *The Male Body at War: American Masculinity during World War II* (DeKalb: Northern Illinois University Press, 2004), 83. For governmental and military policy concerning VD, see Hegarty, *Victory Girls, Khaki-Wackies, and Patriotutes*, 15; Brandt, *No Magic Bullet*, 161–65.

27. Surgeon General of the Army, *Sex Hygiene and Venereal Disease* (Washington, DC: US Department of War, 1942), 4, 7, US National Library of Medicine, digital collection. Marriage rates also soared to record-breaking levels nationally between 1940 and 1945, with 1.5 million more marriages occurring than experts predicted based on peacetime norms. Patriotic culture during World War II encouraged marital unions to strengthen family bonds and the war effort across the home front and the battlefronts. Monogamous marriages also enabled servicemen to enjoy sexual entitlements safely as husbands while legitimately reproducing the national citizenry. See Cornell, "Romanticizing Patriarchy," 2.

28. Brandt, *No Magic Bullet*, 97–98, 164; John F. Patton, ed., *Surgery in World War II: Urology* (Washington, DC: Office of the Surgeon General, 1987), 45–88, 102–3. The 1944 US Navy medical bulletin, M. L. Gerber's "Some Practical Aspects of Circumcision," is cited by Frederick Hodges in "A Short History of the Institutionalization of Involuntary Sexual Mutilation in the United States," in *Sexual Mutilations: A Human Tragedy*, ed. George C. Denniston and Marilyn Fayre Milos (New York: Plenum Press, 1997), 27–28.

29. Brandt, *No Magic Bullet*, 170; "Venereal Disease and Treatment during WW2," WW2 US Medical Research Centre (website), accessed October 10, 2023.

30. Rebecca L. Davis, *More Perfect Unions: The American Search for Marital Bliss* (Cambridge, MA: Harvard University Press, 2010), 66.

31. Leder, *Thanks for the Memories*, 65, 122; Roberts, *What Soldiers Do*, 167.

32. In the European theater of operations between February 1944 and June 1945, the US Army reported 94,305 cases of VD among white troops (incidence rate: 36.9) and 38,103 cases of venereal disease among Black troops (incidence rate: 169.4). See Thomas H. Sternbery et al., "Venereal Diseases," in *Preventive Medicine in World War II*, vol. 5, *Communicable Diseases: Transmitted through Contact or by Unknown Means*, ed. John Boyd Coates (Washington, DC: Office of the Surgeon General, 1961), 264.

33. Roberts, *What Soldiers Do*, 164, 195–238; see also Hegarty, *Victory Girls, Khaki-Wackies, and Patriotutes*.

34. Roberts, *What Soldiers Do*, 9, 187. See also Jarvis, *The Male Body at War*, 83; Clement, *Love for Sale*, 249, 253.

35. Cornell, "Romanticizing Patriarchy," 79–171.

36. Gary Sheftick, "ARNEWS Marks 75 Years of Serving Soldiers," Army News Service, July 5, 2018.

37. Ron Goulart, "World War II Gave Rise to Numerous Comic Strips and Brought Fame to the Artists Who Drew Them," *World War II*, September 1996; Maggie Sansone, "Leonard Sansone, 1917–1963, Cartoonist and Creator of *The Wolf*" (online resource), hosted at MaggiesMusic.com, accessed October 10, 2023.

38. Robert Westbrook, *Why We Fought: Forging American Obligations in World War II* (Washington, DC: Smithsonian Books, 2004), 7–9. See also Nancy Walker, introduction to *What's So Funny? Humor in American Culture*, ed. Nancy Walker (Wilmington, DE: Scholarly Resources, 1998), 3, 4, 10; William Keough, "The Violence of American Humor," in Walker, *What's So Funny?*, 136–37; Louis Rubin, "The Great American Joke," in Walker, *What's So Funny?*, 107–20.

39. Cornell, "Romanticizing Patriarchy," 79–118, 259–301.

40. Milton Caniff, foreword to Sansone, *The Wolf*, n.p.

41. See also Kara Dixon Vuic, *The Girls Next Door: Bringing the Home Front to the Front Lines* (Cambridge, MA: Harvard University Press, 2019); Winchell, *Good Girls, Good Food, Good Fun*; Meyer, *Creating GI Jane.*

42. Melissa McEuen, *Making War, Making Women: Femininity and Duty on the American Home Front, 1941–1945* (Athens: University of Georgia Press, 2011), 21, 23, 26. See also Alex Lubin, *Romance and Rights: The Politics of Interracial Intimacy, 1945–1954* (Jackson: University of Mississippi Press, 2005).

43. Lary May, *The Big Tomorrow: Hollywood and the Politics of the American Way* (Chicago: University of Chicago Press, 2002), 164–65.

44. Satish Chandra, *History of Medieval India* (Himayatnagar, Hyderabad, India: Orient BlackSwan, 2007), 132–33; Swati Detha, "Life inside the Zenani Deorhi of Rajuts during the Medieval Period," *Scholarly Research Journal for Humanity Science and English Language* 9, no. 2 (April–May 2015): 2197.

45. For a discussion of rape during World War II, see Robert Lily, *Taken by Force: Rape and American GIs in Europe during World War II* (New York: Palgrave MacMillan, 2007); Roberts, *What Soldiers Do*, 195–238; Clement, *Love for Sale*, 153–54; Hegarty, *Victory Girls, Khaki-Wackies, and Patriotutes*, 89, 91–92, 160; Estelle Freedman, *Feminism, Sexuality, and Politics* (Chapel Hill: University of North Carolina Press, 2006), 122; Susan Brownmiller, *Against Our Will: Men, Women, and Rape* (New York, Penguin Books, 1975), 64. For a discussion of wartime violence and rape in general, see Cynthia Enloe, *Maneuvers: The International Politics of Militarizing Women's Lives* (Berkeley: University of California Press, 2000), 108–52.

46. Carolyn Apple, "World War II Mission Symbols," Delaware Historical and Cultural Affairs (blog), posted September 3, 2015.

47. John Modell and Duane Steffey, "Waging War and Marriage: Military Service and Family Formation, 1940–1950," *Journal of Family History* 13, no. 2 (April 1988): 196; see also, Walker, introduction to *What's So Funny?*, 5. For examples of how the battle of the sexes was depicted in a civilian publication, see the following cartoons in the *Saturday Evening Post*: "Don't you dare raise your voice to me," September 11, 1943, 44; "Oh, its nothing to worry about. Every marriage requires an adjustment period," August 28, 1943, 61; "Ignorance of the law is not an excuse, Mrs. Reed; the fact remains that you shot and killed your husband," September 18, 1943, 49; "They get married and live happily ever after. He's drafted and she joins the Wacs," August 21, 1943, 76.

Chapter 9

1. Ellen Goodman, "Tailhook Only Part of Backlash," *Birmingham Post-Herald*, July 7, 1992, A4.

2. "The Tailhook Association," *PBS Frontline* (website), accessed October 10, 2023.

3. Michael Winerip, "Revisiting the Military's Tailhook Scandal," *New York Times*, May 13, 2013.

4. "The Tailhook Association," *PBS Frontline*.

5. Susan Faludi, "Going Wild?," *New York Times*, February 16, 1994.

6. Douglas Walter Bristol Jr., "Terror, Anger, and Patriotism: Understanding the Resistance of Black Soldiers during World War II," in *Integrating the US Military: Race, Gender, and Sexual Orientation since World War II*, edited by Douglas Walter Bristol Jr. and Heather Marie Stur (Baltimore, MD: Johns Hopkins University Press, 2017), 28. See also, in the same collection, James Westheider, "African Americans, Civil Rights, and the Armed Forces during the Vietnam War," 102.

7. Kristy N. Kamarck, "Women in Combat: Issues for Congress," Congressional Research Service, report no. R42075, December 3, 2015, 5.

8. Victoria Sherrow, *Women in the Military* (New York: Chelsea House, 2007), 31. See also D'Ann Campbell, *Women at War with America: Private Lives in a Patriotic Era* (Cambridge, MA: Harvard University Press, 1984); D'Ann Campbell, "Women in Combat: The World War II Experience in the United States, Great Britain, Germany, and the Soviet Union," *Journal of Military History* 57, no. 2 (April 1993): 301–23.

9. Betty Friedan, *The Second Stage* (New York: Abacus, 1983), 171 (qtd.), 189.

10. Linda Greenhouse, "Women Join Battle on All-Male Draft," *New York Times*, March 22, 1981.

11. Quoted in Jon Nordheimer, "Women's Role in Combat: The War Resumes," *New York Times*, May 26, 1991.

12. Quoted in Nordheimer.

13. Elaine Donnelly, "What Did You Do in the Gulf, Mommy?," *National Review*, November 18, 1991, 44.

14. James D. Milko, "Beyond the Persian Gulf Crisis: Expanding the Role of Servicewomen in the United States Military," *American University Law Review* 41 (1992): 1329.

15. Elaine Donnelly, July 3, 1992, memo on supplementary travel report, Parris Island, and Fort Bragg trip of June 15–16, 1992, box 3, folder titled "Hearing, August 6–8, 1992—Briefing Book," record group 220, Records of Temporary Committees, Commissions, and Boards, July 13–15 to August 27–29, 1992, National Archives and Records Administration, College Park, MD.

16. Brian Mitchell, *Women in the Military: Flirting with Disaster* (Washington, DC: Regnery, 1997), 175.

17. Thomas Szayna et al., *Considerations for Integrating Women into Closed Occupations in the U.S. Special Forces* (Santa Monica, CA: RAND, 2015), 38.

18. Szayna et al., 35.

19. Szayna et al., 20–21.

20. Szayna et al., 16.

21. Gayle Tzemach Lemmon, "Women in Combat? They've Already Been Serving on the Front Lines, with Heroism," *Los Angeles Times*, December 4, 2015.

22. Jeffrey S. Dietz, "Breaking the Ground Barrier: Equal Protection Analysis of the U.S. Military's Direct Ground Combat Exclusion of Women," *Military Law Review* 207 (Spring 2011): 113.

23. Art. 125, Sodomy, 10 U.S.C. § 925 (1956).

24. John D'Emilio, *Sexual Politics, Sexual Communities: The Making of a Homosexual Minority in the United States, 1940–1970* (Chicago: University of Chicago Press, 1998), 24.

25. *Matlovich v. Secretary of the Air Force*, no. 75-1750 (D.D.C., July 19, 1976), opinion of the Honorable Gerhard A. Gesell, July 16, 1976, box 2, file 58, Leonard Matlovich Papers, Gay Lesbian Bisexual Transgender Historical Society, San Francisco Public Library. See also, in the same box, appellant brief by David F. Addlestone, May 17, 1979, file 56; Gregory Gordon, UPI wire story on Matlovich, November 24, 1980, file 64.

26. Randy Shilts, *Conduct Unbecoming: Lesbians and Gays in the U.S. Military, Vietnam to the Persian Gulf* (New York: St. Martin's Press, 1993), 60–65.

27. Steve Estes, "Ask and Tell: Gay Veterans, Identity, and Oral History on a Civil Rights Frontier," *Oral History Review* 32, no. 2 (Summer–Autumn 2005): 32.

28. Mary Ann Humphrey, *My Country, My Right to Serve: Experiences of Gay Men and Women in the Military, World War II to the Present* (New York: Perennial, 1991), 262.

29. "Gays and the Military," *Newsweek*, January 31, 1993.

30. Aaron Belkin and Melissa Sheridan Embser-Herbert, "A Modest Proposal: Privacy as a Flawed Rationale for the Exclusion of Gays and Lesbians from the U.S. Military," *International Security* 27, no. 2 (Fall 2002): 182.

31. Bernard Rostker, "A Year after Repeal of Don't Ask, Don't Tell," *RAND Blog*, September 20, 2012.

32. Karen DeYoung, "Colin Powell Now Says Gays Should Be Able to Serve Openly in Military," *Washington Post*, February 4, 2010.

33. Bernard D. Rostker, Susan D. Hosek, and Mary E. Vaiana, "Gays in the Military: New Facts Conquer Old Taboos," *RAND Review*, April 29, 2011.

34. Kay Jones and Ray Sanchez, "Pfc. Vanessa Guillen Bludgeoned to Death on Army Base," CNN, July 3, 2020.

35. Quoted in Graham Kates, "14 Fired or Suspended Following Fort Hood Investigation into Vanessa Guillen's Death," *CBS News*, December 9, 2020.

36. Richard A. Serrano, "Gulf War Veteran Executed for 1995 Murder," *Los Angeles Times*, March 19, 2003; Heather Marie Stur, *Beyond Combat: Women and Gender in the Vietnam War Era* (New York: Cambridge University Press, 2011), 95.

37. Department of Defense, *Annual Report on Sexual Assault in the Military: Fiscal Year 2012* (April 2013), 12–13, 25.

38. Ella Torres, "Military Sexual Assault Victims Say the System Is Broken," *ABC News*, August 28, 2020.

39. Torres.

Epilogue

1. Max Boot, "Americans' Ignorance of History Is a National Scandal," *Washington Post*, February 20, 2019.

2. Boot's works include *War Made New: Technology, Warfare, and the Course of History,*

1500 to Today (New York: Penguin, 2006), *Invisible Armies: An Epic History of Guerrilla Warfare from Ancient Times to the Present* (New York: Liveright, 2013), *The Savage Wars of Peace: Small Wars and the Rise of American Power* (New York: Basic Books, 2014), and *The Road Not Taken: Edward Lansdale and the American Tragedy in Vietnam* (New York: Liveright, 2018).

3. Boot, "Americans' Ignorance of History Is a National Scandal."

4. Jim Grossman (@JimGrossmanAHA), "Max Boot is simply wrong about this . . . ," Twitter, February 20, 2019, 4:23 p.m.; Annette Gordon-Reed (@agordonreed), "Nope. Historians are in newspapers . . . ," Twitter, February 20, 2019, 1:58 p.m.; Joanne Freeman (@jbf1755), "1/ I have to join the chorus of historians who disagree . . . ," Twitter, February 20, 2019, 4:10 p.m.; Kevin Kruse (@KevinMKruse), "We're in the public sphere and political history is thriving . . . ," Twitter, February 20, 2019, 5:31 p.m.; Keisha N. Blain (@KeishaBlain), "I see some folks are peddling the same old . . . ," Twitter, February 20, 2019, 3:51 p.m.

5. Max Boot, "I Wrote about the Waning Popularity of History at Universities. Historians Weren't Happy," *Washington Post*, February 26, 2019.

6. Martha S. Jones (@marthasjones_), "The heart of the matter is not whether we engage in public debate . . . ," Twitter, February 20, 2019, 4:13 p.m.

7. James Baldwin, *The Devil Finds Work*, in *The Price of the Ticket: Collected Nonfiction, 1948–1985* (New York: St Martin's Press, 1985), 606.

8. Chad L. Williams, *Torchbearers of Democracy: African American Soldiers in the World War I Era* (Chapel Hill: University of North Carolina Press, 2010).

9. W. E. B. Du Bois, "World War and the Color Line," *Crisis*, November 1914.

10. W. E. B. Du Bois, "The African Roots of War," *Atlantic Monthly*, May 1915.

11. Rayford W. Logan, *The Negro in American Life and Thought: The Nadir, 1877–1901* (New York: Dial Press, 1954).

12. 55 Cong. Rec. S104 (1917).

13. W. E. B. Du Bois, "Close Ranks," *Crisis*, July 1918.

14. Colonel E. D. Anderson to chief of staff, May 22, 1918, box 264, 8142–49, record group 165, Records of the War Department General and Special Staffs, National Archives and Record Administration, College Park, MD.

15. W. E. B. Du Bois, "An Essay toward a History of the Black Man in the Great War," *Crisis*, June 1919.

16. See Williams, *Torchbearers of Democracy*, chap. 3.

17. Robert Lee Bullard, *Personalities and Reminiscences of the War* (New York: Doubleday, Page, 1925), 298.

18. Albert Duham to W. E. B. Du Bois, June 17, 1919, W. E. B. Du Bois Collection, Fisk University Archives, Nashville, TN.

19. W. E. B. Du Bois, "Returning Soldiers," *Crisis*, May 1919.

20. Stanley B. Norvell to Victor F. Lawson, August 22, 1919, Julius Rosenwald Papers, Department of Special Collections, University of Chicago Library, courtesy of Dr. William M. Tuttle Jr.

21. W. E. B. Du Bois, "The Black Man and the Wounded World: A History of the Negro Race in the World War and After," *Crisis*, January 1924.

Further Reading

Chapter 1

Anderson, Gary Clayton. *The Conquest of Texas: Ethnic Cleansing in the Promised Land, 1820–1875*. Norman: University of Oklahoma Press, 2005.

Barr, Juliana. *Peace Came in the Form of a Woman: Indians and Spaniards in the Texas Borderlands*. Chapel Hill: University of North Carolina Press, 2007.

Baumgartner, Alice L. *South to Freedom: Runaway Slaves to Mexico and the Road to the Civil War*. New York: Basic Books, 2020.

Brooks, James F. *Captives and Cousins: Slavery, Kinship, and Community in the Southwest Borderlands*. Chapel Hill: University of North Carolina Press, 2002.

Bryan, Jimmy L. *The American Elsewhere: Adventure and Manliness in the Age of Expansion*. Lawrence: University Press of Kansas, 2017.

DeLay, Brian. *War of a Thousand Deserts: Indian Raids and the U.S.-Mexican War*. New Haven, CT: Yale University Press, 2008.

González Quiroga, Miguel A. *War and Peace on the Rio Grande Frontier, 1830–1880*. Norman: University of Oklahoma Press, 2020.

Greenberg, Amy S. *Manifest Manhood and the Antebellum American Empire*. New York: Cambridge University Press, 2005.

Greenberg, Kenneth S. *Honor and Slavery: Lies, Duels, Noses, Masks, Dressing as a Woman, Gifts, Strangers, Humanitarianism, Death, Slave Rebellions, the Proslavery Argument, Baseball, Hunting, and Gambling in the Old South*. Princeton, NJ: Princeton University Press, 1996.

Guardino, Peter F. *The Dead March: A History of the Mexican-American War*. Cambridge, MA: Harvard University Press, 2017.

Haynes, Sam W. *Unsettled Land: From Revolution to Republic, the Struggle for Texas*. New York: Basic Books, 2022.

Haynes, Sam W., and Gerald D. Saxon, eds. *Contested Empire: Rethinking the Texas Revolution*. College Station: Texas A&M University Press, 2015.

Lack, Paul D. *The Texas Revolutionary Experience: A Political and Social History, 1835–1836*. College Station: Texas A&M University Press, 1992.

Nichols, James David. *The Limits of Liberty: Mobility and the Making of the Eastern U.S.-Mexico Border*. Lincoln: University of Nebraska Press, 2018.

Ramos, Raúl A. *Beyond the Alamo: Forging Mexican Ethnicity in San Antonio, 1821–1861*. Chapel Hill: University of North Carolina Press, 2008.

Reséndez, Andrés. *Changing National Identities at the Frontier: Texas and New Mexico, 1800–1850*. New York: Cambridge University Press, 2005.

Richards, Thomas, Jr. *Breakaway Americas: The Unmanifest Future of the Jacksonian United States*. Baltimore, MD: Johns Hopkins University Press, 2020.

Rodriguez, Sarah K. M. "'The Greatest Nation on Earth': The Politics and Patriotism of the First Anglo American Immigrants to Mexican Texas, 1820–1824." *Pacific Historical Review* 86, no. 1 (February 2017): 50–83.

Sachs, Honor. *Home Rule: Households, Manhood, and National Expansion on the Eighteenth-Century Kentucky Frontier*. New Haven, CT: Yale University Press, 2015.

Schlereth, Eric R. "Privileges of Locomotion: Expatriation and the Politics of Southwestern Border Crossing." *Journal of American History* 100, no. 4 (March 2014): 995–1020.

Shire, Laurel Clark. *The Threshold of Manifest Destiny: Gender and National Expansion in Florida*. Philadelphia: University of Pennsylvania Press, 2016.

Torget, Andrew J. *Seeds of Empire: Cotton, Slavery, and the Transformation of the Texas Borderlands, 1800–1850*. Chapel Hill: University of North Carolina Press, 2015.

Chapter 2

Ashcraft, Allan C. "Confederate Indian Troop Conditions in 1864." *Chronicles of Oklahoma* 41, no. 4 (Winter 1963–64): 442–49.

Carson, James Taylor. *Searching for the Bright Path: The Mississippi Choctaws from Prehistory to Removal*. Lincoln: University of Nebraska Press, 1999.

Finkelman, Paul. "States' Rights, Southern Hypocrisy, and the Crisis of the Union." *Akron Law Review* 45, no. 2 (2012): 449–78.

Fischer, LeRoy H. *The Civil War Era in Indian Territory*. Los Angeles: Lorrin L. Morrison, 1974.

Fortney, Jeff. "Lest We Remember: Civil War Memory and Commemoration among the Five Tribes." *American Indian Quarterly* 36, no. 4 (Fall 2012): 525–44.

Gibson, Arrell M. "Native Americans and the Civil War." *American Indian Quarterly* 9, no. 4 (Autumn 1985): 385–410.

Hauptman, Laurence M. *Between Two Fires: American Indians in the Civil War*. New York: Free Press, 1996.

Kidwell, Clara Sue. *Choctaws and Missionaries in Mississippi, 1818–1918*. Norman: University of Oklahoma Press, 1995.

King, Patricia Jo Lynn. "The Forgotten Warriors: Keetoowah Abolitionists, Revitalization, the Search for Modernity and the Struggle for Autonomy in the Cherokee Nation, 1800–1866." PhD diss., University of Oklahoma, 2013.

Krauthamer, Barbara. *Black Slaves, Indian Masters: Slavery, Emancipation, and Citizenship in the Native American South*. Chapel Hill: University of North Carolina Press, 2013.

Lowery, Malinda Maynor. "The Original Southerners: American Indians, the Civil War, and Confederate Memory." *Southern Cultures* 25, no. 4 (Winter 2019): 16–35.

Naylor, Celia E. *African Cherokees in Indian Territory: From Chattel to Citizens*. Chapel Hill: University of North Carolina Press, 2008.

Saunt, Claudio. *Black, White, and Indian: Race and the Unmaking of an American Family*. New York: Oxford University Press, 2005.

Schreier, Jesse Turner. "Different Shades of Freedom: Indians, African Americans, and Race in the Choctaw Nation, 1800–1907." PhD diss., University of California, Los Angeles, 2008.

Snyder, Christina. *Great Crossings: Indians, Settlers, and Slaves in the Age of Jackson*. New York: Oxford University Press, 2017.

Swanton, John R. *Source Material for the Social and Ceremonial Life of the Choctaw Indians*. 1931. Tuscaloosa: University of Alabama Press, 2001.

Wickett, Murray R. *Contested Territory: Whites, Native Americans and African Americans in Oklahoma, 1865–1907*. Baton Rouge: Louisiana State University Press, 2000.

Chapter 3

Blight, David W. *Frederick Douglass: Prophet of Freedom*. New York: Simon and Schuster, 2018.

Dobak, William A. *Freedom by the Sword: The U.S. Colored Troops, 1862–1867*. New York: Skyhorse, 2013.

Downs, Gregory P. *After Appomattox: Military Occupation and the Ends of War*. Cambridge, MA: Harvard University Press, 2015.

Jones, Martha S. *Birthright Citizens: A History of Race and Rights in Antebellum America*. Cambridge: Cambridge University Press, 2018.

Kantrowitz, Stephen David. *More Than Freedom: Fighting for Citizenship in a White Republic, 1829–1889*. New York: Penguin Books, 2013.

Lang, Andrew F. *In the Wake of War: Military Occupation, Emancipation, and Civil War America*. Baton Rouge: Louisiana State University Press, 2017.

Pinheiro, Holly A., Jr. *The Families' Civil War*. Athens: University of Georgia Press, 2022.

Smith, John David. *Lincoln and the U.S. Colored Troops*. Carbondale: Southern Illinois University Press, 2013.

Taylor, Brian. *Fighting for Citizenship: Black Northerners and the Debate over Military Service in the Civil War*. Chapel Hill: University of North Carolina Press, 2020.

Chapter 4

Edwards, Laura F. *A Legal History of the Civil War and Reconstruction: A Nation of Rights*. New York: Cambridge University Press, 2015.

Foote, Lorien. *Rites of Retaliation: Civilization, Soldiers, and Campaigns in the American Civil War*. Chapel Hill: University of North Carolina Press, 2021.

Gray, Michael P., ed. *Crossing the Deadlines: Civil War Prisons Reconsidered*. Kent, OH: Kent State University Press, 2018.

Grimsley, Mark. *The Hard Hand of War: Union Military Policy toward Southern Civilians*. New York: Cambridge University Press, 1995.

Lee, Wayne E. *Barbarians and Brothers: Anglo-American Warfare, 1500–1865*. New York: Oxford University Press, 2011.

Martinez, Jaime Amanda. *Confederate Slave Impressment in the Upper South*. Chapel Hill: University of North Carolina Press, 2013.

Neff, Stephen C. *Justice in Blue and Gray: A Legal History of the Civil War*. Cambridge, MA: Harvard University Press, 2010.

Pickenpaugh, Roger. *Captives in Blue: The Civil War Prisons of the Confederacy*. Tuscaloosa: University of Alabama Press, 2013.

Sheehan-Dean, Aaron. *The Calculus of Violence: How Americans Fought the Civil War*. Cambridge, MA: Harvard University Press, 2018.

Urwin, Gregory J. W., ed. *Black Flag over Dixie: Racial Atrocities and Reprisals in the Civil War*. Carbondale: Southern Illinois University Press, 2004.

Chapter 5

Adams, Kevin. *Class and Race in the Frontier Army: Military Life in the West, 1870–1890*. Norman: University Oklahoma Press, 2009.

Coffman, Edward M. *The Old Army: A Portrait of the American Army in Peacetime, 1784–1898*. New York: Oxford University Press, 1986.

Dobak, William, and Thomas Phillips. *The Black Regulars, 1866–1898*. Norman: University of Oklahoma Press, 2001.

Foner, Jack. *The United States Soldier between Two Wars: Army Life and Reforms, 1865–1898*. New York: Humanities Press, 1970.

Fox, Richard. *Archaeology, History, and Custer's Last Battle: The Little Big Horn Reexamined*. Norman: University of Oklahoma Press, 1993.

Greene, Jerome. *American Carnage: Wounded Knee, 1890*. Norman: University of Oklahoma Press, 2014.

Jacoby, Karl. *Shadows at Dawn: A Borderlands Massacre and the Violence of History*. New York: Penguin Press, 2008.

Kenner, Charles L. *Buffalo Soldiers and Officers of the Ninth Cavalry, 1867–1898: Black and White Together*. Norman: University of Oklahoma Press, 1999.

Lahti, Janne. *Cultural Construction of Empire: The U.S. Army in Arizona and New Mexico*. Lincoln: University of Nebraska Press, 2012.

Leiker, James. *Racial Borders: Black Soldiers along the Rio Grande*. College Station: Texas A&M University Press, 2002.

Meyerson, Harvey. *Nature's Army: When Soldiers Fought for Yosemite*. Lawrence: University Press of Kansas, 2001.

Ostler, Jeffrey. *The Plains Sioux and U.S. Colonialism from Lewis and Clark to Wounded Knee*. New York: Cambridge University Press, 2004.

Robinson, Charles M., III. *The Fall of a Black Army Officer: Racism and the Myth of Henry O. Flipper*. Norman: University of Oklahoma Press, 2008.

Smith, Sherry. *The View from Officers' Row: Army Perceptions of Western Indians*. Tucson: University of Arizona Press, 1990.

Tate, Michael. *The Frontier Army in the Settlement of the West*. Norman: University of Oklahoma Press, 1999.

Utley, Robert. *Frontier Regulars: The United States Army and the Indian, 1866–1891*. New York: Macmillan, 1973.

West, Elliott. *The Last Indian War: The Nez Perce Story*. New York: Oxford University Press, 2009.

Wooster, Robert. *The American Military Frontiers: The United States Army in the West, 1783–1900*. Albuquerque: University of New Mexico Press, 2009.

———. *The Military and United States Indian Policy, 1865–1903.* New Haven, CT: Yale University Press, 1988.

———. *The United States Army and the Making of America: From Confederation to Empire, 1783–1900.* Lawrence: University Press of Kansas, 2021.

Chapter 6

Alexander, Adele Logan. *Homelands and Waterways: The American Journey of the Bond Family, 1846–1926.* New York: Pantheon Books, 1999.

Alexander, Shawn L. *An Army of Lions: The Civil Rights Struggle before the NAACP.* Philadelphia: University of Pennsylvania Press, 2012.

Andrews, George Reid. *Afro-Latin America: 1800–2000.* New York: Oxford University Press, 2004.

Borucki, Alex. *From Shipmates to Soldiers: Emerging Black Identities in the Rio de la Plata.* Albuquerque: University of New Mexico Press, 2015.

Glasrud, Bruce A. *Brothers to the Buffalo Soldiers: Perspectives on the African American Militia and Volunteers, 1865–1917.* Columbia: University of Missouri Press, 2011.

Lamson, Peggy. *The Glorious Failure: Black Congressman Robert Brown Elliott and the Reconstruction in South Carolina.* New York: W. W. Norton, 1973.

Mixon, Gregory. *Show Thyself a Man: Georgia State Troops, Colored, 1865–1905.* Gainesville: University Press of Florida, 2016.

Morris, J. Brent. "'No Peer In His Race': Robert Brown Elliott and the Politics of Reconstruction Era South Carolina." In *Before Obama: A Reappraisal of Black Reconstruction Era Politicians,* edited by Matthew Lynch, vol. 2, 1–40. Santa Barbara, CA: Praeger, 2012.

Chapter 7

Ferrer, Ada. "Cuba, 1898: Rethinking Race, Nation, and Empire." *Radical History Review,* no. 73 (Winter 1999): 22–46.

Gatewood, Willard B., Jr. *"Smoked Yankees" and the Struggle for Empire: Letters from Negro Soldiers, 1898–1902.* Little Rock: University of Arkansas Press, 1987.

Glasrud, Bruce A., ed. *Brothers to the Buffalo Soldiers: Perspectives on the African American Militia and Volunteers, 1865–1917.* Columbia: University of Missouri Press, 2011.

Hannah, Eleanor L. *Manhood, Citizenship, and the National Guard: Illinois, 1870–1917.* Columbus: Ohio State University Press, 2007.

Keefer, Bradley S. *Conflicting Memories of the River of Death: The Chickamauga Battlefield and the Spanish-American War, 1863–1933.* Kent, OH: Kent State University Press, 2013.

Linderman, Gerald. *The Mirror of War: American Society and The Spanish American War.* Ann Arbor: University of Michigan Press, 1974.

Love, Eric T. L. *Race over Empire: Racism and U.S. Imperialism, 1865–1900.* Chapel Hill: University of North Carolina Press, 2004.

Post, Charles Johnson. *The Little War of Private Post: The Spanish-American War Seen Up Close*. Lincoln, NE: Bison Books, 1999.

Tuccille, Jerome. *The Roughest Riders: The Untold Story of the Black Soldiers in the Spanish-American War*. Chicago: Chicago Review Press, 2015.

Turpie, David C. "A Voluntary War: The Spanish-American War, White Southern Manhood, and the Struggle to Recruit Volunteers in the South." *Journal of Southern History* 80, no. 4 (2014): 859–92.

Chapter 8

Bailey, Beth, and David Farber. *The First Strange Place: Race and Sex in World War II Hawaii*. Baltimore, MD: Johns Hopkins University Press, 1992.

Bederman, Gail. *Manliness and Civilization*. Chicago: University of Chicago Press, 1995.

Brandt, Allan M. *No Magic Bullet: A Social History of Venereal Disease in the United States since 1880*. New York: Oxford University Press, 1985.

Canaday, Margot. *The Straight State: Sexuality and Citizenship in Twentieth-Century America*. Princeton, NJ: Princeton University Press, 2009.

Clement, Elizabeth Alice. *Love for Sale: Courting, Treating, and Prostitution in New York City, 1900–1945*. Chapel Hill: University of North Carolina Press, 2006.

Costello, John. *Virtue under Fire: How World War II Change Our Social and Sexual Attitudes*. Boston: Little, Brown, 1985.

Giesberg, Judith Ann. *Sex and the Civil War: Soldiers, Pornography, and the Making of American Morality*. Chapel Hill: University of North Carolina Press, 2017.

Hegarty, Marilyn E. *Victory Girls, Khaki-Wackies, and Patriotutes: The Regulation of Female Sexuality during World War II*. New York: New York University Press, 2008.

Hoganson, Kristin L. *Fighting for American Manhood: How Gender Politics Provoked the Spanish-American and Philippine-American Wars*. New Haven, CT: Yale University Press, 1998.

Huebner, Andrew J. *Love and Death in the Great War*. New York: Oxford University Press, 2018.

Meyer, Leisa D. *Creating GI Jane: Sexuality and Power in the Women's Army Corps during World War II*. New York: Columbia University Press, 1998.

Roberts, Mary Louise. *What Soldiers Do: Sex and the American GI in World War II France*. Chicago: University of Chicago Press, 2013.

Vuic, Kara Dixon. *The Girls Next Door: Bringing the Home Front to the Front Lines*. Cambridge, MA: Harvard University Press, 2019.

Westbrook, Robert. *Why We Fought: Forging American Obligations in World War II*. Washington, DC: Smithsonian Books, 2004.

Wexler, Laura. *Tender Violence: Domestic Visions in an Age of U.S. Imperialism*. Chapel Hill: University of North Carolina Press, 2000.

White, Kevin. *The First Sexual Revolution: The Emergence of Male Heterosexuality in Modern America*. New York: New York University Press, 1992.

Winchell, Meghan. *Good Girls, Good Food, Good Fun: The Story of USO Hostesses during World War II*. Chapel Hill: University of North Carolina Press, 2008.

Chapter 9

Bailey, Beth, Alesha E. Doan, Shannon Portillo, and Kara Dixon Vuic, eds. *Managing Sex in the U.S. Military: Gender, Identity, and Behavior*. Lincoln: University of Nebraska Press, 2022.

Bérubé, Allan. *Coming Out under Fire: The History of Gay Men and Women in World War II*. Chapel Hill: University of North Carolina Press, 2010.

Enloe, Cynthia. *Bananas, Beaches, and Bases: Making Feminist Sense of International Politics*. Berkeley: University of California Press, 2014.

Estes, Steve. *Ask and Tell: Gay and Lesbian Veterans Speak Out*. Chapel Hill: University of North Carolina Press, 2009.

Herbert, Melissa S. *Camouflage Isn't Only for Combat: Gender, Sexuality, and Women in the Military*. New York: New York University Press, 2000.

Holm, Jeanne. *Women in the Military: An Unfinished Revolution*. Novato, CA: Presidio Press, 1992.

Shilts, Randy. *Conduct Unbecoming: Gays and Lesbians in the U.S. Military, Vietnam to the Persian Gulf*. New York: St. Martin's Press, 1993.

Stiehm, Judith Hicks. *It's Our Military, Too! Women and the U.S. Military*. Philadelphia: Temple University Press, 1996.

Contributors

Kevin Adams earned his undergraduate and graduate degrees at the University of California, Berkeley, and is currently professor of history at Kent State University, where he teaches courses on war and society in US history, Gilded Age America, and the Civil War and Reconstruction. He is the author of *Class and Race in the Frontier Army: Military Life in the West, 1870–1890*, and his research explores the relationship between the US Army and American society in the decades after the close of the Civil War.

Amanda Bellows earned her PhD in history from the University of North Carolina at Chapel Hill. She is a teaching associate and the departmental faculty adviser for history at the New School in the Department of Historical Studies. She is the author of *American Slavery and Russian Serfdom in the Post-Emancipation Imagination* and coeditor of the anthology *South Writ Large: Stories, Art, and Ideas from the Global South*. She has also published articles in academic journals and in general publications like the *New York Times*, and she helped design the recent exhibit *Black Citizenship in the Jim Crow Era* at the New-York Historical Society.

Kari L. Boyd-Weisenberger was born and raised in Michigan, where she graduated from Michigan State University with a BA in history. She earned her MA and PhD from The University of Alabama. Her dissertation, "Disease, Disuse, and Disappointment: The Volunteer Experience and the Modernization of the American National Guard, 1898–1902," explores how disease and feelings of misuse defined the American volunteers' experience of the Spanish-American War and influenced the shape of the National Guard in the years after the war. She is currently an instructor at both the University of Alabama in Tuscaloosa and Anderson University in South Carolina.

Michele Curran Cornell is employed as a military historian with SNA International supporting the Defense POW/MIA Accounting Agency (DPAA), which works to find and identify missing and unknown US service members from World War II, the Korean War, and the Vietnam War. She supports the World War II disinterment identification program, researching associated losses from the Battle of Iwo Jima, Chichi Jima, kamikaze attacks on ships at Okinawa, and more. Previously, Dr. Cornell supported DPAA's identification project for Korean War Unknowns and planned investigative field operations to recover ground losses in the Republic of Korea and the Korean Demilitarized Zone. Dr. Cornell earned her PhD in history from Kent State University, after authoring the dissertation "Romanticizing Patriarchy: Patriotic Romance and American Military Marriages during World War II." While completing her degree, Dr. Cornell worked as an adjunct professor of history at Kent State University and Robert Morris University. She has won grants from Harvard University's Schlesinger Library, Florida State University's Institute on World War II and the Human Experience, and the US Army Heritage and Education Center's Military History Institute. She has published work in several anthologies.

Lesley J. Gordon holds the Charles G. Summersell Chair of Southern History at the University of Alabama. She earned her BA with high honors from the College of William and Mary, and her MA and PhD in American history from the University of Georgia. Her publications include *General George E. Pickett in Life and Legend*, *A Broken Regiment: The 16th Connecticut's Civil War*, and the coedited volume *Inside the Confederate Nation: Essays in Honor of Emory M. Thomas*. In addition, she has published numerous articles and book reviews, and her public talks have been featured on C-SPAN. Her latest book is *Dread Danger: Combat and Cowardice in the American Civil War*.

Andrew J. Huebner is professor of history at the University of Alabama. He earned his graduate degrees in history from Brown University. His publications include *Love and Death in the Great War*, *The Warrior Image: Soldiers in American Culture from the Second World War to the Vietnam Era*, and *The Unfinished Nation: A Concise History of the American People*. He is also coeditor of *Dixie's Great War: World War I and the American South* and the forthcoming edited collection *The Cambridge History of War and Society in America*. Currently he is working on a study of Black regulars and US empire from 1866 to 1917.

Gregory Mixon recently codirected a summer institute for K–12 educators with the Landmarks of American History and Culture program of the National Endowment for the Humanities. Before that, he served as interim director of the Center for the Study of the New South at the University of North Carolina at Charlotte and was the Fulbright Research Chair in North American Studies at York University in Toronto, serving as visiting professor in the Department of History. He is also the winner of the Georgia Historical Records Advisory Council's Award for Excellence in Research Using the Holdings of Archives for his book *Show Thyself a Man: Georgia State Troops, Colored, 1865–1905*. He is additionally the author of *The Atlanta Riot: Race, Class, and Violence in a New South City*. A professor in the Department of History and affiliated faculty with the Department of Africana Studies, the American Studies Program, and the Center for the Study of the New South, all at the University of North Carolina at Charlotte, he teaches African American, southern, and US history and racial violence, with a research focus on the years 1860 to 1930. He is currently working on a comparative study of Black militiamen in North Carolina and South Carolina, 1865 to 1898. He is also a founding member of the Charlotte-based Romare Bearden Branch of the Association for the Study of African American Life and History.

Caroline Wood Newhall is assistant professor at Oberlin College, where she specializes in nineteenth-century US history. Her focus is on North American slavery and captivity, warfare, and the Civil War era. She earned her BA at Trinity College, Hartford, and her MA and PhD in US history from the University of North Carolina at Chapel Hill. Her publications include blog posts, book reviews, and book chapters, and her public talks have been featured on C-SPAN and YouTube. Her current book project explores African American soldiers who became prisoners of war (POWs) in the Confederacy, as well as a digital database and mapping project centered on these POWs' movements throughout the American South and their genealogies. She previously served as the 2020–21 postdoctoral fellow at the Virginia Center for Civil War Studies at Virginia Tech, and as assistant professor of history at Columbus State University in Georgia.

Heather Marie Stur, PhD, is professor of history at the University of Southern Mississippi and codirector of the Dale Center for the Study of War and Society. She is the author of four books, including *21 Days to Baghdad: General Buford Blount and the 3rd Infantry Division in the Iraq War*, *Saigon at War: South Vietnam and the Global Sixties*, *The U.S. Military and Civil Rights since World War II*, and *Beyond Combat: Women and Gender in the Vietnam War Era*. She is also coeditor of *Integrating the US Military: Race, Gender, and Sexual Orientation since World War II*. Stur's op-eds and articles have been published in the *New York Times*, *Washington Post*, *BBC*, *National Interest*, *Orange County Register*, *Diplomatic History*, *War & Society*, and other journals and newspapers. In 2013–14, Stur was a Fulbright scholar in Vietnam, where she was a visiting professor on the Faculty of International Relations at the University of Social Sciences and Humanities in Ho Chi Minh City.

Patrick T. Troester earned his PhD from Southern Methodist University and is assistant professor of history at the University of Pittsburgh at Bradford. He has taught previously at Fort Lewis College, Southern Methodist University, and

Clemson University. His current book project examines the intertwined histories of organized violence and nationalism in the nineteenth-century borderlands of Texas and northeastern Mexico, uncovering how the Mexican and US nation-states emerged at the grassroots level within preexisting frameworks of kinship, honor, and community. His work has appeared in the *Western Historical Quarterly* and the *Pacific Historical Review*.

Chad L. Williams is the Samuel J. and Augusta Spector Professor of History and African and African American Studies at Brandeis University. He earned a BA with honors in history and African American studies from the University of California, Los Angeles, and received both his MA and PhD in history from Princeton University. He specializes in African American and modern US history, African American military history, the World War I era, and African American intellectual history. He is the author of *The Wounded World: W. E. B. Du Bois and the First World War*, named a best book of 2023 by the *Washington Post* and the *New Yorker*, and *Torchbearers of Democracy: African American Soldiers in the World War I Era*, recipient of the Liberty Legacy Foundation Award from the Organization of American Historians and the Distinguished Book Award from the Society for Military History, and designated as a Choice Outstanding Academic Title. He is also coeditor of *Charleston Syllabus: Readings on Race, Racism, and Racial Violence and Major Problems in African American History*. He has published articles and book reviews in numerous leading journals and collections, and earned fellowships from the Radcliffe Institute for Advanced Study at Harvard University, the American Council of Learned Societies, the Schomburg Center for Research in Black Culture, the Ford Foundation, and the Institute for Citizens and Scholars. His op-eds have appeared in the *Atlantic*, the *Washington Post*, *Time*, and *The Conversation*.

Fay A. Yarbrough received her doctorate in American history from Emory University and completed her undergraduate degree at Rice University. She is currently the William Gaines Twyman Professor of History at Rice University. She is the author of *Choctaw Confederates: The American Civil War in Indian Country*, which explores Choctaw Indians' participation in the American Civil War. Her first book, *Race and the Cherokee Nation: Sovereignty in the Nineteenth Century*, argues that Cherokee lawmakers' definitions of interracial sex and policing of this activity served multiple functions: preserving political sovereignty, delineating Cherokee identity, and creating social hierarchy. With Sandra Slater, she coedited *Gender and Sexuality in Indigenous North America, 1400–1850*, a contribution to the growing scholarly interest in the operation of notions of gender and sexuality in Indigenous societies. Her work has also appeared in the *Journal of Social History* and the *Journal of Southern History*, as well as the edited volumes *Race and Science: Scientific Challenges to Racism in Modern America* and *Civil War Wests: Testing the Limits of the United States*. She has served on a number of editorial boards for various journals, and she was recently the visiting editor at the *Journal of Southern History*.

Index